Luke's Rhetorical Compositions

Luke's Rhetorical Compositions

―――――― *Essays in Lukan Studies* ――――――

Paul Elbert

◥PICKWICK *Publications* • Eugene, Oregon

LUKE'S RHETORICAL COMPOSITIONS
Essays in Lukan Studies

Copyright © 2022 The Foundation for Pentecostal Scholarship, Inc. All rights reserved. Except for brief quotations in critical publications or reviews, no part of this book may be reproduced in any manner without prior written permission from the publisher. Write: Permissions, Wipf and Stock Publishers, 199 W. 8th Ave., Suite 3, Eugene, OR 97401.

Pickwick Publications
An Imprint of Wipf and Stock Publishers
199 W. 8th Ave., Suite 3
Eugene, OR 97401

www.wipfandstock.com

PAPERBACK ISBN: 978-1-6667-0283-5
HARDCOVER ISBN: 978-1-6667-0284-2
EBOOK ISBN: 978-1-6667-0285-9

Cataloguing-in-Publication data:

Names: Elbert, Paul, author.

Title: Luke's rhetorical compositions : essays in lukan studies / by Paul Elbert.

Description: Eugene, OR: Pickwick Publications, 2022 | Includes bibliographical references and index.

Identifiers: ISBN 978-1-6667-0283-5 (paperback) | ISBN 978-1-6667-0284-2 (hardcover) | ISBN 978-1-6667-0285-9 (ebook)

Subjects: LCSH: Bible. Luke—Language, style. | Bible. Luke—Criticism, interpretation, etc.

Classification: BS2595.2 E43 2022 (print) | BS2595.2 (ebook)

07/18/22

Contents

Preface | vii
Acknowledgments | ix
Abbreviations | x

1 Luke's Fulfillment-of-Prophecy Theme: Introductory Exploration of Joel and the Last Days | 1

2 An Observation on Luke's Composition and Narrative Style of Questions | 33

3 Acts 2:38 in Light of the Syntax of Imperative-Future Passive and Imperative-Present Participle Combinations | 43

4 Possible Literary Links between Luke-Acts and Pauline Letters Regarding Spirit-Language | 55

5 Luke's Possible Progymnasmatic Improvements on and Employment of Paul's Letter to the Romans | 74

6 Pentecostal/Charismatic Themes in Luke-Acts at the Evangelical Theological Society: The Battle of Interpretive Method | 93

7 Paul of the Miletus Speech and 1 Thessalonians: Critique and Considerations | 117

8 Spirit, Scripture, and Theology through a Lukan Lens: A Review Article | 128

9 Progymnasmatic Examples in Luke-Acts of Salvation Experience: Necessary Narrative Persuasion from Jesus Tradition and History That Clarifies Paul | 142

Bibliography | 149
Index of Persons | 171
Index of Ancient Sources | 177

Preface

I WOULD LIKE TO draw the reader's attention in particular to the articles in two chapters of this collection, namely chapters 3 and 9. The material in chapter 3 is a groundbreaking discussion of Acts 2:38 in which its Greek verb tense speaks to the subsequent reception of the gift of the Holy Spirit *following* salvation, not coincident with salvation. In Acts 2:38 it is Luke's intention to portray Peter as promising the gift of the Holy Spirit to hearers and to those beyond narrative time as a Pentecostal experience.

The previously unpublished article in chapter 9 discusses Luke's use of progymnasmatic examples in his descriptions of the salvation experience. It also discusses Luke's clarification of Paul using narrative persuasion from Jesus tradition and history. Also, Luke's use of basic soteriological vocabulary provides clarity and plausibility. His distinctive selection of examples from the Jesus tradition and his duplication of Paul's soteriological vocabulary is very helpful.

Acknowledgments

I AM GRATEFUL THAT these articles are going to appear in a new format, brought together as a collection. They represent the product of many years of research, study, and reflection. I gratefully recall helpful discussions with three late scholars, Colin Hemer, Graham Stanton, and especially my longtime friend, John Rea. I hope that this collection of essays will be helpful in encouraging present and future scholars. In addition, I appreciate my friend Robert Graves for his help and vision in bringing about the publication of this collection.

Abbreviations

AASF	Annalles Academiae scientiarum fennicae
AB	Anchor Bible
AnBib	Analecta biblica
ANRW	*Aufstieg und Niedergang der römischen Welt: Geschichte und Kultur Roms im Spiegel der neueren Forschung.* Edited by H. Temporini and W. Haase. Berlin, 1972–
AOAT	Alter Orient und Altes Testament
ATR	*Australasian Theological Review*
BDF	*A Greek Grammar of the New Testament and Other Early Christian Literature.* Edited by F. Blass, A. Debrunner, and R. W. Funk. Chicago: University of Chicago Press, 1961.
BETL	Bibliotheca ephemeridum theologicarum lovaniensium
Bib	*Biblica*
BJRL	*Bulletin of the John Rylands University Library of Manchester*
BK	*Bibel und Kirche*
BNGJ	*Byzantinisch-neugriechische Jahrbucher*
BWANT	Beiträge zur Wissensschaft vom Alten und Neuen Testament
BZNW	*Beihefte zur Zeitschrift für die neutestamentliche Wissenschaft*
CBET	Contributions to Biblical Exegesis and Theology
CBQ	*Catholic Biblical Quarterly*
CJ	*Classical Journal*

ABBREVIATIONS

CP	*Classical Philology*
EDNT	*Exegetical Dictionary of the New Testament.* Edited by Horst Balz and Gerhard Schneider. ET. 3 vols. Grand Rapids: Eerdmans, 1990–93.
EKKNT	Evangelisch-Katholischer Kommentar zum Neuen Testament
ET	English Translation
EtB	Etudes bibliques
ETL	Ephemerides theologicae lovanienses
ETS	Erfurter theologische Studien
EvQ	*Evangelical Quarterly*
EvT	*Evangelische Theologie*
ExpTim	*Expository Times*
FRLANT	Forschungen zur Religion und Literatur des Alten und Neuen Testaments
FS	Festschrift
GR	Greece and Rome
GRBS	Greek, Roman, and Byzantine Studies
Greg	*Gregorianum*
HandbAW	Handbuch der Altertumswissenschaft
HeyJ	*Heythrop Journal*
HSCP	Harvard Studies in Classical Philology
HTR	Harvard Theological Review
IB	*Interpreter's Bible.* Edited by G. A. Buttrick et al. 12 vols. New York, 1951–1957
ICC	International Critical Commentary
Int	*Interpretation*
JAC	Jahrbuch für Antike und Christentum
JAOS	Journal of the American Oriental Society
JBL	Journal of Biblical Literature
JETS	Journal of the Evangelical Theological Society

JPT	*Journal of Pentecostal Theology*
JPTSup	Journal of Pentecostal Theology Supplement
JR	*Journal of Religion*
JSNT	*Journal for the Study of the New Testament*
JSNTSup	Journal for the Study of the New Testament: Supplement Series
JSOT	*Journal for the Study of the Old Testament*
JTS	*Journal of Theological Studies*
KEK	Kritisch-exegetischer Kommentar über das Neue Testament (Meyer-Kommentar)
KNT	Kommentar zum Neuen Testament
LCL	Loeb Classical Library
LD	Lectio Divina
LNTS	The Library of New Testament Studies
NCB	New Century Bible
NICNT	New International Commentary on the New Testament
NIGTC	New International Greek Testament Commentary
NovT	*Novum Testamentum*
NovTSup	Supplements to *Novum Testamentum*
NRTh	*La nouvelle revue théologique*
NTAbh	Neutestamentliche Abhandlungen
NTD	Das Neue Testament Deutsch
NTM	New Testament Message
NTS	*New Testament Studies*
OBO	Orbis biblicus et orientalis
Pneuma	*Pneuma: Journal of the Society for Pentecostal Studies*
PW	*Paulys Real-Encyclopädie der classischen Altertumswissenschaft*. New edition by Georg Wissowa and Wilhelm Kroll. 50 vols. in 84 parts. Stuttgart: Metzler and Druckenmüller, 1894–1980

ABBREVIATIONS

RAC	*Reallexikon für Antike und Christentum.* Edited by T. Kluser et al. Stuttgart, 1950–
RB	*Revue biblique*
RHPR	*Revue d'histoire et de philosophie religieuses*
RNT	*Regensburger Neues Testament*
RSR	*Recherches de science religieuse*
SBLSBS	Society of Biblical Literature Sources for Biblical Studies
SBLSP	Society of Biblical Literature Seminar Papers
SBLSymS	Society of Biblical Literature Symposium Series
SBLTT	Society of Biblical Literature Texts and Translations
SBLWGRW	Society of Biblical Literature Writings from the Greco-Roman World
SJT	*Scottish Journal of Theology*
SKKNT	Stuttgarter kleiner Kommentar, Neues Testament
SNT	Studien zum Neuen Testament
SNTSMS	Society for New Testament Studies Monograph Series
ST	*Studia theologica*
SUNT	Studien zur Umwelt des Neuen Testaments
TDNT	*Theological Dictionary of the New Testament*
ThStKr	*Theologische Studien und Kritiken*
TJ	*Trinity Journal*
TRE	*Theologische Realenzyklopädie.* Edited by G. Krause and G. Müller. Berlin, 1977–
TSK	*Theologische Studien und Kritiken*
TU	Texte und Untersuchungen
TWNT	*Theologisches Wörterbuch zum Neuen Testament.* Edited by Gerhard Kittel and Gerhard Friedrich, Stuttgart: Kohlhammer, 1932–79.
TynBul	*Tyndale Bulletin*
VC	*Vigiliae Christianae*
VE	*Vox Evangelica*

ABBREVIATIONS

WUNT	*Wissenschaftliche Untersuchungen zum Neuen Testament*
ZKT	*Zeitschrift für katolische Theologie*
ZNW	*Zeitschrift für die neutestamentliche Wissenschaft und die Kunde der älteren Kirche*
ZTK	*Zeitschrift für Theologie und Kirche*

Chapter 1

Luke's Fulfillment-of-Prophecy Theme

Introductory Exploration of Joel and the Last Days[1]

Introduction

DO YOU BELIEVE THE prophets? That is the question King Agrippa will have to decide (Acts 26:27). However, for Luke, who in Acts interprets Scripture through his characters, not in narrative comment, this question has already received a decisive answer. But Luke has composed his story in the light of an even deeper understanding of the significance of prophetic fulfillment, which he develops in a most artistic and consistent manner. It is this prophetic dimension of his narrative-rhetorical composition that the present study attempts to explore.

Dupont, Schneider, and Berger, for example, incisively note the thematic paradigm of prophetic fulfillment found in Luke-Acts.[2] This narratively attractive conception, which indeed informs the theological plan of Luke-Acts, could be logically connected to the fulfillment motif inherent in Luke's use of the perfect passive verb πληροφορεῖν, compounding πληροῦν with φορεῖν, in his opening preface (Luke 1:1) when weight is given to the idea of "to be fulfilled" over "to be accomplished" or "to be confirmed."[3] By calling Theophilus's attention to the fact that prophecy has been, and, as I will argue here, continues to be, fulfilled, a "to be fulfilled" understanding of πληροφορεῖν is quite narratively harmonious both with the detectable theme of promise and fulfillment itself,[4] as well as with Luke's pastoral desire to provide cred-

---

1. Paper presented to the Society for Pentecostal Studies, Marquette University, 2004.

2. Dupont, "L'utilisation apologetique de l'ancien Testament dans les discourse des Acts," 289–327; Schneider, "Zur Bedeutung von καθεξῆς im lukanischen Doppelwerk," 128–31, underscores Lukan "Verheißung und Erfüllung" within the framework of narrative continuity, observing that the theme is a continuing one, citing Luke 24:47, Acts 1:8, and 28:28. Berger, "Hellenistische Gattungen im Neuen Testament," 1031–432, properly links the theme to Luke's evident recognition of and belief in active divine providence and foreordainment as treated earlier by Schulz, "Gottes Vorsehung bei Lukas," 104–16.

3. With Marshall, *Gospel of Luke*, 41; Fitzmyer, *Gospel according to Luke I-IX*, 238. As to being accomplished and being confirmed, cf. Dillon, "Previewing Luke's Project from His Prologue," 221–22, and Rengstorf, *Das Evangelium nach Lukas*, 43–44, respectively.

4. So too, Parsons, *Departure of Jesus in Luke-Acts*, 83–91.

ible assurance (ἀσφάλεια, 1:4), which the prophetic fulfillment theme also evidently provides.[5]

Talbert, in his study of promise and fulfillment in Luke-Acts,[6] makes the point that while there is no doubt that the theme of prophecy-fulfillment is a major Lukan concern, it is certainly not the only prominent theme in the Lukan perspective. However, a theological and pneumatological plan based upon prophetic fulfillment coupled with narrative prediction is advanced via this theme and accomplished in a specific narrative manner as this present study attempts to demonstrate. Frein, in her contribution to our understanding of Luke's sense of prophetic fulfillment, duly stresses that this thematic pattern functions equally well with respect to predictions made by Lukan characters, interfacing with the fulfillment of LXX prophecy.[7] Both Talbert and Frein observe that the fulfillment-of-prophecy theme in Lukan thought is much more than the past fulfillment of LXX predictions.

For example, the theme includes fulfillment of specific LXX prophecy (Luke 4:16–21, "this scripture has been fulfilled [πεπλήρωται] in your ears" [4:21, Lukan Sondergut]; Acts 13:23, 27–29, 33, "the voices of the prophets . . . they fulfilled [ἐπλήρωσαν]," "God has fulfilled [ἐκπεπλήρωκεν] what has been written" [13:27b, 33]).[8] The application of Joel's prophecy, whose narrative functions I am focusing on here, fall into this category. Then there is the fulfillment of narrative predictions: Luke 1:13–17 fulfilled in 1:57–66 ("the time was fulfilled [ἐπλήσθη]" [1:57]), this first instance being explicitly denoted, making it impossible to be missed, as prophetic words which will be fulfilled (πληρωθήσονται, 1:20c) in due time. In the category of narrative predictions, for example, we see them given by angels (Luke 1:26–37 fulfilled in 1:39–44, and 2:1–2; 2:11–12 fulfilled, with respect to the birth in 2:15–20; Acts 27:23–24 fulfilled in 27:44b and 28:14b); by Jesus (Luke 11:13; 24:49; Acts 1:4, 5, 8, 14 fulfilled in 2:4 with further examples in diverse characters' lives; Luke 9:22, 44 and 18:31–33 fulfilled in chapters 22–24, noting the introductory implementation by Luke [συμπληροῦσθαι, 9:51]; Luke 12:11–12 fulfilled in Acts 5:29; Luke 13:35b fulfilled in 19:38; Luke 22:10–12 fulfilled in 22:13; Luke 22:34 fulfilled in 22:61); by the heavenly Jesus (9:15, fulfilled via various audiences); by a prophet (Luke 1:67–70 fulfilled in

---

5. Frein, "Prophecies," 35, concludes thusly: "That so many of the eschatological prophecies are coupled with prophecies that find their fulfillment within the narrative suggests that one of the purposes of Luke's emphasis on prophecy and fulfilment is to assure his readers that Jesus's prophecies are reliable. Thus, the juxtaposition of these two types of prophecies is one of the ways that Luke accomplishes his stated purpose of giving assurance or certainty about the instructions they have received (Luke 1:4)." Luke 24:49 is of this type. When the first fulfillment is reported, it is a fulfillment of both Joel's prophecy and Jesus's narrative prediction.

6. Talbert, "Promise and Fulfillment," 101.

7. Frein, "Prophecies," 30–31.

8. For discussion and textual comparisons related to this element of prophetic fulfillment as signaled by δεῖ πληρωθῆναι πάντα τὰ γεγραμμένα (Luke 24:44b), as in John the Baptist's ministry (Luke 3:4–6; 7:27) and in Jesus's earthly ministry (Luke 4:18–19, 21, 43; 7:22; 22:37; 24:27, 46; Acts 1:16; 3:18), cf. Rusam, *Das Alte Testament bei Lukas*, 165–253, 265–69.

3:1–20 and 7:24–27); and by prophetic speech (Acts 11:27–28a fulfilled in 11:28b; Acts 20:23 and 21:10–11 fulfilled in 21:27–28).

This detection of this theme, in the case of Joel's prophecy, appears especially relevant to a pastoral and pragmatic purpose, because its fulfillment in the Jerusalem/Petrine tradition as described by Luke goes far beyond the narrative world he portrays. Luke's idea of fulfillment, while serving his narrative development, including the fulfillment of predictions made by characters in the narrative,[9] reaches beyond his characters' lives into the experiential world of his readers. Indeed, the narrative predictions have been composed by Luke so that they repeat or echo past prophecies. This phenomenon could have an interactive effect. Assuming that Luke's addressee[10] is a disciple-believer who, like Apollos in the narrative, is partially familiar with Christian teaching and practice but is in need of further instruction, the past fulfillment of narrative predictions in Luke's story serves to legitimize the teaching of the earthly Jesus and to provide confidence in the heavenly Jesus. This heavenly person (whose action is described at Acts 2:33) could then be looked to as one who is both narratively and pneumatologically connected to the person of the earthly Jesus and to his teaching on personal prayer allied to Lukan expectations for the gift of the Holy Spirit;[11] another way of putting this is to say that Theophilus can be confident that what Luke is telling him about Christian experience via a persuasive narrative format, wherein prediction and prophetic announcement are integral, is true.[12] Consistent with a practical pastoral interest in the experiential world of his readers would be a desire to compose the narrative in such a way so as to clearly delineate the *continuing* fulfillment of prophecy. If Theophilus was a literary minded person, as Luke appears to be,[13] a person educated in the Empire where rhetorical training was mandatory in the schools,[14] he would naturally expect Luke

---

9. Talbert, "Promise and Fulfillment," 94–95; Frein, "Prophecies," 34–36.

10. Luke's address of κράτιστε Θεόφιλε, as with the Roman officials Felix and Festus, both orally and in writing, seems to preclude a symbolic addressee, but rather suggests a real person (as a first-century politarch Θεόφιλος, P. Oxy. 745, 4) with whom Luke is pastorally concerned.

11. The teaching of Jesus on prayer and its narrative connections in characters' lives is noted, for example, by O'Brien, "Prayer in Luke-Acts," 111–27.

12. So too, Talbert, "Promise and Fulfillment," 99; Frein, "Prophecies," 35.

13. Brodie, "Greco-Roman Imitation of Texts," 33, is on target in assessing Luke as a littérateur, employing techniques of the narrative-rhetorical tradition, while obviously influenced by the style of the LXX. As an educated man, influenced by the rhetorical tradition, Luke could then be expected to employ varying literary devices (so too, Unnik, "Luke's Second Book," 46).

14. In the Greco-Roman culture, as in Hellenistic culture, rhetorical training was highly valued and was mandatory at an early stage. In the Roman educational system, the student was introduced to and familiarized with rhetorical concepts; the preliminary rhetorical exercises of the *progymnasmata* were taught before specializing in other topics, cf. Bonner, *Education in Ancient Rome*, 250–53; Webb, "*Progymnasmata* as Practice," 289–316. For an overview of the functionality of this rhetorically sensitive education and the habits of expression it would generate, cf. Marrou, *History of Education in Antiquity*; Cribiore, *Writing, Teachers, and Students*; Cribiore, *Gymnastics of the Mind*; Morgan, *Literate Education*; Hock, "Homer in Greco-Roman Education," 56–58; MacDonald, "Paul and Greco-Roman Education," 198–208. The widespread cultural awareness and appreciation of Homeric epic in Roman

to illustrate ongoing prophetic fulfillment by examples and precedents in characters' lives within the framework of the two scrolls (or papyrus codices) dedicated to him. Such an expectation on Theophilus's part would be quite consistent with the accepted rhetorical procedure of illustrating main points with examples and precedents in the traditional standards of narrative composition, as set out in the contemporary treatise of Theon.[15] Theon's instructional effort builds on solid rhetorical tradition concerning the necessity and the quality of the expected examples and precedents. Any real thematic paradigm that fulfilled prophecy beyond narrative time would bear directly upon relevant instructional matters (πράγματα) cited in the prologue[16] and would, importantly, have to be illustrated by examples and precedents in order to be convincing within Greco-Roman narrative-rhetorical culture.

Assuming Luke expected Theophilus to be sure to comprehend a properly illustrated ongoing prophetic fulfillment currently impacting Christian experience according to conventional narrative-rhetorical tradition, experience deemed connected to the heavenly Jesus as Luke portrays him, Luke would have to be sure that his thematic delineation of prophetic fulfillment would be recognizable in his characters' lives and, to be completely convincing, that it connected to the teaching of the earthly Jesus.[17] Ongoing prophetic fulfillment would be bolstered by making sure that the

---

schools is complemented by inscriptional evidence in Israel, cf. Horst, "Greek in Jewish Palestine," 9, 23–25.

15. Progymnastic categories of narrative composition related to argument and personification, like "thesis" and "speech-in-character," surely predated Theon (c. 50 CE), something Theon himself acknowledges, cf. Stegemann, "Theon," cols. 2037–54. For a comprehensive treatment of Theon of Alexandria, his text, versions, and editions thereof, cf. Patillon, *Aelius Théon Progymnasmata*, vii–clvi, and Butts, "'Progymnasmata' of Theon," 7–95.

The texts of Patillon and Butts (with French and English translations, respectively) now replace that of Spengel, *Rhetores Graeci*, 2:59–130. Patillon retains the Spengel numbering system, which I will employ here, followed by a page number(s) in Patillon. Both Patillon and Butts insert "On Refutation and Confirmation" into Theon's chapter "On the Narrative" and attempt to recapture Theon's original order of the exercises. The Patillon edition includes a reconstruction of chapters 13–17 in Armenian (edited by Giancarlo Bolognesi). Kennedy, *Progymnasmata* also provides English translations of, introductions to, and notes on the work of Theon, Hermogenes, Aphthonius, and Nicolaus. While consulting the translations of Butts, Patillon, and Kennedy, translations presented here are mine based on the critical edition of Patillon.

For discussion of the concerns and categories of the *Progymnasmata*, cf. Hunger, *Die hochsprachliche profane Literatur der Byzantiner*, 1:92–120; Kennedy, *Greek Rhetoric Under Christian Emperors*, 54–73.

16. Confidence-building exemplary descriptions in the matter of prophetic fulfillment accord well with the rhetorical and compositional elements of the Lukan prologue; on this historiographical point see, too, Hagene, *Zeiten der Wiederherstellung*, 29–37.

17. Luke is in accord with the instruction of Theon on this expected method of narrative persuasion via plausible examples and precedents serving to provide Christian expectation. Clarity, understandability, and vividness of examples and precedents are the narrative tools deemed important by Theon; it is unsurprising then that Luke employs such contemporary narrative technique. Lukan portrayal of interaction with, and of Christian expectation of, the divine is quite harmonious with Theonic characterization and personification. The use of examples and precedents on the oratorical side of the rhetorical tradition, surely not unknown to those educated in the Empire, is treated by

heavenly Jesus in this regard was narratively connected to the earthly Jesus as well as to a LXX prophecy and/or narrative prediction. This experiential continuity with ongoing prophetic fulfillment is what I would like to suggest that Luke is intent on portraying with respect to Joel's prophecy. Regarding this narrative strategy of comprehension, Luke could reasonably desire to improve on some Matthean material, which he arguably employed,[18] given, for example, the lack of practical detail between earthly and heavenly ministries of Jesus in Matthew 11:28 and 28:20, along with the pastoral need for realistic narrative implementation and practical examples of the fulfillment of John the Baptist's opening prophecy (Matt 3:11b).

Luke's intention to carry out such an enterprise is probably signaled by the opening sentence of his second installment: "The first account [a διήγησις (a narrative account, Luke 1:1, as in Theon, Περὶ Διηγήματος, διηγεῖσθαι, διήγημα, διηγηματικός, διήγησις)] I composed, Theophilus, about all that Jesus began [ἤρξατο] to do and teach" (Acts 1:1). The imperfect in this self-description may suggest that Luke intended the second account to be about what Jesus now continues to do and to teach, not about something finished or handed over to others, an implication made stronger by the ensuing and narratively prominent connections with the activities of the heavenly Jesus.[19] Luke's rendering of a narrative account, having, as it apparently does, connections of the activities of a heavenly character linked to the teaching and prediction of an earthly character, plus fulfillment scenes in other characters' lives, is rhetorically distinctive, but is entirely consistent and harmonious with contemporary literary standards for narrative composition. Theon's definition of narrative insists that it must be an explanatory account of matters which have occurred (including events of the past, the present, and the future) and that it must portray the intention, importance,

---

Alewell, *Über das rhetorische Παράδειγμα*; Price, "'Paradeigma' and 'Exemplum' in Ancient Rhetorical Theory"; Fiore, *Function of Personal Examples*, 32–44; and Lausberg, *Handbuch der Literarischen Rhetorik*, 37, 227–35.

Other Lukan connections with these compositionally oriented exercises are suggested by Parsons, "Luke and the *Progymnasmata*," and by Penner, "Civilizing Discourse," 66–72, respectively.

18. Understanding parts of Mark and Matthew as Lukan sources certainly has its obvious attractions but cannot be all encompassing. A desire to improve upon the πολλοί (Luke 1:1) would extend to other sources as well. As to Luke's interest in improving upon Matthew, cf. Franklin, *Luke*, 280–375.

19. Ehrhardt's proposal that the "whole purpose" of Luke's second book "is no less than to be the Gospel of the Holy Spirit" would then seem to be a reasonable introductory guide (cf. Ehrhardt, "Construction and Purpose," 45–79, esp. 55, 63); Ehrhardt suggests a title for the second book as "The Gospel of the Holy Spirit in the Church Militant Here on Earth," in his *Acts of the Apostles*, 129. Here Ehrhardt may echo the observation of Jaquier, *Les Actes des Apôtres*, cvii: "The Acts are, so to speak, the Gospel of the Spirit."

On my argument, the writer of this double-work would live on his own terms, as would his readers, *not* in a philosophically and rationalistically confined "apostolic age" or "Pentecostal age" (as in the superimposed periodization of *Pfingstzeit* and associated *Pfingstzeitalter Anwendung* assumed, for example, by Procksch, "ἅγιος im Neuen Testament," *TWNT* 1:101–16 [105]), but *instead* in the time of "Die Zeit der Geistesgabe" (with Pesch, "Die Gabe des Heiligen Geistes [Apg 2, 38]," 53, Pesch assuming, rightly so on my argument here, that the Lukan gift of the Holy Spirit is *not* phenomenologically equivalent to the Lukan soteriological nexus of repentance-forgiveness-faith-salvation-conversion).

and manner of the activity and the reason for it, including motives and action of a main character.[20] Predictive narrative engenders expectations. Since, for Luke, the reason for an ongoing prophetic fulfillment beyond narrative time lies in a LXX text not generally well known to educated Greek-reading Romans (Joel 3:1–5a with Christian modifications), coupled with narrative prediction that he is presenting (by John the Baptist, an angel, Jesus, and Peter), he apparently believes that by making a case for the reason and the cause of Christian experiences, he has then done his best to compose an orderly and truthful explanation for prophetic destiny.[21]

For Luke, the ministry of the earthly Jesus and of the heavenly Jesus are dynamically linked, the soteriological nexus of faith/repentance/forgiveness/salvation in the ministry of the earthly Jesus in characters' lives (prodigal son, woman with ointment, Zacchaeus) continues in characters' lives under the ministry of the heavenly Jesus (Ethiopian eunuch, Sergius Paulus, Lydia, Philippian jailer, Crispus).[22] The former characters can be understood by Luke to fulfill prophetic announcements from heaven and from the Holy Spirit-prompted revelation that Jesus is a Savior, with narrative coupling to that same component of Joel's prophecy (Acts 2:21). The latter characters can be similarly understood. And for Luke, the ministry of the heavenly Jesus also includes the outpouring of the gift of the Holy Spirit, which continues to fulfill the programmatic prophecy by John and its implementation via teaching on prayer and predictions by the earthly Jesus, as well as another main component of Joel's prophecy (Acts 2:17a, 18). This ministry takes its literary place alongside the soteriological nexus in Lukan personification in another collection of experientially descriptive and delicately different phrases, namely the pneumatological nexus of Spirit-reception/Spirit-filling/

---

20. Taken from his Περὶ Διηγήματος, *Progym.* 5.1–38. The definitions of narrative offered by Quintilian, Hermogenes, Aphthonius, and Nicolaus are remarkably similar in various details, suggesting Theonic roots.

21. The concept of prophetic destiny in a Lukan sense is that of divine power fulfilling LXX prophecy and narrative prophetic predictions in a practical and pastorally relevant manner, consistent with Luke's pastoral and urgent purpose. For Luke, this prophetic destiny is the source of Christian experiences as understood and practiced in the Jerusalem/Petrine tradition. For Luke, narrative theology and pneumatology, the actions of God in concert with prophetic fulfillment, are embedded in historiography (see too, Talbert, "Promise and Fulfilment," 94, for Luke's understanding of the divine will).

Similar historiography at a secular level is detectable in the conception of Dionysius of Halicarnassus, *Ant. Rom.* 5.56, who understood competent historiography "to seek the causes of what has happened, the forms of action and the intentions of those who acted, and what happened by the hands of the gods (τὰ παρὰ οὗ δίμονίου συγκυρήσαντα)." For Dionysius, what happened as destiny conformed to the ways of heaven, it was heaven sent, somehow by divine power, whereas for Luke prophetic destiny for Christians includes, on my argument, the ongoing manifestation of divine power according to Luke 3:16; 11:5–13; 24:49; Acts 1:4, 5, 8, 14; 2:4, 33, and a narrative projection controlled by heaven at Acts 2:38c, 39 (see n92 below).

22. During the ministry of the heavenly Jesus in the "last days," until the return of the Son of Man and righteous judge (Luke 21:27; Acts 1:9, 11; 17:31), the concept of Lukan conversion (ἐπιστρέφειν) is added to Luke's descriptive soteriological nexus, cf. Michiels, "La conception lucanienne de la conversion," 42–78; George, *Études sur l'oeuvre de Luc*, 351–68; Talbert, "Conversion in the Acts of the Apostles," 141–53.

Spirit-falling-upon/Spirit-outpouring.²³ This latter pneumatological nexus of the Lukan gift of the Spirit is narratively connected, as we shall see, with distinctly noticeable and prominently placed promissory language. I argue that both the soteriological nexus and the pneumatological nexus are well illustrated by the expected examples and precedents and that both are contained in Luke's programmatic concept of ongoing prophetic fulfillment. I also suggest that prophetic fulfillment is understood by Luke as underpinning the missionary guidance portrayed in Acts.

My discussion, however, must be prefaced by a literary observation. Where did Luke get the idea of improving on the πολλοί (Luke 1:1), who I take literally to be many, including some previous Matthean and Markan material, with respect to his employment of a plan of prophetic fulfillment? The plan encompasses the historical reason for the occurrence of selectively narrated events from the recent past wherein divine words had been fulfilled, *and* now boldly and no doubt for Luke, appropriately and possibly urgently,²⁴ extends this identical prophetic fulfillment beyond narrative time to clarify and support Christian experiences taking place in the present. Given Luke's plentiful use of material from 1 and 2 Samuel and 1 and 2 Kings,²⁵ apparently quoting prophecy (2 Sam 7:13) at Luke 1:32–33; Acts 2:30 and its fulfillment (1 Kings 8:20) at Acts 7:47, and given the theological plan evident there of how historical events occur because God invariably achieves His purpose and builds upon events according to prophetic predictions which He honors according to His power and will,²⁶ we may infer that Luke has seen this thematic approach and

---

23. Odette Mainville builds upon fulfillment of Acts 2:33, cf. "Jésus et l'esprit dans l'oeuvre de Luc," 193–208; Mainville, *L'Esprit dans l'oeuvre de Luc*.

Acts 2:33 is the locus classicus regarding the narrative elucidation of the pneumatological nexus of various linguistically connected descriptions of the promise of the Lukan gift of the Holy Spirit. It briefly describes the initiation of the outpouring of the gift of the Holy Spirit by the heavenly Jesus as He begins to fulfill earlier prophecy, teaching, and narrative predictions about this function from heaven. In keeping with our emphasis on a contextual, contiguous, narrative-rhetorical reading, we may appropriately note that in Acts 2:22–36 Luke constructs his argument on God's oath (steadfast love, covenant, cf. 2 Sam 7:12–16) to David (Acts 2:30). O'Toole, "Acts 2:30 and the Davidic Covenant of Pentecost," 246, 258 is correct to conclude that Luke's "account of Pentecost does not include a single verifiable reference to the Sinai covenant, nor does the Jewish law play any part in his account of the event.... Neither Luke's text nor any valid argument justifies the claim that the Sinai covenant or the Law of Moses are to be seen in Acts 2:33."

24. On the possible use and clarification of Pauline Letters in this regard, cf. Elbert, "Paul of the Miletus Speech," 258–68.

25. Regarding this employment: 1 and 2 Samuel, together with 1 and 2 Kings, are referred to twenty-nine times in Luke; twenty-four times in Acts; twenty times in Matthew; twelve times in Mark; two times in John. First and Second Kings are referred to seventeen times in Luke; fourteen times in Matthew; six times in Mark; once in John.

26. Cf. von Rad, "Die deuteronomistische Geschichtstheologie in den Königsbüchern," 192–96, 203. Von Rad draws attention to eleven prophecies and their fulfillment: 2 Sam 7:13 (prophecy) > 1 Kgs 8:20 (fulfillment); 1 Kgs 11:29–30 > 1 Kgs 12:15b; 1 Kgs 13 > 2 Kgs 23:16–18; 1 Kgs 14:6f > 1 Kgs 15:29; 1 Kgs 1–2 > 1 Kgs 16:12; Josh 6:26 > 1 Kgs 16:34; 1 Kgs 22:17 > 1 Kgs 22:35–36; 1 Kgs 21:21–22 > 1 Kgs 21:27–29; 2 Kgs 1:6 > 2 Kgs 1:17; 2 Kgs 21:10–11 > 2 Kgs 24:2; and 2 Kgs 22:15–16 > 2 Kgs 23:30.

has effectively imitated it because it serves his purpose of illustrating the irrevocable prophetic plan of God. A part of this plan Luke has discerned, I suggest, is revealed by John the Baptist, prophetically implemented by the earthly Jesus, and then moved further beyond narrative time by Peter.

The narrative technique of illustrating prophecy and fulfillment in the Samuel-Kings narrative, as in Genesis, involves making it clear to the reader that a past prophecy in the narrative is being fulfilled. This may be accomplished in several ways. A key word (*Stichwort*) may be used relevant to the initial prediction to help signal its later fulfillment, some narrative statement regarding the veracity of prophecy and its effect on ensuing history may be included, or an initial prophetic event may be coupled to an intervening clarification or implementation before it is stated that fulfillment is occurring. For example, in the case of Joseph's prophetic dreams about bowing sheaves (Gen 37:7, 9, 10), recognition of the fulfillment (43:26b, 28b) is assisted by a repetition of a *Stichwort* (here, προσκυνεῖν). Pharaoh's prophetic dream (Gen 41:2–7) is repeated (41:17–24a) with clarification of how the divine plan works in history ("God has shown to Pharaoh what He is about to do. . . . [T]he matter is determined by God and God will soon bring it about," 41:28b, 32b). This intermediate stage is then followed with a reference to its fulfillment ("Just as Joseph had said," 41:53, 54). And in the case of the prophecy against Eli's seed (1 Sam 2:30–34), the predicted event occurs with the death of his sons (4:11b), there is amplification of the same (4:17b), followed at some distance with a reference to fulfillment ("In order to fulfill the word of the Lord," 1 Kgs 2:27).

At Luke 1:45b we are told that "There shall be a completion (τελείωσις) of those things which were told her from the Lord." At 1 Kings 8:56 it is pointed out that "Not one word has failed of all His good promise," and 2 Kings 10:10 urges the recognition, "Know then that there shall fall to the earth nothing of the word of the Lord." Further, Luke may have considered Samuel as initiating the prophetic order (Acts 3:24; 13:20). And it is reasonably suggested that sections of Luke-Acts bear a special relationship to first and second Kings, Luke being impressed by the lives of the prophets.[27] But in any case, there can be no doubt that Luke must be aware of a venerated narrative tradition of properly understanding the past, the present, and for Luke especially the future, as the fulfillment of prophetic words. Such a narrative compositional plan could be understood to appeal to LXX readers.

What about the literary effect of this theme on educated Greek-speaking gentile readers? Given the prominent use of and familiarity with the Homeric epics as literary

---

Von Rad also points out (192) the similar understanding of history and future by drawing attention to Joshua 21:45; 23:14b, 15, with 1 Kings 8:56; 2 Kings 10:10 (an Elijah prophecy and its fulfillment), together with the idea in Deuteronomy 23:47 that Yahweh's word is "nicht leer."

27. Cf. Dubois, "La Figure d'Elie dans la perspective lucanienne," 155–76; Brodie, "Towards Unraveling Luke's Use of the Old Testament," 247–67; Brodie, "Departure for Jerusalem," 96–109; Öhler, *Elia im Neuen Testament,* 136–39; and, on Luke 17:11–19 and 2 Kings 5, Weissenrieder, *Images of Illness in the Gospel of Luke,* 169–75, 185.

models,[28] a known prophetic-fulfillment theme easily detected therein could also serve and give recognizable credibility to Luke's theological and pneumatological plan. Duckworth shows convincingly that forecasts of the future, whether made by the poet, the gods, or mortal characters of the *Odyssey* and the *Iliad*, definitely foretell certain events to come and are devices to arouse curiosity and suspense but not the suspense of uncertainty.[29] Luke appears to also employ this technique, particularly, as does Homer, with respect to divine action that is prophetically projected to lie outside the narrative action of the poem. Similarly, Haft adroitly captures the theme of prophetic fulfillment by focusing on Homer's idea of "Now all things are being brought to completion."[30] Characters are portrayed as being expected to be aware, through normal human recollection, of previously narrated prophecies which affect them. Prophetic instructions are remembered and acted upon. The past and the future affect the present. This is how great stories are told and how the narrative world is expected to be understood by thoughtful readers. Luke fits remarkably well within this literary framework. With respect to another influential epic within the literary culture of the Roman world, Henry and Botha demonstrate that in Vergil's *Aeneid* the narrative sequencing and connectedness of prophetic fulfillment is prominently displayed.[31] Bonz has argued that Luke's understanding of unfolding prophecy is suitably influenced by the *Aeneid*.[32] In any case, both Homer and Vergil compose in the narrative light of a historical design that is initiated in heaven and finds its fulfillment both in the past and in the future beyond narrative time. Luke of course has the advantage on his literary predecessors in that, while he may employ persuasive narrative devices as they do, his experiential descriptions in an ostensibly similar literary case suggest that he enjoys the clarity and understandability of a more orderly presentation, resulting in the confirmation that comes from the distinctive Christian experiences of his readers.[33] Such a realization of experiential confirmation may have given Luke the boldness and the vision he required

28. Cf. Hock, "Homer in Greco-Roman Education."

29. Duckworth, *Foreshadowing and Suspense*, 6, 28–32, 100.

30. Haft, "τὰ δὴ νῦν πάντα τελεῖται," 223–40.

31. Henry, *Vigour of Prophecy*, 108–200; Botha, "Aspects of Prophecy in Vergil's *Aeneid*," 6–14.

32. Bonz, *Past as Legacy*, 87–128.

33. The present study suggests Luke's familiarity with contemporary rhetoric and narrative-rhetorical practice in terms of the communicative style of his writing, but an arguable Lukan expectation of readers' personal interaction with experience portrayed in characters' lives seems to me also quite Bakhtinian, that is, in accord with a perspective within modern rhetoric as well, cf. Green, *Mikhail Bakhtin and Biblical Scholarship*, 24, 40, 47, 48, 69, 70, 162, 164, 191. Further, an authorial perspective serving to coordinate all the parts of a story and give it unity, while inviting the reader to draw dotted lines to a future continuation (so Newsom, "Bakhtin, the Bible, and Dialogic Truth," 292, 296), is also quite Lukan, harmonious indeed with a desire to demonstrate prophetic fulfillment and to project it beyond narrative time. Writing so that a reader may connect the dots to provide clarity of a theme is also consistent with Theon's advice (83.16—84.5, Patillon, *Aelius Théon Progymnasmata,*, 45, 46) that a narrator must pay attention to the main thrust of the whole subject he is setting forth, employing only those matters contributing to his subject, in contrast to a historian, who will be obliged to relate extraneous details.

to improve upon the πολλοί, to clarify their work, to enhance plausibility rooted in a new genre of prophetic historiography, and then to narratively project the ministry of the heavenly Jesus into the present and the future

Discussion

Brawley is right to observe that understanding Acts 2 entails recognition that it has strong antecedents.[34] Antecedents set the stage for the context of the Lukan Peter's focus on Joel's prophecy. The connection between Luke 24:49 and Acts 1:4, taking reference to the "promise of the Father," together with Jesus's saying "You will be baptized with the Holy Spirit not many days from now" (Acts 1:5), reaches back into the narrative as well as forward.[35] It is wise to point this out, given that there is no doubt that Luke expects Theophilus to read front to back and perhaps to reread back to front, when necessary, in order to grasp the narrative continuity being offered him.[36] One strong invitation for Theophilus to look back is Jesus's claim to recollection in the aorist, "This is what you *have heard* from me" (Acts 1:4, emphasis added).[37] In this way Theophilus is nudged back to recall Jesus's own teaching on prayer for the Lukan gift of the Holy Spirit, "How much more will the heavenly Father give the Holy Spirit to those who ask Him!" (Luke 11:13).[38] Jesus's reference to have spoken in the past will surely at least trigger such recollection, if not reinforce an already ongoing personal practice, even for one who might have put Luke's first book down for a time.

On the point that Luke fully expects Theophilus himself to pray for the gift of the Holy Spirit as it appears at the narrative zenith of the Lord's teaching on prayer,[39] as well as to recall Jesus's teaching when he picks up Luke's second book, it may be noted that Jesus's teaching is described by Luke as the word of God (ὁ λόγος τοῦ θεοῦ, Luke 5:1), a phrase signaling significant information deserving a serious response, specific direction from the Lord himself.[40] People crowd about him to hear

---

34. Brawley, *Text to Text Pours Forth Speech*, 75.

35. Brawley, *Text to Text Pours Forth Speech*, 76.

36. On these narrative-rhetorical points, cf. Gaventa, "Toward a Theology of Acts," 146–57; Alexander, "Reading Luke-Acts from Back to Front," 419–46.

37. With Brawley, *Text to Text Pours Forth Speech*, 76.

38. O'Brien, "Prayer in Luke-Acts," 114, notes Lukan references where it is explicitly or directly mentioned that the Spirit is given in answer to prayer (Luke 11:2 [Marcion], 13; Acts 1:14 with 2:1–4; 4:23–31; 8:15–17), although in other portrayals prayer is an attractive, narratively harmonious, and implicit assumption (Acts 2:38c; 9:17; 19:6). Regarding the origin of the Marcion reference and its narrative connections, cf. Schneider, "Die Bitte um das Kommen des Geistes im lukanischen Vaterunser," 344–73.

39. Ernst, *Das Evangelium nach Lukas*, 273, for example, perceives as well that verse 13 is the *Zielpunkt*, appropriately calling attention to the climactic aim, goal, or bull's eye of the entire pericope on prayer, namely, prayer for the gift of the Holy Spirit.

40. Luke's use of κύριος in his first book demonstrates a significant effort to portray a heavenly origin and regard for the earthly Jesus. Extending that heavenly regard to earth, κύριος is used to

it (Luke 5:1), at his word Simon Peter obeys (5:5), parabolic seed is the word of God (8:11) to which good hearers hold fast and bear fruit in patience, and Jesus lets his disciples know emphatically that those who both hear the word of God and do it (8:11–15, 21; cf. 6:46–49) and those who hear the word of God and keep it (11:28) are his real spiritual family and are disciples who will be blessed. Further, Jesus draws attention to the importance of his teaching by regularly encouraging his audience to pay careful attention to his words, "But I say to you that hear" (6:27). The parables of the sower and of the salt conclude with the exhortation "He who has ears to hear let him hear" (8:8; 14:35). Luke portrays Peter as understandably aware of and impressed by this narrative world, in that Peter appropriately describes Jesus along the same lines with a forceful LXX quote from Moses (Acts 3:22b, 23): "You shall hear him (αὐτοῦ ἀκούσεσθε) in all things whatever he may speak," followed by a dire warning to those who will not hear him (ἐὰν μὴ ἀκούσῃ).[41] Jesus's hearers are challenged to "Take care how you listen" (8:17) since "My mother and brothers are those who hear the word of God and do it" (8:12), Riesner linking 8:12 with obedience to Jesus's teaching on prayer for the gift of the Holy Spirit.[42] As to this teaching within the life of the earthly Jesus, it would be both credible and expected from a narrative-rhetorical perspective, since, with a very understandable awareness of the prophetic prediction of John the Baptist (Luke 3:16), Jesus would, with appreciated narrative veracity, reasonably attempt to actuate or stimulate a response to what soon will be His heavenly ministry to disciple-believer-witnesses.

Overall then it is clear that Luke's portrayal of Jesus and his teaching is geared to generating a genuine and obedient response to what Jesus says to do. When Jesus is asked for teaching on prayer with an initial mention of John the Baptist, it is Luke's understanding that his disciples proceed accordingly, and by inference, Luke writes so that Theophilus will follow suit. Jesus is aware of the prophecy of John about himself (3:16) as future baptizer in the Holy Spirit. Jesus's awareness of this would be anticipated in the narrative world. Therefore, a connected and coherent personification/

---

portray the significance of his person among characters (Luke 1:43, 76; 2:11; 7:13, 19; 10:1, 39, 41; 11:39; 12:42; 13:15; 17:5, 6; 18:6; 19:8, 31, 34; 20:42, 44; 22:61; 24:3, 34), cf. Hagene, *Zeiten der Wiederherstellung*, 189–93; a similar effort is found in his second book, cf. Dunn, "ΚΥΡΙΟΣ in Acts," 363–78, a point germane to the lordship of the heavenly Jesus over the outpouring of the gift of the Holy Spirit upon disciple-believer-witnesses (Acts 2:33, 36).

Given this, and that Luke understands Jesus's teaching as the word of God, it would not be expected that Luke should have to paint an additional scene in which the disciples are shown as praying for the gift of the Holy Spirit or for their daily bread as Jesus specifically directs them to do; such a scene could well be deemed superfluous.

41. For discussion of the rhetorical features of this speech in its connected narrative setting, cf. Dietrich, *Das Petrusbild der lukanischen Schriften*, 223–29; Hagene, *Zeiten der Wiederherstellung*, 114–29.

42. Riesner, *Jesus als Lehrer*, 428, links Luke 8:21, "My mother and brothers are those who hear the word of God and do it," with 11:5–8, 9–13, in that these especially useful promises would surely engender a response by disciples in real life within the province of active imitation (Kreis der Nachfolge) and obedience to Jesus's teaching.

characterization portraying Jesus as saying something about it would be expected rhetorically, something from Jesus that would serve to narratively implement the eventual fulfillment of this programmatic prophecy concerning him. We find this implementation in the Lukan Jesus's teaching on prayer.

Obediently responding to Jesus's direction to pray for the gift of the Holy Spirit at Luke 11:13 with boldness, patience, and persistence/shamelessness,[43] according to Jesus's parabolic motivation leading to the climax of his instruction (11:5–8, 9–13), would be the rightly inferred response of Jesus's immediate disciples. Following suit would then place Theophilus—who might by this time in the story have an eye out for Luke's style of prophetic fulfillment—in the company of distinguished Lukan characters who sought to practice what Jesus said to do.[44] It is difficult to imagine that a first-century, rhetorically minded Christian Theophilus would not be so motivated at this juncture. George is insightful in this culminating context to realize that, for Luke, the gift of the Holy Spirit is the best of its kind, a preeminent gift, "le don de l'Esprit est le don par excellence."[45] Montague observes what I believe would be obvious to Theophilus, namely, "It is apparent that those who are already God's children, children of the Heavenly father, may ask for and receive"[46] the Lukan gift of the Holy Spirit.

In this case, Acts 1:5 becomes the risen Jesus's claim to the superiority of his forthcoming baptism over John's earthly baptism, echoing what John already proclaimed (Luke 3:16). There is careful narrative development to set the stage for prophetic fulfillment: early in the first book John the Baptist promises that Jesus will baptize with the Holy Spirit, in the middle of the story Jesus provides strongly motivational teaching that the disciples should begin prayer for the gift of the Holy Spirit, and at the end of the first book Luke records Jesus's pledge that this promise of the Father is about to be forthcoming. Then, at the beginning of his second book, Jesus synthesizes these previous references and their delicately varied descriptive language, revitalizing readers' anticipations for fulfillment of John's prediction.[47] For Theophilus, reading front to back, armed with some previous instruction as was Apollos, but reading *tabula rasa* with the realization that Luke was attempting to communicate to him the substance of a valued and genuine tradition, this narrative development does indeed set a mood of expectancy.[48]

---

43. The contextual and literary arguments are assessed in favor of ἀναίδεια (Luke 11:8) as persistence in prayer within the exemplary parable of the friend at midnight by Kim, "Lucan Pentecostal Theology of Prayer," 205–17.

44. Cf. Pesch, "Die Gabe des Heiligen Geistes," 53; Pesch, *Die Apostelgeschichte*, 66–67.

45. George, "La prière," 412.

46. Montague, *Holy Spirit*, 259–60.

47. This basic development noted also by Tannehill, *Narrative Unity of Luke-Acts*, 2:12; Brawley, *Text to Text Pours Forth Speech*, 76.

48. Gaventa, "Toward a Theology of Acts," 154.

LUKE'S FULFILLMENT-OF-PROPHECY THEME

The Characterization of a Soteriological Foreground

Before looking at the placement of the Joel passage in Peter's opening programmatic speech and considering how Peter and his hearers would comprehend its prophetic contents, it will be appropriate to evaluate Luke's previous depiction of the 120 disciple-believer-witnesses (Luke 24:48) who are portrayed, compatibly so within a Theonic narrative-rhetorical framework of examples and precedents, as praying for (cf. Luke 24:53; Acts 1:14)[49] and receiving the mysterious power (Acts 1:8) Jesus associates with the Father's promised gift of the Holy Spirit. These characters have already taken their place within the thematic personification of a soteriological nexus. It seems unmistakable that Luke fully intends Theophilus to understand that the disciples who received the first occurrence of the promised gift of the Holy Spirit in his second book had already entered into genuine Christian discipleship and commitment to Jesus, i.e., they had entered into that nexus of experiential concepts: repentance, forgiveness, belief, and salvation which Luke associates with experiencing Jesus.[50] Indeed, Luke writes about his characters' lives in such a plausible and convincing manner so as to convey this very point with great clarity. A convincing portrayal in this regard would be important for Luke from the standpoint of narrative plausibility, so that Theophilus may be assured that the prophecy of Jesus as a Savior was fulfilled in Jesus's earthly ministry.

So, let's review the main points of this personification (προσωποποιΐα or ἠθοποιΐα).[51] The prophetic characterization of Jesus is properly accompanied with ap-

---

49. Marie E. Isaacs correctly observes in *Concept of Spirit*, 88: "It is interesting to note that in the Pentecost story the reception of the Spirit is associated with prayer. It was whilst they were praying that the Spirit filled the room. Cf. Luke 11:13 where, according to Luke, it is πνεῦμα ἅγιον which will be granted in answer to prayer." Similarly, Charles H. Talbert recognizes that "In Acts 1:14 the disciples are praying before the pentecostal gift of the Spirit in Acts 2. Indeed, the evangelist would see this promise of Jesus in Luke 11:13 as the basis for Pentecost," in *Reading Luke*, 139.

50. By experiencing Jesus, I mean that these disciples had experienced Jesus christologically and reflectively as the Son of God (cf. Kilgallen, "Conception of Jesus [Luke 1:35]," 225–46) *and* that they had experienced him pneumatologically as a person anointed with the Holy Spirit (Luke 4:4–19) in as much as the Holy Spirit present in Jesus's earthly ministry impacted and influenced his hearers and disciples. Since Luke clearly indicates the Holy Spirit's presence in Jesus's life and ministry, I suggest that Luke would conclude that the disciples had experienced the Holy Spirit. *Also*, what I mean by experiencing Jesus in the Lukan narrative includes experience of the Father, as suggested by Luke 15:11–32 and the Father's involvement with those who repent. All of this experiential portrayal of Lukan characters *in his first book* who participate in the soteriological nexus lays a conceptual background for characters in this narrative world to obediently pray for, and then receive of, the Lukan gift of the Holy Spirit for empowerment in his second book.

51. Lukan προσωποποιΐα is again quite harmonious with contemporary narrative-rhetorical standards, with words ("speech in character") and actions appropriate to the characters introduced, cf. Theon, Περὶ προσωποποιΐας, *Progym.* 8.1–80; 11.13–18; Patillon, *Aelius Théon Progymnasmata*, xxxiv–xxxvii; "l'action appropriée au sujet" (105); Kennedy, *Progymnasmata*, 34–36, 89, 126.

As to the use and background of the concept, cf. Bühlmann and Scherer, *Stilfiguren der Bibel*, 70; Stählin, "Das Bild der Witwe," 10–11; and *Rhet. ad Her.* 4.53.66, where προσωποποιΐα (*conformatio*) "consists in representing an absent person as present, or in making a mute thing or one lacking

propriate examples of Jesus fulfilling prophecy as God's will is done. Jesus is portrayed in the narrative world as if he is aware of prophecy about himself and is appropriately implementing the same. It would be rhetorically odd, for example, if Jesus is announced from heaven as a Savior and then is portrayed as either never mentioning this or as never explicitly illustrative of this function with respect to characters' lives. Such a portrayal might seem to lack a basis of credibility (*Glaubwürdigkeitsbeweis*),[52] given that in Luke-Acts it is the fulfillment-of-prophecy theme that can be recognized as the underlying cause for the events rendered. So, via a prophetic announcement by an angel, Luke presents the earthly Jesus at the outset as being a Savior (Luke 2:11), with the Lukan Paul repeating this description (Acts 13:23). Not only did the earthly Jesus function as a Savior (σωτήρ), fulfilling the angel's prophecy, being the salvation (σωτήριον) of God (Luke 2:30; 3:6), but so too, in the narrative present, the heavenly Jesus is also Savior (Acts 5:31). In the narrative world, Jesus would be expected to be aware of the angel's prophecy and to be reasonably portrayed as being engaged in its implementation. Lukan *Sondergut* includes then a scene where Jesus applies LXX Isaiah 61:1-2, with Christian overtones of salvific forgiveness, to himself (Luke 4:16-21), the one scripture quotation in the double-work explicitly declared to be "fulfilled" (πεπλήρωται, 4:21). In fact, while other NT authors normally or frequently assign the time of salvation to the future,[53] Luke normally employs salvific concepts with respect to his characters' lives in the present time.[54] It would indeed be strange if Luke believed that during the ministry of the earthly Jesus no one under His ministry had a genuine soteriological experience. Based on what Luke actually writes, such an aggressive thesis appears rhetorically incomprehensible and egregiously anti-Lukan. On the contrary, Theophilus will easily gain the impression that Luke explains the fruits of repentance (Luke 3:8, 10-14), that Jesus does not call the righteous, but sinners, to repent (5:32; cf. 13:3, 5; 15:7, 10; 17:3f), and that disciples are also to then preach repentance for the forgiveness of sins (24:47).[55] Plausibly, as the first book concludes, the disciples' experience of repentance and forgiveness enable them to preach about the

---

form articulate, and attributing to it a definite form and a language of a certain behavior appropriate to its character." Further similar definition is found in Demetrius, *Eloc.* 5.265-66 (following Περὶ Ἑρμηνείας, Roberts, *Demetrius on Style*; Quintilian, *Inst. Or.* 9.2.29-37 (30); 11.1.4; 11.1.47; Martin, *Antike Rhetorik*, 411-13.

52. With Lausberg, *Handbuch*, 230.

53. Observed, for example, by Cadbury, "Names for Christians in Acts," 5:375-92 (383).

54. As observed by Throckmorton, "Σώζειν, σωτηρία in Luke-Acts," 515-26, noting exceptions like Luke 13:23; 18:26. Throckmorton basically concludes (526) that "in Luke-Acts σωτήρ, σωτηρία, and σωτήριον point, almost exclusively, not to the future, not to the End-time or the consummation, but to historical reality met or received during Jesus life," and "experienced" also in post'ascension Christianity where the heavenly Jesus functions as Savior (Acts 5:31). An exception to this present time usage in the latter case is the future salvation in Acts 16:31, which falls within Luke's consistent syntax of imperative-future middle/passive combinations (see n80).

55. Marshall, *Luke*, 193.

significance of these personal responses and divine initiatives after they themselves receive the Lukan gift of the Spirit in the ensuing narrative.

Theophilus will of course believe that some hearers responded to Jesus's mission of calling sinners to repentance (5:32), being aware of the coming destruction if there is no repentance (13:3, 5; cf. Acts 17:30). The story of Lazarus and the rich man (16:19–31) obviously serves as a call for repentance (16:30), suggesting that hearers who repent could also expect eternal comfort in Abraham's bosom when they died. Jesus's knowledge of joy in heaven when a sinner repented (15:7, 10) suggests that some of His hearers did repent. When gentiles at Caesarea were granted repentance unto life (μετάνοια εἰς ζωήν, Acts 11:18), Theophilus would surely think that such spiritual events took place during the ministry of the earthly Jesus as well. Salvation experience, accompanied by deeds of repentance, comes to Zacchaeus's house "today" (19:9, 10).[56] This Lukan *Sondergut* specifically illustrates the Son of Man's claim to forgive sins (5:24; cf. 5:32; 12:8) in the face of opposition (7:34)[57] and fulfills the narrative prediction that Jesus is a Savior (2:11). The woman with the ointment is forgiven and told that her faith has saved her (7:36–50),[58] very appropriate and persuasive as far as narrative characterization or personification is concerned given that salvation entails deliverance from sin (1:68, 69, 71, 77), her forgiveness and her faith and her salvation being inseparable.[59] These specific instances of salvation, forgiveness, and faith in the lives of people during the ministry of the earthly Jesus complement in an inverse manner those who have the word taken from their hearts by the devil, erasing potential belief and salvation.[60] Faith in Jesus separates the

---

56. Fitzmyer, *Gospel according to Luke I–IX*, 1225, notes that here "Salvation, the primary Lucan effect of the Christ-event, surfaces on the lips of Jesus." Note the combination of "today" and "salvation" in this scene: Jesus says, "Today *salvation* has come to this house" (Luke 19:9) and "today it is necessary for *me* to stay in your house" (19:5), my emphasis bringing in the idea that, for Luke, the earthly Jesus is the *salvation* of God (Luke 2:30; 3:6), with Throckmorton, "Σῴζειν, σωτηρία in Luke-Acts," 525. Spicq, *Notes de lexicographie néo-testamentaire*, 629–43 (635), also observes the significance of the fact that this Lukan salvation is portrayed as a present reality (*qui est déjà présent*) in the narrative world.

57. Cf. Hagene, *Zeiten der Wiederherstellung*, 232–36.

58. A comparative observation on Lukan style is quite apropos here: "If the style is the man, then the man with whom we have to do is for his time and station a gentleman of ability and breadth of interest, whatever his past reading and training may have been. His vocabulary no purist could wholly commend, but no ignorant man could entirely equal it, though he could always understand it. It had the qualification, which is the chief requisite of any vocabulary—it could express what its owner wished to express with ease and accuracy" (Cadbury, *Making of Luke-Acts*, 220–21). *Luke's portrayal of this woman's experience places it squarely within Luke's soteriological nexus of repentance, forgiveness, faith, salvation, and Lukan conversion, something Theophilus would readily understand*, cf. also Kilgallen, "Forgiveness of Sins (Luke 7:36–50)," 105–16; Marshall, *Gospel of Luke*, 314. Neale, *None but the Sinners*, 140–47, argues persuasively that she has been restored to God's favor, with forgiveness and repentance dramatically demonstrated as the purpose of Jesus's ministry.

59. With Throckmorton on the last point, "Σῴζειν, σωτηρία in Luke-Acts" 518.

60. The implication seems obvious that Jesus understood some hearers to be able to experience salvation, Luke adding ἵνα μὴ πιστεύσαντες σωθῶσιν to the parable of the sower (Luke 8:12c).

disciples from the living dead who do not respond to Jesus's word (9:60). The joyful response within parables implies a powerful new experience, suggesting forgiveness and salvation (15:4–6, 8–9, 11–32). Those who repent (15:7), like lost and found coins (15:8), set the stage for the younger son who also is lost and found, beginning new life (15:24, 32). The immediate invitation to self-satisfied listeners (15:1) to this latter story is unmistakable,[61] suggesting, via the arrangement of three parables of chapter 15, a pragmatic and coherent rhetorical description of Jesus's soteriological concern for his opponents in the narrative world.[62] The parable of the grand feast (14:15–24) suggests a recognizable experiential outcome in hearers' lives who accept Jesus's invitation, while the rich man's treatment of Lazarus (16:19–31) provides an example of unrepentant behavior based on a rejection of Jesus's message.

Luke understands the kingdom dynamically and forcefully present during the ministry of the earthly Jesus (4:43, connected experientially to 4:18–19; 8:10; 9:2; 10:9, 11; 11:20; 16:16, implying a personal decision to enter; 17:21).[63] These conceptions of the kingdom, which can include salvation, faith, forgiveness, and repentance, are narratively suggestive of the spiritual interactivity of God in bringing the kingdom to those responsive to the message.[64] As in Luke's description of salvation, his concept of the kingdom also combines a present reality with a future expectation.[65]

In the present Satan's power is broken (13:16 [Lukan *Sondergut*]; 7:21, 22).[66] A Samaritan leper (17:11–19) is understandably portrayed as "*saved* by his faith [cf. Acts 2:21] . . . *this man needed and received salvation beyond his disease*, something the others still lacked."[67] Names of disciples have been recorded in heaven (10:20b, τὰ ὀνόματα ὑμῶν ἐγγέγραπται ἐν τοῖς οὐρανοῖς, the perfect passive suggesting continuance of a completed heavenly action, the entrance into salvation, so that, in context, "We have a particularly solemn image which carries with it the thought of the ancient custom of inscribing a list of citizens (a well-known image in Roman civic life). . . . The meaning is that by ὄνομα (name), i.e., as persons of individual worth,

---

61. So, too, Linnemann, *Gleichnisse Jesu*, 84; Schottroff, "Das Gleichnis vom verlorenen Sohn," 42; Pokorný, "Lukas 15,11–32 und die lukanischen Soteriologie," 179–92; Pokorný, *Theologie der lukanischen Schriften*, 165. Luke 5:32; 15:7 are the same as 15:24, 32. Evidently the major themes in the exemplary parable are sin, repentance, forgiveness, grace, joy, and sonship, experiential states obviously intended to be understood and experienced by hearers in the narrative world in response to their parabolic enunciation by the earthly Jesus.

62. Wolter, "Lk 15 als Streitgespräch," 25–56.

63. That Luke portrays the kingdom as present insofar as the earthly Jesus is concerned is stressed by Wolter, "'Reich Gottes' bei Lukas," 549–550, 557, 561–63.

64. Cf. Atkinson, "Prior Work of the Spirit in Luke's Proposal," 107–14; Cho, "Spirit and Kingdom in Luke-Acts," 173–97.

65. On this combination re: the kingdom, cf. Wolter, "'Reich Gottes' bei Lukas," 543; Guy, "Interplay of the Present and Future," 119–37.

66. Healing and exorcism signal the presence of the spiritual kingdom. On these activities in the Third Gospel, cf. Thomas, *Devil, Disease and Deliverance*, 197–226.

67. Stenschke, *Luke's Portrait of Gentiles*, 111 (emphasis and insert his).

those belonging to Jesus are God's possession (*zugehörendes Eigentum*) and therefore citizens of the heavenly πολιτεία (commonwealth)."[68] The recording of names on the heavenly role is cause for present rejoicing (10:20b), similar to the rejoicing over lost sheep, coins, and sons (15:6, 9, 24). Participation in and observation of such personal experience is clearly illustrated within Luke's narrative world. After his resurrection, Jesus tells a group of assembled disciples that they will be proclaiming repentance and forgiveness (Luke 24:47), that they are witnesses of these things (ὑμεῖς μάρτυρες τούτων, 24:48). Not only will they bear witness to the teachings, life, death, and resurrection of Jesus, but also to their own experience of salvation/ repentance/forgiveness/faith, which they, along with other Lukan characters, have themselves experienced during Jesus's earthly ministry.[69]

Further, it is unflattering to Luke's intelligence to believe that he would portray Jesus telling the disciples to proclaim repentance/forgiveness if this was something they themselves did not experientially understand. It is clear from this context that repentance for the forgiveness of sins (24:47) has already occurred in the lives of these witnesses (24:48) and that they understand that their soteriological experience is one experience that Jesus wants them to proclaim and be a witness to, another prophecy-fulfilling, Christocentric experience being yet to come. Overall, then, the deliberate impression given to Theophilus at this juncture, as he reflects backward in time and conjoins the narrative world, is that the obedient characters going to prayer at Acts 1:14 were, from Luke's perspective, Christians, as I have presumed that he is, waiting for the promise of the Father about which Jesus had earlier given instruction (Luke 11:5–13; 24:49; Acts 1:4, 5), believer-disciple-witnesses who have heard the word of God from Jesus and are accordingly seeking the Lukan gift of the Spirit so as to enhance their ability as witnesses.

The Contextualization of Joel's Prophecy within Peter's Speech

Having established the Lukan characterization of the first disciple-believer-witnesses seeking prayerfully to receive the gift of the Holy Spirit, thereby experiencing one of the phenomenological contents of Joel's prophecy to be advanced by the Lukan Peter, I now turn to the event itself. When the promise of the Father is first poured out, there is

---

68. Schrenk, "ἐγγράφω, Zu Lk 10,20," 770, parentheses mine. Luke portrays these persons in a manner that is perfectly consistent with his characterization of other disciple-believers. Plummer, *Gospel according to S. Luke*, 280, translates 10:20 as "your names have been written, and remain written, in heaven," describing these disciples "as citizens possessing the full privileges of the heavenly commonwealth."

69. Following their reception of the gift of the Holy Spirit, they will witness more powerfully to the significance of the supportive events and words in the life of the earthly Jesus (Luke 24:48) via their personal faith in the heavenly Jesus. Strathmann, "μάρτυς, κτλ. im NT," is correct to notice (496) that it is the direct Christian experience (*unmittelbaren Erleben*) of these disciples which will motivate them to proclaim salvation/repentance/forgiveness/faith (Acts 2:21; 4:12, e.g.).

a rushing wind and tongues of fire. Luke does not provide any editorial comment as to any understanding he might have had as to what these first accompanying effects might represent, perhaps because he is more interested in the pastoral dimension, given that he directs his narrative focus on the experiential concept of being filled with the Spirit,[70] which undoubtedly connects to the empowerment-for-missions motif. Nevertheless, perhaps the best and most straightforward clues, if extant, to what he may have thought about the fire and the wind might be found in his own text, but he leaves us to speculate. The fulfillment-of-prophecy theme may be helpful. Luke 3:16 predicts that Jesus will baptize with the Holy Spirit and fire, metaphorical fire in view (3:17). Tongues as of fire resting on inspired xenolalic or glossolalic[71] speakers in the shape like a human tongue (Acts 2:3) suggests that this fire is related first and foremost to the inspired speech of those being baptized (γλῶσσαι ὡσεὶ πυρός, cp.λαλεῖν ἑτέραις γλώσσαις and ἡμετέραις γλώσσαις, 2:3, 4, 11). The increased power (1:8) for witness of disciple-believers so baptized will have a fiery component which could recall "I will make my ministers as a flame of fire" (LXX Ps 103:4). As to the rushing wind (2:2), this clothing with power comes from "on high" (Luke 24:49) according to the risen Jesus. This Jesus has now ascended into the atmosphere (Acts 1:9–11). What better signal could be provided than an abnormal movement of the atmosphere to indicate that the heavenly Jesus was now fulfilling the prophecy of the earthly Jesus? In any case, apart from the significantly narrated interior effects of this baptism/gift of the Holy Spirit reception (perhaps described in concert with an experiential consensus at the time of Luke's composition as tangible "Spirit-filling"), the external prophetic effects may be described as xenolalia, a variation of glossolalia.[72] I agree with Talbert that "tongues of men and angels" (1 Cor 13:1) may refer first to xenolalia and then to glossolalia, and that a sharp distinction between what Luke describes in Acts 2:4 and what he portrays in other events of the gift of the Holy Spirit (like Acts 10:46; 19:6) cannot be drawn. They are as two sides of the same coin.[73] And, they fulfill, as Peter himself takes note of, one of the components of Joel's prophecy, that of inspired prophetic speech.

The speech exhibits discernible argumentative categories or stages set out in response to two short information-seeking questions, a feature of Lukan style.[74] These stages are very compatible with the rhetorical patterns of argumentation found in Cicero's *ratiocinato* (*De Inv.* 1.34.57–41.77) and in the complete argument of the *Ad*

70. Cf. Shelton, "'Filled with the Holy Spirit,'" 81–107.

71. Regarding the possible inclusion of glossolalia at Acts 2:4, cf. Williams, "Speaking in Tongues," 79. For Luke, glossolalia can at times be xenoglossy, cf. Powers, "Missionary Tongues?," 39–55; Hovenden, *Speaking in Tongues*, 103–4.

72. Perhaps similar, in respect to the external result of hearing, with cases of people today who testify of hearing their own language being spoken by persons ministering the interpersonal spiritual gift of tongues, cf. Talbert, *Literary and Theological Commentary*, 43.

73. With Talbert, *Literary and Theological Commentary*, 43.

74. Cf. Elbert, "Observation on Luke's Composition and Narrative Style of Questions," 104–5. [Included in this anthology—Ed.]

Herrenium (2.18.27–29.46). This may be briefly illustrated in the following analysis. A question, "What does this mean?" (Acts 2:12b), serves to introduce what is to be argued, Acts 2:14b–16, concluding with "This [phenomenon] is what was spoken by Joel" (the thesis, *propositio*). Then, 2:17–21, the reconfigured Joel text to suit the occasion is set forth (the reason, *ratio*). This is followed, 2:22–33, by a progymnastic argument from example (ἐκ παραδείγματος) or, as *Ad. Her.* 4.49.62 states it, an argument from example (*exemplum*) which is "the citing of something done or said in the past, along with the definite naming of the doer." This stage is a proof of reason (*rationis confirmatio*), confirming that the heavenly Jesus is indeed responsible for this example of inspired prophetic speech by men, women, sons, and daughters which can now be seen and heard (2:33), promised during the earthly ministry of Jesus to His disciples. Then we have in 2:34–36 an embellishment (*exornatio*) "to enrich the argument after the proof has been established" (*Ad Her.* 2.18.28). Another question, "What shall we do?" (2:37b), prepares the way for the conclusion, the rhetorical nature of which I will discuss below. This concluding response (the resume [*complexio*]) gathers the experientially relevant highlights of the argumentative stages together for the questioners, appropriately recollecting from the first stage the "This is what"[75] and culminating the final stage with a conditional clause promising "you will receive the gift of the Holy Spirit."[76]

Now, if Luke wanted to make sure that his readers would understand how Peter knew, specifically, to go right to Joel in order to support and explain what had occurred, and how Peter would know to prophetically predict what should now be expected to continue to occur as prophetic fulfillment during the ministry of the heavenly Jesus, he has taken care of this concern at Luke 24:27, 44. By including specific instruction from the risen Christ on prophetic fulfillment, he shows Theophilus how Peter began to understand Jesus's prophecy-fulfilling role (δεῖ πληρωθῆναι).[77] The Christian edit-

---

75. Perelman and Olbrechts-Tyteca, *New Rhetoric*, 65, observe that "When a speaker selects and puts forward the premises that are to serve as foundation for his argument, he relies on his hearers' adherence to the propositions from which he will start."

76. Peter's argumentative stages are closely knit (with Evans, "'Speeches' in Acts," 296; Kennedy, *New Testament Interpretation through Rhetorical Criticism*, 117), building upon the reconfigured Joel prophecy, amplifying various Scriptures in order to confirm that the resurrection should inevitably lead to the phenomenon that is presently being observed and contemplated, the "This is what" that is placed first in the argument. The final question (2:37b) then prompts a vivid answer, a concluding answer contiguous with the event motivating the beginning of the speech, an answer appropriate to the speaker's own experience.

77. One senses the implication that the disciple-believer-witnesses at the close of Luke's first book, and at the commencement of the second, were actively engaged in understanding the ministry of the earthly and heavenly Jesus in the light of Scripture. Peter's previous instruction by Jesus, who gave "exegesis classes" (so Sanders, *Luke and Scripture*, 18), could account in this connected story for Peter's immediate recognition and application, in a narrative-rhetorical world where appropriate "speech-in-character" is valued, of the Joel text. Coherent with this narrative implication is its potential bearing on Theophilus's assurance of previous instruction in this matter. To reasonably conclude that Peter's application of the Joel text to a phenomenon directed from heaven had its origin with Jesus himself, as suggested by the contextual train of thought (Luke 24:27, 44–47, 49), could be helpful in bolstering

ing[78] of the LXX text produces the following version (with the important improvements by the Lukan Peter, Acts 2:17-21, in italics): (v. 17) *In the last days, God says,* I will pour out my Spirit upon all people, your sons and daughters will prophesy, your young men will see visions, and your old men will dream *dreams*. (v. 18) Indeed, on *my* servants, both men and women, in those days I will pour out my Spirit, *and they will prophesy.* (v. 19) I will show wonders in the heaven *above* and *signs* on the earth *below*, blood and fire and billows of smoke. (v. 20) The sun will be turned to darkness and the moon to blood before the coming of the great and glorious day of the Lord. (v. 21) And everyone who calls on the name of the Lord will be saved."[79]

Peter attributes v. 18, inspired prophetic speech, phenomena that is seen and heard, to the heavenly Jesus, who having received this ministry from the Father has poured forth the promise (ἐπαγγελία) of the Holy Spirit (Acts 2:33). Based upon Luke's previous soteriological characterization of Peter and his fellow disciple-believer-witnesses which we have reviewed, Peter cannot be applying v. 21, calling for salvation, to himself, rather that will apply to Peter's hearers (who are urged to repent). We should understand Luke in his narrative-rhetorical context where the narrative quality of "speech-in character" (προσωποποιΐα), was a highly valued literary convention which Luke and a Roman-educated Theophilus may have internalized.[80] By this phrase Theon, for example, means attributing suitable words to an actual person; this personification must set forth in a noncontroversial manner words which are suitable to the character, to the subject, and to the occasion.[81] Accordingly, this literary strategy requires that Peter must speak according to his own experience and point

---

confidence in the reliability of Jesus tradition. Given that the appeal to the opening of minds regarding ancient texts is immediately followed by a quotation from the earthly/resurrected Jesus treating the instrumentality (v. 49) of the narratively forthcoming heavenly Jesus in the ministry of the gift of the Holy Spirit (noting the foregrounding of a *Schlüsselwort* [ἐπαγγελία] to be employed in Peter's speech and harkening back to previous teaching on the subject [11:5–13]), a reader could easily conclude that one of the texts being expounded must be relevant to such a forthcoming function of the heavenly Jesus.

78. Kilpatrick, "Some Quotations in Acts," 81–83, notes the variations in Acts 2:16-21 from the LXX, which do not depend on an independent reference to the Hebrew, but appear to be alterations to the LXX "to suit the interests and the purposes of the man making the quotation."

79. For discussion of the improvements from the LXX deemed appropriate to the occasion, cf. Menzies, *Empowered for Witness*, 179–86; Steyn, *Septuagint Quotations in the Context*, 77–89, 91–100; and McQueen, *Joel and the Spirit*, 48–52.

80. It may be appropriate to note that ancient conceptions of rhetorical categories, like "speech-in-character," which would affect the perceived plausibility of speeches, have a distinct advantage in their potential assistance to the reading process over modern conceptions, given that *they are not indebted to the Enlightenment view of rationality* (with Crowley, *Methodical Memory*, 1–14). Neither are ancient conceptions indebted to reading speeches through the lenses of fixed humanistic or speculative philosophical presuppositions, which may exert influence against a contiguous contextual interpretation of Peter's speech in Acts 2. Instead, the ancient literary critics and narrative practitioners of "speech-in-character" evaluated speeches in historiography based on their *perceived plausibility*.

81. As to the Theonic and other similar rhetorical understandings of προσωποποιΐα in the tradition contemporary with Luke's project, see n47.

of view, from the perspective of previous narration which characterizes Peter.[82] Not to do this would violate the very essence of how a narrative is to be composed, with plausibility and consistency.[83] Luke is very Theonic and transparent, as he should be in his rhetorical culture, in that Peter can easily be understood in his narrative context as applying vv. 17a-c and 18 to himself and his fellow prophetic speakers who are men and women ("sons and daughters will prophesy").

When hearers ask, "What should we do?" Peter responds from his own experience, "Repent, be baptized in the name of Jesus Christ for the forgiveness of your sins, and you will receive the gift of the Holy Spirit, for the promise (ἐπαγγελία) is for you and your children, and for all who are afar off, as many as the Lord our God shall call to Himself" (Acts 2:38–39). Luke can here be easily understood as paying attention to one of the three desirable Theonic qualities or virtues of narrative, that of clarity.[84] Avoiding the punctuation of current editions of the GNT, which is not especially sensitive to the context and to narrative-rhetorical "speech-in-character," verse 38a, b, and c flows contiguously into the thought of verse 39. The promise there resonates clearly with the immediately contiguous thought about a future passive reception of the gift of the Holy Spirit, obviously describing the same phenomenon. The promise there (v. 39) resonates with the description of the heavenly Jesus (2:33), with a foregrounded narrative prediction (Luke 24:49), which in turn picks up the earlier teaching of the main character on the same subject and connects to an introductory prophecy by a significant character concerning this same heavenly action, action wedded to the same ἐπαγγελία at 24:49; Acts 1:4; 2:33, and 39.

Ἐπαγγελία is the Lukan *Stichwort* employed in his fulfillment-of-prophecy theme with regard to the gift of the Holy Spirit. We see it in what appears to be a persuasive narrative display. The coupling of the *Stichwort* is easily understood, in a Homeric flowing thought-line, as a credible and plausible implementation of the earlier prophecy of John the Baptist about what Jesus will do. Even though this foregrounding prophecy is some distance away from the heavenly action here, narrative-rhetorical technique demands its connection by remembrance, reading back to front if need be, so as to see the beginning of the sequence which leads to heavenly action beyond narrative time. In the information provided by Jesus after the resurrection and prior to the ascension, the *Stichwort* there may be easily understood as foregrounding a

---

82. Genette, *Narrative Discourse*, 186, while not referring to Theon's narrative exercise on "speech-in-character," refines Theon's exercise a bit by explicitly calling attention to the point of view of the speaker, something Theon does implicitly. Harmonious with Theon, Genette holds that *the speaker's point of view as determined from the narrative must not be compromised.* A competent narrator is well aware of this and must compose so that his readers will easily grasp the point of view of the speaker. Theon notes that his exercise is particularly useful to characters' emotions (*Progym.* 8.75–80), modestly suggesting that students who may wish to handle "speech-in-character" at a more advanced stage can nevertheless make use of the starting points he offers.

83. Theon, *Progym.* 5.187–91.

84. Theon, *Progym.* 5.39–51. Clarity is achieved by the proper style of composition, by a style of articulation that is clear to a reader (*Progym.* 5.57–58, 86).

visible coupling to a main element of Peter's Christianized version of Joel's prophecy, which in turn invokes the progymnastic assumption that a speaker should represent the contiguous and vivid realism of the narrative world of which he/she is a part.[85] And, further enhancing the function of the *Stichwort* in bringing reader's attention to the contiguous narrative sequencing from Luke 3:16, to an exemplary fulfillment at Acts 2:4, to the projection beyond narrative time at 2:39, is a deft employment of gift-language at Luke 11:13 and Acts 2:38c.

The Lukan Peter, I would say as obviously expected in good narrative-rhetorical personification, communicates to his hearers out of his own experiential context.[86] Under the teaching of Jesus, he has prayed for the gift of the Holy Spirit, taking his place in the narrative world of disciple-believers in Luke's first book. At the end of the first book disciple-believer-witnesses are again portrayed as praying, waiting for the promised gift of the Holy Spirit. Further, from the narrated soteriological experience of Lukan characters in the first book, some of whom are picked up at the beginning of the second book, it is clear that the gift of the Holy Spirit is not tied to baptism, a fact the rest of the text makes clear, if any clarification is needed.[87] Calvin captures the intent of the speech when he comments on Acts 2:38c, 39, that "He (Peter) promises them (his hearers) the gift of the Spirit of which they saw an example in the diversity of tongues."[88] Calvin's understanding is contextually sensitive, according well with contemporary guidance that "Exegesis seeks for an interpretation of a passage which will account satisfactorily for all features of that passage, both on its own and in its context."[89] Why should Peter expect his hearers to receive a different gift of the Holy

---

85. As the reader's eye follows the *Stichwort*, which serves as a narrative guide within the schema of prophetic fulfillment, the invocation of an orderly connectedness takes on and enhances a progymnastic sense in that Luke, probably not unlike a number of other educated writers of his day, may have cut his teeth on the *Progymnasmata*, as Parsons, "Luke and the *Progymnasmata*" (n17), Penner, "Civilizing Discourse" (n17), and Elbert, "Observation" (n74) have recently suggested.

86. I have suggested that perhaps Luke renders the interior experience of these characters, who externally manifest inspired prophetic-type speech, with Spirit-filled terminology, because such terminology had become understandable due to similar experience, not because of purely literary motives. Peter's inner sphere of experience would expectedly be connected to his ensuing speech about the promised gift of the Holy Spirit (2:38c, 39), that is, connected to what he would be expected to say about that topic based upon what has just happened to him, as Theonic personification requires, cf. too, Berger, *Identity and Experience in the New Testament*, 71.

87. Cf. Pesch, "Taufe und Geistempfang in der Apostelgeschichte," in his *Die Apostelgeschichte*, 1:281–85. Obviously, the gift of the Holy Spirit is not tied to water baptism or the imposition of hands. However, Pesch underplays the strong previous context of prayer in the narrative life of the speaker relative to the gift of the Holy Spirit. This cannot be underestimated, as this didactic (Luke 11:5–13) and imperative (Luke 24:49, 53; Acts 1:4, 14) context originated with the Lord himself (cf. n40, κύριος note).

88. Calvin, *Acts of the Apostles*, 1:81.

89. So, Marshall, "Introduction," 15. Arguably also, such a "speech-in-character" reading of the speaker's argumentative and experiential intent at 2:38c, 39 suggested in the narrative-rhetorical perspective advocated here accords well with the dispassionate interpretive guidance of Adele Berlin, that the text and its integral parts "make sense." Cf. her "Search for a New Biblical Hermeneutic," 195–207.

Spirit, with a different phenomenological intimacy and interiority, than he with the 120 have just received? Is that a plausible perception? Exploration of this narrative world and the rhetorically sensitive personification of characters within it must take these questions seriously, for I find it difficult to detect any such expectation that is consistent with the train of argumentation within the speech.[90] In his personification of Peter, Luke leaves no noticeable clues that such an expectation exists. The narrative descriptions of fire and wind are not a part of the inspired prophetic speech cited by Joel which is exemplified by the preceding glossolalia and hence are not, in the speaker's view of prophetic fulfillment, part of the promised gift of the Holy Spirit at 2:38c, 39. Yet the compositional culmination of the speech, wherein Peter's answer to his hearers' question, "What shall we do?" (2:37b), serves to provide contextually connected teaching based on Peter's experience.

Actually, paying a bit more attention to the speaker's previous context, and reading back to front, suggests that the Lukan gift of the Holy Spirit at 2:38c, 39 would involve prayer, on the part of those entering the soteriological nexus of repentance/forgiveness/faith/salvation, for the promised gift described by Jesus as empowering and by Luke as interior Spirit-filling. The contextual emphasis is not on speaking with the tongue but waiting and prayer for Spirit-filling and empowerment, exemplified by inspired prophetic speech initiated in heaven by a sovereign Lord (2:33). Marguerat is right to observe that "The giving of the Spirit remains God's doing. One can only wait for it and pray that this grace be given."[91] Further, the imperative-future middle/passive combination, as employed here, is, interestingly, a consistent feature of Lukan style, and when employed clearly connotes, for him, two verbal ideas that are temporally nonsimultaneous. This syntactical combination occurs in conditional sentences, as here with an imperative in the protasis; if the addressees obey the verbal idea framed by the imperative, they will, at some indefinite and unspecified future time, be acted upon. When Luke wants to portray two concurrent verbal actions, one of them being an imperative, he reserves, in a very high percentage of cases, the present participle/main verb combination for such two temporally simultaneous verbal ideas.[92] Luke's consistent imperative-future middle/passive combination syntax is well suited here to the speaker, his subject, and the expectations of his addressees in the narrative world of this scene.

---

90. Including the quite germane observations of Crowley (n80) and Genette (n82), *that the speaker's point of view must neither be compromised nor made subservient to Enlightenment rationalism*, I would additionally have to assess such an expectation as being unharmonious with the narrative-rhetorical spirit of the *Progymnasmata*. This speaker's hearers could reasonably understand that Peter's own expectations would be shared with them. This seems the most plausible extension of his argument and most suitable for the occasion in responding to questions about a heaven-sent phenomenon to believer-disciples.

91. Marguerat, *First Christian Historian*, 127.

92. Elbert, "Syntax of Imperative-Future and Imperative-Participle Combinations." [Included in this anthology—Ed.]

Readers at this juncture may be appreciative of Lukan speech-in-character and of his previously well-grounded narrative of prophetic staging or foregrounding in Homeric/Vergilian style as well as in the style of the Samuel-Kings (and Genesis) narratives. They will understand that Peter's hearers who repent may also participate, like Peter himself has repented, and in an ensuing fulfillment of Joel's prophecy, Acts 2:21, enter into salvation. And then they may be assured that the rest of the prophecy, vv. 17b and 18, applies to them as well in their own future course, as it has just been previously applied to Peter and his colleagues, as they give heed to prayer and the emerging teaching of the Jerusalem/Petrine tradition (Acts 2:42). As the gift of the Holy Spirit was poured out upon Peter, so it is promised to them and to all who are repentant and who are "afar off," even at "the ends of the earth," beyond narrative time.[93]

93. Contra, for example, Neil, *Acts of the Apostles*, 79, who, impervious to all the previously developed levels of context in the narrative world, simply claims, without even an argument or a consideration, that the gift of the Holy Spirit at 2:38c, 39 is "the promise, i.e. salvation, referred to in v. 21."

It goes without saying that Neil's claim displays no cognizance of Luke's theme of prophetic fulfillment, seeming remarkably incurious of context. *Neil's claim is clearly questionable and now appears, on my argument, not entirely reasonable, if not just plainly wrong.* It appears in violation of Luke's sequential ordering of prophetic events and their implementation in his first book, and it is disconnected from portrayals that are ostensibly related to the same prophetic fulfillment in his second book, aside from being at loggerheads with the art of personification. Its narrative incoherence appears substantial, yet it is often repeated as if it was an assured result of scholarship.

It may be observed as well that aggressive scenarios have been foisted upon Luke in order to sustain this traditionally venerated claim, stating that all the clear and vivid soteriologically connected portrayals of characters in Luke's first book with respect to faith, forgiveness, repentance, and salvation are supposedly intended so that readers should see nothing more than either nonexistent or disingenuously vanishing soteriological experiences in character's lives. But such a narrative-rhetorically unattuned hermeneutical style is unlikely to be either comprehensible or convincing. Moreover, such a counterintuitive tact suffers as well from unexamined rationalist presuppositions that arise directly and explicitly from the artificial and anti-authorial epochal periodizations that have uncritically, yet traditionally, been imposed by some upon Luke's text, periodizations which, for example, transform the second installment of Luke's prophetic historiography into paleoreformed paradigms like the "acts of thirteen male witnesses." Such concept-confining and character-confining mischaracterization is prone to other blanket assertions as well, wherein Joel is transformed into Ezekiel or Jeremiah and Joel's words in the mouth of the Lukan Peter are reduced to "the message of salvation," resulting in a willful misreading, and wherein the nonrational components of Joel's prophecy are either naturalistically reinvented or their thematic narrative prominence is marginalized altogether.

However, the argument advanced as reasonable in this present study is that Luke did no intend to be understood in his first book as at all suggesting that the gift of the Holy Spirit serves to initiate an entrance into salvation. Such an argument might be extended in a coherent *Pfingstgeschichte* into the second book so as to include other occasions that Luke has selected, but that is beyond the present scope. We may, however, take note in passing of a few items in support of the position developed here that the gift of the Holy Spirit is portrayed as being received by disciple-believers. For instance, Eduard Schweizer, "πνεῦμα, πνευματικός, κτλ., Lukas und Apostelgeschichte," *TWNT* 6:401–13 (409, 410), concludes that "the outpouring of the Spirit can be repeated whenever men come to faith" whereas "salvation . . . is never ascribed to the Spirit. According to Acts 2:38 the Spirit is imparted to those who are already converted and baptised. Obedience also must precede Spirit-reception (of the promised gift of the Holy Spirit, 2:38c, 39) according to 5:32" (parentheses mine).

Lake, "Holy Spirit," 5:108–9, regarding the Samaritan episode, finds that the Lukan gift of the Holy Spirit "was neither the cause nor the necessary result of salvation," a conclusion quite substantially confirmed by the exegesis of Russell, "'They Believed Philip Preaching,'" 169–76.

Having noted Luke's fulfillment-of-prophecy theme and the deployment of Joel's prophecy to account for a fulfillment of it in characters' lives and its potential application to ensuing characters' lives and given Luke's arguable affinity for the narrative-rhetorical conventions of his day, it is heuristic to also observe that Luke now proceeds not only to provide examples and precedents of his two main thematic experiential nexuses, the soteriological one and the gift of the Holy Spirit one, as expected, but also of other components of Joel's prophecy in disciple-believer-witnesses' ensuing lives, as if to illustrate anew the importance of also realizing the importance of this particular ongoing fulfillment.

This realization can be briefly argued as follows. Luke continues portrayals of the soteriological nexus with scenes, for instance, of the Ethiopian eunuch, Sergius Paulus, Lydia, the Philippian jailer, and Crispus. These can be understood both as fulfillment of v. 21 of the Lukan Peter's programmatic reference to Joel's prophecy and as fulfilling the prophetic announcement from heaven that Jesus is a Savior (Luke 2:11). Luke continues portrayals of examples and precedents of disciple-believers receiving the gift of the Holy Spirit, as if reinforcing the exemplary nature of the first instance, with scenes of Samaritan believers and Ananias ministering the gift of the Spirit to Paul in Damascus, both scenes illustrating the pervasive nature of genuine Jerusalem tradition and practice. Another scene of Roman God-fearers and a cogent scene of Ephesian believer-disciples who, like Apollos before them, have not yet connected with the authentic Jerusalem/Petrine tradition in which Paul stands insofar as the Lukan gift of the Holy Spirit is concerned.[94] All of these portrayals can be understood as fulfilling Luke

---

And as to the twelve Ephesian disciple-believers (Acts 19:1b, 2a), an array of scholarship (A. Ehrhardt, C. Hemer, K. Lake and H. Cadbury, P. Stuhlmacher, M. Wolter, and T. Zahn, for example) rightly concludes that both Luke *and* his character, Paul, understand these addressees of Paul's question (Acts 19:2a) to be Christians, cf. a narratively based stylistic appraisal which is supportive of this conclusion (Elbert, "Observation on Luke's Composition," 106–8). These addressees take their narrative place as exemplifying Christians who, in light of further information befitting the Jerusalem/Petrine tradition, are baptized in the Holy Spirit by the heavenly Jesus, being illustrative of a progymnastic strategy of narrative cohesion via Luke 3:16; Acts 1:5; 11:16; and 19:1–7 (with, on that topical connectedness, Schweizer, *Das Evangelium nach Lukas*, 48, 49). The present study suggests that the quite narratively realistic, perhaps even rhetorically expected, and prophetically supportive implementation found in Luke 11:5–13; 24:49 should also be included within this sequence illustrating prophecy and fulfillment.

An overall contiguous narrative picture arising from this double-work would resonate with Theophilus's experience as a disciple-believer: praying disciples, like him, were not saved via the Lukan gift of the Holy Spirit; instead they should be praying for it in obedience to Jesus's teaching on prayer, since it was a gift that Luke ostensibly believed to be designed for other important purposes, mysterious interior purposes which, according to this narrative, the earthly Jesus had, and now the heavenly Jesus continues to have, in mind.

94. The Lukan Paul and the Paul of the Letters are both, in my judgment, participants in the linguistic heritage of experiential description with respect to Luke's two main foci, the soteriological nexus and the Spirit-reception nexus. As to Paul's continuity with Jerusalem/Petrine tradition, cf. Menoud, "Jésus et ses témoins," 7–20; Fannon, "Influence of Traditions on St. Paul," 292–307. As to Paul's transmission of that earlier tradition which he accepts, cf. Müller, *Der Traditionsprozess im Neuen Testament*, 204–24; Ellis, *Making of the New Testament Documents*, 248–51, 256–60.

3:16 and vv. 17 and 18 of Joel's prophecy. So the twin main foci of Joel's prophecy that Luke decides are being fulfilled by the will of God in the past, the present, and equally into the future, advance both *Heilsgeschichte* and *Pfingstgeschichte*.

With respect to *Pfingstgeschichte*, the projection of the promise of the gift of the Holy Spirit to repentant disciple-believers beyond narrative time at 2:38c, 39 may also be understood as being well represented according to the narrative-rhetorical goal of ἐνάργεια, which is to create a persuasively life-like description with words so as to stimulate the reader's visual imaging and comprehension.[95] The term refers to a vivid description that puts things before our eyes. In this way, the verbal and cognitive ability of an accomplished narrator approximates that of a successful visual artist. Both give form to an unseen and as yet unexperienced object. The former uses the medium of scenes painted in words, the latter paint, clay, stone, or metal. Thus the reader, induced to employ his or her mind's eye, is transformed into a spectator. Such a participatory response between the narrator and the spectator results from a strategy of verbal and visual persuasion and is an achievement of communication. Demetrius thinks of ἐνάργεια in a Homeric manner as being visible and arising from an exact narration, overlooking no detail and cutting out nothing, when all the accompanying circumstances are mentioned and nothing is omitted, the entire description being vivid owing to the fact that no detail which would usually occur and then occurred is deleted.[96] When hearers are provoked to ask, "What should we do?" Peter brings the thrust of his experiential and textually based argument to a dramatic conclusion with details, repetition, and words expressing actuality.

In Luke's narrative, one may see then, I suggest, a strategy broadly applied with respect to clarifying prophetic fulfillment of the gift of the Holy Spirit within Joel's prophecy. The prophecy is introduced by a highly regarded character; it is then

---

95. On the background for this concept, that of a vivid representation used to create a mental picture consistent with the circumstances, cf. Volkmann, *Die Rhetorick der Griechen und Römer*, 158, 276, 442, 447, 452; Lausberg, *Elemente der Literarischen Rhetorik*, 119; Martin, *Antike Rhetorik*, 288–89.

On the narrative-rhetorical side, cf. Theon, *Progym.* 7.53–55; Patillon, *Aelius Théon Progymnasmata*, 119, 31–33. In both narrative and oratory, the characteristics of ἐνάργεια are a desire for clearness, vividness, or "transparency," cf. Woodman, *Rhetoric in Classical Historiography*, 25–28. In Rome, the concept is illustrated by Demetrius, *Eloc.* 4.209–220, and by Quintilian, *Inst. Or.* 6.2.26–33; 8.3.61–71, 88–89; 9.2.40–44, where we are warned that mere narration is not enough for the orator to achieve a positive result. Dionysius of Halicarnassus applauds ἐνάργεια as rendering a character's likely actions and feelings (*Lys.* 7; *Thuc.* 15) and Plutarch (*Mor.* 346f–347c) thinks the best historian renders vivid impressions of emotions and characters like a narrative painting. Cicero's legacy of this descriptive mode (cf. Avenarius, *Lukians Schrift zu Geschichtschreibung*, 130–40) was widely known to the Romans as illumination and actuality, being able to exhibit the actual scene so that insight would be no less actively stirred than if hearers (or readers) were present at the actual occurrence.

96. Demetrius, *Eloc.* 4.209, 210. None of the expected details, expected to be present in order to be persuasive, are omitted in the entire description: Luke 3:16; 11:5–13 with the *Zeilpunct* of v. 13; 24:44–49; Acts 1:4–8; 2:4, 17, 18, 33, culminating, transparently, in Acts 2:38c, 39 so as to present a reader with a vivid picture of Peter projecting the gift of the Holy Spirit, in all its mysterious phenomenological description (power, glossolalia, interior filling), beyond narrative time directly to him or her as a fulfillment of prophecy.

implemented by the main character who, being the subject of the prophecy, would be expected to act accordingly; its progress is moved ahead by teaching and guidance and further description about it by the main character; a prominent *Stichwort* and coupled gift-language are employed for clarity; a fulfillment is portrayed, and a speech-in-character extends the prophetic fulfillment to the reader. All of this foregrounding is complemented by some further examples and precedents of fulfillment in the narrative world as also is expected in a Theonic style. A previously instructed reader, like Theophilus, is thereby motivated to enter these scenes of the narrative world and to participate with his own prayer for the gift of the Holy Spirit, if that is an element of his Christian experience that requires further orderly clarification.[97]

But what of other characterization beyond the examples and precedents illustrating the twin major foci? The gender inclusive prediction of inspired prophetic speech (vv. 17 and 18) is fulfilled, for instance, with Philip's daughters who were prophetesses (Acts 21:8, 9). The fact that Luke does not record their prophetic speech, as he does for some other characters, does not mean that he did not know about it or that it did not occur when he visited Philip's home with Paul or that he thought it uninteresting. Rather, it was probably not useful for his narrative purpose, perhaps just as recording quotes from Paul's letters was also not useful for that purpose.[98]

Prophetic fulfillment can also be appreciated by the numerous dreams and visions Luke records, given that *dreams* are one of the Christianized variations in Joel's prophecy, the ongoing entire fulfillment of which I am suggesting is quite programmatic. Perhaps this extra plural of dreams is a Lukan emphasis, peshering the original text in light of contemporary experience which Luke understands as unfolding under providential influence according to the plan of God for the "last days,"[99] not just the fulfillment of 2:17c in the destiny of particular individuals from the past. Comparatively, Hanson senses a distinctive plausible quality in the Christian dreams and visions Luke describes.[100] In any case, Theophilus in his cultural context would expect

---

97. Lukan ἐνάργεια in this particular respect may be compared with that of Mark and Matthew, perhaps some of the πολλοί (Luke 1:1), who, although stating the initial prophecy by a respected character (Mark 1:8; Matt 3:11), do not develop it by showing how their main character implements or fulfills it. It is not part of their narrative purpose. Perhaps they thought the subject had been treated by others. In any case, their treatment of this prophecy cannot then be subject to analysis via progymnastic narrative-rhetorical procedures, although other aspects of their presentations so arguably lend themselves (as suggested by Robbins, "Progymnastic Rhetorical Composition and Pre-Gospel Traditions," 111–47).

98. On this point, cf. Elbert, "Paul of the Miletus Speech." [Included in this anthology—Ed.]

99. Bovon, "Ces chrétiens qui rêvent," 3:642.

These activities of the Spirit in dreams and visions appear narratively as an eschatological fulfillment of an element of the Christianized Joel prophecy. Their inclusion in narrative time to Spirit-filled disciple-believer-witnesses, who are thereby informed and led by the heavenly Jesus, is suggestive of the contemporary narrative-rhetorical emphasis on examples and precedents. If so, they would be intended to be paradigmatic of prophetic fulfillment beyond narrative time.

100. Hanson, "Dreams and Visions," 1395–1425; cf. Bovon, "Ces chrétiens qui rêvent," 3:642–49.

plausible dream-visions to be prophetic and significant.[101] Luke's fulfillment-of-prophecy theme with respect to 2:17c is borne out functionally in his narrative, where Theophilus can see how these phenomena provide a central role as to motivation and guidance (Acts 5:19–21; 8:26–29; 9:1–19, 27; 10:1–23, 30–33; 11:1–15; 12:1–11; 16:6–12; 18:9–11; 22:6–11, 17–21; 23:11; 26:12–18; and 27:21–26).[102] Perhaps Luke thought of these dream-visions within the multiple categories of prophecy-type phenomena and of signs and wonders, given that dreams and visions can set the stage for prophetic speech (Acts 23:23–24, 34b);[103] if so, vv. 17c and 19b of the Joel prophecy come into play with their editorially improved *signs below*.

According to Luke, signs and wonders are done in ministry (Acts 14:3). Is this prophetic fulfillment of v. 19, *signs below*? Signs and wonders below, that is, on earth during the ministry of the disciples, are cited consistently with awareness of, reliance upon, or reference to the heavenly Jesus (cf. Acts 2:43; 4:30; 5:12; 6:8; 10:38; 14:3; and 15:12), and, interestingly, a reference to them goes back to the earthly Jesus in Acts 2:22. I say *interestingly*, because this suggests that Luke sees no wedge between the ministry of the heavenly and the earthly Jesus; rather he appears to sense continuity between the two. In addition, Luke clearly takes a keen interest in describing, with terms of his own choosing, a number of healings fitting these categories in *both* of his books.[104] This Lukan interest may suggest that the heavenly Jesus is understood to be carrying on the healing ministry of the earthly Jesus in response to prayer.[105] It also may suggest that Luke is attempting to bring clarity to his understanding of prophetic fulfillment wherein signs and wonders are believed to be initiated from heaven in concert with a predictive component of Joel's prophecy, destined to occur for both compassionate and evangelistic purposes until the day of the Lord.[106] It is likely that Luke has a positive expectant attitude toward this category of prophetic-type phenomena, given a reasonable identification with his characters (cf. Acts 4:29, 30). Luke gives no hint in his composition that signs and wonders in his prophetic-fulfillment conception of Joel are confined to a category of Christian persons by the emendation of *signs below* at v. 19 or by any other Lukan passage;[107] rather, he nar-

---

101. Cf. Pelling, "Tragical Dreamer," 201–10; Frenschkowski, "Traum und Traumdeutung im Matthäusevangelium," 5–21. For a survey of OT, Jewish, and NT considerations, cf. Frenschkowski, "Traum II–IV," 33–41, and "Vision II–IV," 124–37.

102. In this way the Christian mission Luke has selected to portray is guided, cf. George, "L'Esprit Saint dans l'oeuvre de Luc," 520; Frenschkowski, *Offenbarung und Epiphanie*, 1:359–66.

103. These prophetic-type categories are related by Kolenkow, "Relationships between Miracle and Prophecy," 1489, 1502.

104. Weissenrieder, *Images of Illness*, 355–57.

105. Such a perceived ministry would pertain to infirmities due to natural causes and to those suggestive of implicit activity of the devil, cf. Thomas, *Devil, Disease and Deliverance*, 227–95.

106. So too, apparently, Bagalawis, "'Power' in Acts 1:8," 1–13.

107. *Pace* Bock, *Proclamation from Prophecy and Pattern*, 167, who intrusively transforms Luke's inclusive gender-insensitive approach of prophetic fulfillment in Joel's nonrational categories into a restricted one for "apostles," as if they were the only ones who were to be witnesses in the last days to

rates in the interests of his purpose to illustrate this fulfillment in characters' lives. In every phenomenological category stemming from Joel's prophecy, Luke portrays instances of fulfillment which are pastorally relevant not just to his characters' lives, but to all who are afar off in the *last days*.

Comparisons and Conclusion

When Luke's double work is evaluated in the light of contemporary narrative-rhetorical practices, his vivid portrayals exhibit not just the desirable quality of ἔκφρᾰσις,[108] where details are brought into view, but also reveal a deeper quality of description, where events are perceived contiguously on the basis of what happened before them and after them.[109] There is clear narrative sequencing and connectivity, and for participants experiential events themselves are part of a divine prophetically fulfilling plan. Luke is perhaps best understood as writing a new genre of prophetic historiography,[110] where prophecy about Jesus as a heavenly and previously earthly character is fulfilled and continues to be fulfilled beyond narrative time. This engenders interactive expectations of disciple-believer-witnesses within Luke's readership. I have attempted to argue that within Luke's schema of the fulfillment of prophecy, there lies at the heart of his enterprise an awareness that before, during, and after he composes, improving on the writers before him, the prophecy of Joel is being fulfilled in all of its practical dimensions within the version of Jerusalem/Petrine Christianity that Luke desires to clarify.

Luke could develop this awareness of prophetic fulfillment from contemporary experience and thus be motivated to compose his narrative so as to inclusively stress this perspective in a thematic manner. On the literary side, he will find the prophetic theme in the theological plan of the Samuel-Kings (and Genesis) narratives, and also in the *Odyssey* and the *Iliad* and in the *Aeneid*. His timing and understanding of progression in such a presentation holds our interest throughout; his repetition of examples and precedents coordinating with fulfillment of the Joel citation in his second book builds excitement and exhibits a design of harmony, connectedness, and orderly

---

those who are "afar off," or the only ones to whom Joel's prophecy applies. This style of reinterpretation, one to which Adele Berlin's guidelines (n89) are apropos, is inconsiderate of Luke's narrative strategy, thematic structuring, and descriptive techniques. As to how this "apostolic age" hermeneutical style, with its unexamined rationalistic presuppositions linked to epochal periodization, appears to affect interpretation of Lukan thought elsewhere, cf. Elbert, "Paul of the Miletus Speech," nn. 35–37 therein.

108. Theon, Περὶ Ἐκφράσεως, *Progym.* 7.53–55.

109. Theon, too, *Progym.* 7.40–41, senses this deeper narrative picture and attempts to train students accordingly.

110. Prophetic historiography would of course also be useful apologetically, providing examples and precedents for use in both defending and in defining Christian experience and tradition (so, too, Sterling, "Luke-Acts and Apologetic Historiography," 341, 342).

arrangement (τάξις as manifested in Lukan καθεξῆς).[111] In addition, Greco-Roman readers of several ethnic backgrounds can find themselves represented by characters who experience this fulfillment. I suggest that Luke is motivated in his unrelenting insistence on holding to this motif, repeating it indefatigably, by two primary reasons, one being literary persuasiveness in concert with the narrative-rhetorical conventions of his day, and the other a pastorally based experiential pragmatism to "get it right" with respect to the mysterious teaching of the risen Lord Jesus which resonated in oral memory as framed in his account at Acts 1:8.

When Luke, in the present, learns of repentance, forgiveness, belief, salvation, conversion, experiential descriptions which he knows may be taken from soteriological characterization of the past, Luke thinks anew and realizes that Joel's prophecy is being fulfilled. He is living in the "last days" himself. When Luke, in the present, learns of Christians receiving the gift of the Holy Spirit, the Holy Spirit falling on believers, of disciples being baptized with the Holy Spirit by the heavenly Jesus, as taken from pneumatological characterization of the past, he again thinks anew and applies the fulfillment of prophecy to this phenomenon, similarly for dreams and visions and signs below (in which he would include healings as a sign of the power of the heavenly Jesus who can both afflict and heal, as well as pour out the gift of the Holy Spirit [e.g., Acts 9:17]). Luke's presentation of fulfillment of the various components of Joel's prophecy, coupled to his narrative predictions which are thereby shown to be reliable, is utterly supernatural and nonrational.

The pragmatic observations of Christian experiences in the present combined with a modest literary background, exposure to narrative-rhetorical learning, and knowledge of past "speech-in-character" predictions by his main characters would provide strong motivation for Luke to compose as he does. Given these postulated factors, Luke can be understood to remedy the many before him who have not yet properly linked

---

111. Order and arrangement in composition (τάξις) is a quite visible concern of the *Progymnasmata* in all the desirable narrative virtues, as in building contiguous and cogent argumentation (Theon, *Progym.* 8.40–42; 11.84–86, 171–76). I have suggested that Luke may be understood as demonstrating an awareness of the virtues of descriptive and contiguous vividness. While Theon does not use the word καθεξῆς (Luke 1:3; Acts 3:24; 11:4; 18:23), for an author who adopts a prophecy-and-fulfillment theme the concept of order and arrangement would be a vital narrative concern. This virtue would apply specifically, for example, to the Lukan gift of the Holy Spirit projected to readers beyond narrative time as a promise from heaven unto all those who are called by God to repent in the "last days," with Luke using the imitative and progymnastic techniques regarding that projection that I have suggested in this study. The contemporary narrative-rhetorical emphasis on τάξις is well suited to Luke's narrative purpose and appears very similar indeed to Luke's envisioning of an orderly arrangement via his concept of καθεξῆς (with O'Fearghail, *Introduction to Luke-Acts*, 107).

Germane to such an impression of Lukan harmony, connectedness and arrangement pertaining to a strategy of prophecy and fulfillment is the observation of Moessner, "Meaning of ΚΑΘΕΞΗΣ in the Lucan Prologue," 2:1528, who concludes that "Theophilus . . . must be instructed by Luke's particular order and arrangement of the two-volume narrative which constantly relates the development of the one part to other parts of the whole. . . . To gain a firm grasp then of the significance of any event along or within this scheme, one must be able to configure or relate it to these beginnings according to the narrato-logical sense or order (καθεξῆς) which Luke has provided through his narrative connections."

the two main themes of Christian experience that Luke portrays (the soteriological and the pneumatological), along with the other phenomena in Joel's prophecy, as stemming from prophetic fulfillment. Perhaps they had not realized the truly astounding basis for these distinctive Christian phenomena in human experience, a basis securely founded upon God's will to fulfill—not just LXX prophecy in general—but prophecy spoken in the recent past by an angel, by John the Baptist, and by Jesus. Perhaps they did not see the larger picture that Luke portrays, hence the need for a narrative illustrating a thematic framework of prophetic fulfillment, a narrative composed with attention to the rhetorical qualities of internal coherence and unity.[112] On this thesis, Christian experience happening in the present (the "last days") is happening, Luke realizes, not just because of Christian ministry and prayer, not just because it can be noticed that in accord with Christian ministry this is what the heavenly Jesus apparently wants to do but, basically, because of God's unwavering desire to fulfill, in an ongoing continuing enterprise, the personal details of Joel's prophecy as edited by Peter and proclaimed in known Jerusalem/Petrine tradition. The observation of a correlation between experiential observations in the present with the prediction and prophecy in the recent past made credible by an ancient LXX text, by well-known people, by heavenly beings, and even by the earthly Jesus himself, would be extremely motivational with respect to composing a narrative with a theme of prophetic fulfillment. Once Luke became convinced that the ministry of the heavenly Jesus should be understood as extending the ministry of the earthly Jesus with respect to fulfilling the role of a Savior, he set out to portray the experience of people in whom this soteriological prediction had been fulfilled. Once he became convinced that Peter's prediction of the gift of the Holy Spirit extended into the present time, was logically connected to the past prophecy of John the Baptist, to the credible and known implementation of it by the earthly Jesus, and was also connected to the present ministry of the heavenly Jesus in an ongoing fulfillment of another element of Joel's ancient prophecy, he set out to portray the experience of Christian people in whose lives this baptizing or outpouring ministry of the heavenly Jesus had been fulfilled. These perceptions, building on those of Kim, if rightly inferred, could motivate a narratively contiguous Lukan ἔκφρασις with respect to his distinctive theme of prophecy and fulfillment.[113]

112. The perception of internal coherence and narrative unity is an outcome that lies very much within the scope of progymnastic teaching. I am suggesting that the main twin foci of the Christianized Joel prophecy (well represented in Lukan portrayal by examples and precedents of a soteriological nexus and by examples and precedents of inspired prophetic-type speech illustrating receipt of the gift of the Holy Spirit) are well illustrated by progymnastic concerns wherein the prophecy and fulfillment theme appears so attractively framed. A similar principle of internal coherence with respect to other issues is discerned by Meynet, *L'Évangile selon Saint Luc*, 2:255–57.

113. I would suggest then that there can be little doubt that a part of the basic motivation for Luke's composition, which is arguably compatible with the analysis of a portion of his text that I have set forth in the present study, is vigorously expressed in his scheme of "Verheißung/Weissagung-Erfüllung" dynamically coupled to an interest in the activity of the Holy Spirit. On the detection of this basic motivation per se, cf. Kim, *Die Geisttaufe des Messias*, 35–47.

However, the difference between both Samuel-Kings and Genesis narratives, and well-known Greco-Roman literary narratives, in which this motif of prophetic fulfillment is preeminently found, and with what Luke has set out to accomplish, is a vast one. In these narratives nothing like what Luke is writing about has actually happened. There had never been a character like the heavenly Jesus. No character in these narratives could be credibly understood to be fulfilling narrative predictions or prophecies beyond narrative time, doing so from beyond the present world. Luke's realization that the heavenly Jesus was fulfilling prophetic predictions and projections vivid in oral memory would provide strong motivation for him to compose his narrative in order to bring out this point clearly in the most persuasive manner that he could muster. This, I suggest, is what he has done.

On my thesis then, the highly appropriate narrative-rhetorical learning by worthy, not paltry, examples and precedents of the past, as I suggest the Lukan examples and precedents of this narrative are selected and designed to promote and encourage, both of personal *Heilsgeschichte* and of personal *Pfingstgeschichte*, are expected by Luke to be combinable with such examples in the present. This expectation may have been the beginning of a narrative theologian's dream! Luke's pastoral purpose then, broadly conceived, is thereby given a good deal of specificity and urgency. This postulated realization and awareness on Luke's part, which may be deduced from his performance as a narrator of connectedness and coherence, lends a certain excitement, surely a mood of expectancy, if Theophilus and other Christian readers temporally "afar off" readily appreciate the spiritually encouraging personal implications of prophetic fulfillment.[114]

---

114. The narrative-rhetorical emphasis on narrative composition by illustrating main points by examples and precedents has already been brought to bear on Luke's performance in this study. Suffice it to say here that the examples of the past were believed, in the rhetorical culture in which Luke lived, to have relevance for the present life, in that these same examples could often be observed for due instruction in different human lives in the present.

The hospitality extended by Maria Pantelia of the Thesaurus Linguae Graecae (University of California at Irvine) and by Trianos Gagos of the Michigan Papyrology Collection (University of Michigan at Ann Arbor) is gratefully acknowledged. I would also like to thank colleagues who have contributed heuristic discussion and criticism on various points of the thesis advanced in this study: Marianne Palmer Bonz, Thomas Brodie, David Gunn, Emerson Powery, and John Walsh. The responsibility for the views herein, and any missteps, are solely my own.

Chapter 2

An Observation on Luke's Composition and Narrative Style of Questions

HENRY CADBURY, IN HIS useful study "Four Features of Lucan Style," called attention to the "Homeric manner"[1] of Lukan style in which the narrative content of an original event is repeated later on the lips of a speaker. Cadbury detects this obvious trait of Homeric style as exemplified (1) by Paul's Damascus road experience in Acts 9 and his subsequent testimony about it on two different occasions (Acts 22 to a Jewish mob and Acts 26 to Festus, King Agrippa, and Bernice), (2) by the gentile Pentecost in Acts 10 reported by Peter in Acts 11:1–2 and 15:7–9, 13–21, and (3) by Luke's quotation from the letter by Claudius Lysias (Acts 23:26–30) which sums up previously narrated events. Cadbury is of course correct in this observation given that many times in the *Odyssey* and the *Iliad* one finds exactly this kind of characterization, previous narrative action, and information repeated in characters' speech. Another way of describing this style is to say that Luke follows the style of Homer's well-read texts by similarly foregrounding narrative content which is then connected to subsequent characterization.[2]

Cadbury concludes with the following observation: "The features of style presented here are not intended to prove any subtle hypothesis. I hope that the time has not yet come when linguistic data are of no interest unless they are relevant to edifying, instructive, or controversial matters. If we may suppose that they show the native and unpremeditated working of an author's mind, that in itself is worth knowing."[3] My study of Lukan composition of questions and how they function in his narrative is offered in this spirit, given that one of the principle stylistic features observed here could be considered a subset of the phenomenon Cadbury noticed earlier.

---

1. Cadbury, "Four Features of Lucan Style," 89.

2. Luke may also be understood as consciously employing other Homeric literary models, as, for example, detailed textual comparisons between *Iliad* 6 and Acts 20 would seem to suggest. This is not surprising, given the impact of the Homeric epics on all levels of education in the Empire, along with the rhetorical use of examples and precedents, cf. Hock, "Homer in Greco-Roman Education," 56–77; Price, "'Paradeigma' and 'Exemplum' in Ancient Rhetorical Theory," 2.

3. Cadbury, "Four Features of Lucan Style," 100.

Looking over the landscape of syntactical and related studies of Luke's double work, from Sophie Antoniadis's Lukan grammar and style in 1930[4] to the present, I am not aware of an investigation into this particular aspect of Lukan style.[5] Personally, I doubt that Luke was unconscious of his literary positioning and style of composition with regard to his narrative use of questions, although a habitual process of written expression would lie in the background of a writer trained to portray or personify characters' speech in a certain way.[6] Some rhetorical training as mandated in Roman schools and practice therein to afford the maximum amount of clarity, persuasiveness, and plausibility would enhance a writer's desire for appropriateness in characterization and his deliberate portrayal of speech-in-character or personification. Such rhetorical categories, which would have a bearing on how the interior thought-life of characters should be portrayed in questions, are set out in general terms by Luke's contemporary, Theon of Alexandria, in his treatise on narrative composition.[7]

There are 152 questions in the Third Gospel. Most are one-clause questions often functioning to introduce further explanation, instruction, dialogue, action, prophecy, or narrative comment. Of the 152 questions, sixty-five may be identified by their two-clause nature; that is, they have a dual-focus determined either by two verbal ideas or two concepts or clauses. They are not a long sentence ending with a short question, which I am treating as a one-clause question. For example, a dual-focus or two-clause type question would be Luke 8:25b, "Who then is this man, that he commands even the winds and the water and they obey him?" The second part of this question picks up the previously narrated content of 8:24b, "He rebuked the wind and the roughness of the water and they ceased." The primary concern to the speaker in posing this question appears to be "Who is this man?" The speaker brings the main point of the question to the attention of the addressees in the forward part of the two-clause question. The rearward part of the question topically connects to previous context, thereby providing narrative cohesion and enhancing understandability. My notation for this dual-focus type question, where the second part reviews or relates to previous contextual material placed in the narrative foreground, is 8:25b (8:24b). This notation means that Luke 8:25b is composed as a dual-focus question and that the rearward or second clause of it is foregrounded by 8:24b. Luke follows

---

4. Antoniadis, *L'Évangile de Luc*.

5. For comment on Lukan style, cf. Antoniadis, *L'Évangile de Luc*, 362–435; Fitzmyer, *Gospel according to Luke I–IX*, 105–27; Delebecque, *Les Actes des Apôtres*, xx–xxxix, xlv–xlix; Boismard and Lamouille, *Texte Occidental des Actes des Apôtres, II*; Boismard and Lamouille, *Les Actes des Deux Apôtres, II*; Boismard and Lamouille, *Les Actes des Deux Apôtres, III*.

6. Minchen, "Verbal Behaviour in Its Social Context," 15–32, probes the issue of how the narrative composition and function of questions may relate to the speech habits of a writer.

7. The latest critical editions are by Patillon, *Aelius Théon Progymnasmata*, and Butts, "'Progymnasmata' of Theon." For discussion of the concerns and categories of the προγυμνάσματα, cf. Hunger, *Die hochsprachliche profane Literatur der Byzantiner*, 1:92–120; Kennedy, *Greek Rhetoric Under Christian Emperors*, 54–73.

Mark in this particular question as he does on one other occasion. Luke follows Matthew on two occasions as well. However, as we shall see, Luke can be reasonably understood to build on earlier Jesus tradition and Christian composition insofar as his question composition is concerned,[8] but he apparently prefers and employs his own style rather elegantly in the majority of cases.

Luke not only follows the compositional nature of these four aforementioned dual-element questions in his sources (note 16 below), he demonstrates a distinctive fondness for a dual-focus narrative style in his own composition and recomposition of questions, a style which picks up previously foregrounded information from the immediate context (very rarely more distant context), topical content which he takes care to provide, and connects that information with the rearward or second aspect of the dual-focus question. The apparent immediate concern of the speaker is placed forward and introduces new narrative content which moves the story on.

The sixty-five dual-focus, two-clause, two-verbal-idea type questions in Luke's first book that I have so identified break down as follows in their Lukan contextual settings.

- Three questions are Lukan and do not exhibit the foregrounding of the rearward component.[9] (These three questions, however, like a very high percentage of the one-clause questions, are used by Luke to set the stage for further instruction or action.)

- One question follows Mark and Matthew, sets stage for explanation, and does not exhibit the foregrounding feature.[10]

- Four questions have the first idea or concept in the question built on previously high-lighted information. Three are Lukan[11] and one has ostensibly improved foregrounding over Matthew.[12]

---

8. For example, as to Luke's use of Matthew, cf. Franklin, *Luke*, 280–375. For attempts to grasp the picture of Lukan sources in this regard, cf. Goodacre, *Case against Q*. Mark and Matthew as Lukan sources certainly has its attractions but cannot be all encompassing as Goodacre realizes. The other major source hypotheses impacting the processes of oral tradition to written gospel are as follows: Lindemann, "Die Logienquelle Q. Fragen an eine gut begründete Hypothese," 3–26; Casey, *Aramaic Approach to Q*; Dunn, "Jesus in Oral Memory," 84–145; that Luke used Mark, Proto-Luke, and Matthew's *Logia* is advanced by Brodie, *Proto-Luke*; and that Luke employed a homogeneous oral and written tradition, q, not a formal Q, in addition to Mark, without strict separation between the words and deeds of the earthly Jesus, is advanced by Hultgren, *Narrative Elements in the Double Tradition*, 310–54. As to the πολλοί (Luke 1:1), early Christian exegesis, preaching, oral memory, tradition, and discursive correspondence seem to have played a role in the composition of Luke's second book, cf. Stanton, *Jesus of Nazareth in New Testament Preaching*; Hultgren, *Narrative Elements in the Double Tradition*, 316–25; Barrett, *Acts*, 1:49–56; 2:xxiv–xxxii; Dunn, "Jesus in Oral Memory," 127; Elbert, "Paul of the Miletus Speech," 258–68. [Included in this anthology.—Ed.]

9. Luke 12:41; 22:35; 22:49.

10. 20:41.

11. 12:20b (12:18); 13:4b (13:4a), 13:15b (13:14b).

12. 12:56 (12:54, 55).

- Seven questions have both foci in the question equally foregrounded. Four are Lukan,[13] two have ostensibly been recomposed by Luke to strengthen the twin foregrounding,[14] and one follows Matthew.[15]

- Fifty questions exhibit topical foregrounding of the second element in the question that is placed in the rearward position. These fifty are amenable to the following analysis.

    - Two follow Mark and two follow Matthew.[16]

    - Eight are understandable as Lukan improvements or recompositions to strengthen the foregrounding that connects with the second focus.[17]

    - Four are provided a foreground for the rearward element by Luke when placed in Lukan contexts but receive no such foregrounding in Matthean contexts.[18]

    - Thirty-four are Lukan, that is, are attributable to his pen or are accepted by him.[19]

From this summary then, statistically speaking, of the sixty-five dual-focus or two-clause type questions in Luke's first narrative book, fifty of them, or 77 percent, have topical foreground provided in the preceding narrative content that serves as a cohesive connection to the second element in the question so composed.

In Luke's second book he has written seventy questions. Of these seventy, thirty-eight may be identified as dual focus, two-verbal-idea type questions. These break down as follows in their Lukan contextual settings.

- Four do not exhibit foregrounding of the rearward element.[20]

---

13. 22:27 (22:24–26); 24:17 (24:14a, 15 and 24:13a respectively); 24:18 (24:14b); 24:38 (24:37 and 24:32–35 respectively).

14. 20:15b (20:13, 14); 20:33 (20:32).

15. 20:44 (20:41–43).

16. 8:25b (8:24b); 8:28b (8:28a) follow Mark and 11:18 (11:17); 12:42 (12:40) follow Matthew.

17. 9:25 (9:24); 18:18b (18:17); 19:22 (19:21b); 19:23 (19:13b); 20:33 (20:33a, 32); 21:7 (21:6); 22:11 (22:8); 22:48 (22:21, 22).

18. 7:31 (7:29–30); 8:28b (8:28a); 12:25 (12:18, 19a, 19b, 20b); 12:51a (12:49a).

19. 1:34 (1:31); 1:43 (1:41–42); 2:48 (2:43–45); 2:49b (2:46); 7:49b (7:48); 9:9b (9:7–8); 10:25b (10:20b); 10:40b (10:40a); 10:36 (10:30); 11:40 (11:39b); 12:14 (12:13); 12:17 (12:16b); 12:26 (12:25); 12:57 (12:56b); 13:2 (13:1); 13:16 (13:14b, 15a, 15b); 14:5 (14:4); 15:4 (15:2); 16:2b (16:2a); 16:3a (16:2b); 16:5b (16:5a); 16:7b (16:7a); 17:8b (17:8a); 17:9 (17:7b); 17:17a (17:14b); 17:18 (17:16b); 18:7 (18:5); 18:8 (18:1); 23:31 (23:29–30); 23:40b (23:33); 24:5 (24:3); 24:17 (24:13a, 14a, 15); 24:26 (24:22b, 23); 24:32 (24:27).

20. Acts 7:49b (a LXX quote); 8:31; 16:30; 21:38 (an appropriate "speech-in-character" question about a non-Lukan character). Two of these (8:31; 16:30) set the stage for further instruction and action as a complement or answer to the question.

- One (11:17) is provided with foreground for the first idea or concept in the question.

- Two have both elements foregrounded (9:21 by 9:13, 14, and 25:9b by 25:3, 5).

- Thirty-one are composed with the second element or clause topically foregrounded in the preceding narrative content.[21]

Quantitatively then, of the thirty-eight dual-focus or two-clause type questions in this writer's second narrative book, thirty-one of them, or 82 percent (compared with 77 percent in his "first account"), have topical foreground provided in the preceding narrative content that serves as a cohesive connection to the second element in the question so composed.

Examples of this style may be found in Homer. Achilles encounters and recognizes the blue-eyed goddess Minerva from heaven, whose eyes shone dreadfully, and then asks her "Why then have you come, O child of Aegis-bearing Jove?" (*Il.* 1.194–201), but the Homeric epics do not at all reveal a relatively uniform style of immediate foregrounding in relation to the second element in reflective, information-seeking questions. However, the high percentages associated with identification of this particular style in Luke-Acts suggest a definite and remarkably consistent style of composition consistent with narrative-rhetorical training. It suggests a set procedure adopted by an individual writer as to how questions were best to be employed as appropriate personification via speech-in-character (προσωποποιΐα), which Theon (himself an admirer of Homeric epic as a pedagogical source) defines as setting forth words suitable both to the character, the subject, and the occasion about which future words will be spoken.[22] While Theon does not comment on exactly how a narrator should compose questions so as to provide narrative cohesion, Luke appears quite harmonious with Theon's general guidelines insofar as how his questions function on the lips of various speakers.[23]

---

21. 1:6 (1:3); 1:11 (1:9, 10); 2:7 (2:6); 2:8 (2:6); 3:12b (3:6); 4:7b (ἐν τῷ Ἰησοῦ, 4:2); 4:25b (4:18, 21a, 23); 5:3b (5:2a); 5:4a (πώλεω, 5:1, foregrounds rearward element πιπράσκω); 5:4b (5:3); 5:8b (land sold [ἀποδίδωμι] foregrounded by property sold [πώλεω], 5:1, by land, 5:3c, and by past participle of πιπράσκω, 5:4a); 5:9a (the Spirit of the Lord foregrounded by the Holy Spirit, 5:3b); 7:28 (7:24b); 7:50 (7:49a); 7:52 (7:51); 8:30b (8:30a); 8:36c (8:36a); 10:21b (10:19b, 20); 10:29b (10:4, 5, divine guidance); 10:47 (10:45b, 46); 13:10b (13:8, 10a); 15:10 (15:5b, synonymous description); 17:19b (17:18d); 19:2a (19:1b); 19:35b (19:34b); 21:13a (21:12b, weeping and weakening foregrounded by narrative content of "besought him"); 22:25b (22:24a); 23:3c (23:2); 23:19b (23:17b, 18b); 26:8 (24:21b, distant but obvious foregrounding of second element in a Homeric manner); 26:27a (26:22b–23).

22. Theon, *Progym*. 8.2–4, 26–29; cf. ch. 13 in Patillon, *Aelius Théon Progymnasmata*, 105. In this study I follow the Butts edition (n7) with respect to line enumeration.

23. Regarding his narrative exercise (Περὶ Διηγήματος), Theon differentiates between asking simple questions (ἐρωτῶντες) and rhetorical questions or inquiries, given that one of the ways to narrate an incident is via simple questions and via dialogue, which in itself involves questions and answers (*Progym*. 5.271–79, 362–64; similarly, Hermogenes of Tarsus speaks of five figures or styles of narratives, one of which is the "interrogative," in Rabe, *Hermogenis Opera*, 5–6). Theon's simple question is one that seeks a response, which a rhetorical question does not (5.303–4). Perhaps Quintilian's discussion of various forms of interrogation (*Inst*. 9.2.6–16) reflects his knowledge of previous rhetorical

However, the fondness or proclivity in Lukan style of linking previous content, content consciously foregrounded, to the second element in dual-focus questions, while placing the main concern of the speaker forward in the first element, indicates that Luke has a real preference for how this dual-element type of question functions cohesively in his narrative. He apparently writes with this in mind.

One may also suggest then, based on his performance, that Luke fully realizes that appropriately composed narrative-rhetorical questions have a direct bearing on the understandability of what future words will be spoken. This seems obvious in that a number of Luke's dual-element twin-verbal-idea questions (for example, Acts 8:31) function directly so as to set the stage for further explanation, dialogue, instruction, action, prophecy, or speeches on the part of his characters, as do a number of his short one-clause type questions in his first[24] and second books.[25] So employed, such questions allow a narrator to present further information emanating from his characters which is of didactic value to his readers.[26]

Before elucidating further the stylistic topical foregrounding of Luke's dual-element questions, this didactic value, which ostensibly serves a theological or pneumatological purpose, may be conveniently illustrated with a few more examples from the collection of short questions. This stage-setting didactic function is striking

---

efforts in this regard, either Latin or Greek, like Theon (so too, Butts, "'Progymnasmata' of Theon," 390–91). Quintilian introduces his discussion by posing the question, "What is more common than to ask or inquire?" He then differentiates between questions employed to get information (Theon's simple question) and those designed to emphasize a point, to excite pity, to strike a comparison, to be answered by the speaker for a pleasing effect (Acts 26:27; Hom., Il. 7.445–53), or to embarrass an opponent by throwing odium on the addressee. With respect to the latter odium-throwing category, aggressive counter or rhetorical questions employed in riposte to engender derailment, cf. Neyrey, "Questions, *Chreiai*, and Challenges to Honor," 657–81; and in Homer, cf. Minchen, "Verbal Behaviour in Its Social Context," 20–26.

24. For example, of the eighty-seven short questions in the first book, Luke 1:66b sets the narrative stage for prophecy; 3:10 and 12 for instruction; 4:22b for debate and prophecy; 10:26 and 29 for teaching, as do 13:20, 23; 14:3b; 22:49b for action; and 24:19a functions as a prelude to information about Jesus.

25. For example, of the thirty-two short questions in the second book, stage-setting of one form or another is apparent at 2:12, 37; 4:16; 8:34b, c; 14:15; 21:37b, c; 22:10a, 227b; and 23:4b. Of the one-clause type questions in Acts that are a prelude to further action, one of them has an adjoining negative expression with a clause serving to rhetorically mark the implied transition to new addressees on the narrative stage: "And now they expel us secretly?" (Acts 16:37b) is followed by "No indeed" (οὐ γάρ), "but (ἀλλὰ) let them bring us out, coming themselves." The negative expression and imperative following the question provide additional rhetorical force, emphasizing the manner in which an answer is expected to be given (cf. Aristides, *Rhet.* 492.2); for similar examples of this phenomenon, cf. Shalev, "Illocutionary Clauses," 531–61.

26. By allowing his characters to pose questions themselves in their own voices, rather than interposing his own questions, say, as a preface to a speech, Luke emulates sound storytelling practice in the narrative-rhetorical tradition. Aristotle, in his commentary on narrative imitation (διηγηματικὸς μίμησις), praises Homer for taking up narrative space himself as little as possible (*Poet.*, 1459b33, 1460a7). Entrusting appropriate questions to his characters and avoiding the potential distraction of a narrator's intervention earns the anonymous writer of the double work prepared for Theophilus a similar commendation.

within Lukan *Sondergut* at Luke 7:44b in the episode of the woman with the ointment where Jesus asks Simon, "Do you see this woman?" Elaboration and important doctrine ensue, Luke painting a scene for readers to "see" the woman. Again, after Jesus's prophetic teaching that "There will be two women grinding together, one will be taken but the other left," Luke inserts a deferential information-seeking short question from hearers, "Where, Lord?" (Luke 17:37a), setting the stage for further explanation in the form of *chreia*/maxim/apothegm type saying, "Where the body (σῶμα) is the eagles (ἀετοί) will also be gathered together (ἐπισυνάγω)" (17:37b). If Luke understands this saying to indicate where the faithful will be taken, rather than where they will be left, Luke may well believe that his version of it is important for spiritual expectation, hence its introduction by a question.[27] Such short questions serve, for Luke, two rhetorical functions. In anticipating a response, they prepare for further useful information befitting the narrative-rhetorical categories of amplification/elaboration, and they enhance vividness (ἐνάργεια), stimulating the reader's cognitive environment, encouraging him or her to think anew, to review previous material and then evaluate their response as the question lingers in the air. As they are with Acts 2:37b, "Brethren, what shall we do?" Both of these literary functions are also apparent in short Homeric questions such as "Which Trojan did blameless Teucer slay first?" (*Il.* 270.5), the difference being the personal theological and pneumatological significance for readers who experientially identify with Lukan characters. Further, in Acts 2:12b a short question, "What does this mean?" sets the stage for Peter's programmatic speech; short questions are also employed (Acts 21:37b, c; 23:4b) to realistically set the stage for speeches by Paul.

In conclusion, I illustrate some of the aforementioned features of Lukan style with respect to dual-element type questions by a few examples. Taken in isolation, the compositional details illustrated by the groupings in notes 16–19 and 21 above

---

27. Luke removes *corpse* (πτῶμα, Matt 24:28), where vultures could conceivably be gathered, improving the saying by the use of body (σῶμα), where eagles might be expected to soar at a heavenly reunion. The pastoral purpose of the Lukan context to live uprightly in expectation of the *parousia* (Luke 17:24, 26, 30) and Luke's editorial enhancement, a clarifying recomposition perhaps done in light of a connection perceived between Matt 24:28 and 31, where the elect are ingathered (ἐπισυνάγω), is enough to suggest that Luke may understand Jesus to offer an encouraging expectation of a heavenly ingathering of disciples who remain dedicated to kingdom service. Theon, *Progym.* 3.12–21, points out that the maxim and *chreia* are useful in many ways for life, just as this saying (Luke 17:37b) could be viewed as contributing to the resolve of expectantly awaiting the return of the Son of Man amid trials and tribulations, especially if Luke believed he understood what the saying really meant. The appearance of this type of saying in Jesus material is connected to rhetorical tradition, cf. Robbins, "Chreia," 1–23; Tannehill, "Types and Functions of Apophthegms in the Synoptic Gospels," 1792–803. Perhaps we have yet to appreciate just how frequently a wise, pithy, or witty saying in the rhetorical tradition was introduced by a question to an honored person in various contexts, cf. Hock and O'Neil, *Chreia in Ancient Rhetoric, I,* 5, 6, 24, 27, 33, 85, 257, 259, 311, 312, 313; *Chreia and Ancient Rhetoric*. Just as a venerated secular quotation is introduced by a question, a fine prophetic saying like this one in Luke's version and context—one both spiritually practical to remember and befitting a highly honored person—surely deserves to be so introduced; so Luke apparently thinks and so his composition would indicate..

might appear insignificant or unconvincing of any pattern, but taken collectively they are, in my estimation, suggestive of a feature of Lukan style. Normatively, it appears that the main concern of the speaker with respect to addressees is forward, the second element of the question being placed rearward, which then connects to previous topical content placed in the foreground prior to the question. In the Lukan conception, the first part of this dual-element type question serves to establish a topic which is then often developed in the immediately ensuing narrative, while the second part functions to enhance contiguity with closely foregrounded material, thus offering a cognitive advantage to the reader.

In Luke 9:25 (9:24), Luke strengthens the rearward element by introducing a participle of a previously foregrounded verb. Also, in the zone of improved recompositions with enhanced foregrounding connecting to the second focus (note 17), at Luke 18:18b (18:17), the kingdom of God, which relates to life eternal, is brought more tightly into the foreground; at Luke 21:7 (21:6), the second-element "things to happen" is foregrounded by "these things which you behold." With respect to Luke's composition at Luke 22:48 (22:21, 22), Ἰούδα, φιλήματι τόν υἱὸν ἀνθρώπου παραδίδως; it is to be noted that both the "Son of Man" and "betrayal" are narratively foregrounded. Understood this way as a matter of Lukan style, Marshall's suggestion that "The saying (22:48) is integral to the narrative"[28] gains support.

Luke reworks Matthew's unforegrounded rendering into the question, "Do you think that I came to give peace on earth?" (Luke 12:51a), providing due foregrounding (note 18) of the rearward element with "I came to cast fire upon the earth" (12:49a). Luke's own examples from his first book (note 19) are "Were none found who turned back to give glory to God except this foreigner?" (17:18), with rearward element foregrounded by "he was a Samaritan" (17:16b), and "For if they do these things in the green tree, what will happen in the dry?" (23:31), with the second focus foregrounded by "the days are coming when they will say 'blessed are the barren' . . . say to mountains 'fall on us' and to hills 'cover us'" (23:29–30).

Three examples from Acts (note 21) which are dramatically effective in the development of action[29] include "Do you understand what things you are reading (ἀναγινώσκεις)?" (Acts 8:30b), where in the immediate foreground (8:30a) Luke places a participle of the same verb (ἀναγινώσκοντος). "What prevents me from being baptized?" (8:36c), is foregrounded by a relational indefinite pronoun and noun

---

28. Marshall, *Gospel of Luke*, 836.

29. I have observed that Luke often employs a question as a dramatic stage-setting device for a speech, prophecy, instruction, or action. With respect to the latter function, Turner, "Rhetoric of Question and Answer in Menander," 5, 21, makes two heuristic observations that do not seem far removed from Lukan characterization and personification. He notices that "An utterance that may be important to the development of the action, or may illustrate character—that utterance will gain immeasurably in vivacity if it can be put as a question," and he wonders "How far is the asking of questions, where the corresponding thought would in English be a statement or a command, a function of the Greek language itself?"

(τι ὕδωρ, 8:36a). "Did you receive the Holy Spirit, having believed (πιστεύσαντες)?" (19:2a), is similarly foregrounded by a relational indefinite pronoun and noun (τινας μαθητάς, 19:1b). From this perspective of consistent Lukan style, the understanding of these disciple-believers Paul encounters at Ephesus as previous believers in Jesus, as is the disciple-believer Apollos encountered and so recognized by Priscilla and Aquila in the lovely "Theonic" and narrative-rhetorically judicious digression that Luke also employs as foreground to Paul's question, gains support. Paul's question to these Christian disciple-believers continues his narratively connected affiliation with the Jerusalem/Petrine tradition and the Spirit-reception language employed by Ananias in his earlier ministry to Paul. Paul is portrayed here as strengthening these disciple-believers, as he was previously portrayed (18:23) immediately before the insertion of the digression, a digression whose intended contextual impact is not well served by paragraph breaks in the Greek New Testament.[30] Luke's style of dual-focus question composition with its accompanying foregrounding of the rearward or postposed element is quite harmonious with how Luke narrates the ministerial concern uppermost on the mind of Paul here with respect to his Christian addressees.[31]

30. It seems probable that the significance of the digression itself (18:24–28) has, historically, been masked in part by the rhetorically insensitive paragraph breaks and by associated intrusive paragraph/chapter entitlements adopted over time by editions of the Greek New Testament at 18:23/18:24 and 18:28/19:1. These two paragraph/chapter breaks at this juncture go against the narrative grain when reading fluently, front to back, and can lend a clumsy disjointedness to the narrative that retards understandability. It is difficult to see how the intended literary purpose for this digression can be served by so detaching it from both of its contexts wherein it was initially located. These inserted breaks are quite unlikely to reflect the train of thought of the writer during his composition and are, I submit, unhelpful insofar as comprehending and appreciating the narratively pleasing impact of the digression with respect to material judiciously placed both immediately preceding and immediately after it. However, these two paragraph/chapter breaks have deeply established roots, going back to Codex Vaticanus and Codex Sinaiticus, where copyists (and possibly dictators) introduced a good number of rhetorically capricious section breaks. Further, my research in Acts shows that the Sinaiticus copyist (or the dictator) introduced 293 such breaks which are reduced to 148 in the current edition of the United Bible Societies' Greek New Testament. The Sinaiticus copyist/dictator also often paused after a *nomen sacrum* that ended a perceived sentence (as at 18:28), often resulting in a break before the next sentence. I suggest that the break at 18:28/19:1 and its counterpart at 18:23/24 are, from the perspectives of rhetorical clarity and stylistic consistency, long overdue for retirement.

31. Lake and Cadbury, *Beginnings of Christianity*, 4:237, point out that "disciples" at Acts 19:1 "must mean Christians, both from the use of μαθητάς in Acts and from the context. Chrysostom's theory that they were disciples of John has nothing to commend it." Luke's remarkable consistency as a matter of rhetorical clarity in his use of this term (Luke 9:16, 18, 54; 10:23; 16:1; 17:22; 18:15; 19:29, 37; 20:45; 22:39, 45; Acts 6:1, 2, 7; 9:10, 19, 26, 35 [feminine μαθήτρια], 38; 11:26, 29; 13:52; 14:20, 22, 28; 15:10; 16:1; 18:23, 27; 19:1, 9, 30; 20:1, 30; and 21:4, 16) is indeed supportive of Lake and Cadbury. Hemer, *Letters to the Seven Churches*, 225, with regard to Luke's usage at 19:1, observes that "the word μαθητάς is used absolutely, as elsewhere of disciples of Jesus; so too, Ehrhardt, "Construction and Purpose," 73. Stuhlmacher, *Biblische Theologie des Neuen Testaments, II*, 278, affords Luke the proper description of these believer-disciples that his narrative clarity deserves, "der Bericht über die (Jesus)-Jünger in Apg 19, 1–7," parentheses his. My stylistic findings on Luke's description of the addressees to Paul's question as foregrounded disciples who are Christian believers prior to the posing of the question finds corroboration with Lake, Cadbury, Hemer, Ehrhardt, and Stuhlmacher, confirming the earlier view of Zahn, *Die Apostelgeschichte des Lucas, II*, 673, who was correct to stress that "Der Text gestattet es nicht,

Lastly, we end our examples of Lukan foregrounding of the rearward or postposed element in dual-focus questions where we began, with Homer. Lukan style is to place the foreground neatly and closely before his character's question, perhaps illustrative of the narrative virtue of description (ἔκφρᾶσις), which according to Theon is an account which brings vividly into view what is being set forth.[32] Desirable qualities of an *ekphrasis* are, most of all, clarity and a vivid impression of all-but-seeing what is described.[33] Close topical foregrounding connections in characters' questions, when not boring or repetitive, are well suited to a skillful practice of this desirable feature of narrative composition. But in one case in Luke-Acts, the narrator departs from his usual style and exhibits again a style to be found in Homer, perhaps a more elegant and intellectually demanding style, where the foreground of the rearward or postposed element in a dual-focus question is a bit further back in the preceding context. Homer's character speaks, "My child, could you not guide me to the house of him they call Alcinous, who is lord among the people here?" (*Od.* 7.22–23, using the common verb ἀνάσσειν, "to be lord"). This passage connects with this previously foregrounded character who is cited regarding "a gift of honor for Alcinous, because he was king (ἄνασσε) over all" (*Od.* 7.10–11). Alcinous as lord, the second element in the question, is distantly but not obscurely foregrounded. Quite similarly, at Acts 26:8 Paul asks, "Why is it judged incredible by you if God raises the dead?" At 24:21b the second element has already been implanted in the preceding narrative as a main issue, "the resurrection of the dead." As compared to Homer in this regard, Luke impresses with his relative consistency of style and with a determined narrative connectedness, exhibiting thereby the desirable narrative-rhetorical virtues of clarity, plausibility, and persuasiveness.[34]

---

sie Johannesjünger zu nennen."

32. Theon, *Progym.* 7.2–3.

33. Theon, *Progym.* 7.54–56. Theon's instruction on appropriate narrative *ekphrasis* may be directly compared with later views on that subject by Hermogenes, Aphthonius, Nicolaus, and John of Sardis in Kennedy, *Progymnasmata*. For discussion of *ekphrasis*, which along with personification (ἠθοποιΐα) may be regarded as "wirklich die grössten ästhetischen Qualitäten" (so Schissal, "Rhetorische Progymnasmatik der Byzantiner," 10), cf. Hunger, *Die hochsprachliche profane Literatur der Byzantiner*, 116–17, 170–88. Luke's stylistic performance with regard to the spirit of narrative description in his composition of questions seems very much in keeping with the desired outcome of a rhetorically minded education. On that elite cultural enterprise in the Empire to which Luke may have been a part, cf. Marrou, *History of Education in Antiquity*, 194–205; Bonner, *Education in Ancient Rome*, 277–327; Morgan, *Literate Education in the Hellenistic and Roman Worlds*.

34. It is a pleasure to recall helpful dialogue with Elizabeth Minchen and Maria Pantelia. An earlier version of this study was presented to the Biblical Greek Language and Linguistics Section of the Society of Biblical Literature, Toronto, 2002.

Chapter 3

Acts 2:38 in Light of the Syntax of Imperative-Future Passive and Imperative-Present Participle Combinations

WHILE CONDITIONAL SENTENCES INVOLVING imperatives are, of course, a standard category of classical and NT grammars,[1] the usage of the particular syntactical structures of imperative-future passive indicative combinations and imperative-present participial combinations are not singled out for discussion in classical and NT grammars because grammarians are occupied with more common linguistic components.[2] These rarer structures are not the basic or standard grammatical categories.

At least at one place in the NT, however, it would specifically be helpful to have a semantic and linguistic appraisal of the syntax of these structures to shed light on how a Greek speaker familiar with narrative composition, one probably educated in Greco-Roman schools with their emphasis on rhetorical exercises, would understand and employ them. This knowledge would help us understand as correctly as possible what Luke, through his important character, intends this language to mean at the conclusion of Peter's narratively programmatic speech at the outset of Luke's second book. Given that 120 disciple-believer-witnesses, including the speaker, have just received the gift of the Holy Spirit, the concluding statement of this speech about this event is

---

1. In this vein, see Caragounis's overall comments on an imperatival protasis in a variety of conditional sentences (Caragounis, *Development of Greek and the New Testament*, 189–90).

2. When imperatives are discussed, an example, like John 2:19, of an imperative-future active indicative combination is sometimes mentioned, as by Schweizer, *Griechische Grammatik*, 344. However, this is not an example of an imperative-future passive indicative combination where the subject of the imperative will be acted upon in the indefinite future if the command to the same subject in the protasis is met. In John 2:19 the subject of the imperative (Jesus's opponents) is also different from the subject of the future active indicative (Jesus himself, who will act in the future on the temple, not on his opponents).

The subject of the present study is especially the conditional imperative-future passive indicative combination in Koine Greek where the subject of the two verbal ideas is the same, namely the addressee(s) of the imperative in the conditional protasis are the same as the subject(s) of the future passive indicative in the apodosis. That same subject of the future passive indicative in such a construction will then be acted upon externally at some indefinite future time, at a time when the command in the protasis is met to the satisfaction of the person(s) acting upon the subject in the apodosis.

43

significant. It is narratively significant both as to what the speaker means by it for his original hearers, and it is significant in understanding the reason why Luke includes the repeated examples and precedents of the gift of the Holy Spirit for his readership that he does.[3]

As Luke addresses Theophilus and his circle of active readers through the narrative, he appears to want to be sure that they understand him with respect to these particular, and undoubtedly carefully chosen, examples and precedents. After the first instance, in response to a question from hearers in Peter's programmatic speech, he tells them: μετανοήσατε, καὶ βαπτισθήτω ἕκαστος ὑμῶν ἐπὶ τῷ ὀνόματι Ἰησοῦ Χριστοῦ εἰς ἄφεσιν τῶν ἁμαρτιῶν ὑμῶν καὶ λήμψεσθε τὴν δωρεὰν τοῦ ἁγίου πνεύματος (Repent, and be baptized each of you in the name of Jesus Christ for the remission of your sins, and you will receive the gift of the Holy Spirit). This Spirit-reception language is immediately quantified (2:39) by identifying it with the narratively prominent ἡ ἐπαγγελία—the promise—contextually invoked at Luke 24:49; Acts 1:4–5, 8; 2:33, and easily traced back to the promise of the gift of the Holy Spirit by Jesus himself at the zenith of his teaching on prayer (Luke 11:13), where the Father will give πνεῦμα ἅγιον in response to persistent prayer. All of this Spirit-reception language is foregrounded by the prophecy of John the Baptist at Luke 3:16,[4] a prophecy with which the earthly Jesus would be familiar in the storyline. Luke is no doubt well aware that ἐπαγγελία functions as a key word in his wider narrative context of Spirit-reception and prophetic fulfillment. Ἐπαγγελία is the Lukan *Stichwort* employed in his fulfillment-of-prophecy theme with regard to the gift of the Holy Spirit. A skillful narrator, Luke employs it here (2:39) in an obvious manner where it will be so recognized by attentive readers at the end of Peter's speech in order to quantify what τὴν δωρεὰν τοῦ ἁγίου πνεύματος actually is, yielding the distinct impression that it is that which has just occurred in the experience of the speaker.

Such an impression would be a reasonable one for a narrator to convey in order to influence and persuade his readership. The Lukan conversation with his readers[5] is such that this speaker is intentionally portrayed in the narration as telling his audience

---

3. For analysis of Luke's narrative strategy with respect to the vital and rhetorically expected use of examples and precedents of the gift of the Holy Spirit in the contemporary progymnasmatic tradition of the first century, see Elbert, "Possible Literary Links," 226–54. [Included in this anthology.—Ed.]

4. Sensitivity to narrative continuity with respect to the sequence of Luke 3:16; 11:13; 24:49 may also be detected in Klein, "Exkurs," 410.

5. Peter's speech seems to be a powerful narrative tool in Luke's conversation with his readers, as it is given by one of the main characters in a thematically connected story of prophetic fulfillment. The thread of the argument in the speech is clear, and its conclusion—as analyzed within Lukan style from structural examples in the present study—is plausible. On this argument a large group of previously Spirit-filled individuals, using Luke's own term of interiority at Acts 2:4, appear, through a concise and well-composed speech by their representative, to promise their own experience conditionally to listeners and to readers beyond narrative time.

and those afar that if they will repent[6] and are baptized,[7] then they will receive at some indefinite future time the same gift of the Holy Spirit[8] that the speaker himself just received and experienced. This understanding of the narration is consistent with the experience of the speaker in the narrative foregrounding of the speech and with Peter's apparent grasp of the meaning of those previous details as set out in the contents of the speech,[9] wherein his own descriptive explanation of what is seen and heard is added to the Joel quote (καὶ προφητεύσουσιν, 2:18b). It is also quite consistent with how the rhetorically minded progymnasmatic teachers framed the subject of speech-in-character (προσωποποΐα or ἠθοποιΐα, otherwise denoted as characterization/personification) for training their students in narrative composition.[10] I have suggested that Luke is familiar with this training.[11] Further, the indefinite future tense employed

---

6. On repentance at Acts 2:38 in the context of Luke 24:47 and Luke-Acts, cf. Nave, *Role and Function of Repentance in Luke-Acts*, 198–202. With Nave, I understand repentance at 2:38 as the entrance into salvation and becoming a disciple-believer; cf. also "Sündenvergebung," in Sellner, *Das Heil Gottes*, 248–49.

7. At Luke 3:3, from which baptism in the name of Jesus Christ probably developed, repentance is a conditional factor as it is here at Acts 2:38. For an overview, cf. Sellner, "Die Taufe auf den Namen Jesu Christi" (*Das Heil Gottes*, 240–47). Elsewhere in Acts, it is clear that for Luke water baptism per se does not convey the gift of the Holy Spirit (8:12–17; 10:44–48). Further, it is not possible to detect from Luke's selected examples of Spirit reception that readers should expect an automatic conveyance of the gift of the Spirit in water baptism, although Acts 9:17–19 and 19:2, 3 do suggest that teaching and prayer concerning the gift of the Holy Spirit was expected at water baptism.

As I will conclude in this study, the procession of verbal ideas at Acts 2:38 in the conditional imperative-future passive syntax suggests a separation in time between the qualifying conditions and the future event of sovereign divine action. This is similar to the understanding suggested by Thiering, "Qumran Initiation and New Testament Baptism," 626, and Brown, "'Water Baptism' and 'Spirit-Baptism' in Luke-Acts," 144, who observes that "Surely it is preferable to interpret the passage [Acts 2:38] in accordance with all the other texts which we have considered and to understand the words 'you shall receive' to point to an event subsequent to baptism."

8. Sellner, "Die Gabe des Heiligen Geists" (*Das Heil Gottes*, 250–66), offers an overview of various understandings of Spirit-reception at Acts 2:38, including those of Pesch, Menzies, and Haya-Prats who suggest that receiving the gift of the Holy Spirit at 2:38 is probably not intended by Luke to be understood here in his conditional sentence as automatically coterminous, temporally, with repentance and/or baptism. Sellner ends his discussion with a reference to Haya-Prats's comment on "l'influx de l'Esprit pentecostal" (266); for a complete English translation of that thesis, cf. Haya-Prats, *Empowered Believers*.

9. For a discussion of contents, cf. Soards, *Speeches in Acts*, 31–38.

10. See, for example, the treatment given to the student exercise of composing narrative with proper attention to speech-in-character by the first-century rhetorical teacher Aelius Theon: "ΠΕΡΙ ΠΡΟΣΩΠΟΠΟΙΙΑΣ" in Patillon, *Aelius Théon*, 70–73. For Theon, a properly composed speech must reflect what is appropriate to the character and the occasion, and exhortation therein must have a suitable starting point (ἀφορμή) and treat what is possible to happen (δυνατὸν γεγέσθαι). Here, the speaker himself is foregrounded as being exhorted to pray and to wait for what he and the 120 disciple-believers have just received (Luke 11:13; 24:49). The starting point for his speech is their common experience (2:4). It is then most rhetorically fitting to personify this speaker by way of exhortation as (1) explaining what his audience has seen and heard and as (2) extending an invitation to his hearers so that they can also possibly receive the same gift.

11. Elbert, "Possible Literary Links."

here in this conditional sentence, a relative gnomic future,[12] does not require and does not seem consistent with temporally pinning the gift of the Holy Spirit from Jesus as sovereign κύριος (Acts 2:36) to either repentance or to baptism. The divine creative action in the future passive indicative here is from the κύριος. Would not a speaker portrayed as giving a speech-in-character think that the κύριος would control the time of reception of this gift of the Holy Spirit, as was done in his own life? It is from the heavenly Jesus as both κύριος and χριστός that what is seen and heard is poured out (2:33–36). Later in this narrative this same speaker observes that God has given the Holy Spirit to those that obey him (5:32), also suggesting sovereignty with respect to the gift of the Holy Spirit to disciple-believers. Wolfgang Dietrich, not employing rhetorical speech-in-character with respect to Peter, gives the narrative-critical and coherent interpretation with respect to him that καὶ λήμψεσθε τὴν δωρεὰν τοῦ ἁγίου πνεύματος at 2:33c should be understood as being phenomenologically equivalent to τὸ ἡ δωρεὰ ... ἐκκέχυται; δωρεὰν ἔδωκεν αὐτοῖς ὁ θεός (10:45; 11:17) and contextually to δωρεὰν τοῦ θεοῦ (8:20) as well.[13] Calvin, although not as familiar with Greco-Roman rhetorical culture as we are today, explicitly recognized that 2:38 indicates that Peter is promising his hearers the same gift accompanied with speaking in tongues that he himself just received, advancing that interpretation in his *Commentariorum Joannis Calvini in Acts Apostolorum*.[14]

Here, as we seek a rhetorically and narratively attuned interpretation at Acts 2:38 that takes into account the nature of the conditional imperative-future passive

---

12. BDF, §349, categorizes the future indicative in two ways according to its normal usage: (1) "in order to express what is to be expected under certain circumstances," a gnomic future—at Acts 2:38 these certain circumstances are generated by the addressees meeting the conditions set out by the imperatives in the syntax of the imperative-future passive indicative combination—and (2) "in declarative sentences after verbs of believing to denote a time subsequent to the acquisition of belief," a relative future. The future passive indicative in the apodosis at Acts 2:38 fits BDF's categorizations like a glove. I grammatically characterize this indefinite future passive indicative (λήμψεσθε, noting that λαμβάνω prefers the future middle form when used in the future passive sense) as a relative gnomic future.

13. Dietrich, *Das Petrusbild der lukanischen Schriften*, 212–15.
In addition to this equivalent language from these two ensuing examples and precedents of Spirit-reception, in the vein of phenomenological interpretation via word recognition, it should not be overlooked that Luke's repeated use of δίδωμι and δωρεά with regard to the Holy Spirit as a gift from God to disciple-believers provides a clear and plausible descriptive pattern of authorial intent readily discernible by active readers: δώσει πνεῦμα ἅγιον τοῖς αἰτοῦσιν αὐτόν (Luke 11:13); δωρεὰν τοῦ ἁγίου πνεύματος (Acts 2:38c); τὸ πνεῦμα τὸ ἅγιον ὃ ἔδωκεν (5:32); ἐλάμβανον πνεῦμα ἅγιον .. . δωρεὰν τοῦ θεοῦ (8:17, 20); ἡ δωρεὰ τοῦ ἁγίον πνεύματος ἐκκέχυται (10:45, cf. ἐξέχεεν, 2:33); and ἴσην δωρεὰν ἔδωκεν (11:17).

14. Calvin, *Commentariorum Joannis Calvini in Acts Apostolorum*, 30. However, possibly for political reasons so as to deny a scriptural basis for the miraculous to his Catholic opponents, Calvin then proceeds to negate his own interpretation by invoking a fanciful imposition of an "apostolic age" or *Pfingstzeit* epoch. Calvin's readers need not bother with his interpretation or with authorial intention; rather, they should dismiss both and accept his overruling hermeneutic of epochal cancellation. For the context of Calvin's tactics toward textual descriptions of nonnatural phenomena, where politically convenient presuppositions about the miraculous and personal revelation may sometimes intrude, see my "Calvin and Spiritual Gifts," 8:303–31.

combination within Lukan syntax, I am personally inspired by an insight from one of the distinguished commentators who labored in the exposition of the Greek text of Acts, namely that we have a duty to press on toward new discoveries whenever possible and appropriate. I refer to C. K. Barrett's insistence that "Other studies have their place, but Christian theology is founded on the study of texts, and exegesis is founded on a precise understanding of grammar—logic in relation to language."[15] In this light, it is to the details of a grammatical and syntactical basis for understanding the imperative-future passive conditional combination as employed at Acts 2:38 and the contextually adverse narrative option of an imperative-participial combination that I now turn.

An unexpected discovery is that in the classical Greek database of the Thesaurus Linguae Graecae no examples of an imperative-future passive indicative combination could be found. Instead, one finds the imperative-aorist passive subjunctive (future) conditional syntax as in the goddess Athene's command to Odysseus and his son: ἴσχεσθε (present middle imperative) . . . διακρινθῆτε (aorist passive subjunctive) in ἴσχεσθε πτολέμου, Ἰθακήσιοι, ἀργαλέοιο, ὥς κεν ἀναιμωτί γε διακρινθῆτε τάχιστα (Cease from painful war, men of Ithaca, so that without bloodshed you may be speedily parted [*Od.* 24.531–32]).[16] Divine action of the goddess plays a role in the verbal idea of the passive subjunctive, as she is an arbiter in the speedy departure of the combatants.

As we shall see, Koine has apparently taken a more direct approach to the protasis-apodosis conditional structure when the subject of the imperative is to be acted upon at some future time. Instead of "Eat your breakfast and you may be taken to the movies," Koine takes the tone of "Eat your breakfast and you will be taken to the movies." However, in this less definite, perhaps more subtle, classical expression of the future action upon the subject of the imperative or in the more definite Koine approach examined below, the subject of the imperative is acted upon at some indefinite time in the future if the condition(s) in the protasis are met. Context may or may not clarify when that time is. In the aforementioned Homeric example, what can be noted is that in this use of the imperative-aorist passive subjunctive conditional combination the same subject is involved for both the verbal idea of the imperative and that of the passive subjunctive, where that same subject will be acted upon at some future time.

Klaus Beyer offers a sketch of imperative-future combinations in sentences with a conditional protasis, detecting a number of interesting Lukan examples[17] which merit further exploration. Rudolf Pesch explicitly raises the implications of a conditional protasis at Acts 2:38[18] by mentioning Spirit-reception at Acts 19:2–6 as being related to 2:38. In Acts 19, Luke portrays a descriptive and quite understandable scene of people

---

15. Barrett, "Biblical Classics IV," 71.
16. Homer, *Odyssey II*, 451.
17. Beyer, *Semitische Syntax im Neuen Testament*, 238–55.
18. Pesch, *Die Apostelgeschichte*, 125, noting that "Uumkehr und Taufe sind Bedingung des Geistempfangs."

in Ephesus who were unfamiliar with what Peter had said earlier in Jerusalem about the Spirit in a programmatic speech that Luke is now recording.[19] I have shown that Luke's question by the Lukan Paul at 19:2 about Spirit-reception is indeed addressed to Christian disciple-believers.[20] Should Peter's audience obey the commands in the protasis of the conditional sentence at 2:38, they too would be Christian disciple-believers and would be the indefinite future subjects of identical divine action as set out in the apodosis at 2:38. Here, different from the Acts 19 narrative, Luke apparently does not feel the need to explicitly detail ensuing Spirit-reception phenomena in the lives of Peter's hearers in the immediately following narrative. As commentators are required to do, Pesch moves ahead at this juncture without taking a critical look at the two long-standing readings of Spirit-reception as being somehow temporally co-terminous with the imperatives, although it seems clear that he is not sympathetic to these readings or an advocate of them.[21]

In order to gain further insight into Luke's syntactical mindset at 2:38, and as background to the relevant Lukan material which we will explore in this study, it will be helpful to first take a look at several examples of imperative-future passive combinations from the papyri, the LXX, and Eusebius.

In a third-century BCE documentary papyrus from Herakleopolites, Egypt (BGU 16 2646, lines 34–37) we read: Ἀσκλᾶν τόν τοῦ Ἀρήου εὔψυχον ποίησον· θεῶν θελόντων τὸ κατὰ αὐτὸν οἰκονομηθήσεται τῇ ἔξω ὡς ὡμολόγησε· (Do encourage Askalos, Areos's agent. The gods willing, his matter will be put in order outside, as he promised.) Askalos, the subject of the back-to-back imperatives is not the subject of the future passive indicative, but the gods are invoked as instrumental in acting in the future upon the matter at hand according to Areos's promise. Here, while the subjects of the two verbal ideas are different, this instance of an imperative-future passive indicative shows that the two verbal ideas in the syntax are not temporally simultaneous, that is, the command to encourage is not temporally coincident with the gods helping to put the matter in order.

From the LXX, 4 Kingdoms 5:10, we have: λοῦσαι . . . ἐπιστρέψει ἡ σάρξ σου σοί καὶ καθαρισθήσῃ (wash . . . your flesh will return to you and you will be cleansed).[22] Here, God committed himself to the action of cleansing after requiring the obedience of washing seven times. At Isaiah 44:1–3, ἄκουσον . . . βοηθήσῃ . . .

---

19. If, for example, these disciple-believers, as Luke describes them at Acts 19:1–2, had read only Mark's Gospel or perhaps some of the other material Luke mentions at Luke 1:1, they would have had no knowledge of the meaning or the fulfillment of John the Baptist's prophecy about the ministry of Jesus who would baptize with the Holy Spirit (Mark 1:8), something important to the Christian faith which Mark's narrative fails to explain.

20. Elbert, "Observation on Luke's Composition," 98–109.

21. See too, Pesch, "Die Gabe des Heiligen Geistes," 52–53.

22. Diehl, *Die Fortführung des Imperativs im biblischen Hebräisch*, 101, observes this to be a classic example of conditional and directive sentence structure, where the washing is the condition for the cleansing.

ἐπιθήσω τὸ πνεῦμά μου ἐπὶ τὸ σπέρμα σου (listen . . . you will be helped . . . I will put my Spirit upon your seed), the time of divine action is indefinite. Similarly, in Sirach 33:4, ἑτοίμασον λόγον καὶ οὕτως ἀκουσθήσῃ (prepare your words and thus you will be listened to), the two verbal ideas with the same subject are temporally nonsimultaneous in concert with indefinite future action.

In Eusebius, *Hist. eccl.* 9.7.14.2, we read: ἀξιώσατε· τεύξεσθε γὰρ αὐτῆς χωρίς τινος ὑπερθέσεως· (Resolve so to do, you will obtain your bounty without delay). Here the imperative of ἀξιόω is combined with the future middle indicative form of τεύχω used in a passive sense. If the citizens will respond with due reverence to the worship of the immortal gods then their petition will be granted. For motivation they are assured that their bounty will then be granted without delay (χωρίς ὑπερθέσεως). The subject of the two verbal ideas is the same, namely the local citizens; obedience to the command will be followed in due time with action from civil administration with regard to their obtaining a bounty.

Speaking of John the Baptist, Mark says "The voice of one crying in the wilderness: prepare (ἑτοιμάσατε) the way of the Lord, make (ποιεῖτε) his paths straight." These commands are to hearers of John the Baptist and by implication to Mark's readers. This is what humans should do. Luke (3:5–6) repeats this verbatim and adds from Isaiah 40 what God will do: "Every valley shall be filled (πληρωθήσεται) and every mountain and hill shall be brought low (ταπεινωθήσεται) and all the crooked shall be (ἔσται) made straight, and the rough ways smooth; and all flesh shall see (ὄψεται) the salvation of God." While humans are the subject of the two imperatives in 3:4b, these verbal ideas would of course not be understood as temporally coincident with the various future actions on various different subjects by God. It might be thought unnecessary to notice this obvious fact, but I do so because this instance illustrates how Luke evidently understood his narrative usage of the conditional imperative-future passive combination with the same subject in both the protasis and the apodosis. His usage throughout is quite consistent with what we see here.

In Lukan *Sondergut* at 6:35 we read ἀγαπᾶτε . . . ἀγαθοποιεῖτε . . . δανείζετε . . . καὶ ἔσται ὁ μισθὸς ὑμῶν πολύς (Love your enemies, and do good, and lend despairing not at all; and your reward will be great). The future middle indicative has a passive sense given that a proper response to the commands will result in sovereign divine action upon the obedient at indefinite future time(s).

Also Lukan is 6:37c–38a: ἀπολύετε, καὶ ἀπολυθήσεσθε· δίδοτε, καὶ δοθήσεται (forgive, and you will be forgiven; give, and it will be given to you). The divine action in the apodosis is not mandated as temporally simultaneous with the verbal idea of the imperative, rather the sovereignty of God is understood to control the fulfillment of the promise.

At 8:50 Luke repeats Mark's μὴ φοβοῦ, μόνον πίστευσον (Do not fear, only believe) and distinctively adds[23] the future passive apodosis καὶ σωθήσεται (and she will

---

23. On the motivation for the addition, other than how Luke instinctively thinks (and speaks)

be healed), raising the syntax to a new level. While the subject of the imperatives is different from the girl in the indefinite future passive, it is clear that for Luke this syntax does not convey temporal simultaneity of the verbal ideas. The divine action in the apodosis occurs in the sovereign timing of God in the ministry of Jesus.

At 10:28, Luke quotes Jesus differently than the Markan version. Instead of "You are not far from the kingdom of God," Luke writes "You have answered right; do this and you will live" (τοῦτο ποίει καὶ ζήσῃ). Here the future middle indicative carries somewhat of a passive sense because the life granted upon obedience to the imperative most probably refers in Luke's thought to life eternal at 10:25b. Again, the two verbal ideas of this conditional syntax are temporally nonsimultaneous.

In the Q passage Luke 11:9=Matt 7:7,[24] we have αἰτεῖτε καὶ δοθήσεται and κρούετε καὶ ἀνοιγήσεται, where it is clear that the intent of the promised divine action in the future passive is not automatically simultaneous with the verbal idea in the protasis, but rather in the indefinite future time of a sovereign God. Ditto again from Q, ζητεῖτε . . . προστεθήσεται ὑμῖν (Luke 12:31=Matt 6:33).

From teaching on humility in Lukan *Sondergut*: κάλει πτωχούς . . . καὶ μακάριος ἔσῃ . . . ἀνταποδοθήσεται (But when you give a feast, *invite the poor*, the maimed, the lame, the blind, and *you will be blessed*, because they cannot repay you. *You will be repaid* at the resurrection of the just, Luke 14:13–14). With the subject of the imperative and the future middle/passives the same, not only are the verbal ideas in the conditional combination temporally nonsimultaneous, but the divine action of blessings in the indefinite future continues on to final repayment in the apodosis.

Aside from 2:38, in the book of Acts we encounter other examples. Simon is told by Peter: μετανόησον . . . καὶ δεήθητι τοῦ κυρίου εἰ ἄρα ἀφεθήσεταί σοι (Repent . . . and petition the Lord if perhaps [the thought of your heart] will be forgiven you, Acts 8:22). Clearly the two imperatives in the conditional protasis here lead to a possible divine action in the future that is expressly in the sovereign providence of the Lord.

At 9:6, the heavenly Jesus addresses Paul: ἀλλὰ ἀνάστηθι καὶ εἴσελθε εἰς τὴν πόλιν, καὶ λαληθήσεταί σοι ὅ τί σε δεῖ ποεῖν (But rise up and enter into the city, and you will be told what you are to do). Three days later, at an indefinite future time as far as Paul is concerned, he was told what to do by Ananias. This syntax is repeated at 22:10 (πορεύου . . . λαληθήσεται).

At 16:31, in response to a question, Paul and Silas reply, "Believe in the Lord Jesus, and you will be saved—you and your household" (πίστευσον ἐπὶ τὸν κύριον Ἰησοῦν καὶ σωθήσῃ σὺ καὶ ὁ οἶκός σου). Paul and Silas speak the word of the Lord (τὸν λόγον τοῦ κυρίου) to them and after their own wounds were attended to, all who heard were baptized. Speech-in-character leads me to think that here the divine

---

when he believes that these syntactical structures are appropriate, cf. Weissenrieder, *Images of Illness*, 283.

24. Schulz, *Q*, 161–64; Schenk, *Synopse zur Redenquelle der Evangelien*, 61–65; Zeller, *Kommentar zur Logienquelle*, 56–59; Robinson et al., *Critical Edition of Q*, 214–15; Fleddermann, *Q*, 454–64.

action of the future passive refers to eschatological salvation[25] as contextually explained in the word of the Lord.

Concluding our analysis of Luke's imperative-future passive combinations, the difference in what Luke chooses to write at Luke 7:7b from what Matthew chooses to write at Matthew 8:8b in their accounts of the centurion's servant story is interesting. Both Matthew and Luke again appear to be following Q at this juncture.[26] Harry Fleddermann is correct that Matthew 7:28a; 8:5–10, 13 and Luke 7:1–10, along with eight other passages, follow a common order in both Matthew and Luke, supporting the conclusion that the author of Q composed the centurion's servant.[27] Here Matthew has ἀλλὰ μόνον εἰπὲ λόγῳ καὶ ἰαθήσεται ὁ παῖς μου (but only say a word, and my servant will be healed [Matt 8:8b, using the future passive indicative of ἰάομαι]), while Luke has ἀλλὰ εἰπὲ λόγῳ καὶ ἰαθήτω ὁ παῖς μου (but say a word, and let my servant be healed [Luke 7:7b, using the aorist passive imperative of ἰάομαι]).

It is clear that Matthew has inserted the adverb μόνον.[28] But after that, which author follows Q, which author edits it, and why? Both the critical edition and Fleddermann's magisterial reconstruction take the text of Q 7:7 to be ἀλλὰ εἰπὲ λόγῳ καὶ ἰαθήτω ὁ παῖς μου.[29] In support, Fleddermann posits that Matthew "switched from Q's ἰαθήτω to the future passive ἰαθήσεται. . . . Luke likes the future passive, so it is unlikely that he would have changed it if he had read it in Q. The third person imperative form appears elsewhere in Q."[30] However, Matthew uses the future passive indicative third person singular on forty-eight occasions and Luke on forty-six. Matthew uses the future passive indicative third person plural on seventeen occasions and Luke on seven. Both Matthew and Luke like the future passive. Assuming that alone would be sufficiently motivational for an emendation, either of them could have switched from ἰαθήτω to ἰαθήσεται or either could have left ἰαθήσεται as it was. Further, the third person imperative form does appear elsewhere in Q, as at Q 11:2=Matt 6:10/Luke 11:2 (ἐλθάτω ἡ βασιλεία σου), but Q 7:7=Matt 8:8/Luke 7:7 is the only occasion where the third person imperative is employed in a conditional sentence following an imperative in the protasis.

---

25. For example, cf. the similar eschatological usage of σωθήσῃ at Romans 10:9. With regard to the imminence of the *parousia*, I do not see any difference between the Paul of the Letters and the Lukan Paul, see too, Porter, *Paul of Acts*, 187–205.

26. Schulz, Q, 236–46; Schenk, *Synopse zur Redenquelle*, 36–39; Zeller, *Kommentar zur Logienquelle*, 37–38; Fleddermann, Q, 335–53.

27. Fleddermann, Q, 52, 353.

28. So too, Gagnon, "Shape of Matthew's Q Text," 138n19, and Fleddermann, Q, 342. Matthew appears to have incorporated μονόν into Markan material at 9:21; 10:42; 14:36; and 21:19, 21, as well as into Q at 5:47 and here at 8:8b. At 24:36 he adds μόνος to Mark 13:32. Luke follows Mark's use of the adverb at Luke 8:50 and uses it frequently in Acts; he would have no reason to remove it from Q at Luke 7:7b.

29. Robinson et al., *Critical Edition of Q*, 110–11, and Fledderman, Q, 346.

30. Fleddermann, Q, 342.

If Luke, as I now will suggest, switched from ἰαθήσεται he found in Q to ἰαθήτω, why would he consciously prefer the aorist passive imperative of ἰάομαι to the future passive indicative ἰαθήσεται of ἰάομαι? I posit that the εἰπὲ–ἰαθήσεται combination, as we find in Matthew, violates Luke's normative pattern or style of thinking about the contents of an imperative-future passive combination. Had he found the conditional sentence ἀλλὰ εἰπὲ λόγῳ καὶ ἰαθήτω ὁ παῖς μου in Q he would be comfortable with it because it is in accord with his syntactical preference. Had he found ἀλλὰ εἰπὲ λόγῳ καὶ ἰαθήσεται ὁ παῖς μου in Q he would have had a syntactical or stylistic motivation to edit it. Even though the subjects of the imperative and the future passive in ἀλλὰ εἰπὲ λόγῳ καὶ ἰαθήσεται ὁ παῖς μου are different, this usage of an imperative-future passive combination is clearly one where there is intentional and immediate temporal simultaneity of the two verbal ideas. This is not how Luke employs this grammatical structure, whether the subjects in the protasis and in the apodosis are the same or not. Therefore, I suggest that here Luke would tend to preserve his normal syntactical choice, namely that in an imperative-future passive indicative conditional structure the two verbal ideas are not temporally simultaneous. Had he found ἀλλὰ εἰπὲ λόγῳ καὶ ἰαθήσεται ὁ παῖς μου in Q he would switch from the future passive to the aorist imperative, obtaining what we now see in Matthew with the added μόνον. Luke's rhetorical consistency in this syntactical style would afford better understandability as far as he is concerned for his conditional sentences where the subjects of the imperative and the future passive are the same. In his own usage of this linguistic structure, it could have been rhetorically instinctive for Luke to avoid the language we find in Matthew 8:8b and, if he found it in Q, to emend it with an imperative of entreaty.

Could Luke have made such a bold move? On my argument he could have done it to avoid the deliberate impression of temporal coincidence between the verbal ideas in the protasis and apodosis of a conditional sentence with an imperative-future passive combination. Such temporal coincidence is contrary to all the rest of Luke's identical grammatical structures that we know. Also, at Mark 11:17/Matthew 21:13 Luke switches from the future passive κληθήσεται to the future indicative ἔσται for no known reason, but at Matthew 8:8b/Luke 7:7b we have a sound stylistic reason for him to alter Q. If this syntactical argument is true, then the best choice of the original text of Q 7:7 is ἀλλὰ εἰπὲ λόγῳ καὶ ἰαθήσεται ὁ παῖς μου, which seems much more probable to me than Matthew changing ἰαθήτω to ἰαθήσεται for no good reason, although certainty in such matters is impossible.

As to the next syntactical topic, for Luke, when a command is intended to be understood as temporally simultaneous with another verbal idea, like "chew your gum while listening to me," the imperative-future passive combination is of course not suitable and instead the imperative-present participle combination is employed. Luke's style in this regard again seems clear and consistent, as illustrated in his syntax of this appropriate linguistic structure which easily communicates that the verbal idea in the imperative is to be understood as temporally coincident with a second verbal idea that accompanies the imperative, as in the scholia on Apollonius Rhodius's *Argonautica*,[31] "λέγων· "ἐπακούσατε οὖν, ὥπερ τὸ χρέος ἀπολαμβάνοντες" (saying: "obey then, so receiving the obligation"); James 5:1, κλαύσατε ὀλαλύζοντες (weep, howling); Jude 21, τηρήσατε προσδεχόμενοι (keep [yourselves in the love of God], anticipating); and Matthew 28:19-20, μαθητεύσατε . . . βαπτίζοντες . . . διδάσκοντες (make disciples . . . baptizing . . . teaching).

Here are Luke's imperative-present participle combinations: δανείζετε υηδέν ἀπελπίζοντες (lend, despairing not at all [Luke 6:35]); ἴσθι ἐξουσίαν ἔχων (you are to be having authority [Luke 19:17]); ἀγρυπνεῖτε . . . δεόμενοι . . . (*Be watchful* at all times, *praying* that you may escape [Luke 21:36]); γρηγορεῖτε μνημονεύοντες (watch, remembering [Acts 20:31]).

Luke could have recorded the conclusion of Peter's speech at Acts 2:38 by using the very common present participle of λαμβάνω following the two imperatives to indicate that receiving the Holy Spirit here accompanied repentance and/or baptism or a cocooning of the two events (μετανοήσατε . . . βαπτισθήτω . . . τὴν δωρεὰν τοῦ ἁγίου πνεύματος λαμβάνοντες). Had he done this he would have misrepresented Peter's intentions as expected from speech-in-character, negated his own narrative emphasis on seeking the gift of the Spirit at the zenith of Jesus's teaching on prayer in Luke 11, and eviscerated the narrative coherence and unity with his own ensuing examples and precedents of receiving the gift of the Holy Spirit which he progymnasmatically provides throughout his narrative. Luke would have had little motivation for employing an imperative-present participle combination in his composition of the conditional sentence at the conclusion of Peter's programmatic speech and he does not do so.

If Luke intends his descriptive examples and precedents of Spirit reception to clarify the unexemplified discursive language of these vitally important Christian experiences in the letters of Paul, and thereby to stimulate fresh rereadings of Paul, as I have argued based upon intertextual comparisons and progymnasmatic concepts about narrative composition,[32] then Luke's recording of the conclusion of Peter's speech is a masterful fit to the entire narrative context of his double-work. His syntax of the conditional imperative-future passive indicative combination at Acts 2:38—with the verbal ideas in the protasis and the indefinite future of divine action in the apodosis being temporally nonsimultaneous as a matter of style—fits very well with believer-disciple-witnesses previously waiting in Jerusalem for the gift of the Holy Spirit in the foregrounded teaching on the subject by the earthly Jesus, and with Luke's plausible examples and precedents of this event in the life of other selected characters who believe later in the narrative.

There is no case in Lukan thought, or anywhere else that I have found, where the conditional imperative-future passive combination is employed—with the same subject(s) of the verbal ideas in the protasis and the apodosis—that implies temporal

---

31. Wendel, *Scholia in Apollonium Rhodium Vetera*, 151, line 3.
32. Elbert, "Possible Literary Links."

simultaneity of the verbal ideas. To the contrary, all the evidence points in the other direction, namely that this particular combination is used when the future action, divine or otherwise, is intrinsically indefinite. Following obedience to the conditional protasis of Acts 2:38 by immediate hearers—and by all who are afar off—is the expectation of an indefinite future divine action, which here is a bestowal of the gift of the Holy Spirit by the heavenly Jesus as described by the relative gnomic future passive indicative in the apodosis. As Pesch correctly intimates,[33] at 2:38 repentance and baptism are not intended by Luke to be understood as automatically conveying the gift of the Holy Spirit. Rather this gift, in this narratively foregrounded context,[34] concluding this speech where Luke's portrayal in concert with speech-in-character suggests that Peter would most probably think that the promised gift he is talking about would be similar in experiential content and manifestation to what he and his fellow 120 disciple-believer-witnesses have just themselves received, will be given when the Lord (2:36) decides to give it.

In summary then, the imperative-future passive indicative combination at Acts 2:38 with its conditional protasis has been analyzed in terms of the syntax of this linguistic structure in broader Koine Greek and in specific Lukan application. The future divine action in the apodosis of Acts 2:38—the impartation of the gift of the Holy Spirit by the heavenly Lord Jesus—is found to be deliberately indefinite and temporally nonsimultaneous with the two verbal ideas, repentance and baptism, in the conditional protasis. In Lukan syntax when a command is meant to be temporally coincident with another action, the imperative-present participle combination is employed. Both of these linguistic findings have been supported by examples.[35] These findings, consistent with speech-in-context and other progymnasmatic narrative-rhetorical qualities, suggest that at Acts 2:38 it is the Lukan intention to portray the speaker as promising the gift of the Holy Spirit to hearers and to those beyond narrative time as a *Pfingsterfahrung*.[36]

33. Pesch, *Die Apostelgeschichte*, 125.

34. Active readers in the early Christian community, whom the narrator of Luke-Acts evidently has in mind, would, in their literary environment, be sensitive to the progymnasmatic narrative-rhetorical qualities of clarity, conciseness, and plausibility (σαφήνεια, συντομία, πιθανοτής in "ΠΕΡΙ ΔΙΗΓΗΜΑΤΟΣ," Patillon, *Aelius Théon Progymnasmata*, 40). Accordingly, they could follow, with anticipation, the prophetic fulfillment theme, beginning with John the Baptist onwards, easily enough (Luke 3:16; 11:13; 24:49; Acts 1:5, 8, 14; 2:4, 18, 33, 38–39).

35. Further, of potential interest to Q studies, the critical reconstruction of Q 7:7=Matt 8:8/Luke 7:7 has been argued to be ἀλλὰ εἰπὲ λόγῳ καὶ ἰαθήσεται ὁ παῖς μου.

36. It is a pleasure to acknowledge the hospitality of the late Traianos Gagos during a working visit to the University of Michigan Papyrology Collection, and the equal hospitality afforded by Maria Pantelia on another working visit to the facilities of the Thesaurus Linguae Graecae, University of California at Irvine. An earlier version of this study was presented at the 2001 international meeting of the Society of Biblical Literature, Rome. Occasional heuristic discussion is also acknowledged with my colleague Emerson Powery and with Francis Gignac, whose third volume on syntax of his *A Grammar of the Greek Papyri of the Roman and Byzantine Periods* is eagerly awaited, with classicist Ronald Ipock and papyrologist Peter Arzt-Grabner. Responsibility for the views advocated in this

Chapter 4

Possible Literary Links between Luke-Acts and Pauline Letters Regarding Spirit-Language

Introduction

THE UNDISPUTED PAULINE LETTERS appeared c. 50–57 CE,[1] Romans being penned from Corinth in 57 CE, with Ephesians written from Rome c. 62 CE.[2] Luke-Acts was probably written some five to twenty years later.[3] Given the obvious literary interest in Paul by Luke,[4] it seems good to continue to explore the construction of a credible text-critical hypothesis or a serious *wissenschaftliche Exegese*, hopefully satisfying methodologically rigorous criteria and comparisons, so as to indicate whether and/or how Luke used Paul's letters in the contemporary literary manner of building upon another respected author. The convincing formation of such an overall hypothesis would be a worthy future goal of scholarship. It would build further literary continuity between these canonical documents and stimulate future theological reflection. In the spirit of such exploration of literary connections, after offering a brief overview of the status of efforts to identify Lukan interaction with Pauline Letters, I discuss the Spirit-reception and Spirit-giving/giftedness language in Paul's discursive correspondence alongside the similar later narrative descriptions in Luke-Acts and offer literary reasons for the similarities. I also discuss the distinctive difference between the Spirit-interiority language of Paul as contrasted with that of Luke and suggest reasons for the dissimilarity. As in any textual exploration, it is easy to get stuck on a detail or two and miss the larger contextual and environmental literary picture, so for now I hope to take wisdom from another context in this endeavor:

---

study is solely mine.

1. Cf. Suhl, "Paulinische Chronologie im Streit der Meinungen," 939–1188; Thornton, *Der Zeuge des Zeugen*.

2. Barth, *Ephesians*, 51, suggests 62 CE, favoring its Pauline authenticity (41–50).

3. For a brief review of the range of suggested possibilities, cf. Fitzmyer, *Acts of the Apostles*, 51–55.

4. So accepting the name Λουκᾶς, with Barrett, *Critical and Exegetical Commentary*, 2:xxx. For discussion of the authorship of the anonymous double-work, cf. Fitzmyer, *Gospel according to Luke I–IX*, 35–62; Fitzmyer, *Acts of the Apostles*, 47–51. I follow Barrett and Fitzmyer in accepting that Luke wrote the Third Gospel as a preface to Acts.

But it is not enough for a learner merely to meet each construction or form in isolated instances; for he may do this repeatedly, and yet know little of the general principle which the single example illustrates. Men saw apples fall and the moon and the planets roll ages before the principle of gravitation was thought of.[5]

Brief Overview of Possible Lukan Literary Use of Paul's Letters

When Chevallier, a French archaeologist and specialist in aerial photography, published the English translation of his great book on Roman roads in 1976,[6] I doubt he anticipated that a quarter century later New Testament scholars would be debating about isolated communities and first audiences and the existence of later audiences.[7] Under Diocletian there were 372 main roads covering 85,000 km, the earliest paved road dating from 174 BCE. Evidence from literature, inscriptions, and archaeology indicates that long journeys by common people were made on foot and that the speed with which people traveled determined the transmission of secular and religious news.[8] Further document-based research on postal systems, the sending of letters or short epistles, and transportation,[9] together with new evidence on the widespread nature of reading and writing at basic levels in secular and religious life,[10] serves to make quite real Quintilian's complaint that his speeches were circulating without his imprimatur.[11] Paul probably produced the letters as a leader of a literary team with the aid of collaborators and stenographers,[12] resulting in circulation among those interested in reading about or documenting the new religion.[13] Since classicists seem to have assumed this background for their analysis of the spread of the Isis cult, which made use of sacred writings in its religious appeal,[14] perhaps it was no surprise to

---

5. Goodwin, *Greek Grammar*, iii.
6. Chevallier, *Roman Roads*.
7. Cf. Plessis, "Lukan Audience—Rediscovered?," 243–61.
8. Chevallier, *Roman Roads*, 191, 205.
9. Llewelyn, "Official Postal Systems of Antiquity," 1–25; Llewelyn, "Sending of a Private Letter," 26–47; Llewelyn, "Letters in the Early Church," 48–57; and Llewelyn, "Provision of Transport for Persons," 58–92; and, with a Christian focus, White, "Ancient Greek Letters," 85–105.
10. Cf. Millard, *Reading and Writing in the Time of Jesus*.
11. Quintilian, *Inst.* 7.2.24.
12. So, Reicke, *Re-examining Paul's Letters*, 30.
13. As to pre-Pauline communication, Paul mentions, unsupportive of an exclusively folklorist oral approach to the transmission of Jesus material, that he has himself both received and handed over early Christian tradition, some of which could have easily circulated in writing as well as via memorization. The list of resurrection witnesses in 1 Corinthians 15 was required so that preachers and teachers could repudiate, with collective force, the official shame-sentence passed on the false messiah from Galilee, cf. Gerhardsson, "Secret of the Transmission of the Unwritten Jesus Tradition," 17.
14. Cf. Witt, *Isis in the Graeco-Roman World*, 56–57, 226 (priest with scroll on an Isaiac altar, from Rome); Beard et al., *Religions of Rome*, 1:260–301; 2:136–37 (scribe with scrolls in a Relief of Isaiac

some when Bauckham argued that Christian literature circulated easily, quickly, and widely in a communicative network.[15] Teachers, pastors, evangelists, deacons and deaconesses, patrons and patronesses, prophets and prophetesses, missionaries, and apostles, who desired to employ written material in their ministries, as the extant papyrological evidence on its own would seem to suggest (with much of it being lost), could produce papyrus codices and/or scrolls which circulated between individuals and groups of Christians in cities and towns.[16]

Because this appears reasonably accurate,[17] it suggests that the Roman world of the Christian gospels, Letters, and theological/historical narratives formed one key community of writers where rewriting and improvement of earlier texts took place as the concept of intertextual clarification emerged.[18] Given the established literary practice of improving, editing, and rewriting previous texts[19] with which a *littérateur* like Luke[20] would be familiar, especially, one would think, with respect to his treatment of Paul,[21] how could it be possible that Luke would not avail himself of Paul's letters? We might rightly ask with Brodie, "In chronicling Jesus, he searched for sources on Jesus; he used the works of other evangelists. Would he do less for Paul? Would he write so much about Paul and never bother getting a copy of any of Paul's own writings?"[22]

A chronological review of previous efforts to offer an explanation for the textual parallels between Paul's letters and Luke-Acts may then be appropriate. Ramsay argued that "It is hard to believe that Paul's letters were unknown to Luke; he was in Paul's company when some of them were written; he must have known about the rest and could readily learn their contents in the intimate intercommunication that bound

---

Procession, from Rome).

15. Bauckham, *Gospels for All Christians*, 44.

16. On these backgrounds, cf. Alexander, "Ancient Book Production" and Thompson, "Holy Internet," in Bauckham, *Gospels for All Christians*, 71–105, 49–70, respectively. On the production and dissemination of books, along with the evidence cited by Millard, *Reading and Writing in the Time of Jesus*, and Alexander (this note), I call attention to discussions by Marrou, "La technique de l'édition à l'époque patristique," 208–24, bespeaking deep roots, and in earlier times by Turner, *Athenian Books in the Fifth and Fourth Centuries B.C.*

17. So too, Brodie, "Schools, Synagogues," 63–71, and Brodie, "Roads and Travel," 72–75.

18. Clarification is one of the semantic effects arising from intertextual interaction with previous texts, cf. Pfister, "Konzepte der Intertextulität," 1–30. While the interpretive and clarifying effect of the improved later text primarily benefits the former text(s), both texts ultimately may individually receive some enhanced contextual meaning (*Sinnpotential*) and contextual resonances (*Sinneffekten*) in this process.

19. Cf. Thomas, "Virgil's *Georgics* and the Art of Reference," 171–98; Hinds, *Allusion and Intertext*; Edmunds, *Intertextuality and the Reading of Roman Poetry*; Finkelpearl, "Pagan Traditions of Intertextuality in the Roman World," 78–90; Zimmerman, "Latinising the Novel"; and "Greco-Roman Tradition: Writing as Rhetorical Imitation," in Brodie, *Birthing of the New Testament*, 3–22.

20. Moulton and Howard, *Grammar of New Testament Greek*, II, 7, asserted that Luke was "the only *littérateur* among the authors of New Testament books."

21. In this regard, cf. Franklin, *Luke*, 33–37, 378–88.

22. Brodie, "Towards Tracing the Gospels' Literary Indebtedness to the Epistles," 109.

together the early churches. We shall try to show that Luke had in mind the idea of explaining and elucidating the letters."[23] Schulz is convinced that there were sufficient parallels in Ephesians, Romans, and particularly 1 Thessalonians to indicate that Luke had employed these documents in his own composition.[24] Martin argues that the parallels between the Miletus speech and Ephesians,[25] along with various other verbal and conceptual connections, suggests that Luke may have written Ephesians. Aejmelaeus, in a detailed comparative study of words and ideas, concludes that there is a detectable literary connection between the Miletus speech and 1 Thessalonians.[26] At this juncture, it is at least evident that Luke and Paul had a similar thought life, but literary dependence based upon Luke's use of Paul's writings may not be an assured fact to some, perhaps awaiting development of more exact criteria.[27] Walker argues that Luke corrected impressions that might be conveyed by Paul in Galatians 2 and that Luke almost certainly knew, in some sense, at least some of Paul's letters, making some use of these in writing his own double-work, and that there are plausible reasons why he did not explicitly mention the letters or indicate that Paul wrote letters.[28] Goulder,[29] with the use of textual comparisons,[30] argues that Luke's first book echoes every chapter of 1 Corinthians between 3 and 11 and the last two chapters of 1 Thessalonians.

Kim sets out a variety of heuristic textual comparisons between Romans and Acts, arguing that "*lukanischen Wortanspielungen sind sehr charakteristisch*"[31] of Paul and that Luke certainly (*freilich*) did take adaptations from Romans, paraphrasing it at will.[32] Given the vivid "we-passages" as indicating personal acquaintance,[33] when Luke and Paul are in Rome, Paul's earlier letter to Christians there might attract Luke's foremost attention. In any case, in addition then to the textual evidence adduced by Kim and Aejmelaeus, I would suggest Romans 1:11, ἵνα τι μεταδῶ χάρισμα ὑμῖν πνευματικὸν εἰς <u>τὸ στηριχθῆναι</u> ὑμᾶς (in order that I may impart to you a gift of spiritual value to strengthen you)[34] in comparison with Luke's portrayal of Paul as

---

23. Ramsay, *St. Paul the Traveller and the Roman Citizen*, 16.

24. Schulze, "Die Unterlagen für die Abschiedrede zu Milet in Apostelgesch. 20,18–38," 119–25.

25. Martin, *New Testament Foundations*, 2:231.

26. Aejmelaeus, *Die Rezeption der Paulusbriefe in der Miletrede*, 89–105. Aejmelaeus also finds conceptual parallels between 1 Thessalonians 3:1–10 and Acts 20:19, 31, and between 1 Thessalonians 2:9 and Acts 20:33–35 (211–24).

27. Cf. Elbert, "Paul of the Miletus Speech," 258–68.

28. Walker, "Acts and the Pauline Corpus Reconsidered," 14.

29. Goulder, *Luke*, 129–46.

30. Goulder, *Luke*, 145–46.

31. Kim, *Die Geisttaufe des Messias*, 196.

32. Cf. Kim, *Geisttaufe des Messias*, 192–96, 205–6.

33. So, Hemer, *Book of Acts in the Setting of Hellenistic History*, 312–34, 353, 389; Porter, *Paul of Acts*, 10–66.

34. The absolute use of οἱ πνευματικοί, a Paulinism, indicating "the people of the Spirit" is Paul's conception in 1 Corinthians, having only Galatians 6:1 as a formal parallel. Given that Romans

στηρίζων μαθητάς (Acts 18:23b). Following the lovely Apollos digression, the Lukan Paul reenters the scene to strengthen other Christian disciple-believers (μαθητάς–οἱ πιστεύσαντες) in a manner reminiscent of Paul's own similarly expressed desire at Rom1:1; namely, he has Spirit-reception on his mind. Perhaps Luke thinks that this is something more clear than χάρισμα πνευματίκος, so Paul asks εἰ πνεῦμα ἅγιον ἐλάβετε πιστεύσαντες; (did you receive the Holy Spirit, having believed?),[35] and Luke promptly clarifies Paul's meaning and intent with an example of Pauline imparting.

Walker presses on to discover verbal and conceptual parallels between Galatians 2 and Acts 15.[36] Brodie, applying three comparative criteria, argues that there are strong reasons for seeing a literary link between the supper texts in Paul and Luke.[37] Leppä, based upon words, expressions, and structural and contextual similarity, demonstrates from textual evidence that Luke probably used Galatians in writing Acts.[38] And, in a forthcoming argument, Aejmelaeus provides a solid justification for continuing these literary investigations.[39]

Possible Lukan Clarification of Paul's Spirit-Reception and Spirit-Giftedness Language

Since Manson and Schnackenburg briefly called attention to some of the Spirit-reception and Spirit-giftedness language of Luke-Acts with its almost identical and

---

was written from Corinth, I suspect that this thought, without the polemic of the Corinthian letter, underpins the idea of χάρισμα . . . πνευματικὸν here in Romans 1:11, hence my rendering, taking into account the verbal idea in the infinitive, of "a gift of spiritual value." Obviously, Paul thought that the Holy Spirit would be involved in this ministry of his to believers since he thought that τὰ πνευματικά (1 Cor 14:1), and especially inspired prophetic speech as well as inspired nonrational speech, were important interior activities of the Spirit.

However, if there were those among Paul's Roman readers who had not read 1 Corinthians, they might have appreciated some help in decoding or unpacking exactly what a χάρισμα . . . πνευματικὸν might be or what they might expect to happen to them when they personally received it. On my hypothesis, having read Romans, Luke keenly and pastorally appreciates these possible questions and sets out the best he can, progymnastically, to clarify this Pauline "strengthening" language with a concrete "strengthening" example for his own Roman readers. Once Luke's readers have both documents, a reality Luke surely must anticipate, they can decide for themselves whether he has got it right or not. On my suggestion about Luke's performance, Luke thinks he has the right answer in mind.

35. This understanding of this Lukan question is supported by Elbert, "Observation on Luke's Composition," 107–8.

36. Walker, "Acts and the Pauline Corpus Revisited," 77–86.

37. His criteria are external plausibility, similarities beyond the normal range of coincidence, and intelligible differences; the supper texts are 1 Corinthians 11:16–19 and Luke 22:14–30, cf. Brodie, "Towards Tracing the Gospels' Literary Indebtedness to the Epistles," 104–16.

38. Leppä, *Luke's Critical Use of Galatians*, 61.

39. Aejmelaeus, "Reopening the Question."

sometimes verbatim similarities with language of Paul's letters,[40] the topic has lain dormant, perhaps for understandable but not uninteresting reasons.[41]

Before setting out the textual evidence, it is appropriate to take note of the rhetorically based educational context from which it originated because this affects how the data may be evaluated. Considering Luke's performance, he appears a well-trained and well-studied writer in the narrative-rhetorical and historiographical tradition of the first-century Roman literary world. This educational world began with standard rhetorical curricula.[42] After learning to read and write, boys went on to a study of Classical literature, composing a series of preliminary exercises in prose called *progymnasmata* which entailed a series of set topics, like "On the Chreia" (Περὶ Χρείας), "On the Narrative" (Περὶ Διηγήματος), "On the Description" (Περὶ Ἐκφράσεως), "On the Comparison" (Περὶ Συγκπίσεως), "On the Speech-in-Character or Personification" (Περὶ Προσωποποιΐα), and "On the Thesis" (Περὶ Θέσεως), taking Theon's order. Theon,[43] who acknowledges that progymnastic categories of concern to narrative-rhetorical writings preceded him,[44] and is cited by Quintilian, prepared a treatise in the

---

40. Manson, "Entry into Membership of the Early Church," 25; Schnackenburg, "Die johanneische Gemeinde und ihre Geisterfährung," 284–85.

41. I would suggest three main reasons for such dormancy within *Acta-Forschung*. First, historical/theological criticism of Acts has only recently consolidated the conclusion that "Rhetorical studies of Acts have given us a greater appreciation for the relationship of Luke to a rich Greco-Roman literary heritage, which he must have shared with an intended audience. We have learned to think of the author of Acts as a recipient of a good Greco-Roman education and an author aware of the persuasive power of literature" (Tyson, "From History to Rhetoric and Back," 41). Second, previous claims that the Lukan Paul and the Paul of the Letters are irreconcilably different have largely been shown to be unsubstantial (Porter, *Paul of Acts*, 187–206). And third, since Gunkel, *Die Wirkungen des heiligen Geistes,* and Schweizer, "πνεῦμα κτλ," *TWNT* 6:401–13, it is only recently that studies of *lukanische Pfingstgeschichte* or *Geisttheologie des Lukas* have appeared which exhibit a renewed interest in appreciating the narrative coherence and connectivity displayed by a narrator whose "literary abilities were of a superior order" (Metzger, "Language of the N.T.," 7:47), as do the following: Haya-Prats, *L'Esprit, force de l'Église*; Mainville, *L'Esprit dans l'oeuvre de Luc* [The previous two sources are now available in English translations: Haya-Prats, *Empowered Believers,* and Mainville, *Spirit in Luke-Acts*—Ed.]; Shelton, *Mighty in Word and Deed*; Kim, *Die Geisttaufe des Messias*; Menzies, *Empowered for Witness*. Given this latter recognition and appreciation, the possible consequences of Luke's active interest in the literary output of a previous writer well-known to him could also face renewed evaluation.

42. Marrou, *Historie de l'éducation dans l'antiquité*; Clark, *Rhetoric in Greco-Roman Education*; Bonner, *Education in Ancient Rome*; Morgan, *Literate Education in the Hellenistic and Roman Worlds*; Cribiore, *Gymnastics of the Mind*.

43. For a comprehensive treatment of Theon, cf. Stegemann, "Theon," cols. 2037–54; Butts, "'Progymnasmata' of Theon," 7–95; Patillon, *Aelius Théon Progymnasmata,* vii–clvi; Heath, "Theon and the History of the Progymnasmata," 129–60. Patillon arranges the chapters in what is believed to be Theon's original order and is assisted by Bolognesi in constructing the five final chapters (13–17) from Armenian texts that had gone missing from the Greek manuscript tradition. Patillon has also prepared an index. I will follow Patillon's critical edition and use, with Patillon, the chapter titles, and textual enumeration set out in Leonard Spengel's edition (Leipzig, 1854).

44. For overviews of the concerns and categories of the *progymnasmata* and what they were designed to accomplish, cf. Schissal, "Rhetorische Progymnasmatik der Byzantiner," 1–10; Hunger, *Die hochsprachliche profane Literatur der Byzantiner,* 2:92–120; Kennedy, *Greek Rhetoric Under Christian*

first century on how to compose proper narratives, not speeches, and was followed by a train of other like-minded teachers.⁴⁵ It is not at all surprising that the concerns and the principles of expression taught in Theon's treatise for teachers of narrative, given the established setting of these exercises in Greco-Roman education and their known lasting influence upon the modes of thought in writers so trained,⁴⁶ could be rightly expected to be detectable in Luke-Acts, as anticipated by Robbins.⁴⁷

Theon believes that his exercises are certainly beneficial to those who take up the narrative-rhetorical craft,⁴⁸ and Parsons concludes, correctly in my opinion, that the *progymnasmata* and the narrative-rhetorical traditions, conventions, and strategies they represent contribute immeasurably to the literary model used by Luke.⁴⁹ For the present study it is necessary to draw attention to Theon's interest in the use of examples and precedents by which a narrative becomes persuasive and attains the three desirable qualities of clarity (σαφήνεια), conciseness (συντομία), and plausibility (πιθανότης).⁵⁰ He applauds the nourishment of style that shapes the soul by good examples (καλῶν παραδειγμάτων) because it motivates readers, including himself, in an imitation of the finest (κάλλιστα μιμησόμεθα) of these.⁵¹ The communicative dynamic in the *chreia* is expressed with an example.⁵² Students must learn by heart effective examples for each exercise,⁵³ Theon noting that, with respect to composing narratives (διηγήσεως), both mythical and factual narratives contain some of the best examples (παραδείγματα τῶν μυθικῶν, παραδείγματα τῶν πραγματικῶν).⁵⁴

As an able practitioner of the communicative conventions of his day, Luke can be expected to have his main points and themes properly illustrated with appropriate

---

Emperors, 54–73; Lausberg, *Handbuch der literarischen Rhetorik*, 532–46; Morgan, *Literate Education in the Hellenistic and Roman Worlds*, 190–226; Cribiore, *Gymnastics of the Mind*, 220–30; and Webb, "*Progymnasmata* as Practice," 289–316.

45. Kennedy, *Progymnasmata*, provides an English translation and brief notes.

46. Gibson, "Learning Greek History in the Ancient Classroom," 105, observes that the introductory stage of narrative-rhetorical training via these exercises "is the stage at which students first learned to compose their own formal prose. And as imperial-era Greek literature richly attests, writers trained in the progymnasmata continued to deploy the forms of these basic exercises long after their formal education was completed." Webb, "*Progymnasmata* as Practice," 292, notes that when students began their composition of the exercises, they engaged in "active use of the linguistic and cultural knowledge they had acquired from the grammarian. Precisely because they [the *progymnasmata*] are elementary, they reveal the lowest common denominator of that training and reveal the basic conceptions of language, categories of composition, and modes of thought which informed both the production and the reception of rhetorical and other texts."

47. Robbins, "Progymnastic Rhetorical Composition and Pre-Gospel Tradition," 111–47.

48. Theon, *Progym.*, Θέωνος Σοφιστοῦ Προγυμνάσματα, 60.1–2.

49. Parsons, "Luke and the *Progymnasmata*," 63.

50. Theon, *Progym.*, Περὶ Διηγήματος, 79.20–21.

51. Theon, *Progym.*, Θέωνος Σοφιστοῦ Προγυμνάσματα, 61.30–34.

52. Theon, *Progym.*, Περὶ Χρείας, 99.16; 100.4–7.

53. Theon, *Progym.*, Περὶ τῆς τῶν Νέων Ἀγωγῆς, 65.31.

54. Theon, *Progym.*, Περὶ τῆς τῶν Νέων Ἀγωγῆς, 66.16–17, 23.

examples and precedents.⁵⁵ The Theonic or progymnastic appreciation for the finest and most effective examples builds on the long-standing recognition of the poetic, narrative-rhetorical, and oratorical virtue of employing *exempla* and παραδείγμα that are suitable to the occasion.⁵⁶ Oehler notes that in Homer examples are placed in speeches with a uniting form and tight structure.⁵⁷ Luke uses examples of Spirit-reception as occasions for speeches and places another example of this phenomena interrupting a speech. Perhaps, given the progymnastic emphasis on the use of Homer, narrative-structural similarities such as these should not be unexpected.

However, now that the stage has been set with respect to the background of education with its expected progymnastic effects upon Lukan narrative, particularly in how examples and precedents are used in the production of a clear presentation, it is time to explore the possible literary linkages between Luke and Paul and see what can be made of the evidence at hand for the hypothesis of Lukan clarification of one aspect of Paul's letters. First, I set out the following data in chronological order.

From Paul's Letters

τὸν Θεὸν τὸν **διδόντα** πνεῦμα αὐτοῦ τὸ ἅγιον εἰς ὑμᾶς (1 Thess 4:8)
(God who gives his Holy Spirit to you)

τὸ πνεῦμα **ἐλάβετε** . . . ἐξ ἀκοῆς πίστεως; (Gal 3:2b)
(have you received the Spirit . . . from hearing by faith?)

ἵνα τὴν ἐπαγγελίαν τοῦ πνεύματος **λάβωμεν** διὰ τῆς πίστεως (Gal 3:14b)
(so that we may receive the promise of the Spirit by faith)

ἡμεῖς . . . **ἐλάβομεν** . . . τὸ πνεῦμα τὸ ἐκ τοῦ θεοῦ (1 Cor 2:12a)
(we have received the Spirit from God)

ὁ καὶ σφραγισάμενος ἡμᾶς καὶ **δοὺς** τὸν ἀρραβῶνα τοῦ πνεύματος (2 Cor 1:22)
(who also sealed us and gave us the pledge of the Spirit)

---

55. This is also the reason why Luke's point of view is normally narrated by "*showing*, as in the Hebrew Bible" (Kurz, "Narrative Approaches to Luke-Acts," 206; emphasis original).

56. Alewell, *Über das rhetorische Παράδειγμα*; Oehler, *Mythologische Exempla in der älterem griechischen Dichtung*; Lumpe, "Exemplum," cols. 1230–57; Price, "'Paradeigma' and 'Exemplum' in Ancient Rhetorical Theory"; Maslakov, "Valerius Maximus and Roman Historiography," 437–96; and Fiore, *Function of Personal Example*, 91, who observes broadly on education by example/precedent that "Example serves as an instructional experience, on the basis of a precedent in personal circumstances or historical events. The example directs attention toward an analogous set of circumstances or conditions in the present or future."

57. Oehler, *Mythologische Exempla in der älterem griechischen Dichtung*, 118.

Θεός ὁ **δοὺς** ἡμῖν <u>τὸν ἀρραβῶνα</u> τοῦ πνεύματος (2 Cor 5:5b)
(God who gave to us the pledge of the Spirit)

πνεῦμα... **ἐλάβετε** (2 Cor 11.4b)
(Spirit ... you received)

ἐκκέχυται ἐν ταῖς καρδίαις ἡμῶν διὰ πνεύματος ἁγίου τοῦ **δοθέντος** ἡμῖν (Rom 5:5b)[58]
([the love of God] has been poured out into our hearts through the Holy Spirit who was given to us)

ἐλάβετε πνεῦμα υἱοθεσίας (Rom 8:15a)
(you have received a Spirit of adoption)

πιστεύσαντες **ἐσφραγίσθητε** τῷ πνεύματι <u>τῆς ἐπαγγελίας</u> τῷ ἁγίῳ (Eph 1:13b)
(having believed, you were sealed with the Holy Spirit of the promise)

τὸ πνεῦμα τὸ ἅγιον τοῦ θεοῦ ἐν ᾧ **ἐσφραγίσθητε** (Eph 4:30)
(the Holy Spirit by whom you were sealed)

πληροῦσθε ἐν πνεύματι (Eph 5:18b)
(be filled with [the] Spirit)

From Luke-Acts

ὁ πατὴρ ... **δώσει** πνεῦμα ἅγιον τοῖς αἰτοῦσιν αὐτόν (Luke 11:13b)
(the Father will give [the] Holy Spirit to those who ask Him)

<u>τὴν ἐπαγγελίαν</u> τοῦ πατρός (Luke 24:49)
(the promise of the Father)

<u>τὴν ἐπαγγελίαν</u> τοῦ πατρός ἣν ἠκούσατέ μου (Acts 1:4)
(the promise of the Father you heard from Me)

ἐπλήσθησαν ... πνεύματος ἁγίου (Acts 2:4a)
(they were filled with [the] Holy Spirit) [Here, disciple-believer-witnesses receive the promise of the Spirit.]

τήν τε <u>ἐπαγγελίαν</u> τοῦ πνεύματος τοῦ ἁγίου...**ἐξέχεεν** τοῦτο βλέπετε καὶ ἀκούετε (Acts 2:33)
(the promise of the Holy Spirit ... He has poured this out which you see and hear)

---

58. See too, ἀνακαινώσεως πνεύματος ἁγίου οὗ ἐξέχεεν ἐφ' ἡμᾶς (Titus 3:5d, 6a) (renewal of the Holy Spirit which he poured out upon us).

λήμψεσθε τὴν <u>δωρεὰν</u> τοῦ ἁγίου πνεύματος (Acts 2:38c)
(you will receive the gift of the Holy Spirit)

ὑμῖν γάρ ἐστιν ἡ <u>ἐπαγγελία</u> καί τοῖς τέκνοις ὑμῶν καὶ πᾶσιν τοῖς εἰς μακρὰν ὅσους (Acts 2:39) (for the promise is to you and to your children and to all who are afar off)

πλήρεις *πνεύματος καὶ σοφίας* (Acts 6:3b)
(full of [the] Spirit and wisdom)

ὅπως **λάβωσιν** *πνεῦμα ἅγιον* (Acts 8:15)
(in order that they might receive [the] Holy Spirit)

ἐλάμβανον *πνεῦμα ἅγιον* (Acts 8:17b) - Baptized believers receive the Spirit.
(they received [the] Holy Spirit)

ᾧ ἐὰν ... **λαμβάνῃ** *πνεῦμα ἅγιον* (Acts 8:19b)
(whomever ... might receive [the] Holy Spirit)

τὴν δωρεὰν τοῦ θεοῦ (Acts 8:20b)
(the gift of God)

ὅπως πλησθῇς *πνεύματος ἁγίου* (Acts 9:17c)
(so that you might be filled [with the] Holy Spirit)–Paul receives the Spirit prior to baptism.

ἐπέπεσεν τὸ πνεῦμα τὸ ἅγιον ἐπ' αὐτοὺς, and **ἐπέπεσεν** τὸ πνεῦμα τὸ ἅγιον ἐπὶ πάντος (Acts 11:15 and 10:44)
(the Holy Spirit fell upon them/upon all)

ἡ **δωρεὰ** τοῦ ἁγίου πνεύματος **ἐκκέχυται** (Acts 10:45b)
(the gift of the Holy Spirit was poured out)

οἵτινες τὸ πνεῦμα τὸ ἅγιον **ἔλαβον** (Acts 10:47)
(who received [the] Holy Spirit)–Believers receive the Spirit.

τὴν ἴσην <u>**δωρεὰν ἔδωκεν**</u> αὐτοῖς ὁ Θεὸς (Acts 11:17a)
(God gave to them the same gift)

πλήσης *πνεύματος ἁγίου* καὶ πίστεως (Acts 11:24a)
(full of the Holy Spirit and faith)

Θεός ἐμαρτύρησεν αὐτοῖς **δοὺς** τὸ πνεῦμα τὸ ἅγιον (Acts 15.8b)
(God bore witness to them, giving them the Holy Spirit)

πνεῦμα ἅγιον **ἐλάβετε** (Acts 19:2a)
(did you receive [the] Holy Spirit)

ἦλθε *τὸ πνεῦμα τὸ ἅγιον ἐπ' αὐτούς* (Acts 19:6a)
(the Holy Spirit came upon them) [Here, disciple-believers receive the promise of the Spirit.]

Some Side-by-Sides

Paul	Luke-Acts
Θεὸν τὸν **διδόντα** πνεῦμα αὐτου τὸ ἅγιον εἰς ὑμᾶς	ὁ πατὴρ ... **δώσει** πνεῦμα ἅγιον τοῖς αἰτοῦσιν αὐτόν
διὰ πνεύματος ἁγίου τοῦ **δοθέντος** ἡμῖν	**λήμψεσθε** τὴν **δωρεὰν** τοῦ ἁγίου πνεύματος
ὁ **δοὺς** ἡμῖν τὸν <u>ἀρραβῶνα</u> τοῦ πνεύματος	τὴν ἴσην **δωρεὰν ἔδωκεν** αὐτοῖς
ἐλάβομεν ... τὸ πνεῦμα τὸ ἐκ τοῦ θεοῦ	**ἐλάβανον** πνεῦμα ἅγιον
	λάβωσιν πνεῦμα ἅγιον
<u>τὴν ἐπαγγελίαν</u> τοῦ πνεύματος **λάβωμεν**	<u>τὴν ἐπαγγελίαν</u> τοῦ πατρός
ἐσφραγίσθητε τω πνεύματι τῆς <u>ἐπαγγελίας</u>	τήν τε <u>ἐπαγγελίαν</u> τοῦ πνεύματος τοῦ ἁγίου ... <u>ἐξέχεεν</u>
πληροῦσθε ἐν πνεύματι	πλησθῆς πνεύματος ἁγίου

In light of these various textual parallels, perhaps the following observations may be apropos. By projecting the promised gift of the Holy Spirit beyond narrative time at Acts 2:38c, 39, Luke shows how two elements of Pauline Spirit-language arise, namely that of "gift" and of "promise." By using the well-known principle of *Stichwörter*, his promise (τὰ ἐπαγγελία) of the Lukan gift of the Holy Spirit, beginning with Luke 11:13b and running through Luke 24:49; Acts 1:4; 2:33, 38c, 39, Luke could conceivably be clarifying, for readers of Paul's letters, the meaning of these descriptive terms with a narrative sequence of good examples and precedents. His Spirit-reception and Spirit-giving language is at times verbatim with Paul's and is always accompanied with a clear example of what the language means. Paul's use of the verbal ideas of the gift of the Spirit as a pledge and of this promise as a sealing may be reasonably understood to be clarified with Luke's account of the Spirit falling upon and coming upon believers. I deem it reasonable to suggest that a progymnastically trained reader of Luke-Acts, who has read Paul's letters, may well appreciate the phenomenon of verbal agreements and strategic improvements as having been undertaken for the sake of clarity. Perhaps then there is a case for literary dependence with a motive of intertextual clarification.

Finally, this progymnastic exemplarity employed by Luke, which is typical of Roman culture, may be understandable as an effort on his part to imitate and replicate Paul's Spirit-language and possibly surpass its communicative value by bringing to it the narrative virtues of clarity, conciseness, and plausibility. Luke's performance is then like a narrative monument, in some sense like an outpost of the past, which he, on my hypothesis, desires to connect with Paul's letters. When reading his double-work, his audience is taken back to earlier times and is invited to feel an impulse to imitate, to experience, similar events for themselves.

Possible Lukan Clarification of Paul's Spirit-Interiority Language

In addition to these similarities/agreements with Lukan description of Spirit-reception and Spirit-giving, we may recognize language that seems to imply dynamic interactive interiority and/or interior perception of the Spirit within the believer. Paul employs this Spirit-interiority language when writing to those whom, like himself, he describes as having been "given the Spirit" or as having "received the Spirit." Namely, I suggest a consideration of the following in this regard:

"Do not quench the Spirit" (1 Thess 5:19)

"Walk by the Spirit . . . if you are led by the Spirit" (Gal 5:16a, 18a)

"You are the temple of God . . . the Spirit of God dwells in you" (1 Cor 3:16)

"We were all given to drink of one Spirit" (1 Cor 12:13c)

"I will pray with the Spirit . . . I will sing with the Spirit" (1 Cor 14:15)

"Walk . . . according to the Spirit" (Rom 8:4b)

"You are . . . in the Spirit if indeed the Spirit of God dwells in you" (Rom 8:9a)

"The Spirit Himself bears witness" (Rom 8:16)

"The Spirit Himself intercedes for us with groanings too deep for words" (Rom 8:26b)

"Do not grieve the Holy Spirit" (Eph 4:30)

"Do not get drunk with wine . . . but be filled (πληρόω) with the Spirit" (Eph 5:18c)

Luke's keen reading, the working hypothesis under investigation here, of this collective background of personification (ἠθοποιΐα) of the Spirit in Paul's Letters, several instances seeming to suggest the involvement of inspired prophetic speech,[59] could easily account for or reasonably explain Luke's decision to portray characters who receive the Lukan gift of the Holy Spirit promised by the Father as being "filled" with the Spirit (Acts 2:4a; 9:17c, Ananias to Paul).

This particular Lukan description (ἔκφρᾰσις), an experientially related interior characterization which he employs in different contexts (Acts 4:8a, 31b; 13:9) with the verb πίμπλημι, along with his similar expression of "full" of the Spirit (Acts 6:3; 7:55; 11:24a) with the noun πλήρης,[60] could well have again been motivated by an assimilation of Paul's previous diverse concepts of interiority by someone with training in and appreciation of the *Progymnasmata* employed in Greco-Roman education. The writer takes one verb-noun combination and, in a connected narrative sequence of examples and precedents, provides an understandable progymnastic or a narrative-rhetorical clarification of Paul by showing where Paul's language of filling and interior dwelling originates. Of course, this assumes that Luke has read Paul and that, because of Luke's rhetorically based education and the anticipated expectations of a literary-minded Theophilus, with whom Luke might have shared a prior draft for criticism,[61] Luke would want to do what I suggest that he does.

It is interesting in this regard that in the preliminary school exercises the composition of an ἔκφρᾰσις in the narrative-rhetorical tradition of the first centuries CE was defined by all the progymnastic writers as a narrative (or speech) which leads

---

59. Quenching the Spirit as a possible source of prophecy (1 Thess 5:19, 20), praying and singing with the Spirit (1 Cor 14:15), participating in intercessory prayer with groanings unfit for (human) words (Rom 8:26, 27), and Paul's figurative language of drinking the Spirit (1 Cor 12:13c), seem to suggest an interior collaboration (or lack thereof) with the Spirit insofar as possible inspired speech is concerned.

Drinking too much wine, as contrasted with the exhortation to be filled with (or by) the Spirit (Eph 5:18), for those who, having believed, were sealed with the Holy Spirit of the promise (Eph 1:13b; 4:30), may recall a similar expression, written from Ephesus, to those who, like himself, had received the Spirit (1 Cor 2:12a). They too, like Paul, had been given to drink of the Spirit (1 Cor 12:13c), an experiential metaphor in contrast to drinking earthly liquids. (Luke later writes that the Spirit is "poured out" [Acts 2:33; 10:45b], since something that is poured out should be drinkable.) I suspect Paul here is thinking along the following lines in his connected expression within the Ephesian letter. Being filled by drinking of the Spirit, as his readers will probably relate to from previous experience-based knowledge, is preferable to drinking too much wine and being filled thereby.

60. For a discussion of Luke's narratively connected performance regarding these two metaphors, cf. Shelton, "'Filled with the Holy Spirit,'" 81–107.

61. In literary circles authors presented gift copies to their friends, cf. Starr, "Circulation of Literary Texts in the Roman World," 213–23. Among the communicative Roman world of writers, the practice of providing a draft at the author's expense served to advance personal friendship and, of course, to enhance understandability upon feedback. Thucydides, Polybius, Tacitus, Plutarch, and Lucian are also suspected of this practice, aside from that documented by rhetoricians Cicero, Pliny, and others, cf. Pelling, "Plutarch's Method of Work in Roman Lives," 94, 95; Johnson, "Oral Performance and the Composition of Herodotus' *Histories*," 243.

one around, bringing the subject matter vividly before the eyes.[62] Luke's precision of style in employing the filled-full description (πίμπλημι–πλήρης), on my hypothesis, serves to explain and clarify the origin of Paul's Spirit-interiority language. Furthermore, Luke's performance in this regard is illustrative of progymnastic interests of clarity. Theon states that the desirable qualities of description are, above all, clarity and vividness.[63] I would suggest that Luke's examples of being filled (Acts 2:4a; 9:17c; with 4:8a, 31b; 13:9) and of being full (6:3; 7:55; 11:24a) are well-rendered with the essential vivid form of narration.[64]

As did Homer, to whom Theon often refers, Luke has a fondness for pictorial effect, for the picturesque scene,[65] especially when it apparently serves to clarify Paul's marginally contextual Spirit-language with vivid examples and precedents. Like Aristides, Luke chooses no paltry or trivial narrative examples, perhaps sharing Aristides's similar oratorical concern in this regard. According to Aristides, the value of oratory should not be shamed by such inadequate and impractical examples (*Def. Or.* 380), hence his own employment of examples touted to be both beautiful and ancient (*Pan. Or.*, 82, 394).[66] Also, we might note that among Theonic subjects suitable for ἔκφρασις are characters, events, and procedures,[67] again quite harmonious with the Lukan ἔκφρᾶσις of events where characters are filled with and/or portrayed as full of the Spirit.

The experiential interior activities of the Spirit mentioned discursively by Paul, which he apparently assumes are understandable by his "in-house" readership, could be appraised from a narrative-rhetorical perspective informed by progymnastic demands and virtues as being deficient. They are progymnastically deficient because they do not provide the reader with any examples and precedents of what experience this Spirit-interiority language arises from.[68] Anyone not an original addressee

---

62. Theon (first century CE), Hermogenes (possibly second century CE), Aphthonios (fourth century CE), and Nikolaos (fifth century CE) are in accord on this point, cf. Webb, "*Ekphrasis* Ancient and Modern," 11.

63. Theon, *Progym.*, Περὶ Ἐκφράσεως. 119.31–32.

64. Webb, "*Ekphrasis* Ancient and Modern," 13, correctly points out that "Narration is the simple account of what happened, while an *ekphrasis* includes the details that tell one how it happened, how it looked (one might add how it sounded and felt)."

65. Shipp, *Studies in the Language of Homer*, 212. As to the influence of the Homeric epics upon the educational and ensuing literary world in which a *littérateur* like Luke would function, cf. Hock, "Homer in Greco-Roman Education," 56–77.

66. Similarly, Cicero, in observing that the past is a source of things worthy of imitation and emulation, and that examples and precedents worked to establish continuity between past and present as a living part of Roman culture, thought they must be chosen with care since they "are vulnerable to the eroding force of time" (Rambaud, *Cicéron et l'histoire romaine*, 164).

67. Theon, *Progym.*, Περὶ Ἐκφράσεως, 118.9, 18, 22.

68. Experience has long been recognized as a significant factor in creating New Testament descriptive language, cf. Voelz, "Language of the New Testament," 928–30. However, Johnson, *Religious Experience in Earliest Christianity*, rightly argues that Christian experience portrayed in these texts is a neglected factor in scholarship.

could easily ask, what does this language mean, where does it come from? These interiority-oriented phrases and their discursive contexts offer no clear *exempla* or παράδειγμα that would be necessarily required, expected, and demanded within a competent first-century Greco-Roman narrative presentation, if the *Progymnasmata* and our knowledge of that educational system be a guide. These scantily clad discursive activities of the Spirit, appearing in these letters as they do, letters which Luke may well know to be widely read by readers who will soon read his double-work, could be assessed by him as unclear to those not "in-house," providing no easily understandable basis for grasping their experiential roots.

This then is a problem that a *littérateur* like Luke, a writer no doubt familiar with the narrative and oratorical culture and its rhetorical priorities on effective communication,[69] with concern for his immediate addressee Theophilus, who like the Lukan Apollos, is in need of further instruction, might choose to correct with a series of well-chosen examples of plausible phenomena that are properly identified with vivid descriptive terms of "being filled" and "full of" (πίμπλημι–πλήρης) the Spirit, terms comprehensive both of interiority and of known Pauline discourse. Perhaps in this narrative-rhetorical and progymnastic manner Luke clarifies this unsatisfactory aspect of Paul insofar as Paul's later readers are concerned.[70]

---

69. Several studies germane to the present thesis may substantiate this point. In chronological order, for example, Stählin, "Das Bild der Witwe," 5–20, detects the rhetorical category of personification or speech-in-character (προσωποποιΐα) in this Lukan *Sondergut*. A point not brought directly into play by Stählin was that προσωποποιΐα and the interrelated quality of characterization (ἠθοποιΐα or χαρακτηρισμός) were among the narrative-rhetorical compositional elements of concern in the progymnastic treatises contemporary with Luke.

Kurz demonstrates "The Likelihood of Luke's Familiarity with Greek Rhetoric," in his "Hellenistic Rhetoric in the Christological Proof of Luke-Acts," 184–95, followed by Berger, "Hellenistische Gattungen im Neuen Testament," 1031–432, who treats ἔκφρασις (1201–4) and other topics addressed in the *Progymnasmata* (1296–98), concluding (1377–78) that such relational backgrounds serve to render a fuller dimension (and *Wirklichkeitsqualität*) of the context of Christian expression. He concludes (1264–68, 1275–81, 1288–89 [1288]) that Luke displays a great affinity for "Die römischen Rede."

Kennedy, *New Testament Interpretation through Rhetorical Criticism*, 114–39, comments on rhetorical features, like προσωποποιΐα, detectable in "The Speeches in Acts," an evaluation of discourse by Lukan characters best seen against the available comparative background, as in Kennedy, *Art of Rhetoric in the Roman World*, where, for example, Cicero's speech, *Pro Milone*, is appraised as the finest of that orator's published speeches (280). Further affinity with rhetorical forms on Luke's part is illustrated by Watson, "Paul's Speech to the Ephesian Elders," 184–208.

As to Luke's interest in *exempla* or παράδειγμα, Kurz, "Narrative Models for Imitation in Luke-Acts," 188–89, crystallizes the interpretive insight that "The Hellenistic rhetorical paradigmatic use of narrative provides a grounding in the text for typical, ethical, homiletic, and other church uses of Lukan stories as models for contemporary Christian behavior. Such paradigmatic uses of Luke-Acts today are in continuity with the paradigmatic uses originally envisaged for such texts."

70. While Paul works admirably from a Christian perspective within the conventions of his time, his discursive medium and the assumed preknowledge of his immediate addressees impose recognizable limitations on later readers.

Further Reflections and Criteria

My two main suggestions regarding the Lukan clarification of Paul as proposed here are based on two further points. First, I suspect that a good ancient *littérateur* writes, inasmuch as communicative desire is concerned, much in the same way as a good modern counterpart would write. Saul Bellow, the 1976 Nobel Prize winner in literature, was once asked, "How much are you conscious of the reader when you write?" to which he replied, "I have in mind another human being who will understand me."[71] So, when assessing Luke's performance and why it is like it is, it may be that his desire to produce an ordered, accurate, and persuasive account, thus building and improving in a clearly understandable manner on previous written efforts already known to his readers, translates, for him, into an urgent pastoral purpose. My sustained impression of that anonymous double-work is that it is written, as Bellow too would write, for a real person, I think already a Christian.[72] That person, based on what we know about the New Testament environment, is going to read some Pauline Letters if he has not already done so. Every effort then, in the mind of a progymnastically trained narrator within Roman literary culture, would be made towards clarity and plausibility (πιθανότης) with respect to a matter of evident concern to Paul, being especially attendant to the employment of effective examples and precedents. Theon reminds students that "If the subject could be naturally difficult, one should resort to clarity and plausibility."[73] From Luke's perspective, who evidently desires to pass on and commend Paul's tradition, how can Paul's Spirit-interiority language be plausible unless Luke's readers understand from what event in Paul's life it originates and within what pre-Pauline Jerusalem/Petrine tradition it is in continuity?[74] Theon presses on to instruct how important it is to

---

71. Hersey, *Writer's Craft*, 290. Similarly, Eagleton, *Literary Theory*, 84, argues that "Every literary text is built out of a sense of its potential audience, includes an image of whom it is written for . . . intimates in its every gesture the kind of addressee it anticipates."

72. Luke's address κράτιστε Θεόφιλε (Luke 1:3), as employed, also, perhaps as "Your Excellency," to address the Roman officials Felix and Festus both orally and in writing (Acts 23:26; 24:3; 26:25), argues against the theory that Theophilus is somehow an unreal symbolic person. Theophilus is simply a common enough name, as the Theophilus addressed by Seneca in his seventh Epistle. Solin, *Die griechische Personennamen in Rom. Ein Namenbuch*, 1:81, 82, lists over forty examples of Theophilus from Rome in the first century.

A search at the University of Michigan Papyrology Collection turned up a citation of Υἱοῦ Θεοφίλου and more instances of Θεόφιλος from the second and third centuries, plus one Θεοφίλα, daughter of Proclus (P. Oxy. 3169, line 61) (174–212 CE), together with another first-century instance in a business letter addressed to a Roman, Gaius Rustius, (P. Oxy. 745, line 4), in which a politarch named Theophilus (τοῦ πολειτάρχου Θεοφίλου) is involved in the business transaction of concern.

73. Theon, *Progym.*, Περὶ Διηγήματος, 79.25–26.

74. When Luke-Acts was written, it was probably known to others besides Luke that Paul had been connected to the mother church of Christendom in Jerusalem and, because of this, to its linguistic heritage. On this point, cf. Menoud, "Jésus et ses témoins," 7–20; Fannon, "Influence of Traditions on St. Paul," 292–307. As to Paul's transmission of earlier tradition, cf. Müller, *Der Traditionsprozess im Neuen Testament*, 204–24; Ellis, *Making of the New Testament Documents*, 248–51, 256–60. Perhaps then, Luke's readers would understand why Luke apparently seeks to pass on and commend Paul's

always maintain plausibility, because if this quality is not present, the narrative will appear that much more incredible to an audience.[75] Indeed, it would seem that to an audience not composed of immediate "in-house" addressees of Paul's correspondence, clarification on this point could again be a priority. This hypothesis is consistent with Luke's preface (Luke 1:1–4), which suggests that he intends to modify, if not correct, the content of previous documents known to Theophilus.[76]

And second, I agree with Eriksson that "Ancient conceptions of rhetoric have a heuristic advantage over modern conceptions in that they are not reduced to the Enlightenment view of rationality."[77] Hence, to some of that latter persuasion, perhaps there might be little resonance with attempting to detect an ancient narrative effort to clarify nonrational and even noncognitive Pauline discourse within a narratively uniform and more understandable way.[78] The Lukan Spirit-reception and Spirit-giftedness language, if imitated and clarified by Luke as I propose, even given the expected and narrative-rhetorical progymnastic exemplification of that language as we see in his performance, may encounter canonically insular and rationalistic readings of Luke-Acts historically unwilling to explore how or why Pauline language of this particular kind could be connected to Lukan exemplification. In fact, given Eriksson's concern, it may be that when the Paul of the Letters employs the same Spirit-reception and Spirit-giftedness language as the Lukan Paul, unseen barriers and distinctions might arise that are *not* just linguistic or intertextual in nature. Hopefully, the framing of my hypothesis here has not been informed by such a rationally exuberant modern notion of rhetoric.

Therefore, I suggest that the rhetorically straightforward Lukan ἔκφρασις of interiority in terms of filling/full, if it be a rewriting of Paul's multifaceted concept, could have been considered by Luke to be a strategic improvement, a thoughtful literary emulation,[79] an inventive imitation,[80] that is, a more easily understandable and progymnastic, pastoral clarification of Paul.

---

tradition, as rightly concluded by Walton, *Leadership and Lifestyle*, 212.

75. Theon, *Progym.*, Περὶ Διηγήματος, 79.28–32.

76. Franklin, *Luke*, 172. Earlier material, perhaps a variety of histories, theological or testimonial tracts, collections of Jesus material, and/or various letters, while no doubt of interest to Luke, is not regarded by him as complete or as entirely satisfactory. I agree with Franklin, "In making the claim he does, Luke sets out to capture the centre of the stage and puts forward his own work as the standard by which all others must be judged" (173).

77. Eriksson, "Enthymemes in Pauline Argumentation," 254.

78. Theophilus, on the other hand, would frame the Lukan Paul's personal relation to, and practices pertaining to, the Holy Spirit in Acts, which is not the subject of this present literary investigation, within the context of the double-work's overall emphasis on the Spirit. On that emphasis per se, cf. George, *Études sur l'oeuvre de Luc*; George, "L'Esprit Saint dans l'oeuvre de Luc," 500–542; Chevallier, "Luc et l'Esprit Saint," 1–19; Ehrhardt, "Construction and Purpose," 45–79.

79. MacDonald, *Does the New Testament Imitate Homer?*, 6.

80. Brodie, *Birthing of the New Testament*, 7.

Luke's narrative characterization or personification of Spirit-interiority, a topic Luke evidently deems important based upon what he actually writes about the Spirit's activities, may then be recognizable as a rhetorical improvement and rewriting of Paul's treatment of the same phenomenon now that we are looking at all the documents from these two authors. As to my hypothesis of literary dependence with respect to this second of my two main suggestions, what criteria does it and does it not satisfy? Of Brodie's "Positive Criteria,"[81] it satisfies "External Plausibility," given the external factors of time and probable circulation of documents among a like-minded and close-knit writing community; and it satisfies his criterion of "Significant Similarities," insofar as similarity of theme, action/plot, linguistic details, and intelligibility of differences are concerned. It fails a positive criterion of "Order," since Paul's Spirit-interiority language does not appear in any order that Luke could reproduce.

Further, with respect to both of my clarification/improvement hypotheses, applying Brodie's "Principles that Can Mislead,"[82] a connection via literary linkage seems, although with some different terminology, strong enough to make the overall connection credible, at least to make it worthy of further study, possibly with other pairs of authors. As to Brodie's criterion of "The Differences Preclude Dependence and Point to a Shared Tradition," my twin hypotheses may be weak here because both Luke and Paul could share the same vibrant oral, experientially based tradition and, as independent authors, vary in their individual expression of shared tradition. But even this sharing should yield to progymnastic clarity over against Paul.

As to MacDonald's criteria of "Density,"[83] or volume of similarities, the Pauline Spirit-interiority antecedents are numerous and proposed instances of Lukan clarification are frequent—both authors were interested in the phenomenon of interiority, both thought their readers would be too. Because of such known practical interest, Luke could have transformed Paul's descriptions for clarity's sake alone. Regarding "Distinctive Traits,"[84] within this criterion my second hypothesis may find a "mimetic flag"[85] in Lukan interiority expression via sustained use of the πίμπλημι–πλήρης combination applied to events evidently impacting upon Spirit-interiority. While Paul employs πληρόω only once among his constellation of interior Spirit expressions, Luke repeats his combination repeatedly with suitable examples, of which Paul has none. Narratively then, Luke's performance illustrates his interest in describing his examples with a distinctive trait, thus binding the two texts together. The recognition of interior phenomena by both writers is not unique to either, but Lukan ἔκφρᾰσις here is distinctive,

---

81. Brodie, *Birthing of the New Testament*, 44–46.
82. Brodie, *Birthing of the New Testament*, 47–49.
83. MacDonald, *Does the New Testament Imitate Homer?*, 5.
84. MacDonald, *Does the New Testament Imitate Homer?*, 5–6.
85. MacDonald, *Does the New Testament Imitate Homer?*, 5. MacDonald defines a "mimetic flag" as a potentially significant phrase or motif.

perhaps tipping the balance toward mimesis, which for Luke yields again to progymnastic narrative-rhetorical clarity and plausibility as well.

Conclusion

Finally, illustrating a point or a theme by showing concrete examples and actions is very much a part of the narrative-rhetorical tradition of Luke's time. Examples offered a lesson, were pragmatic, and could be paradigmatic.[86] Examples were widely understood as being both intended and expected to serve as a model for imitation and, further, they traditionally functioned in narrative by strengthening adherence to a known and accepted rule by providing particular instances which clarified and substantiated a general thesis. This is how Luke appears to be using them in his narrative regarding the Lukan gift of the Holy Spirit and descriptions of Spirit-reception, Spirit-gifting, and associated interiority phenomena. Given his probable knowledge of Paul's letters, I suggest that in these two cases, Luke is improving upon Paul for well-known progymnastic reasons. In doing so, his literary achievement adapts to the new rhetorical situation, which might have been pastorally urgent. Luke's artistic style is neither stodgy nor parasitic, so that a like-minded reader, as Theophilus would seem to be, should be able to recognize and appreciate the skillful borrowing, understanding its necessity.[87] By incorporating inherited and admired discursive expression to a progymnastically suitable narrative context, Luke offers a new, superior, and less skeletal version of the past due to the clarifying virtue of practical and plausible examples and precedents. As to the question, "If Luke knows Pauline letters, why doesn't he quote them?" my response is that to do so directly does not suit his purpose, just like quoting probable prophetic speech by Phillip's daughters (Acts 21:8–9) did not suit his purpose. However, on my twin hypothesis, Luke, to initiate a fresh reading of Paul, is, in his own way, and for good reasons, complementing Paul's letters with an eloquent clarification.

---

86. Brunt, *Studies in Greek History and Thought*, 182, 183, 188, 192.

87. Luke's creative narrative performance is generally harmonious, in a sufficiently transparent manner, with a code of five principles for the reproduction of a literary model in a new setting as deduced by Russell, "De Imitation," 16, namely: "(i) the object must be worth imitating; (ii) the spirit rather than the letter must be reproduced; (iii) the imitation must be tacitly acknowledged, on the understanding that the informed reader will recognize and approve the borrowing; (iv) the borrowing must be 'made one's own,' by individual treatment and assimilation to its new place and purpose; and (v) the imitator must think of himself as competing with his model, even if he knows he cannot win." As to Russell's fifth principle, we may recall that both Seneca and Quintilian encouraged students to seek out both contemporary and past orators so as to be able to imitate more than one model, since the imitator could never match his exemplar, although he should be innovative (cf. Fantham, "Imitation and Decline," 102–16). In the literary case of Luke's narrative improvement and clarification proposed here, Luke does not seek to eclipse Paul's letters or to replace them, but to enhance their understandability with respect to Spirit-language on his own terms in his chosen medium.

Chapter 5

Luke's Possible Progymnasmatic Improvements on and Employment of Paul's Letter to the Romans[1]

FOLLOWING AN OUTLINE OF the contemporary educational and literary environment affecting first-century narrative-rhetorical composition as advocated in Greco-Roman progymnasmatic training, this study suggests that Luke accordingly provides the expected and requisite narrative improvement/clarification of Paul's discursive descriptions at Romans 10:9 and 1:11. Further, it is argued that Luke, in direct consistency with Aelius Theon's instruction on how to compose plausible narrative, employs Romans 2:11 as a *chreia* at the outset of Peter's speech at Acts 10:34 along with accompanying and recognizable imitative context.

Introduction

In Greco-Roman education, after learning to read and write under γραμματικός, in an ensuing tertiary stage of their training in a rhetorically minded culture, most young males, now about fifteen years old, studied rhetorical methods and classical literature and also underwent training in a series of exercises in prose composition. These exercises, the rhetorical categories of the *Progymnasmata*,[2] were a basic component of Greco-Roman education, both practiced and influential in the time of Luke. Exposure to these exercises probably instilled the minimum rhetorical equipment of any literate person from the Hellenistic period onward.[3]

---

1. Versions of this study were presented at the Formation of Luke-Acts Section, Society of Biblical Literature, Washington, DC (2006) and at that society's international meeting, University of Vienna (2007). I am grateful for heuristic comment from L. Aejmelaeus, T. L. Brodie, D. Dorman, R. F. Hock, D. Konstan, H. Leppä, M. C. Parsons, J. Shelton, W. O. Walker Jr., and M. Winninge.

2. Hunger, "Progymnasmata und andere Übungsreden," 1:92–120, and Hunger, "Ekphraseis," 1:170–88; Kennedy, *Greek Rhetoric under Christian Emperors*, 52–73; Berger, "Hellenistiche Gattungen im Neuen Testament," 1296–98; Lausberg, *Handbuch der literarischen Rhetorik*, 532–46; Cichocka, "Progymnasmata as a Literary Form," 991–99; Webb, "*Ekphrasis* Ancient and Modern," 7–18; Kennedy, *Progymnasmata*; Gibson, "Learning Greek History in the Ancient Classroom," 103–29.

3. Berger, "Hellenistiche Gattungen im Neuen Testament," 1296.

As to the time, I take the undisputed Pauline Letters to have appeared c. 50–57 CE,[4] with Luke-Acts probably written some five to twenty years later.[5] Dio Cassius took ten years collecting his material and another twelve to write it up. Perhaps sensing the exigency to provide needed narrative clarification for growing numbers of disciple-believers as to the actual meaning of some early Christian experiential language that Paul's original addressees once better understood, Luke might have tried to finish in a more timely manner. Luke appears to be writing a different kind of history from a new and significant viewpoint on the world, one which conveys for his inscribed reader, Theophilus, both the presumption and the expectation of shared Christian experiences with Lukan characters.[6] Given Luke's awareness of Pauline tradition[7] and, I shall argue, of his Letter to the Romans, perhaps he believed that producing a narrative personification of Paul as a minister participating in the fulfillment of remembered prophecies about the earthly Jesus would stimulate a fresh and more understandable rereading of Paul's correspondence.

With regard to a pastoral purpose behind the narrative-rhetorical composition of such a necessary theological and pneumatological history as a sequential narrative (διήγησις) in contact with previous efforts,[8] the literary effect of a progymnasmatic-based education upon a person previously so trained, perhaps before going on to pursue studies elsewhere as in engineering or medicine,[9] would be reasonably expected to be rather pronounced. Along with Hock, Gibson, and Webb,[10] I propose that these compositional exercises, drills, and critiques, under the direction of a rhetorical teacher, focused as they were on a number of formal categories like description (Περὶ Ἐκφράσεως) and narrative (Περὶ Διηγήματος), would make an indelible imprint on how credible description within narrative-rhetorical composition should best be done in the future, after the pupil left this first stage of Greco-Roman schooling. It would be very difficult to believe otherwise for students so molded. Gibson finds that "as imperial-era Greek literature richly attests, writers trained in the progymnasmata continued to deploy the forms of these basic exercises long after

---

4. Suhl, "Paulinische Chronologie im Streit der Meinungen," 939–1188; Thornton, *Der Zeuge des Zeugen*.

5. For a review of the probabilities in this range, cf. Fitzmyer, *Acts of the Apostles*, 51–55. Regarding this discussion, Barrett, *Acts*, 1:329, argues that "It seems that a strong case can be made for the belief that Jesus did foretell the destruction of the Temple, even if he did not say that he would himself destroy it." If this perception is afforded to Luke, perhaps his implication of the fall of Jerusalem at Luke 21:20–24 should not be taken as evidence that he could not have finished his double work prior to 70 CE.

6. Alexander, "On a Roman Bookstall," 19, and Alexander, *Acts in Its Literary Context*, 163.

7. Klein, "Paulinische Tradition bei Lukas," 13–16.

8. Moessner, "Dionysius' Narrative 'Arrangement,'" 149–64.

9. Weissenrieder, *Images of Illness in the Gospel of Luke*, 335, 355–57, finds that the author of Luke-Acts incorporates considerably more than probable general knowledge of ancient medicine.

10. Hock, "Rhetoric of Romance," 445–65; Gibson, "Learning Greek History in the Ancient Classroom"; Webb, "*Ekphrasis* Ancient and Modern."

their formal education was complete."[11] Going over venerated texts, and composing new ones in that light, with a critical eye toward reexpression, such reexpression or explanation (ἑρμηνεία) having to be both clear (σαφής) and vivid (ἐναργής), would fashion a keen interest in honing a narrative technique that would be the most effective in its communicative intent for a particular audience.

If evident deficiencies in a respected text were detected, improvement and clarification would be in order. Indeed, Webb concludes that the progymnasmatic students made "active use of the linguistic and cultural knowledge they had acquired from the grammarian. Precisely because (the progymnasmata) are elementary, they reveal the lowest common denominator of that training and reveal the basic conceptions of language, categories of composition, and modes of thought which informed both the production and the reception of rhetorical and other texts."[12] Students learn here that in order to be persuasive with their new narrative composition, any elaboration (αὔξησις), amplification (ἐξειργασία), clarification or explanation (σαφηνισμός) of a previous writer who is worthy of imitation and recognition must meet certain well-defined rhetorical goals, namely the three uncompromising virtues or indispensable qualities of a proper narrative presentation: clarity (σαφήνεια), conciseness (συντομία), and plausibility (πιθανότης).

Theon, a first-century progymnasmatic instructor,[13] thinks that the narrative should have all these desired qualities.[14] Students learn as well by correcting mistakes in their own compositions. According to Theon, a great admirer of Homer, the stress on clarity and vividness in the progymnasmatic way of composition is to make the narrative attractive to the mind's eye, so that Homer's saying (*Od.* 11.146) comes true: ῾Ρηΐδιόν τι ἔπος ἐρέω καὶ ἐνὶ φρεσὶ θήσω (I will say an easy word and put it in your mind).[15]

---

11. Gibson, "Learning Greek History in the Ancient Classroom," 105; Morgan, *Literate Education in the Hellenistic and Roman Worlds*.

12. Webb, "*Progymnasmata* as Practice," 292.

13. Quintilian exhibits some kind of dependence on, and development of, Theon's definitions. This and other inferences from Hermogenes, Aphthonius, and Nicolaus suggest that Theon is probably to be placed in the first century CE (cf. Stegemann, "Theon," cols. 2037-54 (37-38); Hock and O'Neil, *Chreia in Ancient Rhetoric, I,* 63-66; Butts, "'Progymnasmata' of Theon," 2-8; Patillon, *Aelius Théon Progymnasmata*, viii-xvi). Nevertheless, Heath, "Theon and the History of the Progymnasmata," 129-60, puts Theon in the fifth century on a questionable version of rhetorical history. However, the roots of progymnasmatic instruction in Greco-Roman rhetorical education are securely established, so that Heath's temporal reassignment of Theon is a conjecture that does not affect the argument of the present study.

14. "Περὶ Διηγήματος," *Théon Progym.*, 38-61 (40, Spengel 79.20-22). Here, my citation of *Théon Progymn.* refers to Patillon's critical edition of the Greek text and his pagination (n13). If line identification might possibly be appropriate, as in this instance, I use the numbering system of Spengel, *Rhetores Graeci*, 2:57-130. Bolognesi prepared five Armenian chapters missing from the Greek texts in *Aelius Théon: Progymnasmata* that I do not cite in the present study.

15. "Περὶ τῆς τῶν Νέων Ἀγωγῆς," *Théon Progymn.*, 9-18 (17), "Je vais dire des mots faciles et te les mettre dans l'esprit."

By writing an easy word and putting it in a reader's mind, authorial intention becomes clear, easy to understand. One communicates effectively; one paints a verbal portrait, especially via exemplarity. One of the well-established techniques in doing this is the effective, essential, and required use of examples (*exempla* and παραδείγματα). Collections of useful *exempla* for rhetorical purposes circulated widely in the Empire before the beginning of the first century BCE.[16] The literary tradition of *exempla* and παραδείγματα as instructional experience that is employed and emphasized in the progymnasmata was built upon narrative practice and ancient rhetorical theory.[17] Aristotle considered the example as one of the most basic forms of proof.[18] Theon teaches narrative composition by showing how examples and precedents may be effectively employed to persuade and describe, using παράδειγμα fifteen times in various formats. Examples help to tell in a believable manner what might otherwise be unbelievable. Examples clarify and correct. They provide a model for future generations. Readers are then enjoined to strive to replicate an example or precedent known to be true. Examples and precedents live on, not being tarnished by time; therefore, the progymnasmatic way is to choose the very finest.

Lastly, in narrative one must always be considerate of what is appropriate for the character you are portraying to say at a certain time and place and on a certain occasion.[19] Theon devotes a chapter in his treatise to this technique, Περί Προσωποποΐίας, giving practical guidelines for composing a plausible, well-argued 'Speech-in-Character' that properly takes into account previous narrated elements between those exhorted and the one who is exhorting as contextually fitting starting-points οἰκείας ἀφορμὰς.[20] Later progymnasmaticists, Hermogenes, Aphthonius, Nicolaus, John of Sardis, and Sopatros[21] offer a chapter on a similar technique of personification, Περί Ἠθοποΐίας.[22] Both προσωποποΐία and ἠθοποΐία concern ap-

16. Nordh, "Historical *exempla* in Martial," 227; Lumpe, "Exemplum," cols. 1230-57; Maslakov, "Valerius Maximus and Roman Historiography," 437-96.

17. Cf. Alewell, *Über das rhetorische Παράδειγμα*; Oehler, *Mythologische Exempla in der älteren griechischen Dichtung*; Price, "'Paradeigma' and 'Exemplum' in Ancient Rhetorical Theory"; Fiore, "Place of Example in Rhetorical Education," 33-37; Lausberg, *Handbuch der Literarischen Rhetorik*, 37, 227-35; Kurz, "Narrative Models for Imitation in Luke-Acts," 171-89.

18. Aristotle, *Rh.* (Τέχνη ῾Ρητορική) 1.2.8, 19; 2.20.1-4, 9; 2.25.8.

19. "Περί Διηγήματος," *Théon Progymn.*, ed. Patillon, 38-61 (46-47). This focus on appropriate characterization and personification led to the progymnasmatic formula "What word would x say upon y event," (Webb, "Poetry and Rhetoric," 346-47).

20. "Περί Προσωποποΐίας," *Théon Progymn.*, ed. Patillon, 70-73 (71-72).

21. Cf. Kennedy, *Progymnasmata*, 63, 89, 126, 161, 163.

22. Προσωποποΐία is closely related to ἠθοποΐία and might best be rendered as "the art of characterization" or "the imitation of the character of person in question." In a world steeped in rhetorical training, ἠθοποΐία "was central from its earliest days" (Whitmarsh, *Greek Literature and the Roman Empire,* 188). Schissal, "Rhetorische Progymnasmatik der Byzantiner," 10, regarded ἠθοποΐία as "wirklich die grössten ästhetischen Qualitäten."

How and why characters are portrayed as speaking as they do according to the narrative virtues of clarity, conciseness, and plausibility/persuasiveness is intimately related to these particular

propriately accurate personification, an important technique relating to plausibility, persuasion, and contiguous characterization.

In narrative-rhetorical education, what a character would actually say, if he were present, has to be suitable to what is known about that character by one's anticipated readers. You had to get this done right, clearly, vividly, and plausibly in your elaboration and, according to Theon, in a noncontroversial way.[23] Since the character is not physically present, you must portray him or her as thinking according to your examples and precedents of what the character speaks about when imitating his or her words. This imitative technique could lead to a fresh rereading and a better understanding of a venerated character's own writings, as well as giving credibility to your own as you improve on the past while retaining descriptive language of a venerated precursor. This technique is applicable if the character is known by your readers to have written what they are probably familiar with. It is not necessary then to mention that the person whom you are imitating wrote anything. This is how some Greek medical writers may treat Hippocrates, as I will illustrate below. In this style they are not writing a *bios* of Hippocrates, but they can mention his name, imitate his words while not mentioning that they are doing this, and not mention that he wrote anything.

I am going to argue that Luke thematically clarifies Paul's Letter to the Romans in important practical areas via needed exemplarity that is probably progymnasmatically motivated.[24] I will also notice that in addition to this intertextual clarification, Luke can also be detected as employing an important statement from Paul he finds in Romans to support a thesis by Peter. The cumulative result is also consistent with both literary and logistic factors within probable widespread Christian communication as observed by Marguerat[25] and by Bauckham et al., Millard, Brodie, and Bird.[26]

---

progymnasmatic elements. For discussion of particular points, cf. Stählin, "Das Bild der Witwe," 5–20; Parsons, "Luke and the *Progymnasmata*," 43–63; Stegman, "Reading Luke 12:13–34," 328–52.

23. "Περί Προσωποποΐιας," *Théon Progymn.*, ed. Patillon, 70.

24. In the two instances (Rom 10:9 and 1:1) where clarification in Luke-Acts via examples and precedents may be arguably detected, the Christian experiences of salvation and Spirit-reception occur within Luke's fulfillment-of-prophecy theme. Here, I take the Lukan Paul as representing a reliable characterization and personification of Paul, known writer of letters, in concert with the arguments of Porter, *Paul of Acts*.

25. Marguerat, "L'image de Paul dans les Actes des Apôtres," 153, demonstrates that Luke's treatment of Paul's life deliberately incorporates diverse phenomena that Paul himself mentions, stemming from Luke's own "réception *canonique* (le corpus des lettres de Paul)." Paul is thereby cast as emblematic (*emblématique du devenit chretien*), his image receiving the necessary Lukan reorientations (*les infléchissements*) consistent with that objective.

26. Bauckham, *Gospels for All Christians*; Millard, *Reading and Writing in the Time of Jesus*; Brodie, "Schools, Synagogues, and Vibrant Scripture-Related Communities," 63–71; Bird, "Markan Community, Myth or Maze?" 474–86.

Three Contemporary Intertextual Performances with Progymnasmatic Flavor from the Scientific Tradition

Before observing how Lukan contemporaries Aretaios and Erotian, and, a little later, Galen, handle respected precursors, thereby illuminating the probable similar use of Paul's letters by Luke, it may be helpful to very briefly substantiate the point that the rhetorical idea of imitation and improvement found in the progymnasmatic tradition has deep roots. Isocrates (*Paneg.* 8.4), who influenced Quintilian in this regard, teaches that it is possible to speak about old things (παλαιά) in new ways (καινῶς) and that one must attempt to speak better on previous subjects than one's predecessors (ἄμεινον ἐκείνων εἰνειν πειρατέον), the goal being to conceive the right sentiments about the predecessors in each instance (*Paneg.* 9.1–6). Giangrande demonstrates how Callimachus clarifies Theocritus.[27] Thomas strengthens the case for Virgil's appropriation and improvement of Apollonius's *Argonautica*.[28] Knight argues that Apollonius shows how Homer may be read, while sometimes drawing attention to inconsistencies in Homer with respect to the interactions of the gods.[29] Finkelpearl highlights literary appropriation by Seneca and Apuleius (b. 123 CE), showing that emulation can stress the digestive metamorphosis of a literary model, rather than simply copying it, and that events could be reshaped in a nonoppositional way.[30] Seneca (*Epistulae morales* 84) advocated recognizable emulation—obviously a desirable result since that brought credit to the known and respected precursor and also to the imitator for any improvement, progress, or clarification involved—which, he reasoned, can clearly be a different thing from whence it came, stamping its own, but harmonious, form on a previous text.

This literary approach was widely practiced among closely contemporary writers as well as on more distant admired ones. It was also expected as due progress in the scientific arts, another genre probably not unknown to Luke, who appears conversant with its literature.[31] The three medical writers, Aretaios, Erotian, and Galen, are particularly germane to Lukan style.

27. Giangrande, "Hellenistic Poetry and Homer," 68.

28. Thomas, "Virgil's *Georgics* and the Art of Reference," 171–98 (cp. *Ap. Rh.* 1.897–98 with *Aen.* 4.327–30; *Ap. Rh.* 3.744–45 with *Aen.* 4.522–23; *Ap. Rh.* 4.355–56 with *Aen.* 4.305–6).

29. Knight, *Renewal of Epic*, 39, 267. Knight argues that the relation of the *Argonautica* to Homer is "intertextual" in the true sense that it is possible to transpose the systems of the *Iliad* and *Odyssey* into the later poem (8). Similarly, Paul's discursive expressions re: the heavenly giving and the personal reception of the Holy Spirit by believers are transposed into Lukan personification and characterization of Spirit-language. Knight shows that at certain points characters in the *Argonautica* demonstrate and use awareness of events recorded in Homer (29) and that the reader is not intended to recall the original Homeric context (14), although the debt to Homer is by no means concealed. This emulation remarkably parallels a probable Lukan conceptual emulation of Paul's letters on my argument of narrative-rhetorical improvement/clarification.

30. So, Finkelpearl, "Pagan Traditions of Intertextuality in the Roman World," 78–90.

31. Complementing the analysis by Weissenrieder, *Images of Illness in the Gospel of Luke*, the writer of Luke-Acts appears to work from within the extant scientific tradition, displaying evidence of

Aretaios of Cappadocia, who is arguably placed in the mid-first century CE,[32] while a medical writer who employs a Hippocratic style like "looking at Hippocrates" (*guardando a Ippocrate*) and whose literary strength lies in his masterly description (*la magistrale descrizione*),[33] mentions no other authors in his large corpus except Homer (once) and Hippocrates (once). On these two occasions he does not inform his readers that Homer and Hippocrates wrote anything. He never says "wie Hippokrates sagt."[34] But in the course of his work he employs material and quotes from both Homer and Hippocrates a number of times without acknowledgement, "simply integrating their words with his text."[35] A careful look at these unattributed occasions of emulation and elaboration shows that they follow the progymnasmatic pattern of instructions I have described above. Aretaios offers recognizable imitation (several words in a row for easy straightforward recognition for those familiar with Homer and Hippocrates), employing slight changes in wording with additions and subtractions to accommodate the new contexts which would then, upon a reconsideration of the precursors, bring interesting improvement and clarification to them.[36]

As to the practice of not citing authors of known and respected texts by name, Erotian (in the time of Nero, 54–68 CE), wrote a dictionary for those who would read medical literature. This was no simple task. He said it would be the best so far, but, in terms of direct quotes or of acknowledgement that any of his predecessors wrote anything, he shows no evidence in that respect of any previous material.[37]

Sluitter shows that Galen undertook the task of necessary improvement when appropriate for more widespread understandability of a previous work he admired, "Since Galen envisaged a wider audience for the works of Hippocrates than just for specialists, he sets himself the task of *eliminating even the smallest obscurities*," namely to clarify the meaning of words and improve contexts to provide a better

---

contact with Greek scientific literature (cf. Enslin, "Luke, the Literary Physician," 142–50; Alexander, "Luke's Preface," 48–74; Alexander, *Preface to Luke's Gospel*, 127–33, 172–76).

32. Oberhelman, "On the Chronology and Pneumatism of Aretaios of Cappadocia," 941–66; Kudlien, *Untersuchungen zu Aretaios von Kappodokien*, 1145–230.

33. Weber, *Areteo di Cappadocia*, 64.

34. Kudlien, *Untersuchungen zu Aretaios von Kappodokien*, 1175.

35. Smith, "From Hippocrates to Galen," 243.

36. Following the critical text of Aretaios by Hude—namely, *Aretaeus*—these unacknowledged but easily recognizable occasions of imitation, improvement and/or clarification are as follows: Aret., 3:7.1.5 (book, chapter, section, line) with Hippolytus, *Aph.* 2.42; Aret., 1:6.2.6 with Hippolytus, *Aph.* 5:2 (Aretaios, ἐπὶ τρώματι γὰρ σπασμὸς θανάσιμον, with Hippocrates, ἐπὶ τρώματι σπασμός ἐπιγεγόμενος θανάσιμον; Aret., 1:7.3.4 with Hippolytus, *De alim.* 14.1; Aret., 6:7.1.7 and 2:7.1.8 with Hippolytus, *De alim.* 31.1; Aret., 3:6.9.3 with Hippolytus, *Epid.* 6.4.18.1; Aret., 4:13.15.9–10 with Hippolytus, Homer, *Il.* 12.463 (Aretaios, ἀλλὰ καὶ νυκτὶ θοῇ ἀτάλαντον ὑπώπια, with Homer, Ἕκτωρ νυκτὶ θοῇ ἀτάλαντος ὑπώπια, memorable words about Hector's countenance fitted to a new context); Aret., 5:2.16.1 with Hippolytus, *De hum.* 1.4; and Aret., 8:6.1.8–9 with Hippolytus, *Epid.* 6:4.7.1.

37. Smith, "From Hippocrates to Galen," 226, 234, 240.

understanding.³⁸ Galen's elimination of obscurities falls within the framework of Theon's insistence that his pupils strive for the narrative-rhetorical virtues of clarity, conciseness, and plausibility when they are elaborating, amplifying, or imitating within their own compositions.

Improvements via Clarification of Paul at Romans 10:9 and at 1:11

Both of these possible clarifications of Paul, that serve to improve expected readings of Romans, are accomplished through Luke's narrative-rhetorical personification (προσωποποιΐα) and interactive characterization of Paul. The portrayal of Paul to this end finds expression within Luke's prominent dual fulfillment-of-prophecy theme.³⁹ Luke may have first come across the fulfillment-of-prophecy theme with exposure to the progymnasmata, which are fond of Homeric citations and illustrations, given the veneration of Homer in rhetorical culture.⁴⁰ The theme is found both in the *Iliad* and the *Odyssey*.⁴¹ Although none of the exercises within the progymnasmatic explicitly mention the theme itself, they do imply that discourse pertaining to a central character, the main character—here the subject of two dramatic and pronounced prophetic descriptions at the outset of the narrative—should be arranged so as to make such matters relative to the prophecy plain and obvious. They suggest that within a practical and direct communicative or rhetorical arrangement, both the credibility and personification of a main character would be well served if his actions were seen as developing the matter of such important prophecies in a sustained manner.

The preliminary exercises accordingly instruct students to address the subject matter within a narrative to explain both the time and the manner of an activity and the reason for these things.⁴² A narrative must thereby maintain plausibility in order to persuade, its most pressing concern when the subject matter has to seem credible to the audience.⁴³ To accomplish this goal the narrative landscape must display a plausible arrangement insofar as connected and consecutive speech and action is concerned that suits the matter at hand (so too, Quint., *Inst. orat.* 1.5.3). Such

---

38. Sluitter, "Embarrassment of Imperfection," 2:532, emphasis mine.

39. Regarding Luke's application of the theme, cf. Berger, "Hellenistische Gattungen im Neuen Testament," 1267, who properly links the theme to Luke's evident recognition of, and belief in, active divine providence and fore-ordainment as treated earlier by Schulz, "Gottes Vorsehung bei Lukas," 104–16. For recent discussion, cf. Talbert, "Promise and Fulfillment in Lucan Theology," 91–103; Frein, "Prophecies and Luke's Sense of Fulfillment," 22–37. As to the dual experiential nature of this thematic plot and its narrative exemplarity in Luke-Acts, cf. Elbert, "Luke's Fulfillment of Prophecy Theme" (ch. 1 of this anthology).

40. Cf. Hock, "Homer in Greco-Roman Education," 56–77.

41. Haft, "τὰ δὴ νῦν πάντα τελεῖται," 223–40; see too, Duckworth, *Foreshadowing and Suspense*, 6, 28–32, 100.

42. Περί Διηγήματος, in Patillon, *Aelius Théon Progymnasmata*, 38.

43. Περί Διηγήματος, in Patillon, *Aelius Théon Progymnasmata*, 40.

required sequencing is quite Theonic and is compatible with his definition of narrative as an explanatory account of matters that have occurred or as if they have occurred, which is virtually identical to Cicero's definition (*Inv. Rhet.* 1.29.27). Quintilian, in another contemporary definition that is highly Theonic, presses the point of persuasion, "The narrative is an exposition, useful for persuasion, of that which either has been done or is supposed to have been done" (*Inst. orat.* 4.2.31). For Luke to compose his narrative with employment of a dual fulfillment-of-prophecy theme is compatible with contemporary literary technique.

The fulfillment-of-prophecy theme also appears in the LXX, easily recognizable to a LXX student like Luke.[44] Luke's fulfillment-of-prophecy theme has a twin focus. He employs the prophecy of an angel (Luke 2:11) to originate his theme of salvation, bound up with forgiveness, faith, and repentance; Luke employs the prophecy of John the Baptist (Luke 3:16) to originate his theme of Spirit-baptism/Spirit-reception. Both foci are amply provided with exemplarity consistent with and appropriate to progymnasmatic προσωποποιΐα and ἠθοποιΐα. Exemplarity of Romans 10:9 falls within Luke's development of the angel's prophecy and Luke's exemplarity of Romans 1:11 may be understood as a prominent component of Luke's portrayal of Paul. In Luke's picture of Paul, he is personified with appropriate speech-in-character so as to provide believable examples and precedents that serve the fulfillment of the angel's and of John's prophecy. Paul's meaning in these two discursive instances is thereby given needed clarity and plausibility within a narratively connected sequence of events that makes believable what would otherwise be naturally difficult (φύσει περισκελές).

Along with others,[45] I have argued that Luke most probably knows and uses the Pauline Letters[46] and that one of the reasons Luke writes is to clarify Paul.[47] Conceptual

---

44. Rad, "Die deuteronomistische Geschichtstheologie in den Königsbüchern," 192–96, 203, draws attention to eleven prophecies and their fulfillment.

45. The following scholars mentioned chronologically may serve to highlight this research: Jacobsen, "Über die lukanischen Schriften," 129–58; Schulze, "Die Unterlagen," 119–25; Soltau, "Die Herkunft der Reden in der Apostelgeschichte," 128–54; Thiering, "Acts of the Apostles as Early Christian Art," 139–89; Enslin, "Once Again, Luke and Paul," 253–71; Enslin, "Emphases and Silences," 219–25; Aejmelaeus, *Die Rezeption der Paulusbriefe in der Miletrede*; Kim, *Die Geisttaufe des Messias*, 192–98; Walker, "Acts and the Pauline Corpus Reconsidered," 3–23; Walker, "Acts and the Pauline Corpus Revisited," 77–86; Leppä, *Luke's Critical Use of Galatians*; Leppä, "Luke's Account of the Lord's Supper," 364–73; Aejmelaeus, "Reopening the Case."

Enslin, "'Luke' and Paul," 83, retorts "Yet we are asked to believe that such a man (Enslin referring to "Luke the littérateur") was either totally unaware that this hero of his had ever written letters—where could he have lived?—or that it never occurred to him that it would be of any value to make use of them." Similarly, Brodie, "Greco-Roman Imitation of Texts," 37, appropriately asks, "Would a researcher like Luke who wanted to highlight Paul and his preaching set to work without bothering to get copies of Paul epistles? In what corner was he marooned that he did not know of these documents? In what literary impoverishment did this elegant writer live that he could not get copies of them?"

46. Elbert, "Paul of the Miletus Speech" (also ch. 7 of this anthology).

47. Elbert, "Possible Literary Links," 226–54 (also ch. 4 of this anthology).

expression in Romans 1–3 may have been especially useful to Luke,[48] although his employment of Pauline language elsewhere in the letter is evident. If anyone among Luke's readership thought that they would not find adequate profit from reading Paul's known correspondence, perhaps after the appearance of his double-work many would probably be prone to reconsider and purchase copies. Luke would anticipate this circumstance given his portrayal of Paul as a person who saw and was personally addressed by the heavenly Jesus, being healed of blindness and being filled, as a Christian brother, with the Holy Spirit. Such matters would be deemed worthy of perusal and Luke's work could stimulate efforts to read past letters directed to believer-disciples by such a famous person, even if occasionally difficult to understand.

However, Paul's discursive style in his occasional, but probably well-known letters among communities of writers and readers, would be immediately perceived by a progymnasmatically inclined Luke as in need of serious narrative-rhetorical clarification via appropriate exemplarity. Luke's anticipated readers must be able to understand Paul's letters either anew or afresh, at least in some practical spiritual matters, as well as Paul's original readers did in a past time when some of them even knew Paul. Romans, for example, is seriously flawed from a narrative-rhetorical perspective, even obscure at critical junctures, with respect to its lack of examples and precedents with regard to two main categories of practical Christian description (ἔκφρᾶσις), categories to which Lukan *ekphrasis* is appropriately attentive, namely salvation and Spirit-reception. These two concepts appear in Romans, but Paul's language comes without any examples whatsoever. Luke's readers, as past and future readers of Paul, will require the progymnasmatic touch of exemplarity within a clear, vivid, and plausible context of Paul's ministry. Luke, following the imprint of his training, on my argument, will reanimate these past inadequate descriptions and thus provide persuasive improvement of Paul.

At Romans 10:9, after noting the urgency of being saved from the coming wrath of God, (5:9),[49] Paul tells God's beloved, called to be saints (1:7), "if you confess with your lips that Jesus is Lord and if you believe in your heart (πιστεύσῃς ἐν τῇ καρδίᾳ σου) that God raised him from the dead,[50] you will be saved (σωθήσῃ)." Two conditional sub-

---

48. Baum, "Paulinismen in den Missionsreden des lukanischen Paulus," 405–36 (434). Observing that "Besonders auffällig ist den juden- und vor allem den heiden- christlichen Missionrede des lukanischen Paulus der starke inhaltliche Bezug zu den ersten drei Kapiteln des Römerbriefs," Baum cites the following occasions: Acts 13:33c (Rom 1:2); Acts 13:33d/17:31c (Rom 1:4a); Acts 13:33b/17:31c (Rom 1:4b); Acts 13:46a/17:31e (Rom 1:16c); Acts 14:17a/17:27c (Rom 1:19a); Acts 14:15b/17:24a (Rom 1:20); Acts 17:29d (Rom 1:23a); and Acts 17:29c (Rom 1:23b).

49. Even to a casual reader of Romans it is evident that Paul considers divine ὀργή as an urgent reality, cf. Eckstein, "Denn Gottes Zorn wird vom Himmel her offenbar werden," 84, 85; Macgregor, "Concept of the Wrath of God," 106; Toit, "Forensic Metaphors in Romans," 240.

50. Baum, "Paulinismen in den Missionsreden des lukanischen Paulus," 417, notes that "Die Formulierung des lukanischen Paulus ὁ θεὸς ἤγειρεν ἐκ νεκρῶν (Act 13,30; vgl. 13,37) findet sich praktisch identisch in Röm 10,9 (ὁ θεὸς αὐτὸν ἤγειρεν ἐκ νεκρῶν) und in ähnlichen Formulierungen an vielen Stellen des *Corpus Paulinum*, auch in 1 Kor 15,4b."

junctives as to confessing and believing in the heavenly Jesus precede a future passive (σωθήση) that is obviously eschatological. For Luke's part, as a prelude to his description of Paul, Lukan *Sondergut* offers believable characterization employing this concept in two examples that promote understandable patterns of action, namely via accounts of a women with ointment (Luke 7:36–50 [σέσωκέν in context of forgiveness and peace]) and of a rich tax-gatherer (Luke 19:5–10 [σωτηρία and σῶσαι in context of joy and deeds of repentance]). Luke then employs the future passive σωθήση, again eschatologically, preceded by an imperative as to believing in the heavenly Jesus (πίστευσον), in his personification of Paul who says (Acts 16:31), also in a context of urgency, "Believe in the Lord Jesus and you will be saved (σωθήση)." What Paul is thinking about at Romans 10:9 is considerably clarified, improving his readability.

At Romans 1:11, Paul desires to see the Roman Christians, "in order that I may impart a gift of spiritual value to strengthen you" (ἵνα τι μεταδῶ χάρισμα ὑμῖν πνευματικὸν εἰς τὸ στηριχθῆναι ὑμᾶς). The unemphatic indefinite pronoun is typically placed forward, second in a sentence and not following its noun,[51] but here it is separated from its subject (χάρισμα πνευματικὸν) by the verbal idea (μεταδίδωμι) Paul has in mind.[52] Perhaps this adds some rhetorical emphasis on what Paul has in mind, suggesting that he does have something specific in mind. The question is, what? Although I still translate the pronoun as "some," it may well lean to "a certain" gift of spiritual value that would apply to all he encountered in Rome who needed prayer for this particular benefit. One notes too that Paul speaks highly of receiving the Spirit, who is from God, and ensuing benefits (1 Cor 2:12, and again at Rom 5:5 written from Corinth). Among those trying to deduce or guess what Paul has in mind, I anticipate that Schenk has got it right in identifying χάρισμα πνευματικὸν (Rom 1:11) as the gift of the Spirit.[53] He suggests that this phrase is a parallel expression for the fullness of all spiritual blessings (εὐλογίᾳ πνευματικὰ) about which Paul speaks at Romans 15:29. However, one might also suggest, perhaps less attractively, that Paul has in mind an unspecific selection from his lists in Romans 12 and 1 Corinthians 12, so an observable clarification by someone perhaps more immediately familiar with Paul's mindset,

---

51. The only other instance of this placement in the Pauline corpus following ἵνα is at Romans 1:13d (ἵνα τινὰ καρπὸν σχῶ).

52. The subjunctive/optative μεταδῶ, "I may/might impart," implies collaboration with the Spirit; Paul appears confident of this collaboration, probably based on his past experience with Christians who are receptive to this aspect of his ministry.

53. Schenk, *Das Sagen im Neuen Testament,* 50, noticing a possible thread of connection of Romans 15:29 to Ephesians 1:3; 3:16, says of χάρισμα πνευματικὸν that "Dieser Segen *ist* das Pneuma" (emphasis his).

On my argument in the present study, however, deducing from narrative-rhetorical practice that Paul understands χάρισμα πνευματικὸν as the gift of the Spirit, is, I suggest, not at all going to fall into the category of a supposed "reduction" of χάρισμα πνευματικὸν (so, Jewett, *Romans*, 124, re: Schenk). Rather, my conceptual identification of τι χάρισμα πνευματικὸν rests as much upon Luke's performance to improve and clarify Paul using contemporary literary conventions as upon the brief contexts of Spirit-reception and Spirit-giftedness language we find in Paul.

someone who could capably portray Paul as personally strengthening believers, would be quite helpful in estimating what χάρισμα πνευματικὸν originally conveyed.

For Luke, based on exposure to progymnasmatic training and concerned with the dearth of a suitable discursive example and with the possibility that some of Paul's past and future readers have not and will not grasp his meaning, and believing that he actually does know and understand Paul's meaning, sets out to make clear what kind of spiritual event Paul is talking about. To accomplish this Luke needs to provide an example of Paul strengthening believers in a recognizable manner, identical to or very similar to Paul's own description of himself here at Romans 1:11 while using Paul's word(s). As I will suggest, this is what Luke appears to be doing.

As a matter of style (λέξις), in harmony with Theon's emphasis on composing a clear, concise, and plausible narrative while guarding against employing words that are unnecessarily figurative (τροπικός),[54] Luke accordingly—as I set out below—replaces Paul's τι χάρισμα πνευματικὸς in his example of Paul with his own thematic and straightforward language of Spirit-reception. On my argument, Luke knows that Paul returns to that very same language as exemplified by the Lukan Paul later in his letter (Rom 5:5; 8:15). Therefore, these two discursive instances will also be illuminated by the narrative example of Paul's actions that Luke provides. However, Paul's Spirit-language at Romans 5:5; 8:15, although foregrounded by 1:11, does not include Paul's personal expressed desire to impart τι χάρισμα πνευματικὸς upon arrival in Rome. All three discursive occasions (Rom 1:11; 5:5; 8:15) need help; progymnasmatic elaboration via exemplarity is in order when narratively imitating and thereby explaining Paul's intended action and meaning. Luke needs an example that also shows this feature of Paul as imparting in order to fully clarify Paul and stimulate fresh understandability when reading Romans.

At Acts 18:23, Paul is portrayed as strengthening disciples (ἐπιστηρίζων πάντας τοὺς μαθητάς0, στηρίζω and Luke's ἐπιστηρίζω), στηρίζω and Luke's ἐπιστηρίζω being cognates.[55] Then, immediately following the rhetorically sophisticated Apollos digression—a short digression serving to support Luke's fulfillment-of-prophecy theme re Spirit-reception and illuminate the immediately ensuing story about Paul while at the same time providing amplification that further confirms his narrative purpose in that respect[56]—Paul immediately encounters more disciple-believers (μαθητάς, 19:1;

---

54. "Περὶ Διηγήματος," Patillon, *Aelius Théon Progymnasmata*, 42.

55. While Spicq properly notes the verbal identity of these cognates at Romans 1:11 and Acts 18:23, he disregards Paul's quantifying language (ἵνα τι μεταδῶ χάρισμα ὑμῖν πνευματικὸν) and, equally, does not consider Luke's own ensuing contextual description of strengthening activity by Paul when Luke returns to Paul (Acts 19:1) immediately following his contextually illuminating Apollos digression (Spicq, "στηρίζω," in his *Notes de lexicographie néo-testamentaire*, 3:614n18).

56. Luke's narratively enhancing and rhetorically delightful Apollos digression (παρέκβασις), following naturally what precedes and favorably foregrounding the next scene where Paul strengthens disciple-believers via imparting or being of ministerial assistance in Spirit-reception, is quite harmonious with Theon's teaching on the proper use of a digression (παρέκβασις). A digression should be short, relate to the subject matter, and not be removed from its literary result (re: an attractive

πιστεύσαντες, 19:2a). He continues his strengthening ministry to these Christians[57] beginning with a question well-framed within Luke's style of composition of questions,[58] namely, "Did you receive the Holy Spirit, having believed?" (εἰ πνεῦμα ἅγιον ἐλάβετε πιστεύσαντες;).[59] Luke vividly and concisely records the phenomenological and experiential outcome. Paul imparts and strengthens. Spirit-reception is evidenced by speaking in tongues and prophecy (19:6).

Paul's figurative Spirit-language at the outset of Romans, perhaps not unappreciated by later readers, but potentially confusing for those not privileged to what Paul thought original readers in Rome would understand, as well as Paul's conceptually related Spirit-reception language at two other instances in his letter, is clarified by a fine example within Luke's narrative-rhetorical performance.

These two possible Lukan clarifications of Paul at Romans 10:9 and 1:11 via progymnasmatic exemplarity and recognizable verbal imitation (*Wortanfehnung*)

---

narrative, "Περὶ Διηγήματος" [41–42]). With a view towards composing a forceful and persuasive argument, the use of παρέκβασις is mentioned right alongside amplification (αὔξησις) four times in Theon's exercises re: training new students, "Περὶ τῆς τῶν Νέων Ἀγωγῆς" (16); re: use of a *chreia*, "Περὶ Χρείας" (30); re: confirming truth in a fable, "Περὶ Μύθου" (38); and re: confirming a thesis, "Περὶ Θέσεως" (94). All pagination is from Patillon's edition (n13).

Based on the available evidence from Luke and Theon, they are both right in line with literary backgrounds on the appropriate use of digressions, as the following studies well illustrate: Canter, "Digression in the Orations of Cicero," 351–61; Austin, "Function of Digressions in the Iliad," 292–312; Gaisser, "Structural Analysis," 1–43; Barker, "Digressions in the 'Theaetetus,'" 457–62; May, "*Ethica Digressio and* Cicero's Pro *Milone*," 240–46; Race, "Some Digressions and Returns in Greek Authors," 1–8; Emmett, "Introduction and Conclusions," 15–33; Ingalls, "Linguistic and Formular Innovation," 201–8; Wiedemann, "Sallust's *Jugurtha*," 48–57; and Härter, "Digression und Rhetorik," 17–52 (Quintilian, 26–52).

57. Lukan disciple-believers at Acts 18:23; 19:1, 2a are Christians. Lake and Cadbury, *Beginnings of Christianity*, 4:237, point out that "disciples" at Acts 19:1 "must mean Christians, both from the use of μαθητάς in Acts and from the context. Chrysostom's theory that they were disciples of John has nothing to commend it." Luke's remarkable consistency as a matter of rhetorical clarity in his use of this term (Luke 9:16, 18, 54; 10:23; 16:1; 17:22; 18:15; 19:29, 37; 20:45; 22:39, 45; Acts 6:1, 2, 7; 9:10, 19, 26, 35 [feminine μαθήτρια], 38: 11:26, 29; 13:52; 14:20, 22, 28; 15:10; 16:1; 18:23, 27; 19:1, 9, 30; 20:1, 30; and 21:4, 16) is indeed supportive of Lake and Cadbury.

Hemer, *Letters to the Seven Churches of Asia*, 225, with regard to Luke's usage at 19:1, observes that "the word μαθητάς is used absolutely, as elsewhere of disciples of Jesus"; so too, Ehrhardt, "Construction and Purpose," 73. Zahn, *Die Apostelgeschichte des Lucas*, 2:673, correctly stresses that "Der Text gestattet es nicht, sie Johannesjünger zu nennen." Stuhlmacher, *Biblische Theologie des Neuen Testaments*, 2:278, affords Luke the proper description of these believer-disciples that his narrative clarity deserves: "der Bericht über die (Jesus)-Jünger in Apg 19, 1–7" (parentheses his).

58. Elbert, "Observation on Luke's Composition," (also ch. 2 in this anthology). My stylistic findings on Paul's description of the addressees to his question as Christian disciple-believers, characters foregrounded as disciples prior to the posing of the question, corroborates the contextual analysis of Lake, Cadbury, Hemer, Ehrhardt, Stuhlmacher, and Zahn (n57 above).

59. My translation follows the context Luke clearly provides (Acts 19:5–6) in the ensuing example of Spirit-reception, substantiated by Williams's analysis of Luke's participial style with regard to the 588 aorist participles in Acts, wherein 540 refer to antecedent action with respect to the main verb as does πιστεύσαντες here with respect to ἐλάβετε (Williams, *Participle in the Book of Acts*, 35, 39).

satisfy several positive intertextual criteria.[60] There are the expected but not at all great differences in expression that are intelligible. Identical key words are employed by Luke to enhance recognition within linguistic similarity. In each case there is not just similarity of theme but an identical theme in both Pauline and Lukan contexts. As to principles that can mislead,[61] Brodie draws attention to the fact that similarities may be due to a shared tradition or to general familiarity rather than to direct literary dependence.[62] In other words, Luke and Paul both were immersed in the same Christian tradition, or, upon reading Paul's correspondence, Luke absorbed Paul's thoughts and phrases that then later unconsciously reappeared in his narrative. While these factors are something to consider, I believe that the probable influence and motivation of a progymnasmatic education and the strong conceptual and verbal identities I have detected between Romans 10:9 and 1:11 and Luke's personification of Paul within a sequential plan of thematic narration are, by far, the dominate factors in each case. Accordingly, I suggest that my argument has a good probability of being the right solution.

Employment of Romans 2:11 as a Maxim at Acts 10:34

It may be interesting first to pinpoint when the literary connection between Acts 10:34 and Romans 2:11 was first noticed in *Acta Forschung*. It is not mentioned by Schwanbeck,[63] Jüngst,[64] or Jacobsen.[65] However, Blass,[66] followed by Preuschen,[67] call attention to Luke 20:21 (οὐ λαμβάνεις πρόσωπον)[68] and the identical Galatians

60. Brodie, *Birthing of the New Testament*, 44–46, lists seven of these.
61. Brodie, *Birthing of the New Testament*, 47–49, lists six of these.
62. Brodie, *Birthing of the New Testament*, 47.
63. Schwanbeck, *Über die Quellen die Schriften des Lukas*.
64. Jüngst, *Die Quellen der Apostelgeschichte*.
65. Jacobsen, "Über die lukanischen Schriften," (n45).
66. Blass, *Acta apostolurum sive Lucae ad Theophilum liber alter*, 129.
67. Preuschen, *Die Apostelgeschichte*, 67. Preuschen suggests that at Acts 10:34, "προσωπολήμπτης ist Neubildung nach Lk 20:21; Gal 2:6, sonst nicht zu belegen."
68. At Luke 20:21 there are three interesting literary alterations. Luke begins by removing Mark's ἀληθής which the Pharisees apply to Jesus, replacing it with "we know that you speak and teach rightly ὀρθῶς" by spies. Luke eliminates the phrase οὐ μέλει σοι περὶ οὐδενός (you care for no man) which Mark places just ahead of his οὐ βλέπεις εἰς πρόσωπον ἀνθρώπων (you do not regard the position of men). He then changes οὐ βλέπεις εἰς πρόσωπον ἀνθρώπων to οὐ λαμβάνεις πρόσωπον.
Luke's three reexpressions here seem progymnasmatically understandable. One, Paul's saying that God does not regard persons accords well as a maxim (γνώμη) useful in life (Patillon, *Aelius Théon Progymnasmata*, "Περὶ Χρείας," 18–30 [18]). A practical maxim can give advice, judgment, or opinion that is believed to be intelligent, good, and true, suggesting that the adjective ὀρθῶς applied to Jesus's speaking and teaching could be a more fitting prelude to a maxim taken from Paul in Luke 20:21b, and also to Jesus's *chreia* at 20:25. Both of these progymnasmatic categories (γνώμη and χρεία) already carry the intrinsic concept of ἀληθής within themselves, so further use of ἀληθής could well be considered redundant and not concise. Two, too much flattery from the spies is not an appropriate

2:6 (πρόσωπον . . . οὐ λαμβάνει) when considering Acts 10:34. Soltau is perhaps the first to observe Luke's employment of recognizable language from Romans at the outset of Peter's speech.[69] We see that at Romans 2:11 Paul writes: οὐ γάρ ἐστιν προσωπολημψία παρὰ τῷ θεῷ. At Acts 10:34 Peter says: οὐκ ἔστιν προσωπολήμπτης ὁ θεός. Paul writes and Luke's character says essentially the very same thing. Paul's language is ever so slightly transformed.[70]

The contexts at Romans 2:11 and Acts 10:34 are different, but they contain one interesting commonality. Paul is pointing out the kindness of God that led to repentance and warning Roman Christians of the danger of sin. Paul's readership consisted of both Jews and gentiles. Both Jew and Greek will receive tribulation for doing evil (Rom 2:9); both Jew and Greek will receive honor for doing good (2:10). Gentiles without the Torah and Jews with it will be treated the same in this regard. Peter, speaking to gentile God-fearers, says that in every nation God welcomes those who do what is right (Acts 10:35) and Luke has in mind many nations (2:9–11). So, the commonality of the two contexts is that Jews and gentiles are mentioned as the recipients of God's lack of partiality (προσωπολημψία), of accepting faces or appearances. In Paul's context this divine attribute applies to the consequences of sin for Jews and gentiles, but it could be understood to apply as well to those who will or have received the gift of the Holy Spirit (Rom 1:1 [Acts 18:23—19:7]; 5:5; 8:15) since they are also the ones

---

starting point for their speech-in-character, so Luke eliminates a phrase that is unnecessary. Then, perhaps humorously, even in the mouths of spies can be found an unattributed maxim which Luke expects his active readers of Paul to recognize as an attribute of the divine (Gal 2:6; Eph 6:9; Rom 2:11, Luke employing the latter on my intertextual argument at Acts 10:34). What is attributed to God by Paul harmoniously befits the Son of God at Luke 20:21 as well.

All of this transformation is especially appropriate since Luke 20:21 serve`s as eloquent progymnasmatic preparation which Luke evidently thought might be helpful to better appreciate one of Jesus's most notable *chreiai*, that of Caesar's coin (Mark 13:17; Matt 22:21; Luke 20:25). Perhaps Luke's rhetorical effort here is designed to magnify the evident point that even Caesar himself, illustrated by his face on the coin, along with the spies, and now all of Luke's readers, are to live in the light of Paul's maxim and of Jesus's esteemed *chreia*. Regarding this particular *chreia* and the contemporary literary context, cf. Mack, *Anecdotes and Arguments*, 9–15, 29–32. For a wider view, cf., Robbins, "Chreia," 1–23; Hock and O'Neil, *Chreia in Ancient Rhetoric, I*; Hock and O'Neil, "Elaborating the Chreia," 79–354. I have also argued that Luke accepts and appreciates Jesus's saying at Luke 17:37a, "Where the body is, the eagles will also be gathered together," as a *chreia*, cf. "Observation on Luke's Composition," 105.

While Luke could be influenced at Luke 20:21 by Leviticus 19:15 οὐ λήψῃ πρόσωπον and some Septuagintal and intertestamental sentiments to that effect, in my opinion his overall communicative performance at Luke 20:21 would seem more likely to be predominantly motivated by his own narrative interest in Paul—the man who had seen and heard the heavenly Jesus—and by his active readers known to be familiar with Paul's Letters.

69. Soltau, "Die Herkunft der Reden in der Apostelgeschichte," 138, observes "Merkwürdig ist vor allem, daß Petrus in seiner Rede 10, 34–35 . . . sicherlich aber auch an Röm 2, 6–13 gehalten hat."

70. At the end of Peter's programmatic speech in Acts 2 Luke mentions that Peter spoke many other words as well (2:40), something Luke probably knew from his oral or written sources. *The important thing for Luke, in selecting what words to include in Peter's speeches, either at Acts 2 or 10, is to follow the narrative-rhetorical convention of speech-in-character appropriate to each occasion.*

being so addressed in Romans. In Luke's context the lack of partiality is reapplied to those who are about to receive the same heavenly person.

Does Luke employ Paul to reinforce Peter's known words for Luke's own contemporary Jewish and gentile readers who may be interested in receiving the gift of the Holy Spirit? Did Luke think that by so employing Paul he would make it more clear to his readers, who he anticipates to be familiar with Romans, that now all Jews and gentiles could receive the same gift as Peter and his addressees received in this story? Luke knows that when his readers reach Acts 10 he has already placed before their mind's eye the end of Peter's programmatic speech in Acts 2. There, in a fine application of progymnasmatic προσωποποιΐα (personification) and ἠθοποιΐα (speech-in-character), Peter, in words quite appropriate to what he would realistically be expected to say on such an occasion, appears to promise the same gift of the Holy Spirit that he himself has just received to immediate Jewish hearers and their children and to all who are afar off, to as many as our God will call (καὶ λήμψεσθε τὴν δωρεὰν τοῦ ἁγίου πνεύματος, Acts 2:38–39).[71] By narrative inference and extension, this same promise would now include Luke's readers, Jew and gentile and all who are afar off. As with his previous Jewish audience, these God-fearers are described by Peter as receiving the Holy Spirit as also we do (οἵτινες τὸ πνεῦμα τὸ ἅγιον ἔλαβον ὡς καὶ ἡμεῖς, Acts 10:47b).

Why not then, when Peter speaks again in another narrative context of Spirit-reception, this time not to Jews but to gentiles, employ Paul, who certainly appears familiar with this subject[72]—if indeed Paul has said something important, excellent, and specifically applicable to composing necessary speech-in-character on this new occasion? If an important Pauline statement could be properly employed to corroborate and support Peter's thesis about the real nature of God regarding lack of

---

71. Calvin, reading this speech and its narrative foreground as I think a student of the Classics could read it, and as a first-century Greco-Roman littérateur would write it, also comes to this conclusion. While Calvin does not mention "speech-in-character," he sees it clearly enough, perhaps the product of his humanist training, wherein he views Acts according to Cicero's *historia magistra vitae*.

In the first volume of the first edition of his commentary on Acts, Calvin interprets Peter's statement at Acts 2:38c, "You shall receive the gift of the Holy Spirit (*accipietis donum Spiritus*)," as follows: "Peter says that they will be partakers of the same gift (*eiusdem doni*), if they pass over to Christ (*siad Christum transierint*). The supreme gifts were the remission of sins and newness of life; but this was something extra (*sed haec erat velut accessio*)—an addition—in order that Christ might show his power in them by some visible gift (*dono visibili*). This passage ought not to be taken to refer to the grace of sanctification that is conferred upon all the godly in common. He promises them the gift of the Spirit (*donum Spiritus*) of which they saw an example in the diversity of tongues (*linguarum diuersitate*)" (*Commentariorum Joannis Calvini in Acta Apostolorum*, 1:30). I follow the translation by J. W. Fraser and W. J. G. McDonald (*Acts of the Apostles 1–13*, 81) of the 1552 text (*ex officina Ioannis Crispini*), suggesting a slight, but accurate, explanatory amplification of Calvin's phrase "*sed haec erat velut accessio*."

72. A tabulation of such language in Paul and Luke helps to indicate this evident familiarity, cf. Elbert "Possible Literary Links," 237–40.

προσωπολημψία as it newly applies to Spirit-reception, an astute progymnasmatic student should be able to spot this and make good use of it.

In addition to Luke's ostensible adaptation at Acts 10:43 of Paul's statement at Romans 2:11, within close proximity in Peter's speech we may also observe four linguistic similarities. I would draw attention to ἐργαζόμενος δικαιοσύνην (Acts 10:35); τῷ ἐργαζομένῳ τὸ ἀγαθόν (Rom 2:10). Doing right in every nation earns a welcome; doing good brings glory, honor, and peace, to the Jew first and then to the Greek. Then, universally: οὗτός ἐστιν πάντων κύριος (Acts 10:36); ὁ γὰρ αὐτὸς κύριος πάντων (Rom 10:12). And again: πάντα τὸν πιστεύοντα εἰς αὐτόν (Acts 10:43); πᾶς ὁ πιστεύων ἐπ' αὐτῷ (Rom 10:11). Also, Peter says here that Jesus has been appointed (ὁ ὡρισμένος) by God as judge of the living and the dead (Acts 10:42b), which incorporates in one forceful statement the points made by Paul at Romans 1:4 (τοῦ ὁρισθέντος υἱοῦ θεοῦ); 2:16; and 14:9.[73]

The answer to the interesting question as to what literary motivation would cause Luke to do what he appears to have done here at Acts 10 probably lies in the impact of a progymnasmatic education. Peter's thesis, quite appropriate to the occasion of the Holy Spirit falling upon gentiles, strikes the opening point that οὐκ ἔστιν προσωπολήμπτης ὁ θεός (10:34). Theon points out that a thesis (θέσις) is about a disputed subject,[74] that the goal of a thesis is to persuade,[75] and that a thesis differs from a hypothesis in not being specific with respect to specified characters, place, time, manner, and reason.[76] In composing a narrative where a character advances a thesis,

---

73. These and other linguistic similarities (*Wortanspielungen*) are deemed by Kim to be very characteristic of Paul. Kim suggests that on several occasions—as in the case I have set out above for Acts 10:34/Romans 2:11 and the four other verbal imitations in the immediate vicinity within Peter's speech—Luke certainly (*freilich*) makes adaptations (*Wendungen*) from Romans (Kim, *Die Geisttaufe des Messias*, 196). Along these lines, in the portion of Peter's speech that treats the death and resurrection of Jesus, Baum ("Paulinismen in den Missionreden des lukanischen Paulus," 417) observes that the Lukan Peter says (Acts 10:40) that God raised him "sichtbar werden lassen (ἐμφανῆ γενέσθαι)" and that only in Paul's speech in Antioch (Acts 13:31a) and 1 Corinthians 15:6, 6a, 7 is the verb-form ὤφθη employed to indicate "daß der auferstandene Christus Menschen 'erschienen' ist."

74. "Περὶ θέσεως," Patillon, *Aelius Théon Progymnasmata*, 82–94 (82).

75. "Περὶ θέσεως," Patillon, *Aelius Théon Progymnasmata*, 82–94 (83), "ὅτι ἐν μὲν τῇ θέσει τέλος ἐστὶ τὸ πεῖσαι."

76. "Θέωνος Προγυμνάσματα," Patillon, *Aelius Théon Progymnasmata*, 1–9 (3). Later progymnasmaticists, like John of Sardis, added developments of Theon's concept of a thesis mentioned here (nn. 67–69). John, for example, who often follows Amphthonius, found it necessary to supplement his discussion of the thesis with material on that topic from Theon and Sopatros, the latter noting that in the thesis there is praise of an action (Kennedy, *Progymnasmata*, 169), a point which affords well with Luke's selection of a praiseworthy maxim from Paul to introduce his portrayal of Peter's speech to Cornelius and company.

Theon instructs that the thesis should be introduced by confirming (κατασκευάζω)⁷⁷ the thesis by a maxim, proverb, or *chreia*.⁷⁸

This is exactly how Luke proceeds. Whether the gentiles can be cleansed is a disputed subject. During Jesus's ministry, Pharisees could have been inwardly cleansed, but they chose not to be (Luke 11:39–40). Peter's vision now persuades him that God cleanses gentiles (Acts 10:15; 11:9), giving repentance unto life to them (Acts 11:18b). A maxim praising and confirming God's new deed—which is strongly unspecific but contextually appropriate to the characters of this occasion—would be progymnasmatically well-suited for Peter to elaborate with respect to Jesus's life, death, and resurrection to the end that everyone believing (πάντα πιστεύοντα εἰς αὐτόν, 11:43b) may receive forgiveness of sins. Accordingly, Luke selects a praiseworthy maxim from Paul: οὐ γάρ ἐστιν προσωπολημψία παρὰ τῷ θεῷ,⁷⁹ reshapes it just a tiny bit, and places it in first position as an introduction, the first sentence in Peter's speech as Theon advises. As far as speech-in-character is concerned, how a character who experiences a revelatory vision would begin a thesis leading to an inclusive *Zielpunkt* (Acts 10:43), knowing beforehand that his hearers can be cleansed, is fully satisfied by Luke's adaptation of a recognizable and now experientially credible maxim that is known to his active readers of Paul. Then, Luke begins to set out Peter's thesis, which might be summarized in two parts, as far as it goes: The nature of God toward humankind (10:35–36); and how God

---

77. Theon stresses the idea that the thesis is to be confirmed, since its goal is to persuade. Κατασκευάζειν, conveying the ideas of to establish, construct a positive argument, to prove and frame it, is used three times in this sense of confirming a thesis about a disputed point in Theon's "Περὶ θέσεως" (83, 84, 87).

78. "Περὶ θέσεως," Patillon, *Aelius Théon Progymnasmata*, 82–94 (83). Examples similar to this Theonic style of thesis structure (θέσεως διαίρεσις), where a *chreia* or maxim introduces a diatribe, upon which a thesis is conversationally worked out, may be illustrated by Epictetus's discourses 2.3 (citing Diogenes); 1.13, 14, 15; 2.14, 24, 25; 3.1, 4, 6, 7, 9, and 22. Regarding this *chreia*/maxim-style thesis format for Epictetus's "On the Cynic Calling" (Περὶ Κυνισμοῦ) 3.22.1–3, cf. Billerbeck, *Epiktet vom Kynismus*, 41–159.

79. Paul's statement, οὐ γάρ ἐστιν προσωπολημψία παρὰ τῷ θεῳ, certainly meets Theon's definition of an unattributed maxim. Theon considers the maxim closely related to the *chreia*, in that a concise γνώμη, if it is attributed to a character, could produce a *chreia*, which if accepted would be an excellent, specific, and concise saying from a known person, memorable and instructive in life: "La chrie est une assertion (ou une action) brève et avisée, rapportée à un personnage défini ... et le *mémorable* est une action ou une parole moralement instructives" (Patillon, *Aelius Théon Progymnasmata*, "Περὶ Χρείας," 18–30 [18], emphasis his). This *chreia*-style statement, when recognized and attributed to Paul, could easily be placed by rhetorically trained readers within Theon's category of *chreiai* that are πρακτικαί, that is, those making their point with action, "les chries d'acte" (19), here praiseworthy, divine action.

On my argument, Luke takes οὐ γάρ ἐστιν προσωπολημψία παρὰ τῷ Θεω as an important saying that can explain the pouring out the gift of the Holy Spirit upon both Jew and gentile alike (K. Berger, "ἡ προσωπολημψία," *EDNT* 3.179–80 [80], sees Acts 10:34 as the reason for admitting gentiles). That a progymnasmatically trained Luke would accept and appreciate Paul's statement at Romans 2:11 as a maxim from a respected person and properly incorporate it in Theonic style, so as to introduce it into a thesis by an important character, should not be surprising.

acted upon this divine attribute recently in Jesus Christ (10:37–43), at which point he is interrupted when the gift of the Holy Spirit is poured out.

Conclusion

I have suggested that Luke, through his narrative-rhetorical presentation of Paul, clarifies and improves him at Romans 10:9 and 1:11 and that Luke's motivation for doing so resides in previous progymnasmatic training. As far as Luke is concerned, with obscurity now eliminated by exemplarity, active readers in light of this clarification may now read Paul more appreciatively.

At Acts 10:34, I have suggested that Luke understands Paul's statement at Romans 2:11 about God's lack of partiality as a useful maxim and progymnasmatically employs it according to Theon's instructions in order to confirm and reinforce Peter's thesis and identical thoughts. In Peter's context, persuasive speech-in-character is especially required because the thesis Peter is advancing—applied to Spirit-reception by gentile believers—would have been controversial in its original setting. Given that Paul had already shown in his letter to Jews and gentiles at Rome that all could be now included in this Christian experience, Luke takes literary advantage of a praiseworthy and experientially verifiable maxim from a respected precursor to help personify Peter. This contemporary literary technique also helps to harmonize, not diversify, the Lukan Peter and Paul.[80]

In all three of these instances I have examined, Luke's probable utilization of basic Greco-Roman rhetorical education, both in his clarifying improvements on, and employment of significant information from, Paul's Letter to the Romans, is interestingly harmonious with Aretaios's similar literary treatment of Hippocrates and Galen's desire to clarify Hippocrates. Luke, along with Erotian and Aretaios, has no literary need to write, "as Paul says." Luke apparently stands in a solid literary tradition where previous venerated authors may be appropriately elaborated upon and also employed so as to benefit the present and bring recognition to the past.

---

80. Cf. Hengel, *Der unterschätzte Petrus*, 140–41.

Chapter 6

Pentecostal/Charismatic Themes in Luke-Acts at the Evangelical Theological Society

The Battle of Interpretive Method

Introduction

ARGUING THAT THERE IS a distinctive Pentecostal hermeneutical paradigm, incorporating a desire to respond experientially to the narrative and discursive theology of NT writers, Paul Lewis advocates a mediating position between the extremes of academic isolation and subsuming Pentecostalism under Evangelicalism (with some Holy Spirit emphasis).[1] Lewis suggests that this paradigm is fundamentally non-Enlightenment without being pre-Enlightenment in orientation,[2] which is harmonious with what DuPree thinks Pentecostalism is[3] and with what Pentecostalism can represent intellectually in the new Era of the Glimpse of God,[4] where the experimental findings of modern science and theology intersect in an age of science and

---

1. Lewis, "Towards a Pentecostal Epistemology," 95–125.

2. Lewis, "Towards a Pentecostal Epistemology," 124.

3. DuPree, "In the Sanctified Holiness Pentecostal Charismatic Movement," 113, namely: "The Azusa Street Revival sparked the Pentecostal and Charismatic movement. The movement is an emotional movement, with behavior ranging from moaning and shouting in the Spirit to the more sophisticated, ordinary behavior like reading the Bible, especially Acts 2:4, and praying." While this Christian behavior encompasses experiences like Lukan conversion, praying for and being filled with the Spirit in concert with glossolalia and prophetic-type phenomena exemplified in the book of Acts (in accord with the teaching of the earthly Jesus on prayer), empowered missionary vision, fasting, seeking and being used as givers of Pauline spiritual gifts, praising God in Spirit-filled worship with uplifted hands, dancing in the Spirit, and sufferings, this spirituality as a descriptive category is explored by Robeck, "Nature of Pentecostal Spirituality," 103–6, and Albrecht, "Characteristic Qualities of Pentecostal/Charismatic Spirituality," 218–51.

4. In the second millennium before Christ, one ancient Near Eastern literary text claimed a beginning for physical reality. In 1963, this cosmic beginning was detected and immediately conveyed the implication of a Beginner. This new "Era of the Glimpse of God," which humankind entered in 1963 with the discovery of the cosmic background radiation, makes the existence of God an attractive speculation and is conducive to an experiential hermeneutic—one open to the supernatural as delineated in biblical characters' lives—perhaps best represented in Christendom by global Pentecostalism, cf. Elbert, "Globalization of Pentecostalism," 96.

technology.⁵ This emerging interpretive paradigm, being articulated by scholars like Lewis and Shelton,⁶ is indeed distinctive with respect to the rationalistic structure of both dispensationalism and sacramentalism,⁷ and perhaps may be likened in its perspective to that of Treebeard in J. R. R. Tolkien's *The Return of the King*, "I am on nobody's side, because nobody is on my side."⁸

From this perspective, Evangelicals⁹ today may be understood as having inherited centuries of suspicion of the supernatural and over a millennium of rationalistic theory¹⁰ as to why selected supernatural activities described in the NT should not and could not be expected to occur.¹¹ To seek and/or to expect these cessationistically filtered supernatural activities of the heavenly Jesus and the Holy Spirit is rationalistically unacceptable or intellectually incredible as far as some Evangelicals are concerned.¹² A wedge between the ministry and the teaching of the earthly Jesus and the ministry of the heavenly Jesus appears to exist in this Evangelical mindset. The heavenly Jesus would not be expected to engage in ministerial activities that contradict the rigid epochs that have traditionally been imposed upon NT texts. Other than as an inert rational proposition, one could be led to wonder whether the

---

5. On this point, cf. Polkinghorne, *Belief in God in an Age of Science*, and Polkinghorne, "Theism," 66–83.

6. Shelton, "Epistemology and Authority in the Acts of the Apostles," 231–47.

7. The epistemology of experience, allied to critical interpretation of NT texts, is more convincing, and possesses more interior motivating power, than some rationally formatted and traditionally venerated conjectures, no matter how firmly ensconced. *On this basis I would suggest that dispensationalism, with its rigid temporal boundaries imposed upon the NT text, and sacramentalism, with its claims of automatic transmission of church-incorporation in paedobaptism and automatic transmission of the forgiveness of sins in personal confession, may both be critiqued as evincing rationalistic excess.*

8. With Lewis, "Towards a Pentecostal Epistemology," 125.

9. With Williams, "Was Evangelicalism Created by the Enlightenment?," 311, I consider the Reformation and Puritanism as Evangelical movements, given that Calvin and the Huguenots were actively concerned for evangelism. However, Evangelicalism today, in my judgment, is yet strongly influenced by a distrust and hostility toward experience, similar to that articulated in Jonathan Edwards's 1746 *Treatise Concerning Religious Affections*.

10. For a succinct yet comprehensive overview of the effects of rationalism throughout church history, cf. McKay, "Pentecost and History," 113–28. In a section on "The Prophets and Modern Ecclesiasticism, Rationalism and Paganism," McKay observes that "The Reformed churches in the main rejected the prophetic way in favor of the doctrinal and the moral, which though biblically founded, came to be set in the context of Enlightenment rationalism. The result was academic aridity and ethical legalism in the church. The situation was exacerbated as theological correctness and moral uprightness became the acknowledged tokens of respectability—and hence a source of pride" (123).

11. Cessationistic theory can be traced to Chrysostom and Augustine, the latter cited by Calvin in this regard, but not to their fourth-century contemporary Basil, cf. Lee, "Relevance of St. Basil's Pneumatology to Modern Pentecostalism," 49–76. Perhaps of equal relevance in the patristic domain would be the late-second-century thought of Irenaeus, who felt that denial of gender-insensitive prophetic gifts robbed Christians of their ability to become fruitful, cf. Robeck, "Irenaeus and 'Prophetic Gifts,'" 104–14.

12. Cf. Elbert, "Globalization of Pentecostalism," 87–92.

heavenly Jesus as a person, as in Acts 2:33, even remembers or takes an interest in the teaching of the earthly Jesus.[13]

The distrust and dismissal of experience brought about by suspicion and rationalistic theory is largely to be attributed, in my judgment, to an anti-Lukan concept known as the "apostolic age" or the "Pentecostal age."[14] So ingrained within some Evangelical mindsets are the concretized ramifications of this traditionally presumed epoch, that a knee-jerk reaction towards those who may challenge this hermeneutical blockade and retardation of Lukan interests is not at all unknown, nor is it always a subsurface phenomenon. Scholarship that may seem to challenge this usually hidden and unarticulated interpretive presupposition[15] may be immediately suspect.[16] An intrinsic impulse may exist with regard to such scholarship, rendering it as likely to be ignored or quickly discarded as to be reflected upon. When challenged, quick and dogmatic "solutions" and position protection emerge from the hermeneutical fog as easily as due reflection. The fanciful epochal dichotomies set in place by Calvin, which he well knew were not "biblical" and which are long overdue for retirement, have not yet been laid to rest, perhaps having served some distant political function. The thoughtfulness normally associated with scholarly enterprise may, even today, seem in short supply when it comes to an intersection with ideas that argue against historically established claims stemming from an "apostolic age."[17] While honoring the

---

13. In contradistinction to such an epochally constrained worldview, the heavenly Jesus apparently does so remember and act accordingly, probably programmatically so, cf. Mainville, "Jésus et l'Esprit dans l'oeuvre de Luc"; Mainville, *L'Esprit dans l'oeuvre de Luc*, 248, 257–82; Dumais, "Ministères, charismes et Esprit dans l'oeuvre de Luc," 413–53.

14. For an assessment of the ecclesial effects and ramifications of this concept within the framework of dispensational theory, cf. Prosser, *Dispensationalist Eschatology*. Dogmatic dispensational periodization receives a harsh critique (269).

15. The long-term deleterious effects of the hidden and unarticulated presupposition is well known, cf. Stanton, "Presuppositions in New Testament Criticism," 60–71; Barth, "Problem of Hidden Persuaders," 164–68.

16. Within scholarly circles historically connected (or wedded) to Calvinistic epochal divisions, and to epochs within epochs, there appears to be little awareness that the continuation of Lukan characters' experience is even an interesting speculation. Ministerial categories like apostleship are equally over a distant horizon, given that the dispensational closure guaranteed by an "apostolic age" settles such matters "once-for-all," but cf. Ruthven, *On the Cessation of the Charismata*, 205–12, 213–20; Ruthven, "'Foundational Gifts' of Ephesians 2:20," 28–43.

17. For example, "The Holy Ghost cannot be the subject for the church as such, to ask for now, seeing He has thus been given," so says Darby, *Notes of Addresses on the Gospel of Luke*, 136. The Darbian theory of the Calvinistic tradition, oft repeated by Evangelical commentators, that Lukan Spirit-receptions are confined to the "old dispensation" and that they functioned "once-for-all" in a mystic process of osmotic permeation, finds expression in the reactionary treatise of Erdman, "Holy Spirit and the Sons of God," 2:338–52. Bruce, *Book of the Acts*, 76, continues the rationalistic exuberance of this "once-for-all" theory, entirely ignoring Luke's prominent efforts to portray characters' lives prior to the first Jerusalem Pentecost within a soteriological nexus. Bruce goes further to claim, without adequate syntactical, grammatical, or contextual investigation, that Acts 2:38c indicates the automatic reception of the Lukan gift of the Holy Spirit upon repentance, "although this is not said in so many words" (79). However, since the traditional conjecture of "once-for-all" and its presumed

legacy of the Reformation has its commendable aspects,[18] the Calvinistic application of the "apostolic age"[19] is still dominant today, both hermeneutically and intellectually, in some Evangelical worldviews. Both Lukan and Pauline cessationism are active and, as yet, critically unexamined concepts in some Evangelical mindsets.[20] Such cessationisms are not necessarily latent or dormant, but near the surface. Historically conforming to centuries of tradition, Lukan and Pauline cessationisms are both discernible backgrounds to some contemporary Evangelical interpretation.[21] In the context of this

---

osmotic transmission of characters' experience to future believers is clearly not to be found in the text of Luke-Acts, one must assume that its source lies elsewhere in some unexamined presupposition that has been historically superimposed onto the text of Luke's double-work.

18. While Pentecostals appreciate the work of the Reformers with respect to the recovery of the use of Scripture, they do not pledge allegiance to Reformed ideas or regard themselves as the spiritual heirs of the Reformation; rather it is more descriptive that "Pentecostals are Protestants, but often Protestants without the Reformation" (so Seytre, "Le pentecôstisme," 101). *While some Pentecostals view themselves as evangelical, most view themselves as evangelistic and as a fourth tradition within Christianity, alongside Catholicism, Orthodoxy, and Protestantism.*

19. On Calvin's explicit introduction of this theory into his commentary on Acts, which then not incidentally appears unarticulated as an assured fact in Calvin's sermons on Acts 1–7, see my "Calvin and the Spiritual Gifts," 8:303–31. The Geneva Divine's willful cessationist theology or ideology not only informs his final exegesis at this point (Acts 2:38), but his reinterpretation is justified by an outright appeal to *his* nonexperience and rationalistic speculation, nonexperience which overrides and denies the validity of his textual exegesis. Whether his original exegesis may be confirmed to be correct or most probable is not the issue, rather this illegitimate hermeneutical style is characterized by the willful imposition of philosophical bias—*not in any way due to the* testimonium *of the Spirit*—in order to suit the nonexperience or convenience of the interpreter. This technique, oft repeated, served to set the intellectual stage for the destructive legacy of a "Calvinistic hermeneutic" wherein biblical texts can be piously and obviously shifted in meaning—under the guise of exegesis—so as to conform to "interpretations" best befitting the presumption of an extrabiblical epoch. Calvin, however unwittingly, became the progenitor of "apostolic age hermeneutics."

20. This modern Evangelical sentiment also has roots in scholastic Protestantism and the deistic Enlightenment which also expressed Christian praxis as a matter of ethics, having cessationistically filtered supernatural components from Luke-Acts and Paul. Ruthven, "'Imitation of Christ' in Christian Tradition," 64, suggests that "With the restriction of the miraculous to the first century on the one hand, and the emphasis on Christianity as morality that developed later, the profile of traditional Christian discipleship was set."

21. These ecclesiastical but unlikely biblical backgrounds are kept alive before the English-speaking Evangelical public through the marketing of the old and new editions of the KJV and NIV Scofield Bible. This dispensationally based tome uncritically propagates, without curiosity for authorial intent and narrative continuity, the traditional "once-for-all" osmosis theory of Lukan cessation, to wit, "For the Christian to go back to Luke 11:13 is to forget Pentecost," cf. English et al., *New Scofield Reference Bible*, 1097. As to Pauline cessationism, English et al. make no attempt to correct the still-popular claim among Evangelicals that the τὸ τέλειον (that which is perfect or complete, 1 Cor 13:10) is the Bible, but rationally encourage it with the unexamined assertion that "Until the NT was written, new revelations suited to the new dispensation were given; tongues and the sign gifts are to cease" (1245). A counterbalance to their theories is offered in similar format by Adams et al., *Full Life Study Bible*, recently revised and retitled as *Life in the Spirit Study Bible* (2003) to complement Arrington and Stronstad, *Life in the Spirit New Testament Commentary*. The *Study Bible* itself is published by Gospel Publishing House (Springfield, MO) in Chinese, Indonesian, Polish, Portuguese, Romanian, Russian, Spanish and Ukrainian, with twenty-six languages pending (Arabic, Czechoslovakian, French, Hindi, Swahili, and Tamil, for example).

perceived environment, a cognitive environmental appraisal that all of my Evangelical friends might not completely share, I offer several reflections after five years of participation with scholars within the Evangelical Theological Society (ETS)[22] focusing on "Charismatic Themes in Luke-Acts and Related Issues."

Discussion, Observations, and Testimony[23]

Luke's second treatise, dubbed the book of Acts, would probably have been considered by his Graeco-Roman literary contemporaries, who were seeking further experientially practical information about Christianity, to be a narrative-rhetorically adroit and pastorally applicable exemplar about what the heavenly Jesus continues to do, about his deeds, given that the first treatise describes what the earthly Jesus did and taught (Acts 1:1). The second book could certainly not have been considered by Luke to be entitled "The Acts of the Apostles," given that it contains no detailed account of any of the apostles except Peter and Paul. John is mentioned briefly on only three occasions, James the son of Zebedee is executed, and much more space is devoted to Stephen and Philip, who are not apostles, than to John and James, similarly for Timothy and Silas.

While understood to be a Gospel of the Spirit by some of its greatest students (here I think of Augustin George and Arnold Ehrhardt),[24] its compositional strengths have been undermined and marginalized in their effect (*Wirkungskraft*) by the long-term superimposition and undeclared presumption of an "apostolic age." The main Lukan theme of prophetic fulfillment[25] and the twin focus upon examples and precedents as displayed via an experiential nexus of salvation/forgiveness/repentance/

---

22. For informative purposes it may be noted that the Evangelical Theological Society has met annually since 1949. ETS consists mainly of a group of North American scholars who doctrinally emphasize biblical inerrancy. Lukan and Pauline cessationisms are prominent traditions among many of its members. Scofieldian editors MacRae and Walvoord are past presidents of ETS. Biblical and theological discussion is characterized by the society in the following manner: "Very rewarding is the experience of subjecting one's own ideas to the criticisms of colleagues who are not only sympathetic but judicious," cf. "Purpose Statement" at http://www.etsjests.org. However, for ETS members whose research interests may not lie in the mainstream of the predominate doctrinal and traditional backgrounds, sympathetic and judicious criticism may not be all that reflective or rewarding. If research interests are perceived as too far from the ETS center of gravity, "criticisms of colleagues" may be less than hospitable as a recurring impulse of excommunicating and disfellowshipping has demonstrated.

23. Let me take this opportunity to thank my Pentecostal colleagues who have served as an advisory board to the Luke-Acts ETS study group and have participated by reading papers: Jim Shelton, my co-worker, together with Ben Aker, Trevor Grizzle, Charles Holman, and Roger Stronstad. In addition to the aforementioned colleagues on the advisory board, other Pentecostal colleagues lent a hand with presentations: Ken Archer, Harold Carpenter, Craig Keener, Julie Ma, Wonsuk Ma, and Keith Warrington. Our Evangelical colleagues whose responses have been gratefully appreciated include Gregg Allison, Bill Larkin, and I. Howard Marshall.

24. George, *Études sur l'oeuvre de Luc*, 500–542; Chevallier, "Luc et l'Esprit Saint," 1–19; Ehrhardt, "Construction and Purpose," 45–79.

25. As recently summarized by Frein, "Prophecies and Luke's Sense of Fulfilment," 22–37.

faith/conversion[26] and via praying for and receiving the gift of the Holy Spirit/being baptized in the Spirit/being filled with the Spirit[27] are matters of comparatively little reflection among ETS attendees today. Luke's soteriological nexus and his Spirit-reception nexus, both masterfully illustrated via examples and precedents, remain unrecognized as narrative-rhetorical requirements. Particularly, Lukan portrayals of Spirit-reception remain locked in a frozen paleo-Reformed time capsule, dismissed as nothing more than historical oddities, instigating a "once-for-all" process of osmosis that trickles down through time to other Christians. Such a perspective may seem confirmed as well by the chapter and paragraph divisions in modern editions of the Greek New Testament (GNT), which do not adequately, and sometimes very inadequately, reflect the thematic emphases of Luke's text and the activity of the Holy Spirit in the text.[28] To think otherwise about these Lukan portrayals of Spirit-reception and their connection to the ministry of the earthly Jesus challenges the Evangelical view that the Holy Spirit is only genuinely at work in Evangelical Christianity within its own focus on revival.[29] However, it may be that gradually, in time, the investigations of biblical scholars in the Pentecostal/charismatic tradition will make these aforementioned Lukan themes more widely considered.[30]

The letters of Paul, albeit with expressions rooted in the Jerusalem/Petrine tradition of past Spirit-reception and Spirit-giving being traditionally eclipsed, have dominated Evangelical discussion for centuries. But demographics are changing within world Christendom. Comparatively as of now, with respect to Evangelicalism,

26. Regarding Lukan conversion, cf. Michiels, "La conception lucanienne de la conversion," 42–78.

27. For discussion of these main thematic categories, cf. Elbert, *Lukan Gift of the Holy Spirit*.

28. Codex Sinaiticus, where the title Acts (Πραξεις) first appears in the NT manuscript tradition to introduce Luke's second treatise, both Codex Vaticanus and Sinaiticus appending ΠΡΑΞΕΙΣ ΑΠΟΣΤΟΛΩΝ as a decorative colophon at the end of the text, exhibits 293 paragraph or section breaks. The current United Bible Societies' Greek New Testament (GNT) reduces this rhetorical effort of 293 to 148, where of course twenty-eight of these begin what that GNT takes as appropriate chapter divisions. Of the 148 paragraph/chapter breaks in this modern edition of the GNT, eighty-seven receive appellations or entitlements by the editors. Only three of these mention the Holy Spirit. This rhetorically insufficient labeling needs to be addressed in future editions.

29. This exclusiveness is also noted by Hocken, "Is Renewal of the Church Possible?," 199. Hocken is also well aware that this particular manifestation of Evangelical exclusivity, with its roots in a paleoreformed paradigm, is potentially dangerous: "Where these rationalist patterns are operative in the realm of theology they cannot help but be reductionist in their effects—taking a richer reality and filtering it through a theological grid that eliminates non-rational, non-logical elements, even at the same time protesting vigorously against those who utilize the same *Zeitgeist* in more blatantly unbelieving ways," cf. his "Charismatic View," 105.

30. In spite of the real threat of the evangelicalization of Pentecostalism with respect to interpretive method, it may be that Lukan scholarship will eventually sense the scholarly impact of these themes if they become further articulated from within the Pentecostal/charismatic tradition. However, it would be unwise to overlook the potential danger of the evangelicalization of Pentecostal reflection and research. Clark Pinnock worries thusly: "What concerns me about Pentecostal theology is that certain evangelicals may infect Pentecostal work with an unrelational virus, hamper Pentecostal theological development and diminish Pentecostal vitality. I fear that Evangelicals may sneeze and Pentecostals catch cold" cf. his "Divine Relationality," 22.

the Pentecostal/charismatic Renewal has only a few scholars, while demographically it has many more adherents. The scholarly ratio between Evangelicalism and this New Reformation could, in time, change and even reverse. Given this projection, scholars intrinsically unwedded to and untutored in "apostolic age" hermeneutics will supervise research dissertations, thereby having the luxury of gaining much needed assistance from their pupils on biblical matters of interest to those with Treebeard's perspective.

While it is now suggested by some that the anonymous writer of the double-work at the heart of the NT has a theology and a pneumatology that probably reflects a widespread early tradition totally alien to "apostolic age" hermeneutics, a tradition accepted and understood by Paul, not distinctive from Paul; such thinking has had little formal impact on ministerial training outside of the global Pentecostal movement and the international charismatic Renewal. While it is clear that Lukan characters in his first book who participate in his soteriological nexus of repentance/faith/forgiveness/salvation are characters who experience the Spirit through Jesus's own anointing and who experience the Father who welcomes sinners, a narrative inference probably taken to be obvious by Luke, it is characterization and personification with respect to the heavenly Jesus and the Holy Spirit that is finally developed in his second book that has undergone an "apostolic age" style of truncation. However, in a modicum of intellectual movement within some Evangelicalism today one may detect some unease with cessationism (abrupt or gradual dispensational closure following enscripturation) and a corresponding more fashionable awareness that "all the Pauline spiritual gifts are for today."[31] Within ETS itself this is apparently not in a context of a response to Pentecostalism or the charismatic Renewal, nor is it in any direct engagement with scholarship treating this subject;[32] rather it would perhaps appear to be demographically driven, or tolerated, if the lack of papers to this effect at annual meetings be a guide. If this detection is now credible as a minor intellectual trend within ETS, it probably does not yet reflect an upsurge among some Evangelical scholars to zealously and actively seek the interpersonal gifts,[33] as I believe Paul intended those addressees to do whom he described as "receiving the Spirit," but instead reflects an admission that, rationally,

---

31. Sam Storms, a charismatic scholar, in his *The Beginner's Guide to Spiritual Gifts*, highlights the ceasing of Pauline cessationism and offers a helpful popular journey into this material. However, in terms of linking Paul's brief discussion of the *charismata* to the tradition underlying Paul's thought to the Jerusalem/Petrine tradition in which he stands, I find that the earlier treatment by Horton, *Gifts of the Spirit*, offers more NT contextuality in that he evidently eschews the incoherence of Lukan cessationism in disconnecting the Lukan Paul from the Paul of the Letters.

32. As, for example, Schürmann, "Die geistlichen Gnadengaben in den paulinischen Gemeinden," 236–67.

33. There are certainly exceptions to this slumber by Evangelical scholars who never bought into the traditional dogma of Calvin's extraordinary-ordinary dichotomies in the first place, cf. the vigorous reflections of Klass Runia, Emeritus Professor of Practical Theology for the Reformed Churches, Kampen, the Netherlands, *Op zoek naar de Geest*, with a review by Cornelius van der Laan.

they can (or may) exist.[34] While the idea that spiritual gifts experientially detected and cataloged by Paul are for interpersonal giving or transmission between believers today is not an integral part of the gospel as portrayed by the Evangelists,[35] it is nevertheless a compromise between the rationalism and suspicion of the past and the demographic trends of today.[36] This idea allows scholars who otherwise ignore Acts theologically and pneumatologically to speculate that certain selected events narrated in Acts may be described in Pauline language. When a Lukan character prophesies or has a vision, a Pauline spiritual gift is quickly adduced, not the contextual Lukan gift of the Spirit or prior Spirit-reception within the narrative continuity of Luke's fulfillment-of-prophecy theme. We will probably see this kind of speculation continue for a time until it begins to become clear that Luke has a pneumatology reflective of the Christians he writes about and that this pneumatology is to be found sequentially in his own double-work, not in Paul's occasional discursive correspondence, which, I have argued, Luke is attempting to clarify, perhaps with some pastoral urgency, with respect to practical matters like Spirit-reception. However, the wholesale interpretation of Luke through Pauline spectacles is probably coming to an end.[37]

What then about our past seminar work within ETS? How did this begin and why does it continue? The former editor of *JETS*, Ronald Youngblood, and I had a good working relationship, even though my first *JETS* piece on the Spirit in Matthew probably engendered the biggest "ho hum" in the history of the society.[38] But we are not dialoging with senior OT scholars like Ronald or sympathetic NT scholars like

---

34. This rational admission should be understood in its historical setting. When Williams, in his "Upsurge of Pentecostalism," 341, asserted that Pentecostalism had rediscovered "a dimension of the Holy Spirit's activity that had been long overlooked," Williams realized full well that this dimension is not captured by the occasional use of an interpersonal spiritual fruit or gift. Further, and this is significant in understanding the trend of admission, in much traditional Reformed/Evangelical scholarship the experiential and/or supernatural elements in Pauline descriptions of interpersonal spiritual gifts has been supplanted by natural perspectives. This is illustrated by Thomas, *Understanding Spiritual Gifts*, along with my review drawing needed attention to the potential introduction of a new divinity unknown to NT writers, courageously printed by Ronald Youngblood, former *JETS* editor. Thomas is a past president of ETS.

35. In saying this, let me clarify by noting that love or charity is not a gift category in Paul, but rather the underlying motivation for seeking and participating in the spiritual practice of a gift process.

36. Cf. the clarification suggested by Aker, "Charismata," 53–69.

37. I am speculating a diminuendo in this approach in spite of yet new theories to recast the Holy Spirit as a clone of a new divinity familiar to Paul, a supposed "spirit of prophecy." This approach will also, in my judgment, have little long-term impact, coupled as it is with the supposed pastoral irrelevancy attributed to Lukan portrayals with delicate variations of Spirit-reception by believer-disciple-witnesses, cessationism that is imposed before Luke picked up his pen.

38. Elbert, "Perfect Tense in Matthew 16:19 and Three Charismata," 149–53. As far as I know, only one ETS member interacted with me (in disagreement) in a Matthew commentary. My suggestion in this study supports the idea that Matthew delineated the difference between the ministry of the earthly Jesus and the heavenly Jesus (cf. Matt 11:28; 28:20b) in terms of revelatory activity from the heavenly Jesus, an idea unharmonious with the proposition that revelation is confined to enscripturation.

Norbert Baumert[39] or with ecclesiastical representatives having charismatic clientele to consider, but with scholars who, with rare exceptions, have not yet actually decided to engage directly in dialogue at all.[40] Perhaps the current trend within ETS is dismissive of scholars who write against dispensational traditions, claiming that to connect Spirit-filling to prophetic inspiration makes illegitimate use of Luke's now supposedly defunct examples and precedents,[41] and further that there are "no scriptural records of 'carnal' Christians shedding their substantial Christian experience by yielding their lives entirely to God" as in the dreaded "second blessing theology."[42]

Against this background, the Lord knew I needed some motivation to get interaction going within ETS, although ETS management has been hospitable. This motivation was not a pleasant experience, but he has kindly let me know subsequent to the first revelatory motivation I am about to describe, that He is pleased with our efforts in the midst of difficulties. I have shared this revelation with several people, believing that collective judgment of revelation is wise and helps get to the right understanding. At first, I did not understand what was revealed to me, the unworthy sinner that I surely am, but now I believe that I do. At the home of a friend in Atlanta, I was standing in his living room when the Lord surrounded me with his presence in an awesome manner. Then strong thoughts entered my mind. Something was dead. This death was very serious and awful. I was somewhat frightened and

---

39. Baumert, *Charisma, Taufe, Geisttaufe*, might provide another perspective for our potential dialogue partners who have inherited the interpretive method responsible for Lukan and Pauline cessationism.

40. As far as I can tell, both the recent Catholic-Pentecostal Dialogue and the recent Reformed-Pentecostal Dialogue are virtually unknown within ETS today, cf. "Evangelization, Proselytism and Common Witness," and "Word and Spirit, Church and Word," 105–51, and 41–72, respectively. Also, apparently little known and uninvestigated by the majority of ETS clientele at present is Menzies and Menzies, *Spirit and Power*.

41. Examples and precedents are very much a part of the narrative qualities expected by a competent narrative performance, properly illustrative of the virtues of clarity and plausibility within narrative persuasion, as highly touted by Luke's contemporary, Theon of Alexandria, cf. Patillon, *Aelius Théon Progymnasmata*.

42. This logic is espoused by the current editor of *JETS*, cf. Köstenberger, "What Does It Mean?," 231. Köstenberger ignores the larger NT picture that might be gained with reference, for example, to Stronstad, *Charismatic Theology of St. Luke,* and to Menzies, *Empowered for Witness*. While Köstenberger begins with Ephesians 5:18, it is exegetically insensitive and extractionary to disconnect language found within the Ephesian letter from its earlier background in the ministry of Paul at Tyrannus' school and from the Spirit-reception by disciple-believers at Ephesus. Köstenberger fails to account for the connections between the text of the letter and that of Acts, connections that are also chronologically significant in light of Paul's relation to Jerusalem/Petrine tradition. Perhaps then Köstenberger's reluctance to countenance or to adequately consider Spirit-filling as portrayed by Luke is influenced by undeclared presuppositions stemming from an "apostolic age," which is inimical to both Paul and Luke. Further, some fair and balanced interaction with scholars on Ephesians 5:18 who do not adopt Köstenberger's extractionist perspective might not have been inappropriate, e.g., Markus Barth in the commentary tradition, and Ervin, *These Are Not Drunken As Ye Suppose*, 74–78; Stronstad, *Charismatic Theology of St. Luke,* 53–55. It may be fairly observed as well that Köstenberger's tactic of dismissing Stronstad by misquoting him is unlikely to be ultimately persuasive.

stood motionless awaiting anything further. My friend stopped talking to me. Then it was repeated; death was serious and had serious effects. Where was this death? The death of what? Of whom? I moved about in the room as if to escape what was being revealed to me, but it came again. I told my friend that something was happening to me. Then, the death was made clear. It was how a certain idea or subject was evaluated, was considered, not on earth where I was, but in heaven. Something is dead in heaven. I moved again. It was very strong and understandable then. Cessationism is dead in heaven. It is not just another bad idea among humankind, but cessationism is dead in heaven. At first, I thought someone had died or was about to die, but that was wrong;[43] the revelation concerned a topic, that topic was cessationism, and cessationism is dead where it really counts, in heaven itself. God dislikes it intensely and I have to conclude that it is now, and has been in the past, regarded in heaven as not just unhelpful, but dangerous.

So, while Evangelicals may claim that "Pentecostal" experience is unrepeatable and cannot be found in Luke's second book and cannot have any connection with his first book, and that in order to countenance experience according to Lukan descriptions we also have to have new Incarnations, these cessationistic proclamations are not as applicable to "all who are afar off" as their proponents believe them to be. Such proponents seem unaware that the "Lord's Prayer," the "Our Father," the "Apostles' Creed," and the "Nicene Creed" do indeed eclipse and ignore the fully developed teaching of the earthly Jesus on prayer and hide his other important teachings and doings, as Moltmann has recently pointed out with respect to the latter two ecclesiastical conceptions.[44] Since the Lord knew I was about to leave for an ETS meeting, He chose to motivate me in this unpleasant way that I would not easily forget. Also, recently, at my home church, where absolutely none of the above is known or even conceived of, a straightforward prophecy which I do not despise made it clear that there was someone present who had made an agreement with the Lord and the Lord expected that contract to be fulfilled.[45] While of course that could apply to others, the Spirit impressed

---

43. The need for community evaluation is critical, cf. Goldingay, "Old Testament Prophecy Today," 44–46; Ellis, "Prophecy in the New Testament Church—and Today," 57.

44. Moltmann, *Der Weg Jesu Christi*, 171.

45. Prophetic information such as this today is fully consistent with the function of prophecy in Luke's narrative and with the ministry of characters like Philip's prophesying daughters (Acts 21:8–9). The fact that these prophetesses do not speak in the narrative does not mean that Luke and Paul, who visited Philip's home, did not listen to their ministries or that Luke was not impressed enough to recall and record what their ministries might have been. Their silence in his story merely reflects the probability that their ministry was not useful for Luke's purpose, although his mention of their ministry was deemed useful in that it connects with his understanding and version of the ongoing gender-insensitive fulfillment of Joel's programmatic prophecy (Acts 2:16–21). *I suggest that Luke did not find it useful for his purpose to quote from or record any prophetic ministry of these prophesying daughters, just like he did not find it useful for his purpose to quote from or cite any written ministry from Paul's discursive correspondence.* Would Paul tell Philip and his four prophesying daughters that they were not to speak when believers gathered for worship? *Such an understanding of the Lukan Paul is of course absurd and utterly unacceptable*, cf. Elbert, "Globalization of Pentecostalism," 98–99. Such a

upon me right then that this information was for me, because, and this was part of the guidance, I had been thinking about discontinuing the ETS ministry, which, for now at least, should be continued in the face of any discouragement. So, I was given some resolve, which in the natural was difficult to find. For example, when a combative questioner aggressively pointed out that my analysis of the Lukan composition of questions like that posed in Acts 19:2a to disciple-believers,[46] in that instance supported by the complementary exegesis of Lake, Cadbury, Hemer, Ehrhardt, Stuhlmacher, Wolter and Zahn with respect to the narratively consistent Christianity of the twelve Ephesians in Acts 19:1 in the eyes of both Luke and Paul, had to be wrong because the great cessationist grammarian, A. T. Robertson, had made a quick uninvestigated dogmatic remark to the contrary, I was calm when responding at length to that questioner. And, as it happened, that same questioner showed up the next day throughout the entire Luke-Acts session, where he remained silent.

Let me close with some personal reminiscences that may be representative of other fellow participants as well; I hope these will be encouraging, perhaps informative, perhaps illuminating. As to the dominance of protecting an established position, particularly one built on the cessationistic and rationalistic assurances stemming from "apostolic" or other "ages" and diverse epochs superimposed presuppositionally upon the text of Luke-Acts at various points, one scholar from Gordon-Conwell Theological Seminary asked Howard Marshall and me to state what we believed Luke to mean by the gift of the Holy Spirit. This question allowed me to restate that, for Luke, characters in his first book were deliberately portrayed as having entered into a faith/forgiveness/repentance/salvation experiential nexus during the ministry of the earthly Jesus; further, for Luke, the gift of the Holy Spirit reflected and built upon an ongoing Jerusalem/Petrine tradition, phenomenologically and narratively. It was, for Luke, certainly not just an unspecific Jewish blessing, not something to be given a reinterpretive shredding, as in current Evangelical commentaries employing "apostolic age" style (à la Darby, imitated recently, for example, by Joel Green[47]), so as to

---

misunderstanding of Paul cannot be varnished over, just as it cannot be harmonized with an interpretation of Paul's discursive correspondence which alleges that Spirit-filled women were to remain quiet when believers gathered. Such a misrepresentation of Paul does not begin with the Lukan Paul or with the women that Luke portrays or with the women that the Paul of the Letters describes. This misrepresentation does not seek, and historically has not sought, to understand Paul in his prophetic setting as we know it, either narratively or discursively. It is simply a wrongheaded and rhetorically insensitive reading of Paul. It is an "apostolic age" reading. *This interpretation, claiming that Spirit-filled women in the Jerusalem/Petrine tradition, in the Lukan and Pauline tradition, should not preach, a ministry consistent with their prophetic talents, must be discarded by Pentecostals in recognition of the ecclesiastically conforming non-Lukan and non-Pauline tradition that lies behind it.* To misrepresent Paul in this way is a tragic distortion of his teaching, conjuring up a cessationistic Paul that Luke never knew.

46. Elbert, "Observation on Luke's Composition," 98–109. In this study the 152 questions in Luke's first book and the seventy in his second book are analyzed in terms of their narrative connectedness and function in light of the Graeco-Roman literary conventions of narrative-rhetorical composition.

47. In Darbian style of "apostolic age hermeneutics" the tactic is twofold: first, to extract the content of Luke 11:13 from the immediately preceding teaching of the earthly Jesus on prayer, then, to

brazenly—in the paleo-Reformed style of "apostolic age hermeneutics"—disconnect the gift of the Holy Spirit at Luke 11:13 from both its narrative foreground and its ensuing development and clarification, reducing it to "what is for the best" or what is nice.[48] This is not biblical interpretation in any logical sense, but merely a pious exercise in the repetitious imitation of the philosophical proclivities of Calvinistic hermeneutics (n19 above). I reviewed the point that, for Luke, the gift of the Holy Spirit was not salvific, but an expected answer to prayer by Christian believers (in concert on this point with, for example, Giblet, Gunkel, Marguerat, Martin, Menzies,

---

reinterpret the gift of the Holy Spirit in Luke's narrative by injecting pleasant speculation supportive of the hidden hermeneutical presupposition of an "apostolic age." This is recently illustrated again by Green, *Gospel of Luke*, 459, who denies outright the persuasive parabolic teaching of the earthly Jesus presented by Luke, assuring his Evangelical readers that "Even if the supplications included no request of the Spirit, God grants the Spirit." *On this method of interpretation, why should obedient prayer in response to Jesus's teaching at Luke 11:2–4 not be similarly dismissed?* Whether Green's contradiction of the earthly Jesus's teaching on prayer is offensive to the heavenly Jesus is apparently of little or no concern, suggesting that the heavenly Jesus portrayed by Luke not only forgets the teaching of the earthly Jesus on prayer to disciple-believer-witnesses, but that this heavenly Jesus himself is transformed into the new Dispensational Jesus. That the heavenly Jesus in Luke's second book is portrayed without any hint of such an "apostolic age"-driven transformation to the divine is, again, apparently of little or no concern. Green, continuing the tactic, converts the narratively contiguous gift of the Holy Spirit in Luke's clearly written texts into the reassuring platitude, "what is for the best" (450)—*fait accompli*! Such obvious and blatantly uncritical reinterpretive shredding, which is offered by scholars without apology, is all the more spectacular given the Evangelical claim to biblical inerrancy, authority, and trustworthiness. *It is quite apparent that none of these concepts in themselves carries enough weight to persuade or to embolden Evangelical scholars, over time, to reverse the more powerful, dogmatic, and insolent grip of hidden and undeclared "apostolic age" presuppositions that have dominated Lukan interpretation in the Reformed tradition.*

48. The cessationistic eclipse or pietistic reinterpretation of the gift of the Holy Spirit, and the propensity to disconnect prayer for the gift of the Holy Spirit from its narrative context, undoubtedly influenced by the ingrained "apostolic age" method of interpretation wherein Luke's second book is approached with the unarticulated assumptions of narrative disconnectedness inherent in Reformed-style *Heilsgeschichte* without *Pneumageschichte*, is a well-established tradition. This "apostolic age hermeneutic" appears grounded in the experience (or nonexperience) of interpreters, not in the experience of Lukan characters, given that Luke, consistent with the narrative-rhetorical conventions of his day, provides a clear and vivid phenomenological description of the gift and of the events, characters, places, and times in which the gift appears. Further, Luke's description places the gift firmly within his theme of prophetic fulfillment, allowing readers to anticipate the gift for themselves. Clarity and vividness are appropriately enhanced by a constellation of co-descriptions, further contributing to Lukan expectations and anticipation on the part of readers. All of this literary performance is closely consistent with the Graeco-Roman narrative-rhetorical category of description (*ekphrasis*) as delineated by Theon (Patillon, *Aelius Théon Progymnasmata*, xxxviii–ix, 66–69) and similar treatises, cf. Hunger, "Progymnasmata und andere Übungsreden" 1:92–120, and Hunger, "Ekphraseis," 1:170–88. *Luke's coherent and ostensibly "Theonic" literary performance in this regard is ignored, a performance to be expected in a rhetorically minded culture, by the extraction of the gift of the Holy Spirit from its multiple narrative contexts and its non-Lukan reinterpretation as "what is for the best."* The erasure of coherent and consistent narrative meaning by the traditional and unexamined paleo-Reformed style of "apostolic age hermeneutics" applied to the Lukan gift of the Holy Spirit is clearly an erasure quite out of place with narrative-rhetorical expectations in Theophilus's literary world (or in any interpretive world where an author's and an addressee's expectations are taken seriously).

Russell, Schweizer, Shelton, Sullivan; *contra* Dunn, Turner).[49] Perhaps Luke would be disappointed to learn how Christians in later centuries would reinterpret the gift of the Holy Spirit, extracting it from his narrative, reinterpreting it as they told their own story instead of Luke's story. Logically, the Lukan gift of the Holy Spirit is connected to the rest of the narrative in which it appears; it is sequentially connected to the rest of Luke's narrative.[50] A scholar from the Reformed Theological Seminary, who had joined me for lunch the previous day, then became somewhat upset and assured me that my interpretation was far too experiential and that any experience associated with such Lukan language could not now be biblical and would create insurmountable problems because the experience of reading might lose significance. In other words, the experience of reading a text might then be accompanied by the same experience that characters have in the text. This appears to be the same fear that the primacy of written revelation makes natural theology dangerous and illegitimate[51] and is related to the tension created by the exclusive primacy of *Sola Scriptura* versus a motif of *In Spiritu Sancto*, with experiential fellowship and inspiration in the Jerusalem/Petrine tradition.[52] When I pointed out that an insurmountable problem does not obviously follow, both experiences (reading and Spirit-reception) being equally valid but simply different, noting that we might want also to be aware of the fact that, for Luke, what Jesus spoke, not what Luke wrote, was the "word of God," a description which Luke would never apply to his own work, a stony silence ensued. So, as is the case with other human endeavors, the first encounter with information seemingly contradictory to an

---

49. Some details of this review may be found in my *Lukan Gift of the Holy Spirit*. See also chapter 9 in this volume. With regard to the former scholars on this point, cf. Giblet, "Baptism in the Spirit in the Acts of the Apostles," 162–71; Gunkel, *Influence of the Holy Spirit*; Marguerat, *First Christian Historian*; Martin, "Le baptême dans l'Esprit," 23–58; Menzies, *Development of Early Christian Pneumatology*; Russell, "'They Believed Philip Preaching' (Acts 8.12)," 169–76; Eduard Schweizer, "πνευμα κτλ," *TDNT* 6:389–455; Schweizer, *Heiliger Geist*; Shelton, *Mighty in Word and Deed*; Sullivan, *Charisms and Charismatic Renewal*; Sullivan, *Charismes et renouveau charismatique*. With regard to Dunn and Turner, see the critique of their positions in Menzies and Menzies, *Spirit and Power*, 69–86, and 87–106, respectively.

50. Cantalamessa, *Mystery of Pentecost*, 30, is correct to pastorally point out that Jesus says the heavenly Father will "give the Holy Spirit to those who ask him" (Luke 11:13). Similar in pastoral intent are Christenson, *Welcome, Holy Spirit*, 85, and Rooney and Faricy, *Lord, Teach Us to Pray*, 84–91, 103. Cantalamessa, Christenson, Rooney, and Faricy continue in the Pentecostal tradition and in the tradition of Augustin George, who stressed that "le don de l'Esprit est le don par excellence" (*Études sur l'oeuvre de Luc*, 412). On the other hand, perhaps the *pervasive erasure* of the Lukan gift of the Holy Spirit within Evangelicalism today is typified by Liefeld, "Parables on Prayer (Luke 11:5–13; 18:1–14)," 240–62, who *fails even to mention* the obvious connection of the gift of the Holy Spirit in the climactic crescendo of Jesus's instruction at verse 13 with the rest of the section (5–12), literally ignoring verse 13 altogether!

51. Polkinghorne, "Theism," 71.

52. That inspiration is better than information, opening better the door to transformation, was pointed out to me by my colleague Lee Roy Martin.

established position can be met with incredulous disbelief, but eventually, if thoughtfulness is given a chance, it might be considered.[53]

One ETS scholar assured me that if texts were interpreted so as to expect experiential events to occur again as they did in the "apostolic age," then we would be left at the mercy of subjectivism. Our role as rational beings would be diminished, and we would be in "bondage." This bondage was no good because it would supplant the experience of reading Scripture—it would compete with written truth. Jack Deere's bondage of a bible deist was unheard of.[54] Would thoughtful dialogue assist in relieving this perceived "bondage," I asked? No way! Bondage was bondage and that was that. For some, the presumptuous claim of automatic divine action through the ecclesiastical administration of sacraments, combined with the cessation of the supernatural following enscripturation, may serve to make Lukan experiential portrayal suspect and bring it into serious question, even though consistent with NT language.[55]

53. Perhaps another way to understand our situation, and I do not take the analogy as a perfect parallel, is to keep in mind that heliocentricity took several hundred years to replace geocentricity on the library shelves of Europe. The interpretation of a stationary earth, like the earlier interpretation of a flat earth, had a comfortable and understandable charm to its Christian adherents. Challenges to stationary-earth theology appeared unrealistic, counterintuitive, unnecessary, divisive, and disturbing. A new physical perspective was needed to understand this challenge to established "biblical" interpretation. Perhaps similarly, "apostolic age hermeneutics" is being challenged today by a new biblical hermeneutic incorporating an experiential paradigm, as well as by a fresh literary appreciation of connectedness and coherency. A new spiritual perspective may be needed to understand this challenge.

54. Cf. Deere's *Surprised by the Voice of God*, 251–69. As to Deere's recent books, one ETS member, representative of unreflective position protection that is closed to dialogue and dissent, reflective of an unfortunate lack of enjoyment with the very vigorous exploratory dissent and interactive debate that is standard fare in the scientific tradition, declared that "We don't want to hear that message, and we don't want to hear it from Deere!"

55. For those in the charismatic Renewal not wedded to the supposed connection between cessationism and enscripturation, a pneumatological ecclesiology (*une ecclésiologie pneumatologique*), correcting the presumptuous sacramental insistence of automatic divine action, would be beneficial. In my judgment, the sovereignty of the Holy Spirit is ill-considered in assuming that sacraments are automatically an ecclesial means of grace, clerically transmitted if ministers are Spirit-filled, as does Congar, "Pneumatologie dogmatique," 2:496. However, Congar's critical efforts toward a pneumatological ecclesiology are to be applauded, cf. Kizhakkeparampil, *Invocation of the Holy Spirit*. The pursuit of a flexible ecclesiology, stressing the freedom of the Spirit, is unharmonious with a tightly constrained sacramental mindset and has little difficulty in describing contemporary NT experience with NT language.

On the other hand, J. I. Packer's claim that charismatic experience cannot be described with NT language, and is therefore "deeply unbiblical," may be challenged and corrected as well, cf. my "Charismatic Movement," 28–33. Packer, undeterred, in a lecture at Rutherford House, Edinburgh, entitled "Charismatic Christianity and Biblical Theology," fails even to surface the possibility that Calvin's arbitrary confinement of the Lukan gift of the Holy Spirit at Acts 2:38, 39 to an artificially devised epoch is quite openly not biblical theology, a point highly germane to his topic. Perhaps this is not surprising since in this lecture he never refers to the narrative theology of Luke-Acts, bypassing Luke-Acts totally, while continuing to mischaracterize the Pentecostal/charismatic movement as a bogus restoration of "sign-gifts." According to Packer any second work of grace (that is, any certain experience viewed from the natural perspective of suspicion) cannot then stem from doctrine nor be described by well-fitting NT texts, new prophetic revelation is nonexistent, supposed "sign-gifts"

Another sincere scholar shared that he does not believe that rationalism exists within Evangelicalism today. It is not subservience to human preconceptions of arbitrary epochs superimposed upon NT texts or anti-supernaturalism or skepticism or the outright denial and/or dismissal of the examples and precedents that Luke sets out in clear detail; rather there is some other factor at work. What then is that factor? Well, he is not sure, but it is not rationalism. Perhaps there are mysterious circumstances afoot other than politics. This sincere scholar wants to actively encourage the usefulness of the book of Acts within Evangelicalism, with main prophetic experiential themes traditionally dampened while emphasizing missions in general terms, hoping that Acts' missionary purpose will not continue to be overlooked and that it will not be employed in sermons to score only moral and ethical points or in classrooms to only argue for historicity and inerrancy. But does not this disconnect the Lukan missionary characters from their narrative world? Might it not be better at this point in time to prepare missionaries in the original version of the Lukan tradition, like, for example, Elva Vanderbout[56] or Elize Scharten[57] or theological educator Alice Luce?[58]

---

are not restored even though the movement's "theological roots" supposedly lie therein (a patently false claim), and everything is satisfactorily explainable via Romans 8:16 and John 14:21–23. *It does seem odd, however, that a Christocentric global movement should develop within a century into a major sector of world Christendom with such scant biblical credentials.* In any case, as Packer well knows, the movement he is discussing did not advance, and is not advancing, along these lines, perhaps a bothersome fact best ignored, similar to how a circular sun and a circular moon were ignored in flat-earth theology based on the four corners passage (Rev 7:1).

56. Ma, "Elva Vanderbout," 121–40.

57. Laan, "Beyond the Clouds," 337–57.

58. Alice E. Luce, formerly an Anglican missionary to India, became a pioneer teacher, evangelist, and dedicated pastor in Hispanic missions. Some of the written legacy of this pioneer theological educator is as follows: "From the Mexican Border," *The Weekly Evangel* (April 28, 1917), 12; "Open Doors in Mexico," *The Weekly Evangel* (Nov 17, 1917), 13; "Mexican Work in California," *The Christian Evangel* (Dec 14, 1918), 14; "Deaf and Dumb Child in Mexico Healed," *The Pentecostal Evangel* (Feb 20, 1932), 11. A rewarding perusal of Luce's contributions, contributions obviously spiritually rich and biblically oriented, during the tenure of her Latin American missionary work makes it clear that her understanding of the NT was not at all a foreground of the fragmented contemporary popularization among some Evangelicals that "not all of the Pauline spiritual gifts are for today." Rather, her written ministry and its lack of appeal to the rationalistic charm of diverse epochs and their heritage of disconnectedness could serve as a refreshing popular balm for the excision of the Paul of the Letters from the complete Lukan Paul and from the Jerusalem/Petrine tradition, other than to argue that Paul's conversion influenced his Christology. As may be observed in her excellent biblical and pastorally able piece "Physical Manifestations of the Spirit" (*The Pentecostal Evangel* [July 27, 1918], 2), she did not just teach only about spiritual gifts, but also appealed to "The Great Physician and His medicine" (*The Pentecostal Evangel* [Sept 6, 1930], 6). Her Christocentric, balanced approach included expectant prayer that regarded the heavenly Jesus as a Savior connected to the earthly Jesus, as a baptizer in the Holy Spirit in accord with prayerful Lukan expectations and sequential narrative portrayal, and as a sovereign healer. She evidently felt in the latter category, for example, contrary to the dictates of "apostolic age hermeneutics" wherein the healing ministry of the earthly Jesus is simply unique, didactic, and "once-for-all," that the merciful, compassionate, and curative dimension of the ministry of the earthly Jesus extended prayerfully to the heavenly Jesus. Further research on Alice Luce may be assisted by the Flower Pentecostal Heritage Center (www.AGHeritage.org).

Another scholar pointed out that we could hardly expect the "Pentecostal" type events in Acts to have been repeated and thereby to have given rise to the same descriptive language that Luke and his contemporaries would later employ and experientially understand.[59] I would expect that most ETS scholars are quite unaware of Thomas Manson's reasonable assumption that the Spirit-reception language employed by Paul has obvious linguistic roots in the Christian heritage which Paul respects and seeks to continue. Linguistic roots imply experiential roots and identification of experience by employing commonly shared language. Since Schnackenburg, in the anniversary volume for the Lukan scholar Heinz Schürmann, linked the Spirit-reception and Spirit-giftedness language of Luke to the almost identical language in the Paul of the Letters,[60] this is a topic awaiting further investigation. In fact, when I asked one prominent Evangelical scholar to engage in a formal dialogue with me in our ETS "charismatic themes" venue on this very point, he declined, stating that "Pentecostals would have to *prove*" (emphasis his), that similar and identical Pauline language was connected to language in Luke-Acts. When I assured him that the goal of dialogue was not intended to fashion a formal proof or to advance or protect ecclesiastical domains, but to advance scholarship, he again declined. Of course, most Evangelical scholars find little or no distinction between the Lukan Paul and the Paul of the Letters, but when the latter employs language of the former as well as the language of the supposedly extinct examples and precedents narrated by his companion and pupil Luke,[61] unforeseen distinctions and barriers seem to arise. Underlying connections between the concepts of power in Luke-Acts (including Luke's portrayal of Paul) and in Paul's letters also suggest a common linguistic tradition within which the two authors operated and communicated. These similarities likewise await fuller investigation.[62] Questions, like where could Luke, who claims to have researched all things thoroughly and was otherwise so informed about Paul's missionary work, have lived to be unaware of Paul's letters,[63] and why would Luke not seek to clarify important Spirit-reception lan-

---

59. Such claims that there was no common linguistic base due to common experience, no creation of descriptive language based on experience, and no connection between the Spirit-reception language employed by Paul in his occasional discursive correspondence and the narrative portrayals of Lukan characters, including Paul, can only be attributed, in my judgment, to cessationistic motivations, not to serious investigation as begun by Manson, "Entry into Membership of the Early Church," 25–33.

60. Schnackenburg, "Die johanneische Gemeinde und ihre Geisterfahrung," 284–85.

61. Regarding this point of association, so too, Tübingen professor Belser, *Die Apostelgeschichte*, 5; Nock, *Essays on Religion and the Ancient World*, 2:827–28; Hengel, "Problems of a History of Earliest Christianity," 135. The "we"-passages of Acts exhibit a common linguistic unity or uniformity of Lukan style with the rest of Acts, cf. Schmidt, "Syntactical Style in the 'We'-Sections of Acts," 300–308. For balanced discussion of the "we"-passages in Acts, cf. Hemer, *Book of Acts in the Setting of Hellenistic History*, 312–34. This connection of Luke with Paul is relevant to the discussion of what common Jerusalem/Petrine tradition of descriptive language, and experiential interaction with the heavenly Jesus related thereto, these two authors would have shared in communication and practice.

62. The recent work of Gräbe, "Pentecostal Discovery," 226–36, is welcome in this regard. Some of this material is explored further in Gräbe, *Power of God in Paul's Letters*.

63. A point also raised, for example, by Leppä, *Luke's Critical Use of Galatians*, 21, and by Brodie,

guage in the letters via explanatory examples and precedents rather than to pastorally confuse with ostensibly similar language conveying a different meaning than that of Paul, are swept under the dispensational rug. Although Luke obviously writes for Theophilus's understanding, using what must have been commonly understandable language for a reader I take to be already familiar with Christian ideas and practices,[64] the inadequately considered version of pre-Lukan cessationism that is quite common among Evangelicals today[65] reflects a hermeneutical bias that Theophilus would, I suspect, find difficult to recognize. According to this bias, we would surely not expect any Lukan language relating to experience that quickly underwent mass extinction, even if contained in Paul's letters, to be relevant in our contemporary application of Paul, even though Paul views himself as part of an earlier preformed tradition.[66] It might be argued that Paul developed an appreciation for the legacy of epochal truncation in Rome, passing it to Luke, although both appear ignorant of it.[67]

"Greco-Roman Imitation of Texts," 37, who goes further: "Would a researcher like Luke who wanted to highlight Paul and his preaching set to work without bothering to get copies of Paul's epistles? In what corner was he marooned that he did not know of these documents? In what literary impoverishment did this elegant writer live that he could not get copies of them?" On the matter of Luke's probable knowledge of Pauline correspondence, which bears on an argument that Luke and Paul were *both* supportive of the Jerusalem/Petrine tradition and that *both* reflected its linguistic heritage, cf. also Soltau, "Die Herkunft der Reden in der Apostelgeschichte," 128–54; Loisy, *Les Actes des Apôtres*, 415, 475; Mundle, "Das Apostelbild der Apostelgeschichte," 44; Thiering, "Acts of the Apostles as Early Christian Art," 139–89; Enslin, "Once Again, Luke and Paul," 253–71; Enslin, "Emphases and Silences," 219–25; Aejmelaeus, *Die Rezeption der Paulusbriefe in der Miletrede*, 267; Walker, "Acts and the Pauline Corpus Reconsidered," 3–23; Walker, "Acts and the Pauline Corpus Revisited," 77–86; Brodie, "Towards Tracing the Gospels' Literary Indebtedness to the Epistles," 105–10; and Aejmelaeus, "Reopening the Question."

64. Cf. my "Spirit, Scripture and Theology through a Lukan Lens," 66–73.

65. Walvoord's and Turner's views are similar within the sphere of narrative disconnectedness, cf. Elbert, "Globalization of Pentecostalism," 90–91. Walvoord and Turner, against the grain of all known narrative-rhetorical convention bearing on understandability, excise the main Lukan character's teaching on prayer from the minds and lives of his disciples. Unhelpful to this narrative excision is its unappealing disconnectedness with narrative facts. This main character is no less than the son of God, the man to whom all the prophets witness, the character who exhorts his hearers to put his teachings into practice and who says that his real relatives are those who obey his teaching. *Perhaps this might suggest that the pervasive erasure of his teaching on prayer from characters' memories would be contrary to Lukan intentions.* Perhaps Walvoord's and Turner's appeal to narrative disconnectedness and incoherence will be as convincing as other cessationistic theories, unless their luster eventually be lost in a scrutiny of the presuppositional basis of "apostolic age" apologetics.

66. Paul's continuity with the mother church of Christendom in Jerusalem and its linguistic heritage is well established, cf. Menoud, "Jésus et ses témoins," 7–20; Fannon, "Influence of Traditions on St. Paul," 292–307. As to Paul's transmission of earlier tradition, cf. Müller, *Der Traditionsprozess im Neuen Testament*, 204–24; Ellis, *Making of the New Testament Documents*, 248–51, 256–60.

67. The content of Paul's Miletus speech does not suggest or imply a Lukan characterization of Paul which is at all truncational toward Luke's own development and application of his prophetic-fulfillment theme. Such a cessationistic interpretation of the Miletus speech is wrongheaded, rather, and here I agree with Walton, that "For Luke, the heart of Christian leadership is to be like Jesus, and the extent to which both the disciples and Paul do and teach what Jesus did and taught—frequently using similar vocabulary—makes this clear" (Walton, *Leadership and Lifestyle*, 135).

In any case, my arguments that pervasive oral memory and a common and ongoing Jerusalem/Petrine tradition is detectable in Paul's discursive correspondence, correspondence that Luke who has researched all things carefully from the beginning surely, in my tentative judgment, knows about, do not seem highly resonant with the current mindset of some Evangelicals.[68] Yet, Luke is an independently minded thinker who, in my view, does not find Paul's letters useful for his theological and pneumatological purpose. A practical telling about the Spirit, rather than elaborate talking about the Spirit,[69] is certainly not, however, a narrative constraint for a writer contemplative of the need for urgent clarification of the discursive correspondence of Paul. Although in light of Reformed tradition, for some, I fear, acceptance of Luke's probable knowledge of Paul's letters, given then his decision not to quote them, would thereby somehow display Luke's narrative inferiority, a perspective highly consistent with the suffocating temporal camouflage long imposed upon Luke's literary accomplishment. Historicity, not narrative theology and pneumatology, has dominated Evangelical scholarship in Acts.[70] And this is of course a proper and important enterprise. But if it becomes an exclusive vision, the interpretation of Paul (dispensational and otherwise) can unduly overshadow the Christian tradition, description, and practice as portrayed by Luke.[71] Perhaps absent such rigid preconceptions and the accompanying allegiance to an alien hermeneutic invoked with respect to Luke's narrative world, due consideration and reflection upon differing ideas would function in a more productive manner. I am not sure how well debate and dissent, as productive tools of progress, are working within Evangelicalism at ETS, which appears to me to be a somewhat insular academic operation. Nevertheless, God is at work, as with Apollos, within ETS and its membership and it is a pleasure to engage in fellowship therein.

As we all know, undue adherence to an established position may prevent, initially at least, otherwise thoughtful scholars, including ourselves, from considering new information. It may also hinder or prevent reflection about previously articulated information that should be considered. After all, we like ourselves the way we are, and when we surround ourselves with those who are like us, then how can differences, dissent, or valid progress be apparent or truly relevant? When my discovery of the consistency of the Lukan syntax of imperative-future middle/passive combinations (as at Acts 2:38) was presented to ETS, a study relevant to Pesch's claim that we live in the time of the Lukan gift of the Spirit (*die Zeit der Geistesgabe*),[72] not in

---

68. As to this Evangelical *Weltanschauung* or worldview through which the NT is read, Wacker, Poloma, Johns, and Archer are undoubtedly correct that a supernatural worldview more akin to that of the NT authors themselves provides an alternate *Weltanschauung* to that motivated by a rational modern society, cf. Archer, "Pentecostal Hermeneutics," 65.

69. With Marguerat, *First Christian Historian*, 128.

70. Perhaps, for some, this dominating interest might not be unfairly paraphrased in its practical dimension as "We believe that the events in Acts happened, we just don't want them to happen to us."

71. Against this possible view, cf. Elbert, "Paul of the Miletus Speech," 258–68.

72. Pesch, "Die Gabe des Heiligen Geistes," 53. One notes the imperative-future passive

the "messianic" or "apostolic" age where Joel's prophecy was supposedly fulfilled,[73]

---

combination at Acts 2:38c, a structure in need of syntactical consideration at least within Lukan and LXX usage.

73. The truncation or confinement of Luke's dynamic understanding of prophetic fulfillment, in the case of selected supernatural categories of inspired speech arbitrarily singled out for extinction in Peter's rendition of Joel's prophecy, to a supposed artificial and prophetic-quenching epoch (Zeit), is standard fare in the commentary tradition on Luke's second book. Occasionally, in the "apostolic age hermeneutics" of the critical commentary tradition, the concealed and unarticulated presupposition driving the truncation explicitly surfaces as it does in Hans Hinrich Wendt's comment on the promise (ἐπαγγελία) of the Spirit at Acts 2:33. Although the promise at 2:33 is rightly connected by Wendt to the same promise (Verheißung) at Luke 24:49 and Luke 3:16, it is disconnected from Jesus's teaching at Luke 11:13 by an established tradition preceding Wendt which has confined Jesus's teaching on prayer to Luke 11:2–4. The promise at 2:33 is also disconnected by Wendt from the same promise at Acts 1:4, from its exemplary fulfillment in 2:4, and from the ongoing prophetic prediction concerning the promise in 2:39 which goes beyond narrative time.

All of these well-placed narrative contextual instances of a specific promise and their delicate co-descriptions (Luke 3:16; 11:13; 24:49; Acts 1:4, 5; 2:4, 33, 39), together with the apparent prophetic extension of this promise to repentant hearers both within and beyond the narrative itself at 2:39, would without a doubt be properly considered in the critical exegesis of a classic epic of narrative fiction involving prophetic fulfillment, had such a construction appeared there. Had 2:17–18 been a prophecy by Zeus or Juno in a Homeric or Virgilian epic, contained within winged words by Minerva or within a speech by bold Aeneas, with all of the obvious narrative linkages carefully afforded this promise, with its delicately nuanced co-descriptions and its experiential example of inspired speech, we would find classical commentators considering the mythic supernatural prediction of the speaker and looking for its repetition in selected lives as the story unfolded. *Indeed, we might find commentators hailing this narrative continuity as a display of Homeric or Virgilian ekphrasis worthy of rhetorical acclaim.* In this hypothetical case, since the narrative prediction beyond narrative time is a technique of fiction, its ambitious extension beyond the narrative makes for arresting and entertaining reading, while in reality it is quite preposterous and would not call for comment.

On the other hand, Wendt, a critical commentator working from the Greek text, like Calvin too at this juncture (n19), reveals that he knows what the well-placed instances of the promise probably suggest, or at least imply; he knows that they are there, *they are just not at all useful to or compatible with his operational agenda,* which is to confine such supernatural prophetic predictions to NT characters. While Wendt does cite 10:45 and 11:17 (and Heb 6:4) as instances of the gift of the Holy Spirit in 2:38c, he apparently sees the need for a comment partially explaining his lack of consideration of the train of promise-markers (Luke 3:16 [Acts 1:5]; 11:13; 24:49; Acts 1:4; 2:33, 39), a comment which also serves to quench any untoward expectations on the part of *his* readers for prophetic fulfillment pertaining to 2:38c beyond the narrative. Wendt offers the truncating assertion re: 2:33 that "Der Messias vermittelt die Geistesbegabung, die nach den Prophetenworte (2:17f) in der messianischen Zeit verwirklicht werden soll" (*Die Apostelgeschichte*, 94).

Historically, the truncation of supernatural components of Joel's prophecy (Acts 2:17–21) is formally inaugurated at 2:39 in the critical commentary tradition on Luke's second book (ditto with hand-me-down assurances in the more popular "Evangelical" tradition). While the critical tradition may sometimes note that at 2:39 the promise is co-described as the baptism in the Spirit, that the Spirit is the object of the promise, that 2:33, 1:4, and Luke 24:49 cite this promise, and that Luke 3:16 and 11:13 are to be recognized as relevant foreground, the contiguous example of the promise (2:4) is marginalized or erased from the scene at 2:39, and ensuing narrative examples—examples which connect to supernatural categories in 2:17, 18—are totally disconnected from prophetic fulfillment. The truncation in the critical commentary tradition at 2:39 (as with Wendt) is accompanied by disconnecting speculation, like "mais le don de l'Esprit appartient aux temps messianiques," the children of the truncated promise being "la future Eglise" (the church of "apostolic age hermeneutics" in a supposedly different epoch than Lukan characters; so Loisy, *Les Actes des Apôtres*, 215).

the reaction seemed mainly "ho hum," together with "who sent for you?" By and large, with two exceptions, consideration and reflection unsurprisingly took a back seat. On the other hand, when this same information was presented at SBL Rome,[74] it was recognized by linguists and sundry NT scholars, as it had been earlier by several classicists with whom I discussed it extensively,[75] to be interesting and, as I suggested, a factor to be considered in interpretation; hence the contrasting attitude, "Let's have coffee together and discuss this further." Similarly, with apologies for mentioning my own work, the aforementioned presentation on Luke's narrative style in his composition of questions and their narrative function seemed to get an ETS "ho hum," but at SBL a warm welcome and a letter of inquiry from a NT faculty member at Westminster Theological Seminary expressing a desire to study the matter further. Ingrained presuppositions can prove difficult to reconsider, but the youthful are open; the dispensational cloak that has long suppressed the Lukan voice and the Pauline connection to that voice is lifting.

Some bright spots are encouraging. At the last ETS session in Toronto, several questioners in the audience asked where they could find more information on Luke's understanding of "being filled with" and "full of" the Holy Spirit. As moderator, I was able to direct them to where such timely and practical information could be found—Jim Shelton's seminal piece in the Horton festschrift, a newly discovered nugget for our Evangelical friends.[76] Evidently these questioners were not convinced, as was suggested by the immediately previous speaker, that Lukan portrayals of personal Spirit-receptions/Spirit-fillings by believers were all but irrelevant before Luke wrote.

While my wife and daughter waited for me in the lobby of the ETS hotel, as we prepared to leave for the SBL hotel, I encountered a lady whom I had observed to be present during our entire Luke-Acts session that same morning. She turned out to be the wife of a dean of an institution of higher education that has a long-standing position of militant Lukan cessationism. Her son had rejected the rationalistic underpinnings of this belief and had been witnessing to her. She was reflective and her mind

---

What is interesting in all of this is that Luke is never said to be a deliberate misleader or an inept bungler. Obviously, he is neither. Instead, his skillful narrative-rhetorical depictions of prophetic fulfillment are—when at variance with ecclesiastical tradition or with neo-Calvinist presuppositions—just presumptuously confined to, or his text divided up into, various arbitrary epochs or ages which, while no more than pneumatological phantoms, function to destroy narrative continuity as in the encapsulating model of von Baer-Dunn, cf. Elbert, *Lukan Gift of the Holy Spirit* (n27).

74. For informative purposes, it may be noted that the Society of Biblical Literature (SBL), founded in 1880 to advance the public understanding of the Bible and biblical scholarship, hosts its annual meeting in North America along with an annual international meeting, cf. http://www.sbl-site.org/.

75. It is a pleasure to acknowledge discussions with Ron Ipock, Department of Classics, University of California at Irvine, and with John Philips, Department of Classics, University of Tennessee at Chattanooga. I would like to thank Maria Pantelia, director of the Thesaurus Linguae Graecae (http://www.tlg.uci.edu/~tlg), for kindly scheduling research time and extending the hospitality of the Thesaurus library at the University of California at Irvine.

76. Filling the bill on this occasion was Shelton, "'Filled with the Holy Spirit,'" 81–107.

had been opened. The two of us stood all alone and talked without interruption for over a half-hour. She asked one question after another and considered the answers. I encouraged her to obey the teaching of the earthly Jesus on prayer in Luke's first book, not to be deterred by ecclesiastical pressures that would surely be brought against her,[77] not to be content with the theoretical admission, independent of Luke-Acts, that spiritual gifts mentioned in Paul's letters may be for today, an admission often equated with natural talent and secular accomplishment by Evangelical scholars like Robert Saucy,[78] who, while "open," rely less on pragmatic Pauline understanding of how these gifts are transmitted and given interpersonally *in the Spirit* and more on notions of epochal boundaries. Rather than scholarly waffling as to whether Paul's first letter to Corinth should be understood by reading front to back,[79] she sought encouragement

---

77. *Traditional Protestant theology deliberately and explicitly eclipses (totally or at best partially) the teaching of Jesus on prayer beyond the "Lord's Prayer" in the Lukan account (cf. nn. 47 and 48 above), that is, Luke 11:2–4 is "for today" and 11:5–13 is for the supposed "apostolic age."* Rationalistically excised as well are the examples of obedient disciples praying for the gift of the Holy Spirit in accord with Jesus's teaching. Under the hidden agenda of "apostolic age hermeneutics" these texts are perceived as ecclesiastically *verboten*, that is, of a nonapplicable, "do-not-touch-under-any circumstances" kind of biblical material. Any practical pastoral application or appropriation of such material in connection with Luke's second book is likely to be met with stout resistance by epochalists imbued by training and ecclesial practice in "apostolic age" interpretive methodology. In this scenario, the examples and precedents within the Spirit-reception nexus in the second book are either divorced from Luke's thematic prophetic-fulfillment theme or are retrofitted to a distant epoch. For a contrary suggestion as to the most effective pedagogic appropriation of such material, cf. Ruthven, "'Between Two Worlds," 283–85, 289–92.

78. Saucy, a past president of ETS, sets out his views on the possibility of the supernatural under various suspicions and constraints, one being to meet his criterion that NT prophecy, to be genuine, must be authoritative, not to meet Paul's criterion that it should edify, cf. his "Open but Cautious View," 97–148.

79. J. Rodman Williams's point that 1 Corinthians 1 and 2 (with its reference to Spirit-reception) precedes 1 Corinthians 12–14 is a valid, rhetorically minded concept rather totally overlooked by Gaffin, "Cessationist Response to C. Samuel Storms and Douglas A. Oss," 284–97. Given the distinctively selective and contextually extractive employment of "prooftexts" in the theory of epochal imposition/truncation, Ruthven's argument, that "The doctrine of cessationism will one day assume its rightful place in the Museum of Theological Curiosities—joining the Gap Theory, the bodily ascension of Mary, and the doctrine that Mussolini is the Antichrist," has the weight of history on its side (cf. Ruthven, Review of *Are Miraculous Gifts for Today?*, 158). However, just when Ruthven's Museum of Theological Curiosities will be fully open to the Christian public to view the biers of Lukan and Pauline cessationism as formerly engendered by experiential suspicion and philosophically based epochal periodization is difficult to anticipate. A guesstimate of several centuries might be apropos, given the grip of underlying rationalistic presuppositions. The current arrogant denial by some of what is reasonably understood to be spiritual reality may not be based entirely upon the rationalistic impulse to divorce the heavenly Jesus from the earthly Jesus, although this disconnectedness is undoubtedly a factor in the denial. The evident conflict with Luke's fulfillment-of-prophecy theme that this tension creates, combined with the non-Pauline fear that somehow revelatory experience will displace the experience of edifying and instructional texts (as in the real Paul, Rom 15:4), reminds me of Robert Jastrow's now-famous poetic picture (*God and the Astronomers*, 116). Jastrow depicts some dogmatic atheists confronted with the beginning of the cosmos in 1963, when humankind entered into the Era of the Glimpse of God: "For the scientist who has lived by his faith in the power of reason, the story ends like a bad dream. He has scaled the mountains of ignorance; he is about to conquer the highest

on how to prayerfully seek and to persist in seeking the Lukan gift of the Holy Spirit, to value and to accept the examples and precedents Luke had provided her, to put herself in the position of Theophilus and to read Luke-Acts *tabula rasa* front to back. I encouraged her to seek the gift of the Holy Spirit and to continue to do so throughout her life and to have Lukan expectations, not to be misled by prayer formulas which deliberately ignore the teaching of the Lukan Jesus and its narrative clarification. All through this conversation, I felt the Lord's gentle presence. I do not know what will happen to this determined woman when she encounters opposition, but her humble curiosity, after spending years in the halls of "apostolic age" academia, was, for me, very encouraging and refreshing. I do wish her well.

Conclusions

I have attempted to draw out some of the ramifications inherent in an anti-Lukan "apostolic age hermeneutic" that may be of some assistance to future students of Luke's interconnected volumes, a double-work obviously composed in light of the narrative-rhetorical conventions of the day which valued clarity, description, and coherence. In contrast to the expectations engendered by Graeco-Roman literary achievement, the truncational method of interpretation concretized in the Reformation remains unresponsive to and reinterpretive of the role of the Holy Spirit in NT texts. In Luke's case, the hidden presupposition of cessationism serves to blot out main themes and destroy narrative cohesion, while in Paul's case it denies the connection of the letters with Jerusalem/Petrine tradition and the examples and precedents described with a common linguistic heritage.

Some conservative evangelicals have historically been better at defending set doctrines of the past rather than constructively changing past blunders. The neo-Calvinist evangelical coalition, whether Wesleyan-Arminian, Baptist, or Reformed, thinks of itself as "biblical" Christianity when, in fact, it evinces a stubborn traditionalism which strongly resists fresh insight into NT texts and their cognitive environment from a new perspective unwedded to rationalism. Perhaps an understandable and commendable desire to defend the existence and practices of Lukan characters within history tended to overshadow a due desire to see things through the eyes of characters in the narrative world, to participate in the connectedness of *their* story.[80] Instead, this preoccupation

---

peak; as he pulls himself over the final rock, he is greeted by a band of theologians who have been sitting there for centuries." *When those wedded to the Dispensational Luke and the Dispensational Paul have explored the last possible tidbits of their thought, perhaps they too, God willing, may be greeted in a similar way by NT theologians: Luke and the Paul of Acts, writer of letters.*

80. The observation of W. C. van Unnik is quite apropos: "Some generations ago it was usual in writing a biography of somebody to say in the subtitle, 'in the framework of his time.' Today such a further indication has fallen into desuetude, but if we wish to come to a correct and fair appreciation of Acts we shall have to see Luke in the framework of his age. I am becoming more and more convinced that much critical study of Acts has been done at a distance from, or even without *living*

with historical and source criticism often leads to the conclusion that what Luke writes is just too difficult to understand, too remote, that is, incompatible with respect to the perspective of an interpreter's story who is locked out of the narrative world because of atomistic readings engendered by exposure to an atomistic commentary tradition, by anti-supernatural bias, or by rational assent to overt or implicit cessationism. It is inevitable that the impulse of reinterpretation in the guise of exegesis, ecclesiastically conforming or not, must come under scrutiny. Yet, the extra-biblical and incoherent practice of "apostolic age hermeneutics"—with its strange residue of disconnectedness—will likely retain a puzzling allure. Nevertheless, future scholars trained to ask, "How do we know?" and "Why do we believe?" should not be intimidated over the long-term by assertions of highly dubious plausibility, assertions intimately and ultimately allied to the narratively uncritical, rationalistic, and exegetically presumptuous epochs presupposed by past generations of scholarship.[81]

I suggest optimistically that scholars who deliberately unsubscribe to "apostolic age" interpretive methodology and embrace a new paradigm, a new perspective on narrative connectedness and of experiential portrayal as shared by the narrative-rhetorical culture in which the NT was composed, will be among those who break new interpretive ground. As they make their work available to the Lord in a ministry useful to pragmatic Christian concerns, they should take their place as partners in progress of a new kind. As to scholarship germinating and becoming productive within the Pentecostal/charismatic Renewal in the new Era of the Glimpse of God, biblical studies emanating from a new paradigm should be of practical assistance in motivating an increase in missionary zeal throughout world Christendom.

---

contact with, Luke's world. It is not sufficient to remind ourselves that he was not a historian in our sense, but in that of antiquity; but we shall have to walk with him along his roads, to see and hear with his eyes and those of his contemporaries" ("Luke's Second Book," 37; emphasis his).

81. Of course a few Evangelicals will continue their attempts to disregard the disciple-believer-witnesses in Luke's first book, and truncate the programmatic narrative force of Acts 1:8 with respect to Luke's chosen examples and precedents of Spirit-reception in his second book, still claiming in a ham-fisted cavalry-style execution of "apostolic age hermeneutics" that only the twelve male apostles received the Spirit as true believers so as to assist their ministry, and that the promise of the Spirit to all others makes them become "believers," not empowered witnesses (so Bolt, "Mission and Witness," 212). However, "Acts 1:8 Reappropriated: Twelve Dispensational Male Apostles Go to the Remotest Part of the Earth, Rewriting the Prophetic Witness of Women, Sons, Daughters, and Other Disciple-Believers Out of Joel's Prophecy," along with other prophetically truncating variants of Lukan cessationism, are unlikely to prove persuasive to the majority of future scholars, even though they conform to a palatable canon of neo-Calvinistic tastes. *On the other hand, future scholars who ask "How do we know?" and "Why do we believe?" should uncover the false paradigms of "apostolic age hermeneutics," namely that Luke-Acts is devoid of pneumatological expectation for disciple-believer-witnesses regarding prayerful Spirit-reception, that a grid of narrative disconnectedness must be superimposed upon Luke-Acts in order to understand it, that reinterpretation, extraction from context, and dismissal of grid-filtered material is "biblical," and that much of the experiential description in Luke-Acts is cognitively estranged both linguistically and conceptually from the letters of Paul.* These hidden persuaders and false paradigms are tied philosophically to a persistent sectarian interpretive method (sectarian vis-à-vis Luke and Paul) which I have attempted, however inadequately, to expose to greater scrutiny.

Paul's familiarity with Jesus material, his conversion and Spirit-reception, and his theological and pneumatological development, place him squarely in the Jerusalem/Petrine tradition narrated in Luke-Acts. The mysterious empowerment of disciple-believer-witnesses through reception of the gift of the Holy Spirit mediated by the heavenly Jesus, according to the examples and precedents afforded by Lukan characters and their ministry (including Paul) who are participating in prophetic fulfillment, appears directly connected to missionary zeal. If biblical scholars now training a further generation of missionaries and gospel workers of all kinds will adopt interpretive methodology that can stand up to the logic of examination, contextually sensitive and culturally sensitive to biblical writers,[82] and seek to be led by the Spirit, diligent not to hold the genuine canons of objective academic enterprise in unnecessary subservience to the great god Tradition, they should be able to contribute evangelistically to the global missionary endeavor.

---

82. In this venture, I recommend serious consideration of Berlin, "Search for a New Biblical Hermeneutics," 195–207.

Chapter 7

Paul of the Miletus Speech and 1 Thessalonians

Critique and Considerations

THE MILETUS SPEECH (ACTS 20:18b–35), Paul's only speech in Acts to a Christian audience, is probably to be understood in the Graeco-Roman narrative-rhetorical setting as providing an example of how an evangelist/pastor in the Jerusalem/Petrine tradition communicates revelatory details to those formerly under his ministry. Perhaps Luke, who presents Paul as a Spirit-empowered evangelist, includes this speech to round out his portrait of Paul as a charismatic missionary to Jews and gentiles. In any case it is full of heuristic concepts worthy of comparison with the Paul of the Letters. Long-standing debate surrounds both the coherence of the Paul of Acts with the Epistles and the state of Luke's knowledge of Paul's occasional, discursive correspondence. Hence the need for the monograph by Steve Walton which brings some fresh ideas to the table.[1]

Walton details the objections of Vielhauer[2] as to coherence of the Lukan Paul with Paul the Epistler in respect to natural theology, Christology, eschatology, and views of the law. Various critical responses to these perceived differences, which are often imprudently overlooked and deserve more consideration, are helpfully cited.[3] Walton mounts a response on two fronts, methodological and evidential.[4] With Hengel[5] and Hemer,[6] Walton argues that some ancient historians were concerned for accuracy (freelance composition not being normative among the great historians) and that the Epistles provide limited knowledge of Paul's preaching. Hence a valid criticism of method: "It is *prima facie* likely that Paul's preaching outside the Christian community would be different from his teaching within that community. Accordingly, it is mistaken to compare

---

1. Walton, *Leadership and Lifestyle*.
2. Vielhauer, "Zum 'Paulinismus' der Apostelgeschichte," 1–15. Walton cites the English version, "On the 'Paulinisms' of Acts."
3. Walton, *Leadership and Lifestyle*, 7.
4. Walton, *Leadership and Lifestyle*, 6–12.
5. Hengel, *Zur urchristlichen Geschichtsschreibung*, the title reminding readers of Lucian's treatise. Walton cites the English version, *Acts and the History of Earliest Christianity*.
6. Hemer, *Book of Acts in the Setting of Hellenistic History*.

the theology of Paul in his speeches in Acts as a whole with that in his epistles as a whole."[7] As to evidence, Walton argues that Paul's circumcision of Timothy (Acts 16:3) does not contradict Paul's hostility to circumcision (Gal 5:3), nor, I might add, does it conflict with Paul's stress on a new creation (Gal 6:15).

However, it may be observed that the implications of Vielhauer's argument go further to the effect that since Paul did eat freely with gentiles in Antioch (Gal 2:12), and since Paul implies that he cannot be accused of preaching circumcision (Gal 5:11), and since Paul has a Christianized loyalty to Judaism (1 Cor 9:19–23), the writer of Acts (had he actually known the real Paul) could not imply (Acts 21:21) that it was a misrepresentation, a false rumor, or a canard that Paul taught Jewish Christians not to circumcise their children. This argument can be countered by observing that we have no evidence that Paul did teach this to Jewish Christians regarding their children[8] and by observing that the writer of Acts appears fully aware of both the Holy Spirit's imprimatur on the resolution for gentiles (Acts 15:23, 28, 29; 21:25) and of misunderstandings by Jewish Christians in the Jerusalem church as to how this written agreement relative to gentiles affected their traditional loyalty to Judaism. The claim that the writer of Acts could not have employed personal reflections of serious differences between the gentile mission and Jewish believers in composing Acts 21 (or the speech in chapter 22), because, had he been present he could not possibly have understood them as portrayed since they supposedly present a serious difference with the Paul of the Letters, seems to lack sufficient *Glaubwürdigkeit*. While James and his colleagues (Acts 21:18) seem insensitive to Paul, the writer of Acts appears aware of the differences in the Christian factions. Such a writer could easily have had contiguous and contemporary awareness of the complicated situation in the Jerusalem church with respect to the law of Moses, probably more so than a distant inventive composer with a desk full of Pauline "traditions." In any case, perhaps Walton's brief treatment may serve to counterbalance, or at least call into question, claims that the incoherence in the two Pauls is so grave that it is necessary to posit other improbable and shadowy "solutions" to avoid this supposed dilemma.[9]

Walton asks: How Lukan does the Miletus speech appear? Given Aejmelaeus's recent conclusion that the tone of the speech is very Pauline (*echt paulinisch*) and that it exhibits many affinities in vocabulary and ideas to material found in 1 Thessalonians,[10] it is timely that Walton also asks: How Pauline does the speech appear? Walton seeks to identify adequate criteria for valid parallels which would

---

7. Walton, *Leadership and Lifestyle*, 9.

8. A point scored as well by Fitzmyer, *Acts of the Apostles*, 693, who observes regarding the charge that Paul taught apostasy from Moses and told Jewish Christians not to circumcise their children, "One will look in vain in the account of Acts so far for such activity of Paul and also for such a formulation in Paul's letters.... What Paul says in Gal 5:2–3, 6, 11, or 1 Cor 7:19 might give a different impression, but also recall the circumcision of Timothy in Acts 16:3."

9. As in Wedderburn, "'We'-Passages in Acts," 85–88.

10. Aejmelaeus, *Die Rezeption der Paulusbriefe in der Miletrede*.

allow the two texts (the Miletus speech and 1 Thessalonians) to be compared side by side. To address how Lukan or how Pauline the speech is, Walton looks for Lukan and Pauline parallels of vocabulary, that is, lexical parallels including cognate words and compounds, parallels of synonyms, as well as for conceptual parallels like narrated actions of Paul or other characters which epitomize teaching, and for parallel styles of argumentation. Walton's agenda, via comparisons, is to look for coherence of the Lukan Paul in only the Miletus speech with the Lukan Jesus, with Lukan narrative, and with only the Paul of 1 Thessalonians.

Walton sees the speech as a tapestry: Acts 20:18–21 (retrospect); vv. 22–24 (future of Paul in Jerusalem); vv. 25–27 (prospect and retrospect); vv. 28–31 (charge to elders); and vv. 32–35 (conclusion). In the charge to the elders of the church Paul reminds them that "The Holy Spirit placed you (as) overseers" (20:28a). In my judgment it is hardly "unusual"[11] that the Spirit should appoint leaders, given that such descriptive language is probably, for Luke, more than mere abstract nonexperiential rhetoric in light of the programmatic agenda of prophecy, dreams, and visions in Peter's opening speech and in light of examples where the Holy Spirit speaks through prophecy regarding individual tasks (13:2). Spirit-appointment fits the context of the speech where the Spirit provides revelatory witness to the speaker himself about his own affairs. Lukan disciples may function in the appointment of leaders in the context of prayer and fasting (14:23; 13:2), a spiritual contextual climate which suggests a strong interest among Lukan characters in seeking prophetic guidance and Spirit-empowerment. Further, since expectation of prophetic-type phenomena in Ephesus, used in an atmosphere of edification as at Thessalonica,[12] is consistent with the lifestyle and practical ministry of the Lukan Paul and since Spirit-appointment is consistent with Pauline Spirit-reception and Spirit-function language in general, this potential thematic connection might have been fruitfully explored in accordance with the comparative ethos of Walton's thesis. In the context of Walton's overall project, Spirit-appointment in the Miletus speech should have received broader consideration in both Lukan and Pauline thought-worlds and should not be quickly dismissed as unusual or unharmonious with either Lukan or Pauline theology.

However, in the charge to these elders of the church (Acts 20:28–31), Walton's focus is not on 20:28a but on the wider meaning of the last clause of the verse because it alludes to the redemptive significance of Jesus's death and Lukan atonement/ransom theology based on that death, "To shepherd the church of God (the Father) which He bought with the blood of His own one (Son)," following Walton's helpful text-critical excursus on the text and meaning of 20:28b.[13] This parallels the saying at Luke 22:20b, "This cup which is poured out for you is the new covenant in my blood." Walton argues for the inclusion of the longer reading (Luke 22:19b–20)

11. So Walton, *Leadership and Lifestyle*, 81.
12. With Walton, *Leadership and Lifestyle*, 154, as so regarding 1 Thessalonians 5:19–21.
13. Walton, *Leadership and Lifestyle*, 94–98.

in another helpful text-critical excursus,[14] making the case for agreement with the fourth UBS edition which raised its evaluation of the longer reading from a "C" to a "B." In light of Acts 20:28b and Luke 22:19b–20, it may be observed that Luke can hardly be accused of not recognizing the centrality of Christ's death,[15] a salient feature of soteriology also found in Paul's letters.[16] Claiming that lack of such recognition makes Luke obtuse and illustrates another supposedly irreconcilable difference between the Christology of Paul and the thought-world of the writer of Acts, who could not therefore have been one of Paul's companions, seems quite awkward and misunderstands the inherent differences between the narrative characterization and the occasional discourse of two individual minds.

Walton details and then discusses four main themes of the speech (faithful fulfillment of leadership responsibility, past and future suffering, attitudes to wealth and work, and Jesus's death) with respect to Luke-Acts. As to the question of how Lukan the Miletus speech is, Walton details the four main themes in the context of Acts, in the context of Luke 22:14–38, and in the context of Luke 12:1–53.[17] This, along with other parallel vocabulary and conceptual linkage in Luke 21:5–36; 7:38, 44; 9:2; 10:3; and 13:32, leads Walton to conclude that Luke's first book yields enough connective material to suggest that he intends to draw attention to the parallel between Jesus and Paul, insofar as leadership is concerned, in the composition of his second book. As to how Pauline the speech is, Walton undertakes a systematic comparison of the speech with 1 Thessalonians, given its pastoral nature and its known and reasonably clear parallels to the four main themes Walton identifies in the speech. Examining his four themes again within 1 Thessalonians, leadership, suffering, money and work, and Jesus's death,[18] Walton finds quite significant verbal parallels in vocabulary and in thought-worlds within 1 Thessalonians to the Miletus speech.

---

14. Walton, *Leadership and Lifestyle*, 137–39.

15. So Wedderburn, "'We'-Passages in Acts," 87, who oddly ignores this textual evidence. Wedderburn might take into account the linguistic unity and uniformity of style in these personalized passages (cf. Schmidt, "Syntactical Style in the 'We'-Sections of Acts," 300–308), which does not do anything to support his distant branch of a Pauline "school" theory of composition. The distant "school" companion of a "companion" of Paul raises as many connective problems to Lukan characterization as does the theory of a supposedly conscious literary "we"-device employed to convey a contiguous and false impression. On the other hand, while not capable of a formal proof, accepting the writer's first-person narration as intrinsically trustworthy, intentional, lifelike, and clearly intelligible seems, in the potentially urgent pastoral and theological context of this anonymous Christian narrator, rather more preferable to these cul-de-sacs.

16. Moule, "Christology of Acts" 159–85, esp. 171, asks if it is significant that the only explicitly redemptive interpretation of the death of Christ in Acts should be on the lips of Paul. Moule sees this as a variation, not a discrepancy, with respect to the Paul of the Letters. He points out that "This is Paul, not some other speaker; and he is not evangelizing but recalling an already evangelized community to its deepest insights. In other words, the situation, like the theology, is precisely that of a Pauline epistle, not of preliminary evangelism."

17. Walton, *Leadership and Lifestyle*, 84–93, 104–17, 119–27, respectively.

18. Walton, *Leadership*, 157–63, 163–67, 167–72, 172–75, respectively.

It may be observed that Walton's dual result regarding 1 Thessalonians is consistent with personal acquaintance and eye-witness recollection as Luke's narration in the first-person plural suggests, and with the internalization of Paul's teaching. Luke may then be reasonably understood as accepting the challenge to move ahead into fresh narrative territory in order to clarify Paul's often-ambiguous discursive language with plausible and concrete experiential examples and precedents, given his undoubted knowledge of Paul. As to assessing the state of that knowledge, from independent accounts or sources, from firsthand experience, from some of Paul's letters (whose existence in the churches the writer of Acts can hardly be expected to be unaware of), or from all of the above, another factor to be considered is the level of communication in Paul's world, with letters sent from one community to another.[19] As to conceptual parallels, Walton discovers that the Lukan and Pauline concepts of leadership, fundamentally about Christlikeness, appear to be mutually conceived (as one might expect from mutual participation in underlying Christian tradition). Overall, unhelpful to the Dibelius-Vielhauer-Haenchen-Conzelmann conception of the Lukan Paul, as also is Porter's analysis of the Paul of Acts and the Paul of the Letters,[20] Walton concludes, "It seems inescapable that Luke and Paul *did* inhabit similar thought-worlds. Luke is clearly capable of presenting Paul speaking in ways that sound very much like the *ipsissima vox* of the apostle himself."[21]

As to additional vocabulary in 1 Thessalonians not covered by the four themes, but paralleled in the speech, Walton draws attention, for example, to μαρτύρομαι (1 Thess 2:12; Acts 20:26) and διαμαρτύρομαι (1 Thess 4:6; Acts 20:21, 23, 24), and τὸ ἐκκλησία τοῦ θεοῦ (1 Thess 1:1; 2:14; Acts 20:28b). Of course, ἐκκλησία needed Christian delimiting, being a secular term for an assembly of citizens. That is how we find it in the speech and in 1 Thessalonians, with reference or allusion to Jesus's death. While it is clear that ἐκκλησία in Acts 20:28b has a Pauline flavor, it should not be overlooked that it also has a strong Lukan flavor, given that Luke in his first book goes to great descriptive lengths to illustrate examples of disciples who experience repentance, faith, forgiveness, and salvation, characters who, for Luke, would be reasonably considered to be assembled by God and bought with Jesus's blood. For Luke, characters in his first book who participate in the soteriological nexus of repentance, faith, forgiveness, and salvation appear experientially identical in this regard to those

---

19. On this point, cf. Llewelyn and Kearsley, "Official Postal Systems of Antiquity," 7:1–57; Thompson, "Holy Internet," 49–70; Millard, *Reading and Writing in the Time of Jesus*.

20. Porter, *Paul of Acts*, 187–206.

21. Walton, *Leadership and Lifestyle*, 185; Walton finds further that the Lukan Paul, "When he speaks to Christians as a pastor, sounds like Paul writing as a pastor. Further, when Paul himself writes about pastoral ministry in 1 Thessalonians he sounds similar to Luke's portrayal of him teaching pastors about pastoral ministry. Therefore, the Vielhauer/Haenchen view, that the 'two Pauls' are at variance, is over-stated, for our research suggests that at this point Luke's Paul sounds like the Paul of the epistles. It would require further work to demonstrate this for other Pauline letters, but our conclusion implies that such a quest would be worthwhile" (213).

characters in his second book who experience this nexus and Lukan conversion, as have Paul and the addressees of the Miletus speech. Here, at 20:28b, the Lukan Paul and the Paul of 1 Thessalonians reflect underlying soteriological similarities from the same cognitive experiential environment.

Walton reviews the evidence for connections between Ephesians and 2 Timothy and the Miletus speech and finds, perhaps as expected, the distance between them and the speech to be considerably greater (but, I might say, certainly not limitless) than is the case for 1 Thessalonians, where there is a clear and valid parallelism in both words and ideas. Nevertheless, it may be observed that the identical language in Acts 20:19, 28 and Ephesians 4:1–2 and 4:11–12 is striking; Martin could even argue that Luke wrote Ephesians.[22] As to the setting of the speech in Luke-Acts, Walton maintains that we cannot assume Luke believes Paul to be dead at the time of the final draft of Acts, and he further points out that the Paul for whom this speech may be a farewell is the church-planting missionary Paul (the Lukan Paul up to Acts 21:26, who thereafter becomes the prisoner Paul). In the Miletus speech, "Paul models for Luke's readers how to lead and pastor a church at a time when he has planted many churches, and when he has recently (Acts 20:7–12) taught a church, raised a church member from the dead and broken bread."[23] Perhaps Paul's recent Asian and Ephesian ministry in Acts 18:23—19:7 is a bit too obviously overlooked here. Does not this practical ministry epitomize relevant contextual teaching to the elders being addressed?[24]

---

22. Based on linguistic and conceptual parallels, so Martin, "Epistle in Search of a Life-Setting," 296–302. However, Barth, *Ephesians* 1–3, 4–50, 53–59 (here: 49) concludes that it is advisable to consider Paul as the author. A thorough study of similar components of style, of similar Jewish and Hellenistic Jewish concepts, and of the substantial correspondence of ideas found in other letters of Paul by Roon, *Authenticity of Ephesians*, motivates the conclusion that "It is not only plausible but even probable that Paul was the author of Ephesians" (440).

23. Walton, *Leadership and Lifestyle*, 202.

24. Wolter, "Apollos und die ephesinischen Johannesjünger," 49–73, correctly admires Luke's portrayal of the Twelve as Christians as being one of scintillating clarity, "Lukas entwirft . . . ein schillerndes Bild: Auf der einen Seite bezeichnet er sie als μαθηταί (v. 1) sowie als 'gläubig Gewordene' (πιστεύσαντες v. 2) und qualifiviert sie damit eindeutig als Christen" (67). It may be observed here that Luke, and his character, Paul, understand these disciple-believers addressed at Acts 19:2a as Christians, not as a special category of *Johannesjünger*, a coherent narrative reading in line with a distinguished train of Lukan scholarship (with Wolter, for example, T. Zahn, K. Lake, H. Cadbury, A. Ehrhardt, C. Hemer, P. Stuhlmacher). Luke's rhetorical clarity in his consistent and uniform characterization of believer-disciples throughout both of his books is indeed remarkable and unmistakable. Wolter observes that Luke wishes to contrast Apollos and Paul, showing that Paul is the superior pneumatic character, and again he is correct. From the preceding Apollos digression it is clear that these twelve Christians lacked information, as did Apollos, about the ministry of the heavenly Jesus and Spirit-reception, perhaps not an unknown problem in the Empire which Luke is attempting to correct. Yet Wolter seems to suggest that Luke must be motivated here by some vague or impractical ecclesiastical concern, whereas I suggest that Luke is motivated by narrative-rhetorical literary concerns, to give another practical example of one of his main narrative themes—the application of the Jerusalem/Petrine tradition regarding reception of the gift of the Holy Spirit by believer-disciples. Perhaps Wolter, who offers no compelling reason for Lukan creativity at this particular juncture and only invokes Lukan invention at the close of his argument, finds it difficult to trust his own analysis

Since the close similarity of the Paul of the Miletus speech and of 1 Thessalonians raises the question of Luke's possible sources, Walton examines the list of detailed textual comparisons[25] adduced by Schulze[26] and by Aejmelaeus.[27] However, Walton does not examine the textual comparisons between Acts and Romans set out by Kim[28] or the heuristic Romans 1:11; Acts 18:23f verbal and ministerial comparison. If Luke remained in Rome after arriving there with Paul, as the 'we'-passages easily suggest, and finished his double-work there as a *littérateur* concerned with sources and writings (Luke 1:1–3), he would have plausibly taken the time to read Romans, a letter which had been in Rome for several years, a letter probably known to have been read by Luke's Roman readership. Neither does Walton consider Walker's and Kim's comparisons with respect to Acts and Galatians.[29] In the future, the additional contribution of these two letters as potential precursors to progressive intertextual enrichment, particularly with respect to Lukan clarification of Paul's Spirit-reception language, will have to be duly considered as well.

Based on detailed textual comparisons, Schulze argues for Luke's literary usage of 1 Thessalonians based on verbal parallels alone; to him it seems obvious that Luke knew some Pauline Letters. Similarly, Aejmelaeus argues for Luke's memory of Pauline Letters he has had occasion to read, pressing this idea a bit hard but agreeing with Schulze on the likelihood of a detectable literary connection. Aejmelaeus[30] also adduces two conceptual comparisons (Acts 20:19, 31; 1 Thess 3:1–10 and 20:33–35; 1 Thess 2:9) and discusses the possible relation of Acts 17:1—18:17 to 1 Thessalonians,[31] concluding that comparisons between that section of Acts and 1 Thessalonians are not against the hypothesis that Luke utilized 1 Thessalonians. Walton apparently does not consider much of this to be very substantive and does not interact with it, although others, examining just the textual evidence alone, could argue for detection of the residue of intertextuality, beyond memory or shared vocabulary. A fair question is, how much verbal parallelism, usually but not always in different contexts, is required

---

insofar as it might logically apply (in Luke's mind) to Spirit-receiving and Spirit-imparting characters whose conduct Luke believes to epitomize the teaching of the Lukan Jesus (cf. the narrative dynamic introduced by Luke 11:13; 24:49; Acts 1:5, 8); otherwise, why must Luke's description be fictitious, somehow psychological (73)?

25. Walton, *Leadership and Lifestyle*, 204–8.
26. Schulze, "Die Unterlagen für die Abschiedsrede zu Milet in Apostelgesch, 20:18–38," 119–25.
27. Aejmelaeus, *Die Rezeption der Paulusbriefe in der Miletrede*, 89–195.
28. Kim, *Die Geisttaufe des Messias*, 193–94, 196.
29. Walker, "Acts and the Pauline Corpus Revisited," 77–86; Walker, "Acts and the Pauline Corpus Reconsidered," 3–23; Kim, *Die Geisttaufe des Messias*, 197. Regarding Galatians, Leppä observes that Luke employs the same rare words and expressions which Paul uses in the same context, arguing that there is significant textual evidence that Luke knew the letter. The structural similarity and, occasionally, similar wording show that Luke employs Paul's story in Galatians when writing about Paul's life up to Acts 15,2a, cf. Leppä, *Luke's Critical Use of Galatians*, 35–61, 183.
30. Aejmelaeus, *Die Rezeption der Paulusbriefe in der Miletrede*, 211–24.
31. Aejmelaeus, *Die Rezeption der Paulusbriefe in der Miletrede*, 196–210.

to weigh the probabilities for a literary decision? Another question in the methodology of comparisons and criteria is what bias, although perhaps not expressly overt, may lie in past scholarly reluctance to delve into the possibility that Lukan experiential descriptions may be used to understand Paul, rather than (sometimes quickly and dogmatically) taking unexampled Pauline language out of often scant epistolary context to supposedly understand Luke?

Walton asks, "If Luke had access to the letters as Aejmelaeus envisages, why does he never even hint that Paul wrote letters?"[32] Aejmelaeus suggests this is because Luke does not see Paul's letters as of particular interest or value for his task. This seems reasonable for a final draft of Acts, but Walton demurs on the argument that since Luke obviously somehow makes use of the contents of at least one of them in the Miletus speech, he would have more noticeably used others elsewhere if he had known them. But this may presuppose that Luke, in his great project, should have to inflexibly function in a predetermined and unnecessarily prescribed manner and not be allowed to freely function in the expected tradition of narrative-rhetorical composition, as illustrated by Theon of Alexandria (c. 50 CE).[33] Another answer to Walton's question (who does not want to envisage any literary "dependence" at all, if that be the right concept, in Luke's compositional improvement on the πολλοί, Luke 1:1) is that perhaps Luke's primary and urgent theological and pneumatological desire with respect to some of the letters is to clarify Paul rather than to quote him. Perhaps the answer is that Luke sees his own task, in part, as being to improve on the inherent deficiencies of illustration in Paul's previous style of discursive communication to exclusively in-house audiences. Lukan narrative thus serves as a pastoral remedy in providing urgently needed vivid examples and precedents[34] in order to make commonly used descriptive Christian experiential language (employed discursively by Paul) more widely understandable. This narrative proclivity certainly lies within the pastoral province of an independently thoughtful Roman-trained intellectual functioning in Theonic tradition. In reply to Walton's question I would ask, among the many details Luke omits, why would he want to portray Paul as a writer of letters? What importance would that add to his portrayal of Paul as a Spirit-receiving, Spirit-imparting, suffering, prophesying,

---

32. Walton, *Leadership and Lifestyle*, 211.

33. In a recent edition, Patillon, *Aelius Théon Progymnasmata*. Patillon's edition includes the five chapters (hg.v. G. Bolognesi) of Theon's treatise on narrative composition in Armenian not included in the edition of Butts, "'Progymnasmata' of Theon."

34. Luke is in accord with the instruction of Theon on this expected method of narrative persuasion via plausible examples and precedents serving to provide Christian expectation. Clarity, understandability, and vividness of examples and precedents are the narrative tools deemed important by Theon; it is unsurprising then that Luke employs such contemporary narrative technique. Lukan portrayal of interaction with, and of Christian expectation of, the divine is quite harmonious with Theonic characterization and personification. The use of examples and precedents on the oratorical side of the rhetorical tradition, surely not unknown to one educated in the Empire, is treated by Alewell, *Über das rhetorische Παράδειγμα*; Price, "'Paradeigma' and 'Exemplum' in Ancient Rhetorical Theory"; and Fiore, *Function of Personal Examples*.

and determined visionary missionary in the Jerusalem/Petrine tradition? As to Paul's letters not being of particular value for Luke's task (with Aejmelaeus), if Luke as a narrative theologian and historian wants to clearly portray, in the second volume of his double-work, both Paul's practical ministerial examples and Paul's speeches in narrative continuity (reading front to back) with the teaching of the earthly Jesus and with Jerusalem/Petrine experience, examples, and teaching, then quoting Paul could well be deemed superfluous. From his perspective Luke could easily consider that it would be best to have Paul speak for himself rather than to quote him.

One might also observe that if the writer of Acts composes from a first-century narrative-rhetorical perspective, as his self-implied context and work suggests, and if he does so with personal recollection, acquaintance, and experiential participation, he then likely does this as well from information received about Paul from Paul or from others, and perhaps, reasonably so, from possible perusal of Paul's occasional correspondence (which he could naturally seek out to confirm the professed accuracy of his portrayals). He is certainly not intellectually attuned to, or might I even say impaled upon, the quite non-Lukan concept of an "apostolic age"[35] with both its often dogmatic fixation on the epochal truncation and cessation of Lukan examples and precedents and its often rationalistic over-emphasis on the supposedly more refined (and accordingly supernaturally and experientially filtered) intellectual discourse of Paul.[36] From

---

35. As a contiguous and contemporary participating historian-theologian of a practical pastoral double-work, Luke might be disappointed to learn that his second untitled book became dubbed as the "acts of the apostles" and the "acts of the two apostles," or even understood in novel characterization-confining and concept-confining interpretation as if it were the "acts of thirteen male witnesses." Instead of these arguably misleading appellations or contentions, if this narrative would be properly entitled, Ehrhardt's thesis that the "whole purpose" of Luke's second book "is no less than to be the Gospel of the Holy Spirit" seems a far more appropriate guide (cf. Ehrhardt, "Construction and Purpose," 45–79, esp. 55, 63); Ehrhardt proposes a title for the second book as "The Gospel of the Holy Spirit in the Church Militant Here on Earth," in his *Acts of the Apostles*, 129. On my argument, the writer of this double-work would live, as would his readers, not in a supposed "apostolic age" or "Pentecostal age" perhaps conceptually germinated by a spirit of cessationistic and rationalistic exuberance, but instead in the time of "Die Zeit der Geistesgabe" (with Pesch, "Die Gabe des Heiligen Geistes" 52, 53, esp. 53, Pesch assuming that the Lukan gift of the Holy Spirit is not phenomenologically equivalent to the Lukan soteriological nexus of repentance-forgiveness-faith-salvation-conversion).

36. The writer of Luke-Acts portrays himself in an easily understandable and persuasive manner to his readers as being a contiguous and contemporary participant in some events in his text. This narrative cohesion of events and characters exhibits what Hemer calls an "integration which is *latent in the narrative*" insofar as the "we"-passages are concerned (*Book of Acts in the Setting of Hellenistic History*, 312–34, esp. 333, emphasis original). Consistent with this vein of personalized narration, our writer, whose careful depiction of his characters' experiences with the divine, might then be disappointed to learn just how dismissive and extreme the concretized perspective from an explicitly imposed, theoretically distant, and impersonal epoch can sometimes become, a perspective deliberately disjoined from the world of his personalized text which is then dubbed the "apostolic age" or the "Pentecostal age." Instead of his characters' actions epitomizing teaching so as to set examples and precedents for the time of his world and beyond via prophetic fulfillment (one of his keen interests), his characters and their vividly narrated experiences are entombed in a supposedly disjointed, altogether different, and experientially truncated epoch from the lives of his readers, a ploy, in my judgment, that he would find surprising as well as disappointing. The perspective of his characters' lives conceptually

such a distant paleoreformed perspective, it might even seem inconceivable to some, if it be accepted that Luke saw a pastoral need to clarify common discursive language of the letters for those in need of further instruction, that Luke would not have quoted Paul had he known his letters or at least have pointed out that Paul wrote letters.[37]

---

encapsulated in an artificial age or epoch bolted to his text, as in a stodgy work of modern fiction, is certainly not a perspective which emerges from this writer's own dynamic narrative-rhetorical and prophecy-fulfilling world, not one that is at all suggested by his text itself, but one externally superimposed from a distant orb where characters' experiences in his double-work are perpetually frozen in their own time frame as if they were fashioned as marionettes of no exemplary significance. Contact with the Christian experience of Lukan characters is thereby minimalized (contra Johnson, *Religious Experience in Earliest Christianity*) and intellectual aspects of Pauline Letters become the *sine qua non* for Christianity. For the writer of Acts not to cite Paul's Letters, had he known them, may even then implicitly display his ignorance of what is really important (although I would certainly not attribute this underlying attitude to Walton). Such an artificial perspective from the imposition of entrenched epochal division is aptly illustrated by Jervell, *Theology of the Acts of the Apostles*, 124, 133. Jervell wrongly attributes impersonal orientation to both the deliberately personal descriptions and personal characterizations of the Holy Spirit's interactions with disciples in Lukan portrayals. An ultra-rationalistic and condescending appraisal of Luke's considerable narratively prominent contextual efforts at clarity and plausibility is mistakenly advanced: "He considers the past the ideal time of the church and as a norm. . . . There is, however, not much rationality in the way Acts describes the Spirit. The Spirit is an impersonal and dynamic force, God's creative presence in the church, visible and manifesting itself in miracles, wonders, glossolalia, inspiration, visions, auditions and, above all, prophetic sayings. . . . Even if there has been a revival of the charismatic in some (established) churches in the last years these phenomena cannot be regarded as any kind of proof for the divine character of the church, not least as they are known from many religions, and not even reserved for religions. In his comprehension of the Spirit Luke is far behind the depths of Paul's understanding, which is of far greater contemporary significance."

37. This appears not to be the case, historically at least, with W. M. Ramsay, who argues that "It is hard to believe that Paul's letters were unknown to Luke; he was in Paul's company when some of them were written; he must have known about the rest and could readily learn their contents in the intimate intercommunication that bound together the early Churches. We shall try to show that Luke had in mind the idea of explaining and elucidating the letters," in his *St. Paul the Traveller and the Roman Citizen*, 16. However, Ramsay's adherence to Lukan explaining and elucidating of Pauline Letters seems confined (albeit unnecessarily) to historical matters, perhaps because this is where his interests lie. Nevertheless, the methodology Ramsay advocates need not, and should not, be confined to historical matters of an "apostolic age," as if this concept, itself at odds with Luke's obvious interest in the ongoing fulfillment of prophecy, should be allowed to truncate even the proposed methodology itself. As an example of this presupposed epoch's rationalistic appeal and hence its interpretive power, when it comes to Luke's portrayal of Paul as either a Spirit-receiving or as a Spirit-imparting missionary to Lukan believer-disciples, Ramsay exhibits no inclination in either instance to explore any experiential explanation or elucidation of the connectivity with similar Pauline epistolary language. Instead of appreciating the mutual cognitive environment of the two writers in this regard, on one such occasion (Acts 19:2-7) Ramsay claims that the Lukan Paul's deportment is supposedly "distinctly below the level on which Luke's conception of Paul is pitched" (270). Ramsay would remove Acts 19:2-7 both from its context, artfully illuminated with the conventional narrative foregrounding of Luke's lovely Apollos digression, and from the New Testament itself on textual grounds if that were possible! Ramsay, in the contextually unharmonious and narratively disjointed style of anti-Lukan (Calvinistic) dispensational imposition/dichotomization, supports his extraction and disappearance of an unwelcome Lukan Paul by positing that Paul here be relegated to "early history of the Ephesian church" (270), completely overlooking and discounting the Lukan emphasis of narrative-rhetorical examples and precedents. Ramsay's extraction/disappearance thesis here, while befitting the narratively foreign interpretive presupposition of an "apostolic age," is a far cry from his otherwise intellectually attractive

In any event, given the need to sharpen methodology, understand backgrounds, and develop criteria for detailed textual comparisons, further interaction on comparative issues may be expected in this emerging area of research.[38]

Walton's judicious and careful study, for which all students of Luke-Acts will be appreciative, achieves three solid conclusions: one, Luke knows Pauline tradition independently of the Epistles; two, Luke knows Pauline tradition "rather better than is sometimes suggested;"[39] and three, Luke "seeks to pass on and commend Paul's tradition."[40] However, when Walton combines these reliable conclusions with the additional assessment that it is improbable that Luke knew any of Paul's letters, he may, in weighing this latter judgment, have overreached the cumulative impression of all the strands of suggestive evidence.

---

attempt to show that "Luke had in mind the idea of explaining and elucidating the letters."

38. For example, cf. Brodie, "Towards Tracing the Gospels' Literary Indebtedness to the Epistles," 104–16; Aejmelaeus, "Reopening the Question."

39. Walton, *Leadership and Lifestyle*, 212.

40. Walton, *Leadership and Lifestyle*, 212.

Chapter 8

Spirit, Scripture, and Theology through a Lukan Lens

A Review Article

THE LATE COLIN HEMER once observed that we must "evaluate Luke rather by his performance than by any literary *Vorverständnis*."[1] So true. Along with Colin's mentor, F. F. Bruce, a distinguished group of scholars have devoted their lives and now continue to labor in a great tradition in order to place Luke's work in its historical context, building confidence in Luke's historicity, as illustrated recently by the important *The Book of Acts in Its First-Century Setting* series. Since Luke's performance with respect to various historical backgrounds has been shown to be so reliable, it is timely to observe that one phenomenon in which he clearly took a keen interest and which set Christianity apart from, rather than making it consistent with, the Greco-Roman religion and Palestinian spirituality within these backgrounds was the distinctive work of the Holy Spirit which he narratively detailed. Yet much remains to be done to try to get a handle on how Luke would have expected Theophilus to react to these narrative descriptions of activities of the Spirit. Should Theophilus become a Christian, he could ignore them or expect them. Are there clues in Luke's performance in this regard which point the way to his intentions and expectations for divine actions?

Onto this comparatively untrodden ground comes Roger Stronstad with a work focusing on hermeneutics which could be of use to the broad evangelical community for discussion and progress in Lukan studies.[2] *Spirit, Scripture, and Theology* attempts to sort out Luke's mixture of history and theology, his self-understanding of his prophetic position, and his rationale for documenting activities of the Holy Spirit within the primitive evangelical mission.

The volume opens with an excellent foreword by William Menzies (iii–vi), who sets into recent historical focus the task of trying properly to understand and interpret Luke's writing about the Holy Spirit as an independent and consistent complement to Paul.[3] Stronstad himself wants to move beyond the "Pentecost-as-pattern" hermeneutic of early Pentecostalism and engage recent discussion by Gordon Fee, Howard Ervin,

1. Hemer, *Book of Acts in the Setting of Hellenistic History*, 42.
2. Stronstad, *Spirit, Scripture, and Theology*. [Now in its second and expanded edition (2018).—Ed.]
3. This builds briefly on Menzies's earlier work, "Holy Spirit in Christian Theology," 67–80.

and William Menzies in his opening piece on "Trends in Pentecostal Hermeneutics" (11–30). Fee begins his criticism of the simplistic "Pentecost-as-pattern" approach with his "The Genre of New Testament Literature and Biblical Hermeneutics,"[4] in which he argues that historical precedent cannot be used as an analogy to establish a normative pattern or even what might be normal in Christian experience, although he leaves token room for the distinctive genre of Luke-Acts to carry some theological weight. Since the reasonable concepts of *Sprachereignis* (occurrence of distinctive speech) or *Wortgeschehen* (descriptive word event) can legitimately be supplemented by an explicit articulation of experience, it is not surprising that interpreters have sought to move on from unnecessarily confining and historically minimizing approaches like that of Fee. I say "unnecessarily confining" and "historically minimizing" because it strains credulity to believe that Luke intended Theophilus to read Acts 2:38 and 39, where he might rightly ask his writer, "What is the gift of the Holy Spirit?," only to be told that events in the manuscript which Theophilus would reasonably think should shed some more light on his question were no longer reliable guides since they had become "historical precedent."[5] On the contrary, Ervin has attempted to integrate reason and sensory experience into interpretation while Menzies advocates the incorporation of experiential verification with both exegetical practice and the construction of biblical theology (which includes theology based on historical narrative).[6] Stronstad serves us well in setting out these three visions (Fee, Ervin, Menzies) as we attempt to formulate a genuine Lukan understanding of the theology present within Luke's two scrolls. (By theology here I mean inscripturated information related to how God might act, because Luke is obviously not just a political historian.)

Stronstad continues his interaction with Fee in "The Hermeneutics of Lukan Historiography" (31–52). Conceding to Fee that the "Pentecost-as-pattern" hermeneutic of Pentecostalism does disregard scientific exegesis and does not seem to be carefully thought out, he argues that it has Pauline traits, namely that all Scripture is profitable for teaching, training, instruction, and example. Luke uses narrative to introduce theological themes, and having established these themes, narrative is again used to illustrate and reinforce the themes via historical episodes (42). The episodes are examples of Luke's theme, activities of the Holy Spirit in the evangelical mission. While narrative has a complex function, it can function paradigmatically; treating both the Gospel and Acts

---

4. Fee, "Genre of New Testament Literature," 105–27; continuing this approach in his "Hermeneutics and Historical Precedent," 119–32; Fee, *Gospel and Spirit*, 83–104.

5. I venture to say that neither Luke nor Theophilus would recognize Fee's agenda, since divine actions in conjunction with ongoing missionary work would reasonably be perceived as setting the tone for a new epoch of history wherein the invisible God would act in concert with the resurrected Christ and with the Holy Spirit poured forth, not only in salvation (e.g., Acts 4:8–12) but poured out in a prophetic manner and in diverse matters within individuals, giving new possibilities to act and to serve, as appreciated also by Bonnard, "L'Esprit saint et l'Église selon le Nouveau Testament," 84.

6. Cf. Ervin, "Hermeneutics," 23–35, and Menzies, "Methodology of Pentecostal Theology," and 1–14.

as narrative, Stronstad concludes that Luke definitely had an instructional rather than a merely informational purpose (51) so that "because historical narrative is Luke's vehicle of instruction, he is also a theologian of the Spirit" (52).

In "Pentecostal Experience and Hermeneutics" (53–78), Stronstad admits that Pentecostals have flaunted the emotional dimension of their experience, but he wonders whether they are "devoid of any real grasp of the Bible that goes beyond mere proof-texting."[7] Carson sees raw triumphalism,[8] and Fee, with a modern conception of Luke's idea of history, obviously sees Pentecostals exegeting their own experience. These personalized assessments, based on a valid but incomplete set of observations, seem to have motivated textual conclusions that seem a bit too neat and hasty, reminiscent of the simplistic and unproductive dispensational theories of the past. But in spite of these criticisms, Stronstad sees the obvious, the exegeting of nonexperience in the evangelical tradition and a lack of recognition of the latent presuppositional underpinnings of cessationist theology in that exegesis.[9] Stronstad's thesis here is a sober one: that spiritual and/or charismatic experience gives the thoughtful interpreter a presupposition that transcends the rational or cognitive presuppositions of scientific exegesis, one consistent with Menzies's supplement of experiential verification, resulting in "an understanding, an empathy, and sensitivity to the text, and priorities in relation to the text which other interpreters do not and cannot have" (59). This is not as ambitious as it seems in that the early church was built on Christocentric experience, as well as upon reflection on the meaning of the life, death, and resurrection of the historical Jesus, experience which motivated and required the creation of language to describe activities of the Holy Spirit.[10] So too the contemporary church, when it decides that it has valid Christocentric experience, which is reasonably described by New Testament language, can and should assume that these experiences are the same as detected and described by the producers of early Christian texts (contra Packer[11]).

7. Carson, *Showing the Spirit,* 12.

8. For a critique of the triumphalism which Carson detects, cf. Penney, "Disturbing Echoes of the Past in Some Pentecostal Prophecy," an Afterword in his "Testing of New Testament Prophecy," 82–84.

9. On these latent presuppositions, see Ruthven, *On the Cessation of the Charismata*. [Revised and expanded in 2011 (Tulsa, OK: Word & Spirit).—Ed.] Barth, "Christ and All Things," 160–72, deals eloquently with the problem of hidden persuaders.

10. E.g., the enthusiastic worship of the early church not only distinguished it from typical synagogue worship but also most probably included experiences of visions, glossolalia, prophecy, and the creation of hymnody used to praise the Lord Jesus, giving early roots to the hymnodic fragments we can detect in New Testament texts, cf. Hengel, "Hymn and Christology," 190–95. Against the contemporary religious backgrounds, these diverse experiences—thoughtfully shared and described with what would have been deemed to be appropriate language—would have contributed, along with salvation experience, to a recognition of unity in Christ; cf. a couple of Paul's descriptions of this experiential-based idea: πάντες ἓν πνεῦμα εποτίσθημεν (1 Cor 12:13b) and ἡ ἀγάπη τοῦ θεοῦ ἐκκέχυται ἐν ταῖς καρίαις ἡμῶν διὰ πνεύματος ἁγίου (Rom 5:5b).

11. J. I. Packer denies this and argues that to describe contemporary Christocentric experience with New Testament language is "deeply unbiblical," because Christians in this century, for example, who would do this are, in fact, just the theologically naive victims of a "restorationist theory of

Since charismatic experience, according to Stronstad, is helpful in interpreting information in Lukan texts, it is odd that he does not identify the category of suffering, since this approach has something significant to offer to our understanding of this aspect of Christian life.[12] Would not this perspective also help in understanding the charismatic experience of the Lukan Paul, a main player in Stronstad's hermeneutical search, since it was God's will for Paul to suffer, as he himself tells us?[13] Further, the suffering of Christ is a concept which Luke makes distinctive as well.[14] Perhaps, Stronstad is reluctant to cite this obvious experiential category in support of his hermeneutical argument because Pentecostals in particular among evangelicals have been victimized in this area by functional heresy from pamphleteers, charlatans, and televangelists. (However, in fairness to them, harmful doctrines and heretics have been exposed[15] and there is willingness to reconsider and/or pastorally reformulate old ideas.[16]) But Stronstad's point is well taken; one component of properly understanding experientially descriptive texts coming from Luke's pen can be contemporary experience, God willing, or as van Unnik observes, "much critical study of Acts has been done at a distance from, or even without living contact with, Luke's world. It is not sufficient to remind ourselves that he was not a historian in our sense, but in that of antiquity; but we shall have to walk with him along his roads, to see with his eyes and those of his contemporaries."[17] In "'Filled with the Holy Spirit' Terminology in Luke-Acts" (79–97), we find Stronstad's careful treatment of the Greek terms Luke

---

sign-gifts"; cf. his "Theological Reflections on the Charismatic Movement, Part 2," 103–25. Packer is, in my judgment, deeply influenced by latent and unexamined presuppositions or hidden persuaders which are rooted in a contemporary dispensational worldview. Cf. my response to Packer in "Charismatic Movement in the Church of England," 28–33. Moreover, shared Christocentric experience (not just an experience identified as salvation, but diverse prophetic-phenomena which can accompany it) plays a fundamental role in the contemporary church; cf. Bittlinger, "Der neutestamentliche charismatische Gottesdienst im Lichte der heutigen charismatischen Emeuerung der Kirche," 186–209; and Grudem, *Gift of Prophecy in the New Testament and Today*.

12. Cf. the challenge to develop a theology of suffering by Nissen, "Problem of Suffering and Ethics," 227–87, together with the work of Luhman, "Belief in God," 326–48; and Kim, "Salvation and Suffering According to Jesus," 204n32. Charismatic experience within a Lukan theology of suffering relates directly to a competent understanding of the gift of the Holy Spirit today.

13. Cf. the insightful incorporation of the charismatic Lukan Paul with this aspect of the historical Paul by Jervell, "Der schwache Charismatiker," 185–98 ; also, Hafemann, *Suffering and Ministry in the Spirit*, 176–77.

14. Moule, "Christology of Acts," 167–70. Also, the Lukan Jesus has a prophetic identity with prophets who suffer (Luke 4:24; 13:33) and this prophetic dimension is a factor, for Luke, in Jesus's suffering and death. Cf. Frein, "Prophecies and Luke's Sense of Fulfilment,"32. Stronstad could have drawn out many ramifications of this for charismatic vocation today.

15. Smail et al., "'Revelation Knowledge,'" 57–77. Exaggerations and distortions beyond orthodoxy, while certainly not pervasive, are perhaps at least as harmful today, with the advent of television, as were the claims of the Marcionites.

16. Petts, "Healing and the Atonement," 23–37. (This is an excerpt of a thesis of the same title at Nottingham.)

17. Unnik, "Luke's Second Book," 60 (emphasis his).

uses to speak of "full of the Holy Spirit" and "filled with the Holy Spirit." Stronstad's result is that the former describes enabling for ministry and the latter describes prophetic office and potentially repetitive experience (95, 97). Interaction with the only other major study of this material, done by Shelton,[18] is missing and is much needed to codify and compare the results. Other distinctive Lukan terminology is investigated, like "received" the Holy Spirit, "the gift" of the Spirit and "baptized" in the Spirit, the latter signifying the consecration of the disciples for a prophetic evangelical mission (97), although this is not Luke's preferred term (98). As to Luke's meaning of one of these widely used phrases, perhaps the pastoral observation of dogmatic theologian Francis Sullivan is apropos:

> The proof, of course, of whether a real "baptism in the Holy Spirit" has taken place will be the subsequent transformation of a person's life, not his speaking in tongues when prayed over. The merely natural factors, I believe . . . cannot account for a deep spiritual renewal. Speaking in tongues, then, is a work of grace when it is a sign of such genuine renewal in the Spirit. The phenomenon of speaking in tongues, as such, is not an authenticating sign of spiritual renewal, but itself needs to be authenticated by subsequent evidence that a real spiritual renewal has taken place.[19]

Stronstad includes a useful picture of how Lukan terms are interpreted in various traditions and argues that our current task "is not to make our pneumatology Reformed, Wesleyan, or Pentecostal, per se, but, to make it biblical" (98).

In "Signs on the Earth Beneath" (99–141), Stronstad corrects Fee's claim that Acts is unique by arguing that Luke's term διήγησις (Luke 1:1) applies to his entire two-volume history, a conclusion not unlike that reached by others.[20] Further, Acts

---

18. Shelton, "'Filled with the Holy Spirit,'" 81–107. On these shades of meaning in Lukan thought, cf. also Menzies, *Empowered for Witness*, 173–228, and Penney, *Missionary Emphasis of Lukan Pneumatology*, 96–110; contra Köstenberger, "What Does It Mean?," 229–40, who ignores relevant episodes in Acts and characterizes Stronstad as limiting Spirit-filling to prophetic inspiration and vocation (although Köstenberger's understanding or acceptance of this vocabulary or categorization for Luke seems in doubt), dismissing him as unconvincing (231n9). However, Köstenberger is not nearly as interested in the spiritual experiences of Luke's characters (including Paul), where a phenomenological context is given, as he is in attempting to identify descriptions of these and similar experiences in Paul's letters so as to address the question he poses in the title of his article.

19. Sullivan, *Charisms and Charismatic Renewal*, 143. The pastoral theologian Donal Dorr also contributes here, in spite of his lack of awareness of attempted exegesis in Acts by evangelicals, cf. *Remove the Heart of Stone*, 35–68; as do the pastoral efforts of Mühlen, *Einübung in die christliche Grunderfahrung* 147–66, and of Williams, *Renewal Theology*, 2:137–409.

20. E.g., Tannehill, *Narrative Unity of Luke-Acts*; Marshall, "Acts and the 'Former Treatise,'" 1:182. While Acts is unique in that it has no obvious secular precedents, the idea that use of historical narrative precludes a serious *Lukan* interest in building theology/pneumatology is not Lukan. There is an intentional narrative sequence here and, therefore, it is reasonable to believe that Luke expects Theophilus to recognize and to seek to understand a message with respect to the activities of the Holy Spirit, to recognize experiences which shaped the story. However, this common-sense point has proven to be elusive, as John Goldingay notes: "Narrative, story, dominates scripture. . . . At one level, Christian

should not be shut out of contemporary relevance by a hermeneutic that "is either hostile or antipathetic to the contemporary applicability of historical narrative" (117), and several guidelines are offered on how to apply the lessons and principles inherent within Luke's historical episodes. Stronstad notes that on the first Jerusalem Pentecost the disciples "speak in languages other than their native language(s), speak in languages hitherto unlearned but now momentarily mediated to them by the Holy Spirit" (123), but he does not address the xenolalia/contemporary glossolalia issue, which he probably feels is included in the prophetic dimension of the Spirit.

Lukan christology is examined as a basis for "The Holy Spirit in Luke-Acts" (143–67), where it comes up a little short, in my judgment, with respect to the categories of lordship and sovereignty, while I agree that Luke's pneumatology does serve and complement his christology. However, Stronstad needs to realize more fully that Lukan pneumatology, with its varied descriptions of activities of the Holy Spirit, is controlled by Luke's recognition of Jesus as sovereign Lord. In Luke 24:49, Jesus says, "*I* send the promise of my Father" (emphasis mine).[21] Yet Stronstad detects an overall charismatic theology in Lukan writings which has the following implication for contemporary readers:

> If the gift of the Spirit was charismatic for Jesus and the early church, so it ought to have a vocational dimension in the experience of God's people today. . . . If Jesus was the charismatic Christ, and the disciples were a charismatic community, so the church in our generation is also charismatic, whether or not it functions at the level of our charismatic potential. (167)

I can agree with this concept of "charismatic potential" as long as it is understood that the Lukan/historical Paul, the suffering and weak apostle (weak and sick charismatic, so Jervell n13 above), the dynamic charismatic miracle worker, teacher, and pastoral theologian, was functioning up to his "charismatic potential" when he left Trophimus sick at Miletus.

The volume wraps up with a piece on "Unity and Diversity: Lucan, Johannine, and Pauline Perspectives on the Holy Spirit" (169–92), wherein Stronstad defends himself against Carson who seems to believe that interpreting Luke independently of

---

tradition has indeed always recognized the importance of story, but you would not guess this from the nature of Christian theology, or from the nature of much writing on spirituality. . . . It is a natural and biblical way to do theology; it takes up the discourse methods of Paul. Yet narrative is scripture's more dominant way of doing theology" ("Biblical Story," 5, 6).

21. Also, cf. τὸ πνεῦμα Ἰησοῦ, Acts 16:7; τὸ πενῦμα κυρίου, Acts 5:9, 8:39, Luke 4:18; ὁ λόγος τοῦ κυρίου, Acts 8:25, 12:24, e.g., and Franklin, *Christ the Lord*, who concludes that Luke's "interest was centred upon the exalted Lord who brings men into salvation as a present act" (182). This evidence, together with Luke's distinctive use of ὁ κύριος many times in his Gospel, his documentation of the resurrection, the ascension, and the thrice-mentioned conversion of Paul by the Lord, suggests a mindset which thinks of κυριότης in terms of sovereignty with respect to divine actions (of diverse description) which fulfill his edition of the prophecy of Joel and empower the evangelical mission.

Paul makes it impossible to "speak of canonical theology in any holistic sense."[22] But earlier, many scholars had already noted[23] that the Lukan data regarding the Spirit did not easily fit any one model (like the Pauline-oriented von Baer-Dunn model which many evangelicals had embraced[24]), so Carson's protestations here do seem overdrawn. Further, Schweizer, in particular, had set out a competent case to the effect that while Luke was not given to as much theological reflection as John or Paul, he understood the Spirit in an Old Testament way as a gift that does not so much create faith as grant those who already believe the strength to do special things.[25] Given this widely held consensus on Luke's distinctive and varied New Testament thought—which is consistent with his alleged independence—I see no reason for disagreeing with Stronstad that for Luke, John, and Paul the Spirit is "vocational-charismatic" as well as personal. However, since the descriptions by these writers vary, I would speculate that some of their spiritual experiences contained some variation as well, one factor accounting for the variation in linguistic description. And why leave out Matthew? If when Matthew wrote his Gospel he intended that it should replace Mark and become the Gospel for Christians of his day,[26] it is likely that he would have carefully considered the role of the Holy Spirit at that time and would have used language to capture correctly the intention of the historical Jesus in that regard. If, then, my earlier argument is right about his theological understanding of charismatic distribution[27] and if Charette is right concerning his theology of the

---

22. Carson, *Showing the Spirit*, 151. In fact, Stronstad's earlier work on Lukan thought is complementary, not antithetical, to Paul (as suggested by Carson).

23. In that time frame, cf. Giblet, "Baptism in the Spirit," 162–71; Sullivan, "Baptism in the Spirit," 49–66; Haya-Prats, *L'Esprit, force de l' Église*; Turner, "Spirit Endowment in Luke/Acts," 45–63; and Quesnel, *Baptisés dans l'Esprit*, 24.

24. As is well known, this appeared in 1970 as a Cambridge thesis by Dunn, *Baptism in the Holy Spirit*, and while an early attempt, it had an easy appeal, with its compression of data into neat compartmental cocoons; apparently less well known is the cogent criticism by Giblet, "Baptism in the Spirit," 168, who detects an "element of fantasy" and the devastating exegetical argument of Russell, "'They Believed Philip Preaching' (Acts 8.12),'" 169–76, which alone should have generated a retraction, or at least a reconsideration, but as is often the case, an "established" position, even one created in just a few years, is, in the theological world, too often protected rather than modified. However, Dunn has proven to be a good dialogue partner, issuing replies on various occasions, which have borne some fruit. For example, cf. Shelton, "Reply to James D. G. Dunn's 'Baptism in the Spirit,'" 139–43. Dunn's "conversion-initiation" model is best considered a useful effort which is neither as explanatory nor predictive as it first appeared to be; rather it broke new ground against the supposed simultaneity of water baptism and Spirit reception.

25. With Stronstad, *Spirit, Scripture, and Theology*, 84, 183. Schweizer, *Heiliger Geist*, 171; Schweizer, "πνεῦμα κτλ," *TWNT* 6:402–12. However, Schweizer's "special things" need not be limited to charismatic vocation or empowering for mission but could include a category which might be called "personal edification," like, for example, Acts 7:51, 11:24, 13:52, and 15:28; cf. George, "L'Esprit Saint dans l'oeuvre de Luc," 500–542, and Haya-Prats, *L'Esprit, force de l'Église* [ET: *Empowered Believers*—Ed.].

26. As argued by Stanton, "Fourfold Gospel," 341.

27. Elbert, "Perfect Tense in Matthew 16:19 and Three Charismata," 149–55. (Research on the

Spirit being reflective of Old Testament expectation,[28] then Matthew also thought of the Spirit as vocational, personal, and charismatic. Stronstad, then, sees the activity of the Spirit for Luke in terms of charismatic vocation or service, for John in terms of service and salvation (ditto for Matthew, given the veracity of Elbert and Charette),[29] and for Paul in terms of service, salvation, and sanctification (189, 190)—unity and diversity.

In conclusion, I return to Theophilus, who would have been aware not only of the scandal of the incarnation and the crucifixion but also, as I suggested above, of the distinctiveness of spiritual phenomena within the Christian movement against the contemporary backdrop.[30] In Luke's second scroll, he would read of divine events of fundamental significance to the movement and of miraculous acts of power and intervention in circumstantial contexts, and he would understand that, for Luke, these things happened in the name of Jesus and that activities of the Spirit were made manifest within Jesus's followers.[31] He could have detected as well a distinctive Christian flavor in Luke's reports of dreams and visions.[32] As an educated person, he would have appreciated Luke's work as coming from a man operating within the scientific tradition, where respect for accuracy was believed to be a significant feature,[33]

Greek perfect tense since this work was prepared is consistent with and supportive of my earlier observations; for background context which does not address Matthew's possible charismatic interests, see Duncan and Derrett, "Binding and Loosing [Matt 16:19; 18:18; John 20:23]," 112–17.) It is important to keep in mind here that Matthew's understanding of Jesus would have included the recognition of his spiritual authority, power, and/or influence, as well as the experiences of his spiritual presence delineating these personality traits (Matt 28:18, 20b). These charismatic understandings would motivate some pastoral linkage, correlation, or connectedness between the divine actions of the spiritual Jesus and those ministerial actions of the historical Jesus described by Matthew. The operations of the Spirit, which I believe Matthew is portraying via his use of the perfect tense, would serve well the need for identification and validation in the charismatic activities of discernment, exorcism, healing, and prophetic utterance within the Matthean community, thus enabling the disciples to continue, in a limited way, the ministry of the historical Jesus. Cf. also Thomas, "Kingdom of God in the Gospel according to Matthew," 143.

28. Charette, "'Never Has Anything Like This Been Seen in Israel,'" 31–51.

29. For some other recent discussion regarding possible charismatic activity in the Matthean community, cf. Holman, "Lesson from Matthew's Gospel for Charismatic Renewal," 48–63; and Smith, "Matthew's Message for Insiders," 229–39.

30. E.g., Ferguson, *Religions of the Roman Empire*, 224–43; Witt, *Isis in the Graeco-Roman World*, 255–68; Witt, *Isis and Sarapis in the Roman World*, where distinctiveness can be seen in worship, cultic practice, and prophetic claims; Aune, *Prophecy in Early Christianity*, 23–79; and Forbes, *Prophecy and Inspired Speech*, 229–60.

31. Cf. Hemer, *Book of Acts*, 433–43.

32. Hanson, "Dreams and Visions," 1395–425, detects such a distinction.

33. Alexander, "Luke's Preface in the Context of Greek Preface-Writing," 48–74, makes a very strong case for Luke as a writer within the scientific tradition. She points out—correctly, I think—that within the first-century scientific context, "Respect for tradition is a prime value in scientific texts, and especially respect for the passing on of tradition by direct personal contact from master to disciple" (71). In her *Preface to Luke's Gospel*, 127–33, 172–76, she argues that the writer of Luke-Acts must have had some direct contact with Greek scientific literature, while showing little interest in the school

and he would have known that in the Empire the best doctors commanded great prestige.[34] More recently, we have learned that Greek epitaphs for itinerant, well-respected doctors are consistent with Luke (Col 4:14), as a traveling physician, practicing his profession on the move with Paul.[35] Horsley notes an honorific inscription to one such respected physician from the first century or the reign of Trajan: "He is the first from ages past who is both doctor and historian."[36] Given these facts, all very likely to be in the forefront of Theophilus's appraisal of Luke's credibility and reliability insofar as divine actions are concerned, he might well have thought of Luke as a promising guide,[37] a trusted and respected man of science with the added prestige of doctor and scientific historian. Should he become a Christian and contemplate the choice, to ignore or expect the workings of the Holy Spirit which the writer of his scrolls describes, I believe the background evidence favors the latter decision. He would choose to investigate, to expect. His guide, in this event, would then be Lukan optimism and this optimism would, I think, for him, outweigh both religious skepticism engendered by divinities of his day and any interior needs he might have felt to protect a personal religious position.

Stronstad is to be commended for trying to take a tiny step in suggesting procedures and reasons for discovering Lukan pneumatology. In this quest it is clear that

---

classics of Greek education; cf. also Enslin, "Luke, the Literary Physician," 142–50.

34. Scarborough, "Doctor and His Place in Roman Society," 109–21, and Scarborough, "Roman Medical Education," 122–33; Phillips, "Medicine from the Alexandrians to Galen," 161–71. The documentation of Scarborough and Phillips is highly consistent with Alexander's result (see n33 above) with respect to the passing on of, and respect for, tested tradition, a framework that suits the book of Acts well.

35. Marx, "Luke, the Physician, Re-examined," 168–72; and Horsley, "Doctors in the Graeco-Roman World," 2:19–21, 24, 25. For identification of the author of Acts with Paul's friend, "the physician, the beloved," cf. Nock, *Essays on Religion and the Ancient World*, 2:827, 828. While the medical aspect of the author of Acts suggested here remains an assessment of probabilities, it is consistent with the "we-passages" and, in my judgment, is the most harmonious solution; for a thorough treatment of the "we-passages," cf. Hemer, *Book of Acts*, 312–34.

36. This particular doctor-historian, from Rhodiapolis in Lykia, was honored by his hometown with a gold portrait and a statue of education. He was a priest of Asklepios and Hygieia, a benefactor honored by other cities as well. The relevant part of the inscription from the statue base reads: "He is the first from the ages past who is both doctor and historian and poet of works on medicine and philosophy; they recorded that he is the Homer of medical verse, honoured with exemption from liturgies, having served as a doctor without charging fees," Horsley, "Doctors in the Graeco-Roman World" (2:24–25).

37. Perhaps, in his religious context, a reliable spiritual guide, cf. Hadot, "Spiritual Guide," 436–59. I agree with Downing, "Theophilus' First Reading of Luke-Acts," 109, that Theophilus would perceive the new faith to be "eminently respectable" within the contemporary religious context, but I doubt that he, whether he was a disciple or not (Downing assumes the former), would passively appraise the scrolls to be just merely "entertaining and reassuring." Rather, I believe his main response, given the distinctiveness of the material vis-à-vis the religious context, would be curiosity and inquiry into the activities of the Holy Spirit and the various experiences pertaining thereto described with Lukan language—given the astounding fact, according to Luke, that the son of God himself had recently appeared on earth due to involvement from that Spirit. Regarding Luke's keen interest in the identity of Jesus, cf. Kilgallen, "Conception of Jesus (Luke 1,35)," 225–46.

Stronstad wants to bring the help of the Spirit to bear in a logical way into our task—evaluating Luke's theological performance—via positive ideas, argument, and challenging dissent in order to stimulate thinking and dialogue in an area of significance for contemporary Christianity.[38] With a better formulated Lukan vision of the gift of the Spirit and its prophetic dimension[39] (harmonious with but not necessarily identical to that of his great theological friend), perhaps his contemporary readers would more fully recapture the eschatological potential for prophetic discipleship and the desire for Spirit-empowered witness and mission portrayed in Luke's writings.

As efforts toward Lukan pneumatology are made it is important to keep in mind that the prophetic dimension for Luke may not be equivalent to the broad concept of "spirit of prophecy" which can be constructed and gleaned from Old Testament and Jewish backgrounds. The Lukan Jesus sends the promise of the Father, not the promise of the Spirit of prophecy. Luke thinks in terms of the Spirit of Jesus. The concepts are similar but not identical. The main idea behind the concept of the gift of the Spirit for Luke may not be the inclusive constellation of spiritual experiences detected within the rubric of Jewish contexts, but it might include some of these as a subset. Evidently, however, the main components seem to include empowerment for mission (sovereignly provided, like Acts 20:23), visions, dreams, prophecy, prophetic

---

38. In this respect he is akin to Thomas, "Current Hermeneutical Trends" 253, who asks "Why should we deny the help of the Holy Spirit in a comparable ministry of removing subjectivity in our quest for the objective meaning of Scripture?" Obviously, we should not deny such possible help. But Thomas is responsible, along with other dispensational closure model inventors and supporters (e.g., Gaffin, cf. n47 below) for creating the confusion and skepticism which leads many to such denial. It is clear that large and significant portions of Scripture portray Jesus and the early church confronting the world soteriologically by manifesting the charismatic power of the Spirit, markedly out of phase with Thomas's postcanon epoch of "church maturity" (into the Dark Ages!). Inhabitants of Thomas's creative epoch, having matured, are epochally constrained so as to deny, evade, and/or be without the help of the Spirit in many functional categories cited or implied in these large and significant portions of Scripture as they serve their world. Thomas truncates the operations of the Holy Spirit as described by Paul and substitutes prescribed functions of a postcanon Holy Spirit, where "functions" of the new spirit are legitimated by nonexperience in order to discontinue any New Testament pattern; cf. an assessment of this influential model (as in the *Ryrie Study Bible*) by Grudem, *Gift of Prophecy in 1 Corinthians*, who argues that Thomas's suggestions "trivialize the whole passage in an unconvincing way" (216), and my critique of other misunderstandings in a review of Robert L. Thomas's *Understanding Spiritual Gifts*, 182–85.

39. Theophilus, regardless of whom he might have been, would attune to this Lukan prophetic dimension as distinctive with respect to contemporary secular and/or dormant Jewish backgrounds (with Forbes, *Prophecy and Inspired Speech*, 338–42, 346). For perceptions of this prophetic dimension, cf. Ellis, "Role of the Christian Prophet in Acts," 55–67; Crone, *Early Christian Prophecy*, 189–204; Robeck, "Gift of Prophecy in Acts and Paul"; Bovon, *Luc le théologien*, 234; and Bovon, "Le Saint-Esprit," 339–58; Jervell, "Sons of the Prophets," 96–121; Turner, "Jesus and the Spirit in Luke," 3–42; Turner, "Spirit of Prophecy and the Power of Authoritative Preaching," 66–68; Turner, "Spirit of Prophecy and Ethical/Religious Life," 166–90; Turner, *Power from on High*, 86–137; Shelton, *Mighty in Word and Deed*; Menzies, *Development of Early Christian Pneumatology*, 112–279; Menzies, *Empowered for Witness*, 48–228; Menzies, "Spirit and Power in Luke-Acts," 11–20; and Penney, "Testing of New Testament Prophecy," 55–59.

speech and/or glossolalia, and salvation experience.[40] Clearly, more quantitative work needs to be done as to the weight of possible categories like "personal edification" which could encompass diverse possibilities to act and serve. And, equally clear, more exegetical work needs to be done on episodes and contexts where Luke records an external appearance of the gift of the Holy Spirit like the "Ephesian Pentecost," where the Spirit is received with glossolalia and prophetic speech (again demonstrating a fulfillment of Luke's vision of Joel's prophecy), for these episodes need and deserve more than cursory explanations in order to estimate their Lukan significance.[41] Lukan pneumatology is ripe for fresh discoveries, having suffered relative neglect since the Reformation. Luke clearly wants to introduce Theophilus to responsible Christian life in a time of perseverance in suffering and ongoing missionary work prior to the judgment of the world, an agenda which does not in any way preclude a conservative theological agenda on his part.[42] For Luke, it matters whether the events he described really happened as a result of the interaction of the Spirit (conveying the presence of the historical Jesus) with the disciples whose experiences he narrates. He is not blasé or content to report a mere chronicle of happenings. He is obviously

40. Marshall, "Significance of Pentecost," 362, cogently observes that "the crucial point is the use of Joel 2:28–32 as a commentary on the gift of the Spirit." Jacob Kremer had earlier observed that Luke understood the Spirit from Jesus (Acts 2:33; 16:7) to be fulfilling Joel's prophecy by motivating prophetic gifts or "charismatischen Begabungen der Urkirche," correctly perceiving that "Daraus geht hervor, dass der Verfasser allem Anschein nach nicht nur das Pfingstgeschehen vor Augen hat" (*Pfingstbericht und Pfingstgeschehen*, 172), and Schweizer suggests that Luke thinks of a kind of prophetic *Eingebung* which the Spirit imparts on specific occasions (*Heiliger Geist*, 83). Menzies, *Development of Early Christian Pneumatology*, 213–29, has studied Luke's editorial work on the Joel text in some detail and concludes that Luke thinks that the gift of the Spirit, appearing in prophetic form, which Menzies calls "the Spirit of prophecy," is given exclusively to the people of God in that "The gift does not produce faith, it is given to faith . . . a heart for God is the pre-condition rather than the result of the prophetic gift" (225).

41. For example, with respect to the Acts 19 event, Ramsay, *St. Paul the Traveller and the Roman Citizen*, 270, thought the best solution would be to remove it from the New Testament if it were possible to do so on textual grounds, and Kirsopp Lake dubbed it "an important but disconcerting episode," in *Beginnings of Christianity*, 5:56. Turner, *Power from on High*, follows on from the von Baer-Dunn model of "conversion-initiation" at this juncture, where scholars employing sound grammatical practice in looking to context to identify the temporal significance of the aorist participle πιστύσαντες (Acts 19:2) with respect to the main verb are still guilty of making an "uninformed assumption" (392). But perhaps grammatical concerns have made a slight advance with respect to model-building, in that, earlier, these scholars "betrayed an inadequate grasp of Greek grammar" (Dunn, *Baptism in the Holy Spirit*, 87). In any case, for Turner, *Power from on High*, this episode is "alleged" (388), which is consistent with his criticism of those who are convinced that Acts represents historical tradition as having an "obvious methodological problem" (25). Menzies, *Development of Early Christian Pneumatology*, 274, is also too quick to characterize this episode as a "Lukan construction" because it seems to disagree with an aspect of his model. These procedural views do not seem to be Lukan, being inconsistent and inharmonious with ἀσφάλεια (Luke 1:4). If Theophilus was told that Luke created this episode for political or evangelistic reasons, something which Luke never implies, he would have had about as much interest in it as in a literary text of Akkadian hymns or Sumerian proverbs insofar as developing theology is concerned, since the "theology" developed, while having a certain antiquarian charm, would be neither explanatory nor predictive of divine actions.

42. So, too, Hengel, *Zur urchristlichen Geschichtsschreibung*, 59, 60.

quite interested in both the fulfillment of Old Testament prophecy and of predictions made in his narrative within historical events.[43] He is faithful to his distinctive and unambiguous theme of prophecy and fulfillment all the way, from the beginning to the close of his entire narrative history (even the final scene fulfills earlier prophecy of Acts 23:11). Not only is his treatment of his sources conservative, but it is motivated, I believe, by a blend of his own Christocentric experiences and by those in his sources and contacts (experience with respect to salvation and vocation), to the end that his evangelistic purpose is probably built considerably more on theological and scientific rather than on literary concerns.[44] Luke has literary ability and sophistication, but as a writer in the scientific tradition who is also a careful historian, his main focus was to make clear the reality of salvation experience and the reality of vocational/missiological experience—due to diverse activities of the Holy Spirit—so that Theophilus and future readers might be optimistic about the entire nexus of these divine actions. Theophilus would then appreciate that the charismatic vocation within the evangelical mission (e.g., Luke's last dramatic example, Acts 28:31)[45] was the distinctive signature of the new movement, where Jesus was the sovereign Lord and central figure.[46] Luke's consistent narrative evaluation and inclusion of prophetic phenomena implicitly signals his own interest in prophetic fulfillment, not fulfillment just in charismatic vocation within the lives of his characters in a literary sense, but in the life of Theophilus and in the lives of future readers in the "last days" (Acts 2:17, 39). The literary impact is vivid, Luke personally expects that as yet unfulfilled prophecies, especially his narratively significant edited version of Joel's prophecy, which I. Howard Marshall ("The Significance of Pentecost") has rightly understood to be a commentary on the Lukan gift of the Spirit, will be sovereignly fulfilled.[47]

43. An active area of Lukan studies has documented this beyond question, e.g., Schubert, "Structure and Significance of Luke 24," 176, 178; Talbert, "Promise and Fulfillment in Luke-Acts," 94, 95; Kurz, "Narrative Approaches to Luke-Acts," 215; and Frein, "Prophecies and Luke's Sense of Fulfilment," 34, 35.

44. Marshall, "Luke and his 'Gospel,'" 289–308, may focus too exclusively on categories like "experience of salvation" and "salvation history" and not enough on the blend of specific experiences of Luke's characters which seem to me perhaps more conveniently characterized by additional descriptive categories, as well as by those Marshall employs, like "vocational charismatic" or "prophetic" or perhaps by categories we yet need to create. Marshall detects aright Luke's distinctive interest in the spiritual idea of salvation rather than in a word group as such; cf. his *Luke*, 92–94.

45. Mealand, "Close of Acts and Its Hellenistic Vocabulary," 596, compares the triumphant ending of Acts with its "unhindered freedom" of daring speech to the conclusion of a Plutarch medical treatise (*Tu. san.* 137e.10) with its "unhindered exercise of virtue" and similar placement of ἀκωλύτως. Due to the tremendous strength of this concluding word, he suggests that "Acts 28:31 at a literary level may also be an allusion to the unstoppable sovereign action of God" (595).

46. Cf. also, Schweizer, "Gegenwart des Geistes und eschatologische Hoffnung," 505.

47. The God which Luke knew, whose sovereign experiential activities are portrayed to Theophilus, is, by strong inference, a God who will fulfill unfulfilled prophetic categories spoken by Lukan characters. To deny this by arbitrarily positing a dispensational closure epoch following Acts' final scene, is, in essence, to invalidate Luke's work and reinvent a god whose performance is unknowable because Lukan texts must then be theoretically sanitized through a dispensational lens. One modern

Our proper service then, if this be so, is to give Luke the credit and the respect he is due. He does not deserve to be marginalized by the dispensationally bizarre or by the historically minimalizing, nor to have his texts dismissed as creative because they seem to be out of phase with a pneumatological model, but he deserves to be understood (with van Unnik, "Luke's Second Book") as a narrative scientific theologian on his own terms, which were: a strong recognition of Jesus as supernatural Lord; and, following from this recognition, a desire to serve by preparing an accurate historical account. With regard to the dispensationally bizarre, once an extra-biblical epoch is superimposed upon the teaching of the New Testament writers in order to truncate spiritual gifts and fulfill other obscure notions and once this presumptuous claim becomes invested with the authority of print for many years (as in the Scofield Reference Bible and Ryrie Study Bible), it is difficult for those enamored with this rationalistic approach, unduly influenced by nonexperience stemming from what they have rejected and have not sought, to break out and embrace the credal sovereignty of God in this regard. Rejection of the tissue-paper theory circumscribing the Spirit via this dispensational closure model involves rejection of a dogmatic fixation on apostles and inscripturation (as well as rejection of zany extrapolations emanating from this dogmatic fixation) and opening up to, making space for, and encouraging the ministries of Christians to be sovereignly and prayerfully energized with *charismata* and *pneumatika* as the New Testament writers no doubt intended. To argue then, from within epochal constraints, that the Lord gives gifts as he determines, not as we determine, and when he decides, not as we decide, is provocative.[48] Since both Lukan and Pauline thought has been long victimized by the unintentionally arrogant demands and muddle of extra-biblical epoch invention, Poythress's insistence on sovereignty (with prayerfulness) vis-a-vis spiritual gifts is refreshingly scriptural and challenging.[49] Such insistence on sovereignty might presumably, God willing, also be extended to the complementary Lukan gift of the Spirit,[50] to salvation, and

---

conception of Luke's idea of history does exactly that and can only be characterized as thoroughly disconnected with Luke's unambiguous narrative theme of prophecy and fulfillment. This creative agenda contains the emphatic claim that "the history that interests Luke is *finished*" (emphasis his), so Gaffin, "Cessationist View," 38. Luke does not offer any palpable hint that the history he narrates is a unique epoch (37), whereafter divine actions were to be truncated, perturbed, and redescribed with respect to those he documents. Gaffin's vision does not spring from Lukan texts. Had both of Luke's scrolls been lost or destroyed, the model Gaffin seeks to build (which neither Luke nor Theophilus would recognize) would be virtually unaffected. Editor Grudem includes two sober rejoinders to Gaffin which take the clues in Luke's performance seriously: "A Third Wave Response," by C. Samuel Storms (72–85, 185–206) and "A Pentecostal/Charismatic Response," by Douglas A. Oss (86–93, 264–80). Both Storms and Oss offer reproof and correction to the false reasoning which declares that artificially selected categories of New Testament charisms were confined to the apostolate or to inscripturation.

48. So Poythress, "Modern Spiritual Gifts," 92, 94.

49. However, if apostolic teaching does have "exclusive divine authority" (Poythress, "Modern Spiritual Gifts," 71), then why not abandon epochal dogma and constraints altogether and use apostolic language to describe spiritual gifts as I have argued elsewhere (n11)?

50. On the complementarity of Lukan and Pauline pneumatology, cf. Menzies, "Holy Spirit in

to related prophetic revelatory activities of the Spirit described in Luke's narrative, thus making Stronstad's efforts all the more timely. In any case, it is clear that the way ahead toward a genuine understanding of Luke, with his soteriological and prophetic/pneumatic emphases,[51] needs to remain open to the possibility of the divine actions which he prophetically envisions. As we continue the challenging task toward formulating that conservative and noncreative Lukan theological agenda with regard to the involvement of the Spirit,[52] we need to realize that we are dealing with a text that is not just historically interesting, but with one which is in the process of being fulfilled.

Christian Theology," 67–80, and Menzies, "Spirit-Baptism and Spiritual Gifts," 48–59. Turner, *Power from on High*, offers a synthesis via the von Baer-Dunn model plus a broad application of the "Spirit of prophecy," 445–46, 450–51.

51. Cf. a summary of this latter emphasis in Stronstad, "Prophethood of All Believers," 62–74. Although the Lukan prophecy-fulfillment theme (see n43) is not explicitly identified here, it may be implicit, beneath the surface.

52. The service of F. F. Bruce in this regard sets the proper tone: "As one who, many years ago, made the transition from classical to biblical learning by writing a commentary on Acts, I welcome these indications that the study of this important book is emerging from a generation of unnecessary skepticism and entering a new phase in which its value is better appreciated as a trustworthy source for our knowledge of the history *as well as the theology of primitive Christianity*" (emphasis mine) in his "Acts of the Apostles Today," 56. On the theological side of this observation lies Bruce's recognition of the important idea that for Luke and for Paul the age of the Holy Spirit had dawned: "For both of them, the presence and activity of the Spirit constituted the great new fact of their time," in his "Holy Spirit in the Acts of the Apostles," 177.

Chapter 9

Progymnasmatic Examples in Luke-Acts of Salvation Experience

Necessary Narrative Persuasion from Jesus Tradition and History That Clarifies Paul

It is clear that Luke has searched through the Jesus tradition of previous narratives and probably oral memory to find examples of characters in his own gospel narrative whose experience serves to describe the important Christian experience of salvation. In the rhetorical schools of Luke's time, narrative examples were considered essential in order to persuade and to clarify. Someone trained in these elementary rhetorical schools would retain their teaching on how to properly compose narratives with the essential use of persuasive examples and precedents. Active readers in the early Christian community, whom the narrator of Luke-Acts evidently has in mind, whether they had formal rhetorical training or not, would, in their literary environment, be sensitive to the highly valued progymnasmatic narrative-rhetorical qualities of clarity (σαφήνεια), conciseness (συντομία), and plausibility (πιθανότης), (so too Theon, for example, the first-century rhetorical teacher on literary prose composition in his chapter narrative, πιθανότης, as at Luke 1:1).[1] In order to achieve these qualities Luke's narrative would have to include carefully chosen examples (παραδείγματα),[2] which is what we find there, or else it would probably fail to persuade.

In Luke's gospel narrative we find two persuasive examples of characters who experience salvation (σωτηρία). At 7:36–50 Luke vividly expands on the woman with the ointment from Jesus tradition, making it a persuasive example of someone whose

---

1. Theon, "Ἀρεταὶ δὲ διηγήσεως τρεῖς, σαφήνεια, συντομία, πιθανότης," in his chapter ΠΕΡΙ ΔΙΗΓΗΜΑΤΟΣ, cf. Patillon, *Aelius Théon Progymnasmata*, 38–61 (40 [79.20–21]), where the square brackets cite the page and line numbers from Spengel, *Rhetores Graeci*, 1:40 of the Patillon-Bolognesi critical edition. See Heather M. Gorman, in chapter 2, "Tools for a Rhetorical Analysis" (29–73), in her thesis *Interweaving Innocence*.

2. Cf. "Explicit Exempla in the Lukan Corpus" in Kurz's "Narrative Models for Imitation in Luke-Acts," 174–76. Both Aristotle and Quintilian used the term "example" (παράδειγμα) for comparative devices. I would expect Aelius Theon and the writer of Luke-Acts, e.g., would think along these lines for παράδειγμα and *exemplum*. Cf. Tucker, *Example Stories*, 413, 412.

sins are many, who is forgiven much, who then loves much, and who behaves accordingly. This grateful behavior from deep internal feelings is emphasized by repetition in his narrative, in contrast to Mark and Matthew. At the end of the story, Luke records that she is explicitly told by Jesus that "Your sins are forgiven (ἀφίημι [3X]) . . . Your faith has saved you, go in peace" (7:50). Ἄφεσις, πίστις, and σωτηρία are linked together here in the Jesus tradition. Σωτηρία is a major theme of Luke and he introduces it early on at 2:11, 2:30—Jesus, who is Christ the Lord even before he is born, is the Savior (a theme continued in Acts 13:26 where Paul, in a synagogue speech at Antioch, tells how God raised unto Israel a Savior, Jesus). In Luke's description of the woman with the ointment, readers/hearers get a persuasive description (or ἔκφρασις)[3] of a salvation experience. Active readers who are aware of the progymnasmatic criteria of narrative composition would treat this as a required example and/or precedent (παράδειγμα),[4] a necessary illustration of ἄφεσις, πίστις and σωτηρία. A basic Christian experience—found in Jesus tradition and again set out with other examples in Luke's second book—is described here as a plausible example. Σωτηρία is also written about in various discursive contexts by Paul in his letters, something we would expect by someone who is familiar with the oral gospel tradition—a familiarity well demonstrated by my late friend Traugott Holtz in his "Paul and the Oral Gospel Tradition."[5] But the discursive Paul provides no examples of this basic Christian experience—a circumstance that would present a serious problem to a progymnasmatically trained Christian narrator of history and theology who also appreciated the letters of Paul, something that I will return to later in this chapter.

However, his discursive communications provide no examples of this Christian experience. He speaks of Jesus in whom we have redemption, the forgiveness of sins (ἐν ᾧ ἔχομεν τὴν ἀπολύτρωσιν, τὴν ἄφεσιν τῶν ἁμαρτιῶν, Col 1:14) and of having been saved through faith (ἐστε σεσῳσμένοι διὰ πίστεως, Eph 2:8). In Romans 1:16, the gospel is the power of God for salvation to everyone who has faith (εἰς σωτηρίαν παντὶ τῷ πιστεύοντι). He teaches that repentance leads to salvation (μετάνοιαν εἰς σωτηρίαν, 2 Cor 7:10), that he and these addressees are being saved (τοῖς δὲ σῳζομένοις ἡμῖν, 1 Cor 1:18), and that one becomes a son of God through faith in Christ Jesus (υἱοὶ θεοῦ ἐστε διὰ τῆς πίστεως ἐν Χριστῷ Ἰησοῦ, Gal 3:26). So, while Paul employs essentially the same language as in the Jesus tradition—evidently experientially understood by his first readers—he gives no descriptive examples of how one feels or behaves when one becomes saved or obtains forgiveness. I suggest that for the later readers and for

---

3. Ἔκφρασις and how to compose a narrative with this persuasive description in mind occupies a chapter in the preliminary rhetorical exercises of Theon (ch. 7), Hermogenes (ch. 10), Aphthonius (ch. 12), Nicolaus (ch. 11), and in John of Sardis's commentary on the *Progymnasmata* of Aphthonius (ch. 12) (cf. Kennedy, *Progymnasmata*, chs. 1–5).

4. For progymnasmatic training in Greco-Roman education cf. my "Narrative-Rhetorical Aspects of Literary Hermeneutics," 105–106n80. Webb, *Ekphrasis, Imagination and Persuasion*, 86, 105, 145. Penella, "*Progymnasmata* in Imperial Greek Education," 77–90.

5. Holtz, "Paul and the Oral Gospel Tradition," 380–93.

narrative composition influenced by contemporary rhetorical standards this would not do. It would not be enough, for example, to speak of turning to God (ἐπεστρέψατε πρὸς τὸν θεόν, 1 Thess 1:9). Persuasive examples would be required.

The second narrative example of a character that experiences salvation appears in the narrative of Jesus and Zachaeus (Luke 19:1–10). This is entirely Lukan *Sondergut*. Once again the experience produces very distinctive personal behavior which readers or hearers will want to consider. The narrator obviously believes that this response to salvation is plausible. Active readers could ask: "If I experience salvation could this happen to me?" Luke's description is again consistent with convincing rhetorical *ekphrasis* which serves to bring this scene—as in the scene of the woman with the ointment—directly to the readers' or hearers' mind's eye. The story again punctuated at the end by a statement from Jesus. Here, in conclusion, Jesus states that "Today *soteria* has come to this house . . . For the Son of Man came to seek and to save (ζητῆσαι καὶ σῶσαι) the lost (τὸ ἀπολωλός) (Luke 19:9–10).

As to τὸ ἀπολωλός (that which is lost), in the Parable of the Lost Sheep or the example story thereof, Luke retains the language of Q of a sheep that is lost, whereas Matthew edits Q to going-astray language (I follow Fleddermann's reconstruction of Q here).[6] In Luke's account (15:1–7) a single sheep is lost, it is found, and there is rejoicing that the one sheep that was lost has been found. In Luke's particular account this is connected to there being more joy over one sinner who repents than over ninety-nine righteous persons who need no repentance. Τὸ ἀπολωλός appears three times in Luke's version of Q (Luke 15:4 [2X], 6). While it is not surprising that Luke's treatment of Q here is harmonious with his later example of salvation in the Jesus and Zachaeus account—where this character is described as being one among τὸ ἀπολωλός—it is also noticeable that in Paul's letters the image of those who are lost occurs several times (τοῖς ἀπολλυμένοις, 1 Cor 1:18, 2 Cor 2:15, and 2 Thess 2:10) where in the latter two instances τοῖς ἀπολλυμένοις is contrasted with τοῖς σῳζομένοις and with τὸ σωθῆναι αὐτούς, respectively. So, we may begin to see that not only does Luke exemplify salvation experience from the Jesus tradition, but he can also be understood to be concerned as a trained narrator with the need to provide needed exemplarity to the identical conceptual language of Paul's letters.[7]

Lukan *Sondergut* includes two more example stories, the Parable of the Lost Coin (15:8–10) and the Parable of the Prodigal Son (15:11–32) which also describe the lost being found. Although the Parable of the Prodigal Son does not explicitly mention repentance, this personal experience is a critical factor in the portrayal of the central character and Luke locates this story immediately after the parables of the lost sheep and lost coin which both cite repentance (ἐπὶ ἑνὶ ἁμαρτωλῷ μετανοοῦντι,

---

6. Fleddermann, *Q*, 906.

7. Aejmelaeus, "Pauline Letters as Source Material in Luke-Acts," 74–75. See too Baum, "Paulinismen in den Missionsreden des lukanischen Paulus," 405–36. Baum shows that Luke is quite aware of Romans 1:2–23b and of Romans 2:5a—3:28.

15:7, 10). Like the parable of the lost sheep, the stories of the lost coin and the prodigal son from Jesus tradition are also aimed at readers/hearers who can compare themselves to what these stories depict. Angels are joyful over one sinner who repents. The stories ask: Am I a lost coin or lost son? Have I been found? Both of these example stories also employ forms of the verb ἀπόλλυμι at critical junctures to describe a Christian experience, which in Luke's narrative flow must be salvific (15:8, 9 and 15:24, 32). These verbal ideas are also identical to those in Paul's language that I cited above, but there this language is quantified via personal exemplarity, where in Paul's letters it is not. There, Paul's being-lost language, while no doubt understood by his original readers/hearers who were familiar with Paul, could not be so easily grasped by a current generation of wider readership as his letters were copied and distributed. Paul had seen the heavenly Jesus. What he thinks and says must be important. Would a progymnasmatically minded Luke want to clarify some of the basic Christian concepts and experiences that Paul writes about by including examples of them in this narrative? I am suggesting that he would and that this rhetorical precept of persuasion via the finest examples—argument from example (παράδειγμα) being firmly established in the rhetorical tradition (Arist., *Rhetorica* 1356b3, 20; 1393a27; 1403a5; Hermog., Περὶ εὑρέσεως 4.1)—is a practice on the art historians (λογοποιῶν) that did contribute to the formation of Luke-Acts.

In this regard, Gibson is right to inquire "How can an ancient historian ever write a single word without relying on the compositional skills, knowledge of historical details and parallels, and assumptions about history acquired during his training in the progymnasmata?[8] Roller suggests that such examples provide the invitation to replicate and an impulse to imitate.[9] And, with reference to a set of verbal comparisons between Luke and Paul, I note that "As an able practitioner of the communicative conventions of his day, Luke can be expected to have his main points and themes properly illustrated with the appropriate examples and precedents. The Theonic or progymnasmatic appreciation for the finest and most effective examples builds on the long-standing recognition of the poetic but narrative-rhetorical and oratorical virtue of employing *exempla* and παραδείγματα that are suitable to the occasion."[10]

In Luke's second book, he begins with an example of a different kind, not a salvific example like the ones I have previously discussed, but one that describes and explains a Christian Spirit-reception experience for 120 witnesses who were already disciple-believers. This is, I think, worth mentioning here because this example of and the ensuing speech-in-character description of Spirit-reception at the first Jerusalem Pentecost (Acts 2:1–39) is one which accords very well with the same Spirit-reception language found in Paul's letters. I have argued that this fact indicates that Luke is going about his historical and theological enterprise with an eye not only to

---

8. Gibson, "Learning Greek History in the Ancient Classroom," 126.
9. Roller, "Exemplarity in Roman Culture," 32.
10. Elbert, "Possible Literary Links," 236–37.

exemplify the material on Spirit-reception he finds in the Jesus tradition but also with an eye toward progymnasmatically necessary clarification of Paul's language on this subject via examples in order to stimulate fresh rereadings of Paul's letters.[11] For our purposes here it is helpful to notice that this first example in Luke's second book also continues the Lukan stress on the personal experience of repentance (μετανοήσατε) and the forgiveness of sins (ἄφεσιν τῶν ἁμαρτιῶν) as called for by Peter.[12] Luke also portrays Paul as announcing a very significant fact that Luke's non-Christian and Christian readers alike may ponder, namely that the fact that God now commands all men everywhere to repent (μετανοεῖν, Acts 17:30). Luke's own special examples of this experience in his first book can now be understood as providing the necessary narrative complement of clarification to this portrayal of Paul speaking with his own soteriological language, language that Paul's letters also duplicate, but do not exemplify (μετάνοια: God's kindness leads you to repentance [Rom 2:4]; godly grief produces a repentance that leads to salvation [2 Cor 7:10]).

The same argument of Pauline clarification and stimulus to reread his letters can be made now with regard to Luke's other use of soteriological language and his distinctive exemplarity thereof. Luke makes good use of the examples of salvation that he has collected both from the Jesus tradition and from history (in the book of Acts) by reinforcing their vivacity with strong statements from main characters in his second book. Peter says that "There is salvation in no one else, for there is no other name under heaven given among men by which we must be saved" (Acts 4:12) and "To him all the prophets bear witness and everyone who believes in him receives forgiveness (ἄφεσις) of sins through his name" (Acts 10:43). Paul makes it clear that "Through this man [Jesus] forgiveness of sins (ἄφεσις ἁμαρτιῶν) is proclaimed to you, and by him everyone who believes is justified (δικαιοῦνται) from everything from which you could not be justified (δικαιωθῆναι) by the law of Moses" (Acts 13:38–39). (Not incidentally, in my view, the Antioch speech also clarifies the concept of justification, which Paul mentions several times without adequate explanation in his letters.) For the active reader these universal salvific statements serve to call attention to and generate personal interest in Luke's chosen examples of salvation/faith/repentance experience.

From history, in the Imprisonment of Philippi story, Paul and Silas are praying and singing hymns when an earthquake opens the doors. The jailer trembles with fear, falls down with evident anticipation and sincerity, and says "Men, what must I do to be saved?" (Acts 16:30). The answer is: "Believe in the Lord Jesus, and you will be saved" which leads to water baptism and communal rejoicing about this belief in God (ἠγαλλιάσατο πανοικεὶ πεπιστευκὼς τῷ θεῷ). This example of characters who experience salvation contains the communal element of joy which also appears in Lukan *Sondergut* in the parables of the lost sheep and lost coin (συγχάρητέ μοι, Luke 15:6, 9) and in the parable of the prodigal son, where the lost son is found and they

---

11. Elbert, "Possible Literary Links," 253–54.
12. For analysis, see my "Acts 2:38 in Light of the Syntax," 94–107.

began to make merry (Luke 15:24). Paul strongly encourages believers to rejoice in the Lord (χαίρετε ἐν κυρίῳ, Phil 3:1; 4:4). Luke's example of salvation at Philippi gives the evidence of the root of that joy—the experience of salvation.

In conclusion, I am suggesting that in addition to Luke's narrative-rhetorical skills that are much in line with previous training in the progymnasmatic exercises as set out by Theon and probably many others, Luke's knowledge of Paul's letters also plays a role in his composition. His knowledge of these documents would serve to motivate him all the more to include examples and precedents that clarify Paul's language on the basic Christian experience of salvation. Luke employs Paul's language and language from Jesus tradition in his composition. While the oral tradition known to Paul would have included this language, the cumulative force of Luke's persuasive examples using Pauline language suggests that *Luke is attempting to clarify Paul's discourse.*

Luke, in my view, is working in an urgent enterprise with an urgent purpose. I do not see the anonymous author of this historical and theological double-work as someone sitting on vital information for years as he gradually polishes it for publication. Here known history and known experience must be documented in the best narrative style and, since Paul's letters would be widely circulated, Luke's use of this basic soteriological vocabulary must be given as much clarity (σαφήνεια) and plausibility (πιθανοτής) as possible.

Given the working hypotheses that Luke did know and use Paul's language to clarify some of his basic thoughts via exemplarity, I have explored in a preliminary manner how Luke could have done this while also subscribing to the narrative compositional techniques of his day. Luke's motivation for doing this, as one component of his purpose, is consistent with his distinctive selection of examples from the Jesus tradition and from history and with his duplication of Paul's soteriological language.

Bibliography

Adams, Wesley, et al., eds. *Full Life Study Bible: An International Study Bible for Spirit-Filled Christians.* Grand Rapids: Zondervan, 1993.

Aejmelaeus, Lars. *Die Rezeption der Paulusbriefe in der Miletrede, Apg 20:18–35.* AASF series B. Helsinki: Suomalainen Tiedeskatemia, 1987.

———. "The Pauline Letters as Source Material in Luke-Acts." In *The Early Reception of Paul*, edited by Kenneth Liljeström, 54–75. Helsinki: The Finnish Exegetical Society, 2011.

———. "Reopening the Question of Luke's Use of the Pauline Letters." In *Lukan Use of Pauline Letters and 1 Clement*, edited by Heikka Leppä, . Helsinki: Suomalainen Tiedeskatemia, forthcoming.

Aker, Benny C. "Charismata: Gifts, Enablements, or Ministries?" *JPT* 11 (2002) 53–69.

Albrecht, Daniel E. "Characteristic Qualities of Pentecostal/Charismatic Spirituality." In *Rites in the Spirit: A Ritual Approach to Pentecostal/Charismatic Spirituality*, 218–51. JPTSup 17. Sheffield: Sheffield Academic Press, 1999.

Alewell, Karl. *Über das rhetorische Παράδειγμα: Theorie, Beispielsammlungen, Verwendung in der römischen Literatur der Kaiserzeit.* Leipzig: Hoffman, 1913.

Alexander, Loveday C. *Acts in its Literary Context: A Classicist Looks at the Acts of the Apostles.* LNTS 298. London: T. & T. Clark, 2005.

———. "Ancient Book Production and the Circulation of the Gospels." In *The Gospels for All Christians: Rethinking the Gospel Audiences*, edited by Richard Bauckham, 71–105. Grand Rapids: Eerdmans, 1998.

———. "Luke's Preface in the Context of Greek Preface-Writing." *NovT* 28 (1986) 48–74.

———. *The Preface to Luke's Gospel: Literary Convention and Social Context in Luke 1:1–4 and Acts 1:1.* SNTSMS 78. Cambridge: Cambridge University Press, 1993.

———. "Reading Luke-Acts from Back to Front." In *The Unity of Luke-Acts*, edited by Jos Verheyden, 419–46. BETL 142. Leuven: Leuven University Press, 1999.

Antoniadis, Sophie. *L'Évangile de Luc: Esquisse de Grammaire et de Style.* Collection de l'institute néo-hellénique de l'Université de Paris 7. Paris: Société d'édition "Les Belles Letters," 1930.

Archer, Ken. "Pentecostal Hermeneutics: Retrospect and Prospect." *JPT* 8 (1996) 63–81.

Arrington, French, and Roger Stronstad, eds. *Life in the Spirit New Testament Commentary.* Grand Rapids: Zondervan, 2003.

Atkinson, William P. "The Prior Work of the Spirit in Luke's Proposal." *Australasian Pentecostal Studies* 5–6 (2001) 107–14.

Aune, David E. *Prophecy in Early Christianity and the Ancient Mediterranean World.* Grand Rapids: Eerdmans, 1983.

Austin, Norman. "The Function of Digressions in the Iliad." *GRBS* 7 (1966) 292–312.
Avenarius, Gert. *Lukians Schrift zu Geschichtschreibung*. Meisenheim: Hain, 1957.
Bagalawis, Manuel A. "'Power' in Acts 1:8: Effective Witnessing Through Signs and Wonders." *Journal of Asian Mission* 3 (2001) 1–13.
Barker, Andrew. "The Digressions in the 'Theaetetus.'" *Journal of the History of Philosophy* 14 (1976) 457–62.
Barrett, C. K. *Critical and Exegetical Commentary on the Acts of the Apostles*. 2 vols. ICC. Edinburgh: T. & T. Clark, 1994.
———. "Biblical Classics IV. J. H. Moulton: A Grammar of New Testament Greek: Prolegomena." *ExpTim* 90 (1978) 68–71.
Barth, Markus. "Christ and All Things." In *Paul and Paulinism: Essays in Honour of C. K. Barrett*, edited by M. D. Hooker and S. G. Wilson, 160–72. London: SPCK, 1982.
———. *Ephesians*. AB 34a. Garden City, NY: Doubleday, 1974.
———. "The Problem of Hidden Persuaders," in his "Christ and All Things." In *Paul and Paulinism: Essays in Honour of C. K. Barrett*, edited by M. D. Hooker and S. G. Wilson, 164–68. London: SPCK, 1982.
Bauckham, Richard, ed. *The Gospels for All Christians: Rethinking the Gospel Audiences*. Grand Rapids: Eerdmans, 1998.
Baum, A. D. "Paulinismen in den Missionreden des lukanischen Paulus: Zur inhaltlichen Authentizität der *oratio recta* in der Apostelgeschichte." *ETL* 82 (2006) 405–36.
Baumert, Norbert. *Charisma, Taufe, Geisttaufe*. 2 vols. Würzburg: Echter, 2001.
Beard, Mary, et al. *Religions of Rome*. 2 vols. Cambridge: Cambridge University Press, 1998.
Belser, Johann E. *Die Apostelgeschichte*. Biblische Zeitfragen 1/7. Münster: Verlag der Asschendorffsschen Buchhandlung, 1908.
Berger, K. "ἡ προσωπολημψία." *EDNT* 3:179–80.
Berger, Klaus. "Hellenistische Gattungen im Neuen Testament." *ANRW* 2 (1984) 1031–432.
———. *Identity and Experience in the New Testament*. Translated by Charles Münchow. Minneapolis: Fortress, 2003.
Berlin, Adele. "A Search for a New Biblical Hermeneutics: Preliminary Observations." In *The Study of the Ancient Near East in the Twenty-First Century: The William Foxwell Albright Centennial Conference*, edited by Jerrold S. Cooper and Glenn M. Schwartz, 195–207. Winona Lake, IN: Eisenbrauns, 1996.
Beyer, Klaus. *Semitische Syntax im Neuen Testament*. SUNT 1. Göttingen: Vandenhoeck & Ruprecht, 1968.
Billerbeck, Margarethe. *Epiktet vom Kynismus. Herausgegeben und Übersetzt mit einem Kommentar*. Philosophia Antiqua 34. Leiden: Brill, 1978.
Bird, Michael F. "The Markan Community, Myth or Maze? Bauckham's *The Gospel for All Christians* Revisited." *JTS* 57 (2006) 474–86.
Bittlinger, Arnold. "Der neutestamentliche charismatische Gottesdienst im Lichte der heutigen charismatischen Erneuerung der Kirche." In *Prophetic Vocation in the New Testament and Today*, edited by J. Panagopoulos, 186–209. SNT 45. Leiden: Brill, 1977.
Blass, F. *Acta apostolorum sive Lucae ad Theophilum liber alter*. Göttingen: Vandenhoeck & Ruprecht, 1895.
Bock, Darrell L. *Proclamation from Prophecy and Pattern: Lucan Old Testament Christology*, JSNTSup 12. Sheffield: JSOT, 1987.
Boismard, M. É., and A. Lamouille. *Les Actes des Deux Apôtres, II: Le Sens des Récits*, EtB Nouvelle série 13. Paris: Librairie Lecoffre, 1990.
———. *Les Actes des Deux Apôtres, III: Analyses Littéraires*. EtB Nouvelle série 14. Paris: Librairie Lecoffre, 1990.

———. *Texte Occidental des Actes des Apôtres, II*. Synthèse 17. Paris: Editions Recherche sur les civilizations, 1984.

Bolt, Peter G. "Mission and Witness." In *Witness to the Gospel: The Theology of Acts*, edited by I. Howard Marshall and David Peterson, 191–214. Grand Rapids: Eerdmans, 1998.

Bonnard, Pierre. "L'Esprit saint et l'Église selon le Nouveau Testament." *RHPR* 37 (1957) 81–87.

Bonner, Stanley F. *Education in Ancient Rome: From the Elder Cato to the Younger Pliny*. London: Metheun, 1977.

Bonz, Marianne Palmer. *The Past as Legacy: Luke-Acts and Ancient Epic*. Minneapolis: Fortress, 2000.

Botha, A. D. "Aspects of Prophecy in Vergil's *Aeneid*." *Akroterion* 37 (1992) 6–14.

Bovon, François. "Ces chrétiens qui rêvent. L'autorité du rêve dans les premiers siècles du christianiame." In *Geschichte—Tradition—Reflexion: Festschrift für Martin Hengel zum 70. Geburtstag*, edited by Hubert Cancik et al., 3:631–53. 3 vols. Tübingen: Mohr, 1996.

———. "Le Saint-Esprit: L'église et les relations humaines selon Actes 20:36–21:16." In *Les Actes des Apôtres: Traditions, rédaction, théologie*, edited by Jacob Kremer, 339–58. Paris-Gembloux: Leuven University Press, 1979.

———. *Luc le théologien: Vingt-cinq ans de recherches 1950–1975*. Paris: Cerf, 1975.

Brawley, Robert L. *Text to Text Pours Forth Speech: Voices of Scripture in Luke-Acts*. Indiana Studies in Biblical Literature. Bloomington/Indianapolis: Indiana University Press, 1995.

Brodie, Thomas L. *The Birthing of the New Testament: The Intertextual Development of the New Testament Writings*. New Testament Monographs 1. Sheffield: Sheffield Phoenix, 2004.

———. "The Departure for Jerusalem (Luke 9,51–56) as a Rhetorical Imitation of Elijah's Departure for the Jordan (2 Kgs 1,1–2,6)." *Bib* 70 (1989) 96–109.

———. "Greco-Roman Imitation of Texts as a Partial Guide to Luke's Use of Sources." In *Luke-Acts: New Perspectives from the Society of Biblical Literature Seminar*, edited by Charles Talbert, 17–46. New York: Crossroads, 1984.

———. *Proto-Luke: A Christ-centered Synthesis of Septuagintal Historiography and a Deuteronomy-based Alternative to Q*. Limerick, UK: Dominican Biblical Centre, University of Limerick, 2002.

———. "Schools, Synagogues, and Vibrant Scripture-Related Communities: Towards a Writing-Oriented Paradigm." In *The Birthing of the New Testament: The Intertextual Development of the New Testament Writings*, by Thomas L. Brodie, 63–71. NTM 1. Sheffield: Sheffield Phoenix, 2004.

———. "Towards Tracing the Gospels' Literary Indebtedness to the Epistles." In *Mimesis and Intertextuality in Antiquity and Christianity*, edited by Dennis R. MacDonald, 104–16. Harrisburg, PA: Trinity Press International, 2001.

———. "Towards Unraveling Luke's Use of the Old Testament: Luke 7,11–17 as an *Imitatio* of 1 Kings 17,17–24." *NTS* 32 (1986) 247–67.

Brown, Schuyler. "'Water Baptism' and 'Spirit-Baptism' in Luke-Acts." *ATR* 59 (1977) 135–51.

Bruce, F. F. "The Acts of the Apostles Today." *BJRL* 65 (1982) 35–56.

———. *The Book of the Acts*. NICNT. Grand Rapids: Eerdmans, 1954.

———. "The Holy Spirit in the Acts of the Apostles." *Int* 27 (1973) 166–83.

Brunt, P. A. *Studies in Greek History and Thought*. Oxford: Clarendon, 1993.

Bühlmann, Walter, and Karl Scherer. *Stilfiguren der Bibel*. Biblische Beiträge 10. Freiberg: Schweizerisches Katholisches Bibelwerk, 1973.

Butts, James R. "The 'Progymnasmata' of Theon: A New Text with Translation and Commentary." PhD diss., The Claremont Graduate School, 1987.

Cadbury, Henry J. "Four Features of Lucan Style." In *Studies in Luke-Acts: Essays Presented in Honor of Paul Schubert*, edited by Leander E. Keck and J. Louis Martyn, 87–102. London: SPCK, 1968.

———. *The Making of Luke-Acts*. New York: Macmillan, 1927.

———. "Names for Christians in Acts." In *The Beginnings of Christianity: The Acts of the Apostles*. Edited by F. J. Foakes Jackson and Kirsopp Lake, 5:375–92. 5 vols. London: Macmillan, 1923–33.

Calvin, John. *The Acts of the Apostles*. Translated by John W. Fraser and W. J. G. McDonald. 2 vols. Grand Rapids: Eerdmans, 1965.

———. *The Acts of the Apostles 1–13*. Translated by John W. Fraser and W. J. G. McDonald. Edited by D. W. Torrance and T. F. Torrance. Edinburgh: n.p., 1965.

———. *Commentariorum Joannis Calvini in Acts Apostolorum*. Geneva: Ex officinal Ioannis Crispini, 1552.

Cantalamessa, Raniero. *The Mystery of Pentecost*. Translated by Glen S. Davis. Collegeville, MN: Liturgical, 2001.

Canter, H. V. "Digression in the Orations of Cicero." *American Journal of Philology* 52 (1931) 351–61.

Caragounis, Chrys C. *The Development of Greek and the New Testament: Morphology, Syntax, Phonology, and the Textual Transmission*. WUNT 2/167. Tübingen: Mohr Siebeck, 2004.

Carson, Donald A. *Showing the Spirit: A Theological Exposition of 1 Corinthians 12–14*. Grand Rapids: Baker, 1987.

Casey, Maurice. *An Aramaic Approach to Q: Sources for the Gospels of Matthew and Luke*. SNTSMS 122. Cambridge: Cambridge University, 2002.

Charette, Blaine. "'Never Has Anything Like This Been Seen in Israel': The Spirit as Eschatological Sign in Matthew's Gospel." *JPT* 8 (1996) 31–51.

Chevallier, Max-Alain. "Luc et l'Esprit Saint: A la mémoire du P. Augustin George (1915–1977)." *RSR* 56 (1982) 1–19.

Chevallier, Raymond. *Roman Roads*. Translated by N. Field. Berkeley/Los Angeles: University of California Press, 1976.

Cho, Youngmo. "Spirit and Kingdom in Luke-Acts: Proclamation as the Primary Role of the Spirit in Relation to the Kingdom of God in Luke-Acts." *Asian Journal of Pentecostal Studies* 6 (2003) 173–97.

Christenson, Larry, ed. *Welcome, Holy Spirit: A Study of Charismatic Renewal in the Church*. Minneapolis: Augsburg, 1987.

Cichocka, H. "Progymnasmata as a Literary Form." *Studi italiani di filologia classica* 10 (1992) 991–99.

Clark, Donald L. *Rhetoric in Greco-Roman Education*. New York: Columbia University Press, 1957.

Congar, Yves. "Pneumatologie dogmatique." In *Initiation à la pratique de la théologie*, edited by Bernard Lauret and François Refoulé, 2:485–516. 5 vols. Paris: Cerf, 1982.

Cribiore, Rafaella. *Gymnastics of the Mind: Greek Education in Hellenistic and Roman Egypt*. Princeton: Princeton University Press, 2001.

———. *Writing, Teachers, and Students in Greco-Roman Egypt*. American Studies in Papyrology 36. Atlanta: Scholars, 1996.

Crone, Theodore M. *Early Christian Prophecy: A Study of Its Origin and Function*. Baltimore: St. Mary's University Press, 1973.

Crowley, Sharon. *The Methodical Memory: Invention in Current-Traditional Rhetoric*. Carbondale: Southern Illinois University Press, 1990.

Darby, J. N. *Notes of Addresses on the Gospel of Luke*. London: Race, 1922.

Deere, Jack. *Surprised by the Voice of God: How God Speaks Today through Prophecies, Dreams, and Visions.* Grand Rapids: Zondervan, 1996.

Delebecque, Edouard. *Les Actes des Apôtres.* Collection D'Études Anciennes. Paris: Société d'édition "Les Belles Letters," 1982.

Diehl, Johannes Friedrich. *Die Fortführung des Imperativs im biblischen Hebräisch.* AOAT 286. Münster: Ugarit-Verlag, 2004.

Dietrich, Wolfgang. *Das Petrusbild der lukanischen Schriften.* BWANT 5/14. Stuttgart: Kohlhammer, 1972.

Dillon, Richard J. "Previewing Luke's Project from His Prologue." *CBQ* 43 (1981) 205–27.

Dorr, Donal. *Remove the Heart of Stone: Charismatic Renewal and the Experience of Grace.* Dublin: Gill & Macmillan, 1978.

Downing, G. "Theophilus' First Reading of Luke-Acts." In *Luke's Literary Achievement: Collected Essays*, edited by C. M. Tuckett, 91–109. JSNTSup 116. Sheffield: Sheffield Academic Press, 1995.

Dubois, Jean-Daniel. "La Figure d'Elie dans la perspective lucanienne." *RHPR* 53 (1973) 155–76.

Duckworth, George Eckel. *Foreshadowing and Suspense in the Epics of Homer, Apollonius, and Vergil.* Princeton: Princeton University Press, 1933.

Dumais, Marcel. "Ministères, charismes et Esprit dans l'oeurve de Luc." *Église et Théologie* 9 (1978) 413–53.

Duncan, J., and M. Derrett. "Binding and Loosing [Matt 16:19; 18:18; John 20:23]." *JBL* 102 (1983) 112–17.

Dunn, James D. G. *Baptism in the Holy Spirit: A Re-examination of the New Testament Teaching on the Gift of the Spirit in Relation to Pentecostalism Today.* London: SCM, 1970.

———. "Jesus in Oral Memory: The Initial Stages of the Jesus Tradition." In *Jesus: A Colloquium in the Holy Land*, edited by Doris Donnelly, 84–145. New York: Continuum, 2001.

———. "ΚΥΡΙΟΣ in Acts." In *Jesus Christus als die Mitte der Schrift: Studien zur Hermeneutik des Evangeliums, FS für Otfried Hofius*, edited by C. Landmesser et al., 363–78. BZNW 86. Berlin: de Gruyter, 1997.

Dupont, Jacques. "L'utilisation apologetique de l'ancien Testament dans les discourse des Acts." *ETL* 29 (1953) 289–327.

DuPree, Sherry Sherrod. "In the Sanctified Holiness Pentecostal Charismatic Movement." *Pneuma* 23 (2001) 97–114.

Eagleton, Terry. *Literary Theory: An Introduction.* Minneapolis: University of Minnesota Press, 1983.

Eckstein, Hans-Joachim. "Denn Gottes Zorn wird vom Himmel her offenbar werden: Exegetische Erwägungen zu Röm 1:18." *ZNW* 78 (1987) 74–89.

Edmunds, Lowell. *Intertextuality and the Reading of Roman Poetry.* Baltimore: John Hopkins University Press, 2001.

Ehrhardt, Arnold. *The Acts of the Apostles: Ten Lectures.* Manchester: Manchester University Press, 1969.

———. "The Construction and Purpose of the Acts of the Apostles." *ST* 12 (1958) 45–79.

Elbert, Paul. "Acts 2:38 in Light of the Syntax of Imperative-Future Passive and Imperative-Present Participle Combinations." *CBQ* 75 (January 2013) 94–107.

———. "Calvin and Spiritual Gifts." In *Articles on Calvin and Calvinism: A Fourteen-Volume Anthology of Scholarly Articles*, edited by Richard C. Gamble, 8:303–31. 14 vols. New York: Garland, 1992.

———. "The Charismatic Movement in the Church of England: An Overview." *Pneuma* 6.1 (1984) 28–33.

———. "The Globalization of Pentecostalism: A Review Article." *TJ* 23 (2002) 81–101.

———. *The Lukan Gift of the Holy Spirit: Understanding Luke's Expectations for Theophilus.* Canton, GA: The Foundation for Pentecostal Scholarship, 2021.

———. "Luke's Fulfillment-of-Prophecy Theme: Introductory Exploration of Joel and the Last Days." Paper presented to the Society for Pentecostal Studies, Marquette University, 2004.

———. "Narrative-Rhetorical Aspects of Literary Hermeneutics: Leaving Questionable Methods Behind and Retaining What Greco-Roman Christian Writers Appreciated and Respected." In *Essays in Biblical Studies: New and Penetrating Ideas on the Work of the Holy Spirit*, 69–107. Canton, GA: The Foundation for Pentecostal Scholarship, 2021.

———. "An Observation on Luke's Composition and Narrative Style of Questions" *CBQ* 66 (2004) 98–109.

———. "Paul of the Miletus Speech and 1 Thessalonians: Critique and Considerations." *ZNW* 95 (2004) 258–68.

———. "The Perfect Tense in Matthew 16:19 and Three Charismata." *JETS* 17 (1974) 149–53.

———. "Possible Literary Links between Luke-Acts and Pauline Letters Regarding Spirit-Language." In *Intertextuality in the New Testament: Explorations of Theory and Practice*, edited by Thomas L. Brodie et al., 226–54. NTM 16. Sheffield: Sheffield Phoenix, 2006.

———. Review of *Understanding Spiritual Gifts* by Robert L. Thomas. *JETS* 23 (1980) 182–85.

———. "Spirit, Scripture and Theology through a Lukan Lens: A Review Article." *JPT* 13 (1998) 55–75.

———. "The Syntax of Imperative-Future and Imperative-Participle Combinations in Luke-Acts and Possible Narrative Implications." Paper read at the Society of Biblical Literature International Meeting, Pontifical Gregorian University, Rome, 8–12 July 2001.

Ellis, E. Earle. *The Making of the New Testament Documents.* 2nd ed. Leiden: Brill, 2002.

———. "Prophecy in the New Testament Church—and Today." In *Prophetic Vocation in the New Testament and Today*, edited by J. Panagopoulos, 46–57. NovTSup 45. Leiden: Brill, 1977.

———. "The Role of the Christian Prophet in Acts." In *Apostolic History and the Gospel: Biblical and Historical Essays Presented to F. F. Bruce*, edited by W. Ward Gasque and Ralph P. Martin, 55–67. Grand Rapids: Eerdmans, 1970.

Emmett, A. "Introduction and Conclusions to Digressions in Ammianus Marcellinus." *Museum philologum Londiniense* 5 (1981) 15–33.

English, E. Schuyler, et al., eds. *The New Scofield Reference Bible.* New York: Oxford University Press, 1967.

Enslin, Morton S. "Emphases and Silences." *HTR* 73 (1980) 219–25.

———. "'Luke' and Paul." *JAOS* 58 (1938) 81–91.

———. "Luke, the Literary Physician." In *Studies in the New Testament and Early Christian Literature*, edited by David E. Aune, 142–50. Leiden: Brill, 1972.

———. "Once Again, Luke and Paul." *ZNW* 61 (1970) 253–71.

Erdman, W. J. "The Holy Spirit and the Sons of God." In *The Fundamentals: A Testimony to the Truth*, edited by R. A. Torrey, 2:338–52. 12 vols. Los Angeles: Bible Institute of Los Angeles, 1917.

Eriksson, Anders. "Enthymemes in Pauline Argumentation: Reading Between the Lines in 1 Corinthians." In *Rhetorical Argumentation in Biblical Texts: Essays from the Lund 2000 Conference*, edited by Anders Eriksson et al., 243–59. Emory Studies in Early Christianity. Harrisburg, PA: Trinity Press International, 2002.

Ernst, Josef. *Das Evangelium nach Lukas*. 6th ed. RNT. Regensburg: Pustet, 1993.

Ervin, Howard M. "Hermeneutics: A Pentecostal Option." In *Essays on Apostolic Themes: Studies in Honor of Howard M. Ervin*, edited by Paul Elbert, 23–35. Peabody, MA: Hendrickson, 1985.

———. *These Are Not Drunken as Ye Suppose*. Plainfield, NJ: Logos, 1968.

"Evangelization, Proselytism and Common Witness: The Report from the Fourth Phase of the International Dialogue (1990–1997) between the Roman-Catholic Church and Some Classical-Pentecostal Churches and Leaders." *Asian Journal of Pentecostal Studies* 2 (1999) 105–51.

Evans, C. F. "'Speeches' in Acts." In *Mélanges Bibliques en hommage au Béda Rigaux*, edited by Albert Descamps and André de Halleux, 287–302. Gembloux: Duculot, 1970.

Fannon, P. "The Influence of Traditions on St. Paul." In *Studia Evangelica, IV: Papers Presented to the Third International Congress on New Testament Studies*, edited by F. L. Cross, 292–307. TU 102. Berlin: Akademie, 1968.

Fantham, Elaine. "Imitation and Decline: Rhetorical Theory and Practice in the First Century after Christ." *CP* 73 (1978) 102–16.

Fee, Gordon. "The Genre of New Testament Literature and Biblical Hermeneutics." In *Interpreting the Word of God*, edited by Samuel Schultz and Morris Inch, 105–27. Chicago: Moody, 1976.

———. *Gospel and Spirit: Issues in New Testament Hermeneutics*. Peabody, MA: Hendrickson, 1991.

———. "Hermeneutics and Historical Precedent." In *Perspectives on the New Pentecostalism*, edited by Russell P. Spittler, 119–32. Grand Rapids: Baker, 1976.

Ferguson, John. *The Religions of the Roman Empire*. Ithaca, NY: Cornell University Press, 1970.

Finkelpearl, Ellen. "Pagan Traditions of Intertextuality in the Roman World." In *Mimesis and Intertextuality in Antiquity and Christianity*, edited by Dennis R. MacDonald, 78–90. Harrisburg, PA: Trinity Press International, 2001.

Fiore, Benjamin. *The Function of Personal Examples in the Socratic and Pastoral Epistles*. AnBib 105. Rome: Pontifical Biblical Institute, 1986.

———. "The Place of Example in Rhetorical Education." In *The Function of Personal Example in the Socratic and Pastoral Epistles*, 33–37. AnBib 105. Rome: Biblical Institute, 1986.

Fitzmyer, Joseph A. *The Acts of the Apostles*. AB 31. New York: Doubleday, 1998.

———. *The Gospel according to Luke I–IX*. AB 28. New York: Doubleday, 1981.

Fleddermann, Harry T. *Q: A Reconstruction and Commentary*. Biblical Tools and Studies 1. Leuven: Peeters, 2005.

Forbes, C. *Prophecy and Inspired Speech in Early Christianity and Its Hellenistic Environment*. WUNT 2/75. Tübingen: Mohr, 1995.

Franklin, Eric. *Christ the Lord: A Study in the Purpose and Theology of Luke-Acts*. London: SPCK, 1975.

———. *Luke: Interpreter of Paul, Critic of Matthew*. JSNTSup 92. Sheffield: JSOT, 1994.

Frein, Brigid Curtin. "Prophecies and Luke's Sense of Fulfillment." *NTS* 40 (1994) 22–37.

Frenschkowski, Marco. *Offenbarung und Epiphanie*. 2 vols. WUNT 2/79. Tübingen: Mohr, 1995.

———. "Traum II–IV." *TRE* 34 (2002) 33–41.

———. "Traum und Traumdeutung im Matthäusevangelium." *JAC* 41 (1998) 5–47.

———. "Vision II–IV." *TRE* 35 (2003) 124–37.

Gaffin, Richard B., Jr. "A Cessationist Response to C. Samuel Storms and Douglas A. Oss." In *Are Miraculous Gifts for Today? Four Views*, edited by Wayne A. Grudem, 284–97. Grand Rapids: Zondervan, 1996.

———. "A Cessationist View." In *Are Miraculous Gifts for Today? Four Views*, edited by Wayne A. Grudem, 25–64. Grand Rapids: Zondervan, 1996.

Gagnon, Robert A. J. "The Shape of Matthew's Q Text of the Centurion at Capernaum: Did It Mention Delegations?" *NTS* 40 (1994) 122–45.

Gaisser, Julia Haig. "Structural Analysis of the Digressions in the *Iliad* and the *Odyssey*." *HSCP* 73 (1969) 1–43.

Gaventa, Beverly Roberts. "Toward a Theology of Acts: Reading and Rereading." *Int* 42 (1988) 146–57.

Genette, Gérade. *Narrative Discourse: An Essay in Method*. Translated by Jane E. Lewin. Ithaca, NY: Cornell University Press, 1983.

George, Augustin. "La prière." In *Études sur l'oeuvre de Luc*, by Augustin George, 395–427. Sources bibliques. Paris: Gabalda, 1978.

———. "L'Esprit Saint dans l'oeuvre de Luc." *RB* 85 (1978) 500–542.

Gerhardsson, Birger. "The Secret of the Transmission of the Unwritten Jesus Tradition." *NTS* 51 (2005) 1–18.

Giangrande, Giuseppe. "Hellenistic Poetry and Homer." *L'Antiquité classique* 39 (1970) 46–77.

Giblet, J. "Baptism in the Spirit in the Acts of the Apostles." *One in Christ* 10 (1974) 162–71.

Gibson, Craig A. "Learning Greek History in the Ancient Classroom: The Evidence of the Treatises on Progymnasmata." *Classical Philology* 99 (2004) 103–29.

Goldingay, John. "Biblical Story and the Way It Shapes Our Story." *Journal of the European Pentecostal Theological Association* 17 (1997) 5–15.

———. "Old Testament Prophecy Today." *The Spirit and Church* 3 (2001) 27–46.

Goodacre, Mark. *The Case against Q: Studies in Markan Priority and the Synoptic Problem*. Harrisburg, PA: Trinity Press International, 2002.

Goodwin, William W. *A Greek Grammar*. 2nd ed. London: Macmillan, 1894.

Gorman, Heather M. *Interweaving Innocence: A Rhetorical Analysis of Luke's Passion Narrative, Luke 22:66—23:49*. Eugene, OR: Pickwick, 2015.

Goulder, Michael D. *Luke: A New Paradigm*. 2 vols. JSNTSup 20 Sheffield: JSOT, 1989.

Gräbe, Petrus J. "Pentecostal Discovery of the New Testament Theme of God's Power and Its Relevance to the African Context." *Pneuma* 24.2 (2002) 225–42.

———. *The Power of God in Paul's Letters*. WUNT 123. Tübingen: Mohr Siebeck, 2000.

Green, Barbara. *Mikhail Bakhtin and Biblical Scholarship: An Introduction*. Semeia Series 38. Atlanta: Society of Biblical Literature, 2000.

Green, Joel B. *The Gospel of Luke*. NICNT. Grand Rapids: Eerdmans, 1997.

Grudem, Wayne A., ed. *The Gift of Prophecy in 1 Corinthians*. Washington, DC: University Press of America, 1982.

———. *The Gift of Prophecy in the New Testament and Today*. Eastbourne, UK: Kingsway, 1988.

Gunkel, Hermann. *Die Wirkungen des heiligen Geistes nach der populären Anschauung der apostolishen Zeit und der Lehre des Apostle Paulus*. Göttingen: Vandenhoeck & Ruprecht, 1888.

———. *The Influence of the Holy Spirit: The Popular View of the Apostolic Age and the Teaching of the Apostle Paul*. Translated by Roy A. Harrisville and Philip A. Quanbeck II. Philadelphia: Fortress, 1979.

Guy, Laurie. "The Interplay of the Present and Future in the Kingdom of God (Luke 19:11–44)." *TynBul* 48 (1997) 119–37.

Hadot, I. "The Spiritual Guide." In *Classical Mediterranean Spirituality: Egyptian, Greek, Roman*, edited by A. H. Armstrong, 436–59. New York: Crossroad, 1986.

Hafemann, Scott J. *Suffering and Ministry in the Spirit: Paul's Defense of His Ministry in II Corinthians 2, 14—3, 3*. Grand Rapids: Eerdmans, 1990.

Haft, Adele J. "τὰ δὴ νῦν πάντα τελεῖται: Prophecy and Recollection in the Assemblies of *Iliad* 2 and *Odyssey* 2." *Arethusa* 25 (1992) 223–40.

Hagene, Sylvia. *Zeiten der Wiederherstellung: Studies zur lukanischen Geschichtstheologie*, NTAbh 42. Münster: Aschendorff, 2003

Hanson, J. "Dreams and Visions in the Graeco-Roman World and Early Christianity." *ANRW* 2 (1980) 1395–425.

Härter, A. "Digression und Rhetorik." In *Digressionen: Studien zum Verhältnis von Ordnung und Abweichung in Rhetorik und Poetic–Quintilian–Opitz–Gottsched–Friedrich Schlegel*, 17–52. Munich: Fink, 2000.

Haya-Prats, Gonzalo. *Empowered Believers: The Holy Spirit in the Book of Acts*. Translated by Scott Ellington. Edited by Paul Elbert. Eugene, OR: Cascade, 2011.

———. *L'Esprit, force de l'Église: Sa nature et son activité d'après les Actes des Apôtres*. Translated by J. Romeo and H. Faes. LD 81. Paris: Cerf, 1975.

Heath, Malcolm. "Theon and the History of the Progymnasmata." *Greek, Roman, and Byzantine Studies* 43 (2002–03) 129–60.

Hemer, Colin J. *The Book of Acts in the Setting of Hellenistic History*. Edited by Conrad H. Gempf. WUNT 49. Tübingen: Mohr, 1989.

———. *The Letters to the Seven Churches of Asia in Their Local Setting*. JSNTSup 11. Sheffield: JSOT, 1986.

Hengel, Martin. *Acts and the History of Earliest Christianity*. London: SCM, 1979.

———. *Der unterschätzte Petrus. Zwei Studien*. Tübingen: Mohr Siebeck, 2006.

———. "Hymn and Christology." In *Studia Biblica III: Papers on Paul and Other New Testament Authors*, edited by E. A. Livingstone, 190–95. JSNTSup 3. Sheffield: Sheffield Academic Press, 1980.

———. "Problems of a History of Earliest Christianity." *Bib* 78 (1997) 131–44.

———. *Zur urchristlichen Geschichtsschreibung*. Stuttgart: Calwer, 1979.

Henry, Elisabeth. *The Vigour of Prophecy: A Study of Vergil's Aeneid*. Carbondale: Southern Illinois University Press, 1989.

Hersey, John, ed. *The Writer's Craft*. New York: Random House, 1974.

Hinds, Stephen. *Allusion and Intertext: Dynamics of Appropriation in Roman Poetry*. Roman Literature and Its Contents. New York: Cambridge University Press, 1998.

Hock, Ronald F. "Homer in Greco-Roman Education." In *Mimesis and Intertextuality in Antiquity and Christianity*, edited by Dennis R. MacDonald, 56–77. Harrisburg, PA: Trinity Press International, 2001.

———. "The Rhetoric of Romance." In *Handbook of Classical Rhetoric in the Hellenistic Period (330 BC–AD 400)*, edited by S. E. Porter, 445–65. New York: Brill, 1997.

Hock, Ronald F., and Edward N. O'Neil. *The Chreia in Ancient Rhetoric, I: The Progymnasmata*. SBLTT 27. Graeco-Roman Religion Series 9. Atlanta: Scholars, 1986.

———. *The Chreia and Ancient Rhetoric: Classroom Exercises.* Writings From the Greco-Roman World 2. Atlanta: Scholars, 2002.

———. "Elaborating the Chreia: The Use of the Chreia in the Rhetorical Curriculum." In *The Chreia and Ancient Rhetoric: Classroom Exercises,* edited by Ronald F. Hock and Edward N. O'Neil, 79–354. Atlanta: Scholars, 2002.

Hocken, Peter D. "A Charismatic View." In *Pentecostalism in Context: Essays in Honor of William W. Menzies,* edited by Wonsuk Ma and Robert P. Menzies, 96–106. JPTSup 11. Sheffield: Sheffield Academic Press, 1997.

———. "Is Renewal of the Church Possible?" *The Spirit and Church* 3 (2001) 183–208.

Holman, Charles. "A Lesson from Matthew's Gospel for Charismatic Renewal." In *Faces of Renewal: Studies in Honor of Stanley M. Horton,* edited by Paul Elbert, 48–63. Peabody, MA: Hendrickson, 1988.

Holtz, Traugott. "Paul and the Oral Gospel Tradition." In *Jesus and the Oral Gospel Tradition,* edited by Henry Wansbrough, 380–93. Sheffield: JSOT, 1991.

Homer. *Odyssey II.* Translated by A. T. Murray and George E. Dimock. 2nd ed. LCL 105. Cambridge: Harvard University Press, 1995.

Horsley, Greg H. R. "Doctors in the Graeco-Roman World." In *New Documents Illustrating Early Christianity, II. A Review of Inscriptions and Papyri Published in 1977,* 2:10–25. 10 vols. North Ryde, Australia: Ancient History Documentary Research Center, Macquarie University, 1982.

Horst, Peter W. van der. "Greek in Jewish Palestine in the Light of Jewish Epigraphy." In *Japeth in the Tents of Shem: Studies on Jewish Hellenism in Antiquity,* by Peter W. van der Horst, 9–26. Contributions to Biblical Exegesis and Theology 32. Leuven: Peeters, 2002.

Horton, Harold. *The Gifts of the Spirit.* Nottingham: Assemblies of God, 1934.

Hovenden, Gerald. *Speaking in Tongues: The New Testament Evidence in Context.* JPTSup 22 London: Sheffield Academic Press, 2002.

Hude, Karl. *Aretaeus.* Edited by J. Zwicker. Berlin: n.p., 1958.

Hultgren, Stephen. *Narrative Elements in the Double Tradition: A Study of Their Place within the Framework of the Gospel Narrative.* BZNW 113. Berlin: de Gruyter, 2002.

Hunger, Herbert. *Die hochsprachliche profane Literatur der Byzantiner.* 2 vols. 3rd ed. HandbAW 12.5.1–2. Munich: Beck, 1978.

———. "Ekphraseis." In *Die hochsprachliche profane Literatur der Byzantiner,* 1:170–88. 2 vols. 3rd ed. HandbAW 12.5.1–2. Munich: Beck, 1978.

———. "Progymnasmata und andere Übungsreden." In *Die hochsprachliche profane Literatur der Byzantiner,* 1:92–120. 2 vols. 3rd ed. HandbAW 12.5.1–2. Munich: Beck, 1978.

Ingalls, W. B. "Linguistic and Formular Innovation in the Mythological Digressions in the *Iliad.*" *Phoenix* 36 (1982) 201–8.

Isaacs, Marie E. *The Concept of Spirit: A Study of Pneuma in Hellenistic Judaism and Its Bearing on the New Testament.* HeyJ 1. London: University of London Heythrop College, 1976.

Jacobsen, A. "Über die lukanischen Schriften." *ZKT* 31 (1888) 129–58.

Jaquier, Eugène. *Les Actes des Apôtres.* EtB. Paris: Gabalda, 1926.

Jastrow, Robert. *God and the Astronomers.* New York: Norton, 1978.

Jervell, Jacob. "Der schwache Charismatiker." In *Rechtfertigung: Festschrift für Ernst Käsemann,* edited by Johannes Friedrich et al., 185–98. Tübingen: Mohr, 1976.

———. "Sons of the Prophets: The Holy Spirit in the Acts of the Apostles." In *The Unknown Paul: Essays on Luke-Acts and Early Christianity,* by Jacob Jervell, 96–121. Minneapolis: Augsburg, 1984.

———. *The Theology of the Acts of the Apostles*. Cambridge: Cambridge University Press, 1996.

Jewett, Robert. *Romans*. Hermeneia. Minneapolis: Fortress, 2007.

Johnson, Luke Timothy. *Religious Experience in Earliest Christianity: A Missing Dimension in New Testament Studies*. Minneapolis: Fortress, 1998.

Johnson, William A. "Oral Performance and the Composition of Herodotus' *Histories*." *Greek, Roman and Byzantine Studies* 35 (1994) 229–54.

Jüngst, Johannes. *Die Quellen der Apostelgeschichte*. Gotha, Germany: Perthes, 1895.

Kennedy, George A. *The Art of Rhetoric in the Roman World*. Princeton: Princeton University Press, 1972.

———. *Greek Rhetoric Under Christian Emperors*. Princeton: Princeton University, 1983.

———. *New Testament Interpretation through Rhetorical Criticism*. Chapel Hill: University of North Carolina Press, 1984.

———, ed. and trans. *Progymnasmata: Greek Textbooks of Prose Composition and Rhetoric*. SBLWGRW 10. Atlanta: Society of Biblical Literature, 2003.

Kilgallen, John L. "The Conception of Jesus (Luke 1,35)." *Bib* 78 (1997) 225–46.

———. "Forgiveness of Sins (Luke 7:36–50)." *NovT* 40 (1998) 105–16.

Kilpatrick, G. D. "Some Quotations in Acts." In *Les Actes des Apôtres: Traditions, rédaction, théologie*, edited by Jacob Kremer, 81–97. Paris-Gembloux: Leuven University Press, 1979.

Kim, Dongsoo. "Lucan Pentecostal Theology of Prayer: Is Persistent Prayer Not Biblical?" *Asian Journal of Pentecostal Studies* 7 (2004) 205–17.

Kim, Hee-Seong. *Die Geisttaufe des Messias: Eine kompositionsgeschichtliche Untersuchung zu einem Leitmotiv des lukanischen Doppelwerks. Ein Beitrag zur Theologie und Intention des Lukas*. Studien zur klassischen Philologie 81. Frankfurt: Lang, 1993.

Kim, Seyoon. "Salvation and Suffering According to Jesus." *EvQ* 68 (1996) 195–207.

Kizhakkeparampil, Isaac. *The Invocation of the Holy Spirit as Constitutive of the Sacraments according to Yves Congar*. Rome: Gregorian University Press, 1995.

Klein, Hans. "Exkurs: Gebet bei Lukas." In *Das Lukasevangelium*, by Hans Klein, 410. Göttingen: Vandenhoeck & Ruprecht, 2006.

———. "Paulinische Tradition bei Lukas." In *Lukasstudien*, by Hans Klein, 13–16. FRLANT 209. Göttingen: Vandenhoeck & Ruprecht, 2005.

Knight, Virginia. *The Renewal of Epic: Responses to Homer in the Argonautica of Apollonius*. Leiden: Brill, 1995.

Kolenkow, Anitra B. "Relationships between Miracle and Prophecy in the Greco-Roman World and Early Christianity." *ANRW* 2 (1980) 1470–506.

Köstenberger, Andreas J. "What Does It Mean to Be Filled with the Spirit?" *JETS* 40 (1997) 229–40.

Kremer, Jacob. *Pfingstbericht und Pfingstgeschehen: Eine exegetische Untersuchung zu Apg 2, 1–13*. SBS 63.63. Stuttgart: KBW, 1973.

Kudlien, Fridolf. *Untersuchungen zu Aretaios von Kappadokien*. Wiesbaden: Steiner, 1964.

Kurz, William S. "Hellenistic Rhetoric in the Christological Proof of Luke-Acts." *CBQ* 42 (1980) 171–95.

———. "Narrative Approaches to Luke-Acts." *Bib* 68 (1987) 195–229.

———. "Narrative Models for Imitation in Luke-Acts." In *Greeks, Romans, and Christians: Essays in Honor of Abraham J. Malherbe*, edited by David L. Balch et al., 171–89. Minneapolis: Fortress, 1990.

Laan, Cornelius van der. "Beyond the Clouds: Elize Scharten (1876–1965), Pentecostal Missionary to China." In *Pentecostalism in Context*, edited by Wonsuk Ma and Robert P. Menzies, 337–57. Eugene, OR: Wipf & Stock, 2008.

———. Review of *Op zoek naar de Geest*, by Klass Runia. *Journal of the European Pentecostal Theological Association* 21 (2001) 138–40.

Lake, Kirsopp. "The Holy Spirit." In *The Beginnings of Christianity: The Acts of the Apostles*, edited by F. J. Foakes Jackson and Kirsopp Lake, 5:96–111. 5 vols. London: Macmillan, 1933.

Lake, Kirsopp, and Henry J. Cadbury, eds. *The Beginnings of Christianity: The Acts of the Apostles*. Edited by F. J. Foakes Jackson and Kirsopp Lake. 5 vols. London: Macmillan, 1923–33.

Lausberg, Heinrich. *Elemente der Literarischen Rhetorik*. Munich: Hübner, 1963.

———. *Handbuch der Literarischen Rhetorik: Eine Grundlegung der Literaturwissenschaft*. 3rd ed. Stuttgart: Steiner, 1990.

Lee, Sang-Whan. "The Relevance of St. Basil's Pneumatology to Modern Pentecostalism." *The Spirit and Church* 1 (1999) 49–76.

Leppä, Heikki. "Luke's Account of the Lord's Supper." In *Lux Humana, Lux Aeterna: Essays on Biblical and Related Themes*, edited by Antti Mustakallio et al., 364–73. Göttingen: Vandenhoeck & Ruprecht, 2005.

———. *Luke's Critical Use of Galatians*. Vantaa, Finland: Dark Oy, 2002.

Lewis, Paul. "Towards a Pentecostal Epistemology: The Role of Experience in Pentecostal Hermeneutics." *The Spirit and Church* 2 (2000) 95–125.

Liefeld, Walter L. "Parables on Prayer (Luke 11:5–13; 18:1–14)." In *The Challenge of Jesus's Parables*, edited by Richard N. Longenecker, 240–62. Grand Rapids: Eerdmans, 2000.

Lindemann, Andreas. "Die Logienquelle Q. Fragen an eine gut begründete Hypothese." In *The Sayings Source Q and the Historical Jesus*, edited by A. Lindemann, 3–26. BETL 158. Leuven: Leuven University Press, 2001.

Linnemann, Eta. *Gleichnisse Jesu: Einführung und Auslegung*. 3rd ed. Göttingen: Vandenhoeck & Ruprecht, 1964.

Llewelyn, Stephen R., ed. *New Documents Illustrating Early Christianity, 7: A Review of the Greek Inscriptions and Papyri Published in 1982–83*. With R. A. Kearsley. Sydney: Macquarie University Ancient History Documentary Research Centre, 1994.

Llewelyn, Stephen R. "Letters in the Early Church." In *New Documents Illustrating Early Christianity, Volume 7: A Review of the Greek Inscriptions and Papyri Papyri Published in 1982–83*, 7:48–57. 10 vols. Grand Rapids: Eerdmans, 1998.

———. "The Official Postal Systems of Antiquity." In *New Documents Illustrating Early Christianity, Volume 7: A Review of the Greek Inscriptions and Papyri Papyri Published in 1982–83*, 7:1–25. 10 vols. Grand Rapids: Eerdmans, 1998.

———. "The Provision of Transport for Persons." In *New Documents Illustrating Early Christianity, Volume 7: A Review of the Greek Inscriptions and Papyri Papyri Published in 1982–83*, 7:58–92. 10 vols. Grand Rapids: Eerdmans, 1998.

———. "The Sending of a Private Letter." In *New Documents Illustrating Early Christianity, Volume 7: A Review of the Greek Inscriptions and Papyri Papyri Published in 1982–83*, 7:26–47. 10 vols. Grand Rapids: Eerdmans, 1998.

Loisy, Alfred. *Les Actes des Apôtres*. Paris: Nourry, 1920.

Luhman, Reginald. "Belief in God and the Problem of Suffering." *EvQ* 57 (1985) 326–48.

Lumpe, A. "Exemplum." *RAC* 6 (1966) cols. 1230–57.

Ma, Julie C. "Elva Vanderbout: A Woman Pioneer of Pentecostal Mission among Igorots." *Journal of Asian Mission* 3 (2001) 121–40.

MacDonald, Dennis R. *Does the New Testament Imitate Homer? Four Cases from the Acts of the Apostles*. New Haven: Yale University Press, 2003.

———. "Paul and Greco-Roman Education." In *Paul in the Greco-Roman World*, edited by J. Paul Sampley, 198–227. Harrisburg, PA: Trinity Press International, 2003.

Macgregor, G. H. C. "The Concept of the Wrath of God in the New Testament." *NTS* 7 (1961) 101–9.

Mack, Burton L. *Anecdotes and Arguments: The Chreia in Antiquity and Early Christianity*. Claremont, CA: Institute for Antiquity and Christianity, 1987.

Mainville, Odette. "Jésus et l'Esprit dans l'oeuvre de Luc: Eclairage à partir d'Ac 2,33." *Science et Esprit* 42 (1990) 193–208.

———. *L'Esprit dans l'oeuvre de Luc*. Héritage et Projet 45. Montreal: Fides, 1991.

———. *The Spirit in Luke-Acts*. Translated by Suzanne Spolarich. Eugene, OR: Wipf & Stock, 2016.

Manson, Thomas W. "Entry into Membership of the Early Church." *JTS* 48 (1947) 25–33.

Marguerat, Daniel. *The First Christian Historian: Writing the 'Acts of the Apostles.'* Translated by K. McKinney et al. SNTSMS 121. Cambridge: Cambridge University Press, 2002.

———. "L'image de Paul dans les Actes des Apôtres." *Les Actes des Apôtres: Histoirie, récit, théologie*, edited by M. Berder, 121–54. Paris: Cerf, 2005.

Marrou, Henri Irénée. *Historie de l'éducation dans l'antiquité*. Paris: Seuill, 1950.

———. *A History of Education in Antiquity*. Translated by G. Lamb. New York: Sheed & Ward, 1956.

———. "La technique de l'édition à l'époque patristique." *VC* 3 (1949) 208–24.

Marshall, I. Howard. "Acts and the 'Former Treatise.'" In *The Book of Acts in Its Ancient Literary Setting, Vol. 1: The Book of Acts in Its First Century Setting*, edited by Bruce W. Winter and Andrew D. Clarke, 1:163–82. 5 vols. Grand Rapids: Eerdmans, 1993.

———. *Gospel of Luke*. NIGTC. Exeter: Paternoster, 1978.

———. "Introduction." In *New Testament Interpretation: Essays on Principles and Methods*, edited by I. Howard Marshall, 11–18. Exeter: Paternoster, 1977.

———. *Luke: Historian and Theologian*. Exeter: Paternoster, 1970.

———. "Luke and His 'Gospel.'" In *Das Evangelium und die Evangelien*, edited by Peter Stuhlmacher, 289–308. WUNT 28. Tübingen: Mohr, 1983.

———. "The Significance of Pentecost." *SJT* 30 (1977) 347–69.

Martin, Francis. "Le baptême dans l'Esprit." *NRTh* 106 (1984) 23–58.

Martin, Josef. *Antike Rhetorik: Technik und Methode*. HandbAW 2.3. Munich: Beck, 1974.

Martin, Ralph P. "An Epistle in Search of a Life-Setting." *ExpTim* 79 (1968) 296–302.

———. *New Testament Foundations*. 2 vols. Exeter: Paternoster, 1978.

Marx, Werner G. "Luke, the Physician, Re-examined." *ExpTim* 91 (1980) 168–72.

Maslakov, G. "Valerius Maximus and Roman Historiography: A Study of the *exempla* Tradition." *ANRW* 2 (1984) 437–96.

May, J. M. "The *Ethica Digressio* and Cicero's *Pro Milone*: A Progression of Intensity from *Logos* to *Ethos* to *Pathos*." *CJ* 74 (1979) 240–46.

McKay, John. "Pentecost and History." *The Spirit and Church* 3 (2001) 113–28.

McQueen, Larry R. *Joel and the Spirit: The Cry of a Prophetic Hermeneutic*. JPTSup 8. Sheffield: Sheffield Academic Press, 1995.

Mealand, D. L. "The Close of Acts and Its Hellenistic Vocabulary." *NTS* 36 (1990) 583–97.

Menoud, Philippe H. "Jésus et ses témoins." *Eglise et Théologie* 23 (1960) 7–20.

Menzies, Robert P. *The Development of Early Christian Pneumatology with Special Reference to Luke-Acts*. JSNTSup 54. Sheffield: JSOT, 1991.

———. *Empowered for Witness: The Spirit in Luke-Acts*. JPTSup 6. Sheffield: Sheffield Academic Press, 1994.

———. "The Holy Spirit in Christian Theology." In *Perspectives on Evangelical Theology*, edited by Kenneth Kantzer and Stanley N. Gundry, 67–80. Grand Rapids: Baker, 1979.

———. "Spirit and Power in Luke-Acts: A Response to Max Turner." *JSNT* 49 (1993) 11–20.

———. "Spirit-Baptism and Spiritual Gifts." In *Pentecostalism in Context: Essays in Honor of William W. Menzies*, edited by Wonsuk Ma and Robert P. Menzies, 48–59. JPTSup 11. Sheffield: Sheffield Academic Press, 1997.

Menzies, William W. "The Methodology of Pentecostal Theology: An Essay on Hermeneutics." In *Essays on Apostolic Themes: Studies in Honor of Howard M. Ervin*, edited by Paul Elbert, 1–14. Peabody, MA: Hendrickson, 1985.

Menzies, William W., and Robert P. Menzies. *Spirit and Power: Foundations of Pentecostal Experience*. Grand Rapids: Zondervan, 2000.

Metzger, Bruce M. "The Language of the N.T." In *The Interpreter's Bible*, edited by Bruce M. Metzger, 7:43–59. 12 vols. Nashville: Abingdon, 1978.

Meynet, Roland. *L'Évangile selon Saint Luc: Analyse rhétorique Commentaire*. 2 vols. Paris: Cerf, 1988.

Michiels, Robert. "La conception lucanienne de la conversion." *ETL* 41 (1965) 42–78.

Millard, Alan. *Reading and Writing in the Time of Jesus*. New York: New York University Press, 1990.

Minchen, Elizabeth. "Verbal Behaviour in Its Social Context: Three Question Strategies in Homer's Odyssey." *Classical Quarterly* 52 (2002) 15–32.

Moessner, David P. "Dionysius' Narrative 'Arrangement' (οἰκονομία) as the Hermeneutical Key to Luke's Re-Vision of the 'Many.'" In *Paul, Luke and the Graeco-Roman World: Essays in Honour of Alexander J.M. Wedderburn*, edited by Alf Christophersen et al., 149–64. London: T. & T. Clark, 2003.

———. "The Meaning of ΚΑΘΕΞΗΣ in the Lucan Prologue as a Key to the Distinctive Contribution of Luke's Narrative Among the Many." In *The Four Gospels 1992: FS Franz Neirynck*, edited by F. van Segbroeck et al., 2:1513–28. 3 vols. Leuven: Leuven University Press, 1992.

Moltmann, Jürgen. *Der Weg Jesu Christi: Christologie in messianischen Dimensionen*. Munich: Kaiser, 1989.

Montague, George T. *The Holy Spirit: Growth of a Biblical Tradition*. New York: Paulist, 1976.

Morgan, Teresa. *Literate Education in the Hellenistic and Roman Worlds*. Cambridge: Cambridge University Press, 1998.

Moule, C. F. D. "The Christology of Acts." In *Studies in Luke-Acts: Essays Presented in Honor of Paul Schubert*, edited by Leander E. Keck and J. Louis Martyn, 159–85. London: SPCK, 1968.

Moulton, James Hope, and Wilbert Francis Howard. *A Grammar of New Testament Greek, II: Accidence and Word-Formation*. Edinburgh: T. & T. Clark, 1920.

Mühlen, Heribert. *Einübung in die christliche Grunderfahrung*. Mainz: Matthias-Grunewald, 1975.

Müller, Paul-Gerhard. *Der Traditionsprozess im Neuen Testament: Kommunikationsanalytische Studien zur Versprachlichung des Jesusphänomens*. Freiburg: Herder, 1982.

Mundle, Wilhelm. "Das Apostelbild der Apostelgeschichte." *ZNW* 27 (1928) 36–54.

Nave, Guy D., Jr. *The Role and Function of Repentance in Luke-Acts*. Academia Biblica 4. Atlanta: Society of Biblical Literature, 2002.

Neale, D. A. *None but the Sinners: Religious Categories in the Gospel of Luke*. JSNTSup 58. Sheffield: Sheffield Academic Press, 1991.

Neil, William. *The Acts of the Apostles*. NCB. London: Marshall, Morgan & Scott, 1973.
Newsom, Carol. "Bakhtin, the Bible, and Dialogic Truth." *JR* 76 (1996) 290–306.
Neyrey, Jerome H. "Questions, *Chreiai*, and Challenges to Honor: The Interface of Rhetoric and Culture in Mark's Gospel." *CBQ* 60 (1998) 657–81.
Nissen, J. "The Problem of Suffering and Ethics in the New Testament." In *Studia Biblica III: Papers on Paul and Other New Testament Authors*, edited by E. A. Livingstone, 227–87. JSNTSup 3. Sheffield: Sheffield Academic Press, 1980.
Nock, Arthur Darby. *Essays on Religion and the Ancient World*. 2 vols. Edited by Zeph Stewart. Cambridge: Harvard University Press, 1972.
Nordh, A. "Historical *exempla* in Martial." *Eranos* (*Acta philologica Suecana*) 52 (1954) 224–38.
Oberhelman, S. M. "On the Chronology and Pneumatism of Aretaios of Cappadocia." *ANRW* 2:27.2 (1994) 941–66.
O'Brien, P. T. "Prayer in Luke-Acts." *TynBul* 24 (1974) 111–27.
Oehler, Robert. *Mythologische Exempla in der älterem griechischen Dichtung*. Aarau, Switzerland: Sauerländer, 1925.
O'Fearghail, Fearghus. *The Introduction to Luke-Acts: A Study of the Role of Lk 1,1–4,44 in the Composition of Luke's Two-Volume Work*. AnBib 126. Rome: Pontifical Biblical Institute, 1991.
Öhler, Markus *Elia im Neuen Testament, Untersuchungen zur Bedeutung des alttestamentlichen Propheten im frühen Christentum*. BZNW 88. Berlin: de Gruyter, 1997.
Oss, Douglas A. "A Pentecostal/Charismatic Response." In *Are Miraculous Gifts for Today? Four Views*, edited by Wayne A. Grudem, 86–93, 264–80. Grand Rapids: Zondervan, 1996.
O'Toole, Robert. "Acts 2:30 and the Davidic Covenant of Pentecost." *JBL* 102 (1983) 245–58.
Packer, J. I. "Charismatic Christianity and Biblical Theology." *Rutherford House Tape 103* (dated 1989/1990).
———. "Theological Reflections on the Charismatic Movement, Part 2." *Churchman* 94 (1980) 103–25.
Parsons, Mikael C. *The Departure of Jesus in Luke-Acts: The Ascension Narratives in Conflict*. JSNTSup 21. Sheffield: JSOT, 1987.
———. "Luke and the *Progymnasmata*: A Preliminary Investigation into the Preliminary Exercises." In *Contextualizing Acts: Lukan Narrative and Greco-Roman Discourse*, edited by Todd Penner and Caroline Vander Stichele, 43–63. SBLSymS 20. Atlanta: Society of Biblical Literature, 2003.
Patillon, Michel, ed. *Aelius Théon Progymnasmata, Texte établi et traduit*. Collection des Universités de France. Paris: Les Belles Lettres, 1997.
Pelling, Christopher. "Plutarch's Method of Work in Roman Lives." *Journal of Hellenistic Studies* 99 (1979) 74–96.
———. "Tragical Dreamer: Some Dreams in the Roman Historians." *Greece and Rome* 44 (1997) 201–10.
Penella, Robert J. "The *Progymnasmata* in Imperial Greek Education." *Classical World* 105 (2011) 77–90.
Penner, Todd. "Civilizing Discourse: Acts, Declamation, and the Rhetoric of the *Polis*." In *Contextualizing Acts: Lukan Narrative and Greco-Roman Discourse*, edited by Todd Penner and Caroline Vander Stichele, 65–104. SBLSymS 20. Atlanta: Society of Biblical Literature, 2003.
Penney, John. *The Missionary Emphasis of Lukan Pneumatology*. JPTSup 12. Sheffield: Sheffield Academic Press, 1997.

———. "The Testing of New Testament Prophecy." *JPT* 10 (1977) 35–84.
Perelman, Chaïm, and Lucie Olbrechts-Tyteca. *The New Rhetoric: A Treatise on Argumentation*. Translated by John Wilkerson and Purcell Weaver. Notre Dame: University of Notre Dame Press, 1969.
Pesch, Rudolf. *Die Apostelgeschichte, Apg 1–12*. 2 vols. EKKNT 5/1. Zürich: Benziger, 1986.
———. "Die Gabe des Heiligen Geistes [Apg 2, 38]." *BK* 21 (1966) 52, 53.
Petts, David. "Healing and the Atonement." *Journal of the European Pentecostal Theological Association* 12 (1993) 23–37.
Pfister, Manfred. "Konzepte der Intertextulität." In *Intertextualität: Formen, Functionen, anglistische Fallstudien*, edited by Ulrich Broich and Manfred Pfister, 1–30. Konzepte der Sprach-und Literaturwissenschaft 35. Tübingen: Niemeyer, 1985.
Phillips, E. D. "Medicine from the Alexandrians to Galen." In *Greek Medicine*, by E. D. Phillips, 161–71. Ithaca, NY: Cornell University Press, 1973.
Pinnock, Clark. "Divine Relationality: A Pentecostal Contribution to the Doctrine of God." *JPT* 16 (2000) 3–26.
Plessis, Isak J. du. "The Lukan Audience—Rediscovered? Some Reactions to Bauckham's Theory." *Neotestamentica* 34 (2000) 243–61.
Plummer, Alfred. *The Gospel according to S. Luke*. 5th ed. ICC. Edinburgh: T. & T. Clark, 1922.
Pokorný, P. "Lukas 15,11–32 und die lukanischen Soteriologie." In *Christus bezeugen. Festschrift für Wolfgang Trilling zum 65. Geburtstag*, edited by K. Kertelge et al., 179–92. Erfurter Theologische Studien 59. Leipzig: St. Benno, 1989.
———. *Theologie der lukanischen Schriften*. FRLANT 174. Göttingen: Vandenhoeck & Ruprecht, 1998.
Polkinghorne, John. *Belief in God in an Age of Science*. New Haven: Yale University Press, 1998.
———. "Theism." In *Science and Theology: An Introduction*, by John Polkinghorne, 66–83. Minneapolis: Fortress, 1998.
Porter, Stanley E. *The Paul of Acts: Essays in Literary Criticism, Rhetoric, and Theology*. WUNT 2/115. Tübingen: Mohr, 1999.
Powers, Janet Evert. "Missionary Tongues?" *JPT* 17 (2000) 39–55.
Poythress, Vern Sheridan. "Modern Spiritual Gifts as Analogous to Apostolic Gifts: Affirming Extraordinary Works of the Spirit within Cessationist Theology." *JETS* 39 (1996) 71–101.
Preuschen, Erwin. *Die Apostelgeschichte*. Tübingen: Mohr Siebeck, 1912.
Price, Bennett J. "'Paradeigma' and 'Exemplum' in Ancient Rhetorical Theory." PhD diss., The University of California at Berkeley, 1975.
Procksch, Otto. "ἅγιος im Neuen Testament." *TWNT* 1:101–16.
Prosser, Peter E. *Dispensationalist Eschatology and Its Influence on American and British Religious Movements*. Texts and Studies in Religion 82. Lewiston, NY: Mellen, 1999.
Quesnel, Michel. *Baptisés dans l'Esprit: Baptême et Esprit Saint dans les Actes des Apôtres*. LD 120. Paris: Cerf, 1985.
Rabe, Hugo, ed. *Hermogenis Opera*. Leipzig: Teubner, 1913.
Race, W. H. "Some Digressions and Returns in Greek Authors." *CJ* 76 (1980) 1–8.
Rad, Gerhard von. "Die deuteronomistische Geschichtstheologie in den Königsbüchern." In *Gesammelte Studien zum Alten Testament*, by Gerhard von Rad, 189–204. Munich: Kaiser, 1971.
Rambaud, Michel. *Cicéron et l'histoire romaine*. Collection d'études latines. Série scientifique 28. Paris: Les Belles Lettres, 1953.
Ramsay, William M. *St. Paul the Traveller and the Roman Citizen*. New York: Putnam, 1896.

Reicke, Bo. *Re-examining Paul's Letters: The History of the Pauline Correspondence.* Edited by David P. Moessner and Ingalisa Reicke. Harrisburg, PA: Trinity Press International, 2001.

Rengstorf, Karl H. *Das Evangelium nach Lukas.* NTD 3. Göttingen: Vandenhoeck & Ruprecht, 1974.

Riesner, Rainer. *Jesus als Lehrer: Eine Untersuchung zum Ursprung der Evangelien-Überlieferung.* WUNT 2/7. Tübingen: Mohr, 1981.

Robbins, Vernon K. "The Chreia." In *Greco-Roman Literature and the New Testament*, edited by David E. Aune, 1–23. Atlanta: Scholars, 1988.

———. "Progymnastic Rhetorical Composition and Pre-Gospel Traditions: A New Approach." In *The Synoptic Gospels: Source Criticism and the New Literary Criticism*, edited by Camille Focant, 111–47. Leuven: Leuven University Press, 1993.

Robeck, Cecil M., Jr. "The Gift of Prophecy in Acts and Paul, Part I and II." *Studia Biblica et Theologica* 5.1 (1975) 15–38 and 5.2 (1975) 37–54.

———. "Irenaeus and 'Prophetic Gifts.'" In *Essays on Apostolic Themes: Studies in Honor of Howard M. Ervin*, edited by Paul Elbert, 104–14. Peabody, MA: Hendrickson, 1985.

———. "The Nature of Pentecostal Spirituality." *Pneuma* 14 (1992) 103–6.

Roberts, W. Rhys. *Demetrius on Style: The Greek Text of Demetrius De Elocutione.* London: Cambridge University Press, 1902.

Robinson, James M., et al., eds. *The Critical Edition of Q.* Hermeneia. Minneapolis: Fortress, 2000.

Roller, Matthew B. "Exemplarity in Roman Culture." *Classical Philology* 99 (2004) 1–56.

Roon, A. van. *The Authenticity of Ephesians.* NovTSup 39. Leiden: Brill, 1974.

Rooney, Lucy, and Robert Faricy. *Lord, Teach Us to Pray: Leaders Manual.* 2nd ed. Vatican City: International Catholic Charismatic Renewal Services, 1998.

Runia, Klass. *Op zoek naar de Geest.* Kampen: Kok Pharos, 2000.

Rusam, Dietrich. *Das Alte Testament bei Lukas.* BZNW 112. Berlin: de Gruyter, 2003.

Russell, D. A. "De Imitation." In *Creative Imitation and Latin Literature*, edited by David West and Tony Woodman, 1–16. Cambridge: Cambridge University Press, 1979.

Russell, E. A. "'They Believed Philip Preaching' (Acts 8.12)." *Irish Biblical Studies* 1 (1979) 169–76.

Ruthven, Jon. "'Between Two Worlds: One Dead, the Other Powerless to Be Born?' Pentecostal Theological Education vs. Training for Christian Service." *The Spirit and Church* 3 (2001) 273–97.

———. "The 'Foundational Gifts' of Ephesians 2:20." *JPT* 10 (2002) 28–43.

———. "The 'Imitation of Christ' in Christian Tradition: Its Missing Charismatic Emphasis." *JPT* 16 (2000) 60–77.

———. *On the Cessation of the Charismata: The Protestant Polemic on Postbiblical Miracles.* JPTSup 3. Sheffield: Sheffield Academic, 1993.

———. Review of *Are Miraculous Gifts for Today? Four Views*, edited by Wayne Grudem. *Pneuma* 21 (1999) 155–58.

Sanders, James A. *Luke and Scripture: The Function of Sacred Tradition in Luke-Acts.* Minneapolis: Fortress, 1993.

Saucy, Robert. "An Open but Cautious View." In *Are Miraculous Gifts for Today? Four Views*, edited by Wayne A. Grudem, 97–148. Grand Rapids: Zondervan, 1996.

Scarborough, John. "The Doctor and His Place in Roman Society." In *Roman Medicine*, 109–21. Ithaca, NY: Cornell University Press, 1976.

———. "Roman Medical Education." In *Roman Medicine*, by John Scarborough, 122–33. Ithaca, NY: Cornell University Press, 1976.

Schenk, Wolfgang. *Das Sagen im Neuen Testament. Eine begriffsanalytische Studie.* Theologische Arbeiten 25. Berlin: de Gruyter, 1967.

———. *Synopse zur Redenquelle der Evangelien.* Düsseldorf: Patmos, 1981.

Schissal, Otmar. "Rhetorische Progymnasmatik der Byzantiner." *Byzantinisch-neugriechische Jahrbücher* 11 (1934–35) 1–10.

Schmidt, Daryl D. "Syntactical Style in the 'We'-Sections of Acts: How Lukan Is It?" In *Society of Biblical Literature 1989 Seminar Papers*, edited by D. J. Lull, 300–308. Atlanta: Scholars, 1989.

Schnackenburg, Rudolf. "Die johanneische Gemeinde und ihre Geisterfahrung." In *Die Kirche des Anfangs: Festschrift für Heinz Schürmann zum 65 Geburtstag*, edited by Rudolf Schnackenburg et al., 277–306. Freiburg: Herder, 1978.

Schneider, Gerhard. "Die Bitte um das Kommen des Geistes im lukanischen Vaterunser (Lk 11,2 v. 1.)." In *Studien zum Text und zur Ethik des Neuen Testaments: Festschrift zum 80. Geburtstag von Heinrich Greeven*, edited by Wolfgang Schrage, 344–73. Berlin: de Gruyter, 1986.

———. "Zur Bedeutung von καθεξῆς im lukanischen Doppelwerk." *ZNW* 68 (1977) 128–31.

Schottroff, Louise. "Das Gleichnis vom verlorenen Sohn." *ZTK* 68 (1971) 27–52.

Schrenk, Gottlob. "ἐγγράφω, Zu Lk 10,20." *TWNT* 1:769–70.

Schubert, Paul. "The Structure and Significance of Luke 24." In *Neutestamentliche Studien für Rudolf Bultmann*, edited by Walther Eltester, 165–86. Berlin: Töpelmann, 1957.

Schulz, Siegfried. "Gottes Vorsehung bei Lukas." *ZNW* 54 (1963) 104–16.

———. *Q: Die Spruchquelle der Evangelisten.* Zürich: TVZ, 1972.

Schulze, H. "Die Unterlagen für die Abschiedsrede zu Milet in Apostelgesch. 20,18–38." *ThStKr* 73 (1900) 119–25.

Schürmann, Heinz. "Die geistlichen Gnadengaben in den paulinischen Gemeinden." In *Ursprung und Gestalt: Erörterungen und Besinnungen zum Neuen Testament*, by Heinz Schürmann, 236–67. Düsseldorf: Patmos-Verlag, 1970.

Schwanbeck, E. A. *Über die Quellen die Schriften des Lukas: ein kritischer Versuch.* Darmstadt: Leske, 1847.

Schweizer, Eduard. *Das Evangelium nach Lukas.* 18th ed. NTD 3. Göttingen: Vandenhoeck & Ruprecht, 1982.

———. "πνευμα κτλ." *TDNT* 6:389–455.

———. "Gegenwart des Geistes und eschatologische Hoffnung." In *The Background of the New Testament and Its Eschatology*, edited by W. D. Davies and D. Daube, 482–508. Cambridge: Cambridge University Press, 1956.

———. *Griechische Grammatik: Auf der Grundlage von Karl Brugmanns Griechischer Grammatik, II. Syntax und Syntaktische Stilistik.* Edited by Albert Debrunner. Handbuch der Altertumswissenschaft 2/1. Munich: Beck, 1950.

———. *Heiliger Geist.* Stuttgart: Kreuz, 1978.

———. "πνεῦμα, πνευματικός, κτλ., Lukas und Apostelgeschichte." *TWNT* 6:401–13.

Sellner, Hans Jörg. *Das Heil Gottes: Studien zur Soteriologie des lukanschen Doppelwerks.* BZNW 152. Berlin: de Gruyter, 2007.

Seytre, Christian. "Le pentecôstisme." In *En compagnie de beaucoup d'autres: Guide théologique du protestantisme contemporain*, edited by Geoffroy Turckheim, 93–104. Paris: Les Bergers et les Mages, 1997.

Shalev, Donna. "Illocutionary Clauses Accompanying Questions in Greek Drama and in Platonic Dialogue." *Mnemosyne* 54 (2001) 531–61.

Shelton, James B. "Epistemology and Authority in the Acts of the Apostles: An Analysis and Test Case Study of Acts 15:1–29." *The Spirit and Church* 2 (2000) 231–47.

---. "'Filled with the Holy Spirit' and 'Full of the Holy Spirit,' Lucan Redactional Phrases." In *Faces of Renewal: Studies in Honor of Stanley M. Horton*, edited by Paul Elbert, 81–107. Peabody, MA: Hendrickson, 1988.

---. *Mighty in Word and Deed: The Role of the Spirit in Luke-Acts*. Peabody, MA: Hendrickson, 1991.

---. "A Reply to James D. G. Dunn's 'Baptism in the Spirit: A Response to Pentecostal Scholarship on Luke-Acts.'" *JPT* 4 (1994) 139–43.

Shipp, G. P. *Studies in the Language of Homer*. 2nd ed. Cambridge Classical Studies. Cambridge: Cambridge University Press, 1972.

Sluitter, Ineke. "The Embarrassment of Imperfection: Galen's Assessment of Hippocrates' Linguistic Merits." In *Ancient Medicine in Its Socio-Cultural Context*, edited by Philip J. van der Eijk et al., 2:519–35. 2 vols. Amsterdam: Rodopi, 1995.

Smail, Thomas, et al. "'Revelation Knowledge' and Knowledge of Revelation: The Faith Movement and the Question of Heresy." *JPT* 5 (1994) 57–77.

Smith, Robert H. "Matthew's Message for Insiders: Charisma and Commandment in a First-Century Community." *Int* 46 (1992) 229–39.

Smith, Wesley D. "From Hippocrates to Galen." In *The Hippocratic Tradition*, by Wesley D. Smith, 177–246. Ithaca, NY: Cornell University Press, 1979.

Soards, Marion L. *The Speeches in Acts: Their Content, Context, and Concerns*. Louisville: Westminster John Knox, 1994.

Solin, Heikki. *Die griechische Personennamen in Rom. Ein Namenbuch*. 3 vols. Berlin: de Gruyter, 1982.

Soltau, W. "Die Herkunft der Reden in der Apostelgeschichte." *ZNW* 4 (1903) 128–54.

Spengel, Leonard, ed. *Rhetores Graeci*. 3 vols. Leipzig: Teubner, 1854–56.

Spicq, Ceslas. *Notes de lexicographie néo-testamentaire*. 3 vols. OBO 22/3. Fribourg: Editions Universitaires, 1982.

Stählin, Gustav. "Das Bild der Witwe: Ein Beitrag zur Bildersprache der Bibel und zum Phänomen der Personifikation in der Antike." *JAC* 17 (1974) 5–20.

Stanton, Graham N. "The Fourfold Gospel." *NTS* 43 (1997) 317–46.

---. *Jesus of Nazareth in New Testament Preaching*. SNTSMS 27. Cambridge: Cambridge University Press, 1974.

---. "Presuppositions in New Testament Criticism." In *New Testament Interpretation: Essays on Principles and Methods*, edited by I. Howard Marshall, 60–71. Grand Rapids: Eerdmans, 1977.

Starr, Raymond J. "The Circulation of Literary Texts in the Roman World." *Classical Quarterly* 37 (1987) 213–23.

Stegemann, W. "Theon." PW 5/2 (1934) cols. 2037–54.

Stegman, Thomas D. "Reading Luke 12:13–34 as an Elaboration of a Chreia: How Hermogenes of Tarsus Sheds Light on Luke's Gospel." *NovT* 49 (2007) 328–52.

Stenschke, Christoph. *Luke's Portrait of Gentiles Prior to Their Coming to Faith*. WUNT 2/108. Tübingen: Mohr Siebeck, 1999.

Sterling, Gregory E. "Luke-Acts and Apologetic Historigraphy." SBLSP 1989, edited by David J. Lull, 326–42. Atlanta: Scholars, 1989.

Steyn, Gert J. *Septuagint Quotations in the Context of the Petrine and Pauline Speeches of the Acta Apostolorum*. CBET 12. Kampen: Kok Pharos, 1995.

Storms, C. Samuel. "A Third Wave Response." In *Are Miraculous Gifts for Today? Four Views*, edited by Wayne A. Grudem, 72–85, 175–223. Grand Rapids: Zondervan, 1996.

Storms, Sam. *The Beginner's Guide to Spiritual Gifts*. Ann Arbor, MI: Servant, 2002.

Strathmann, Hermann. "μάρτυς, κτλ. im NT." *TWNT* 4:492–511.

Stronstad, Roger. *Charismatic Theology of St. Luke*. Peabody, MA: Hendrickson, 1984.

———. "The Prophethood of All Believers: A Study in Luke's Charismatic Theology." In *Pentecostalism in Context: Essays in Honor of William W. Menzies*, edited by Wonsuk Ma and Robert P. Menzies, 62–74. JPTSup 11. Sheffield: Sheffield Academic Press, 1997.

———. *Spirit, Scripture, and Theology: A Pentecostal Perspective*. Baguio City, Philippines: Asian Pacific Theological Seminary, 1995.

Stuhlmacher, Peter. *Biblische Theologie des Neuen Testaments, II. Von der Paulusschule bis zur Johannesoffenbarung*. 2 vols. Göttingen: Vandenhoeck & Ruprecht, 1999.

Suhl, Alfred. "Paulinische Chronologie im Streit der Meinungen." *ANRW* 2.26/2 (2016) 939–1188.

Sullivan, Francis A. "Baptism in the Spirit." *Greg* 55 (1974) 49–66.

———. *Charismes et renouveau charismatique: Etude biblique et théologique*. Loir-et-Cher: Nouan-le-Fuzelier, 1988.

———. *Charisms and Charismatic Renewal: A Biblical and Theological Study*. Ann Arbor, MI: Servant, 1982.

Talbert, Charles H. "Conversion in the Acts of the Apostles: Ancient Auditors' Perceptions." In *Literary Studies in Luke-Acts: Essays in Honor of Joseph B. Tyson*, edited by Richard P. Thompson and Thomas E. Phillips, 141–53. Macon, GA: Mercer University Press, 1998.

———. *A Literary and Theological Commentary on the Acts of the Apostles*. New York: Crossroad, 1997.

———. "Promise and Fulfillment in Lucan Theology." In *Luke-Acts: New Perspectives from the Society of Biblical Literature Seminar*, edited by Charles Talbert, 91–103. New York: Crossroads, 1984.

———. *Reading Luke: A Literary and Theological Commentary on the Third Gospel*. New York: Crossroad, 1982.

Tannehill, Robert C. *The Narrative Unity of Luke-Acts: A Literary Interpretation*. 2 vols. Minneapolis: Fortress, 1990.

———. "Types and Functions of Apophthegms in the Synoptic Gospels." *ANRW* 2.25/2, (1984) 1792–803.

Thiering, B. E. "The Acts of the Apostles as Early Christian Art." In *Essays in Honour of G. W. Thatcher*, edited by E. C. B. MacLaurin, 139–89. Sydney: Sydney University Press, 1967.

———. "Qumran Initiation and New Testament Baptism." *NTS* 27 (1981) 615–31.

Thomas, John Christopher. *The Devil, Disease and Deliverance: Origins of Illness in New Testament Thought*. JPTSup 13. Sheffield: Sheffield Academic Press, 1998.

———. "The Kingdom of God in the Gospel according to Matthew." *NTS* 39 (1993) 136–46.

Thomas, Richard F. "Virgil's *Georgics* and the Art of Reference." *HSCP* 90 (1986) 171–98.

Thomas, Robert L. "Current Hermeneutical Trends: Toward Explanation or Obfuscation?" *JETS* 39 (1996) 241–56.

———. *Understanding Spiritual Gifts*. Chicago: Moody, 1978.

Thompson, M. B. "The Holy Internet: Communications Between Churches in the First Century Generation." In *The Gospels for All Christians: Rethinking the Gospel Audiences*, edited by Richard Bauckham, 49–70. Grand Rapids: Eerdmans, 1998.

Thornton, Claus-Jürgen. *Der Zeuge des Zeugen: Lukas als Historiker der Paulusreisen*. WUNT 56. Tübingen: Mohr, 1991.

Throckmorton, B. H. "Σώζειν, σωτηρία in Luke-Acts." In *Studia Evangelica, VI: Papers Presented to the Fourth International Congress on New Testament Studies*, edited by Elizabeth A. Livingstone, 515–26. 7 vols. Berlin: Akademie-Verlag, 1973.

Toit, Andrie B. du. "Forensic Metaphors in Romans and Their Soteriological Significance." In *Salvation in the New Testament: Perspectives on Soteriology*, edited by Jan G. van der Watt, 213–46. Leiden: Brill, 2005.

Tolkien, J. R. R. *The Return of the King: Being the Third Part of The Lord of the Rings*. New York: Ballantine, 1980.

Tucker, Jeffrey T. *Example Stories: Perspectives on Four Parables in the Gospel of Luke*. JSNTSup 162. Sheffield: Sheffield Academic Press, 1988.

Turner, Eric G. *Athenian Books in the Fifth and Fourth Centuries B.C.* London: University College London Press, 1952.

———. "The Rhetoric of Question and Answer in Menander." In *Drama and Mimesis*, edited by James Redmond, 1–23. Cambridge: Cambridge University Press, 1980.

Turner, Max. "Jesus and the Spirit in Luke." *TynBul* 32 (1981) 3–42.

———. *Power from on High: The Spirit in Israel's Restoration and Witness in Luke–Acts*. JPTSup 9. Sheffield: Sheffield Academic Press, 1996.

———. "Spirit Endowment in Luke/Acts: Some Linguistic Considerations." *VE* 12 (1981) 45–63.

———. "The Spirit of Prophecy and Ethical/Religious Life of the Christian Community." In *Spirit and Renewal: Essays in Honor of J. Rodman Williams*, edited by Mark M. Williams, 166–90. JPTSup 5. Sheffield: Sheffield Academic Press, 1994.

———. "The Spirit of Prophecy and the Power of Authoritative Preaching in Luke-Acts: A Question of Origins." *NTS* 38 (1992) 66–88.

Tyson, Joseph B. "From History to Rhetoric and Back: Assessing New Trends in Acts Studies." In *Contextualizing*, edited by Todd Penner and Vander Stichele, 23–42. Atlanta: Society of Biblical Literature, 2003.

Unnik, W. C. van. "Luke's Second Book and the Rules of Hellenistic Historiography." In *Les Actes des Apôtres: Traditions, rédaction, théologie*, edited by Jacob Kremer, 37–60. BETL 48. Leuven: Leuven University Press, 1979.

Vielhauer, P. "On the 'Paulinisms' of Acts." In *Studies in Luke-Acts: Essays Presented in Honor of Paul Schubert*, edited by Leander E. Keck and J. Louis Martyn, 33–50. London: SPCK, 1968.

———. "Zum 'Paulinismus' der Apostelgeschichte." *EvT* 10 (1950/51) 1–15.

Voelz, James W. "The Language of the New Testament." *ANRW* 2.25/5 (1984) 893–997.

Volkmann, Richard. *Die Rhetorick der Griechen und Römer*. Leipzig: Teubner, 1885.

Walker, William O., Jr. "Acts and the Pauline Corpus Reconsidered." *JSNT* 24 (1985) 3–23.

———. "Acts and the Pauline Corpus Revisited: Peter's Speech at the Jerusalem Conference." In *Literary Studies in Luke-Acts: Essays in Honor of Joseph B. Tyson*, edited by Richard P. Thompson and Thomas E. Phillips, 77–86. Macon, GA: Mercer University Press, 1998.

Walton, Steve. *Leadership and Lifestyle: The Portrait of Paul in the Miletus Speech and 1 Thessalonians*. SNTSMS 108. Cambridge: Cambridge University Press, 2000.

Watson, Duane F. "Paul's Speech to the Ephesian Elders (Acts 20:17–38) Epideictic Rhetoric of Farewell." In *Persuasive Artistry: Studies in New Testament Rhetoric in Honor of George A. Kennedy*, edited by Duane F. Watson, 184–208. Sheffield: JSOT, 1990.

Webb, Ruth. "*Ekphrasis* Ancient and Modern: The Invention of a Genre." *Word and Image* 15 (1999) 7–18.

———. *Ekphrasis, Imagination and Persuasion in Ancient Rhetorical Theory and Practice*. Surrey, UK: Ashgate, 2009.

———. "Poetry and Rhetoric." In *Handbook of Classical Rhetoric in the Hellenistic Period (330 BC–AD 400)*, edited by Stanley E. Porter, 339–69. New York: Brill, 1997.

———. "The *Progymnasmata* as Practice." In *Education in Greek and Roman Antiquity*, edited by Yun Lee Too, 289–316. Leiden: Brill, 2001.
Weber, Giorgio. *Areteo di Cappadocia: interpretazioni e aspetti della formazione anatomo-patologica del Morgagni*. Florence: n.p., 1996.
Wedderburn, A. J. M. "The 'We'-Passages in Acts: On the Horns of a Dilemma." *ZNW* 93 (2002) 78–98.
Weissenrieder, Annette. *Images of Illness in the Gospel of Luke: Insights of Ancient Medical Texts*. WUNT 2/164. Tübingen: Mohr Siebeck, 2003.
Wendel, Carl, ed. *Scholia in Apollonium Rhodium Vetera*. 3rd ed. Berlin: Weidmann, 1974.
Wendt, Hans Hinrich. *Die Apostelgeschichte*. 5th ed. KEK 3/9. Göttingen: Vandenhoeck & Ruprecht, 1913.
White, John L. "Ancient Greek Letters." In *Greco-Roman Literature and the New Testament: Selected Forms and Genres*, edited by David E. Aune, 85–105. Atlanta: Scholars, 1988.
Whitmarsh, Tim. *Greek Literature and the Roman Empire: The Politics of Imitation*. Oxford: Oxford University Press, 2001.
Wiedemann, Thomas. "Sallust's *Jugurtha*: Concord, Discord, and the Digressions." *GR* 40 (1993) 48–57.
Williams, Charles Bray. *The Participle in the Book of Acts*. Chicago: n.p., 1909.
Williams, C. G. "Speaking in Tongues." In *Strange Gifts? A Guide to Charismatic Renewal*, edited by David Martin and Peter Mullen, 72–83. Oxford: Basil Blackwell, 1984.
Williams, Garry J. "Was Evangelicalism Created by the Enlightenment?" *TynBul* 53 (2002) 281–312.
Williams, J. Rodman. *Renewal Theology: Salvation, the Holy Spirit, and Christian Living*. 3 vols. Grand Rapids: Zondervan, 1990.
———. "The Upsurge of Pentecostalism." *The Reformed World* 31 (1971) 340–44.
Witt, R. E. *Isis and Sarapis in the Roman World*. Leiden: Brill, 1995.
———. *Isis in the Graeco-Roman World*. Aspects of Greek and Roman Life. Ithaca, NY: Cornell University Press, 1971.
Wolter, Michael. "Apollos und die ephesinischen Johannesjünger." *ZNW* 78 (1987) 49–73.
———. "Lk 15 als Streitgespräch." *ETL* 78/1 (2002) 25–56.
———. "'Reich Gottes' bei Lukas." *NTS* 41 (1995) 541–63.
Woodman, A. J. *Rhetoric in Classical Historiography: Four Studies*. London: Croom Helm, 1988.
"Word and Spirit, Church and Word: The Final Report of the International Dialogue between Representatives of the World Alliance of Reformed Churches and Some Classical Pentecostal Churches and Leaders (1996–2000)." *Asian Journal of Pentecostal Studies* 4.1 (2001) 41–72.
Zahn, Theodor. *Die Apostelgeschichte des Lucas, II*. 2 vols. 1st and 2nd ed. KNT 5. Leipzig: A. Deichertsche Verlagsbuchhandlung Werner Scholl, 1921.
Zeller, Dieter. *Kommentar zur Logienquelle*. SKKNT 21. Stuttgart: Katholisches Bibelwerk, 1984.
Zimmerman, Maaike. "Latinising the Novel. Scholarship since Perry on Greek 'Models' and Roman (Re-)Creations." *Ancient Narrative* 2 (2002) 123–42.

Index of Persons

Adams, Wesley, 96n21
Aejmelaeus, Lars, 58(2x), 59n39, 74n1, 82n45(2x), 109n63(2x), 118, 123(3x), 124, 125, 127n38, 144n7
Aker, Benny C., 97n23, 100n36
Albrecht, Daniel E., 93n3
Alewell, Karl, 5n17, 62n56, 77n17, 124n34
Alexander, Loveday C., 10n36, 57n16, 75n6, 80n31, 135n33
Antoniadis, Sophie, 34, 34n4, 34n5
Archer, Ken, 97n23, 110n68
Aristotle, 38n26, 77, 142n2,
Arrington, French, 96n21
Atkinson, William P., 16n64
Aune, David E., 135n30
Austin, Norman, 86n56
Avenarius, Gert, 26n95

Baer, H. von, 112n73, 134, 138n41, 141n50
Bagalawis, Manuel A., 28n106
Barker, Andrew, 86n56
Barrett, C. K., 35n8, 47, 55n4
Barth, Markus, 53n2, 95n15, 101n42, 122n22
Bauckham, Richard, 57, 78
Baum, A. D., 83n48, 83n50, 90n73, 144n7
Baumert, Norbert, 101
Beard, Mary, 56n14
Belser, Johann E., 108n61
Berger, Klaus, 1, 22n86, 69n69, 74n2, 74n3, 81n39, 91n79
Berlin, Adele, 29n107, 116n82
Beyer, Klaus, 47
Billerbeck, Margarethe, 91n78
Bird, Michael F., 78
Bittlinger, Arnold, 131n11
Blass, F., 87
Bock, Darrell L., 28n107
Boismard, M. É., 34n5
Bold, Peter G., 115n81

Bonnard, Pierre, 129n5
Bonner, Stanley, 3n14, 42n33, 60n42
Bonz, Marianne Palmer, 9, 32n114
Botha, A. D., 9
Bovon, François, 27n99, 27n100, 137n39
Brawley, Robert L., 10, 12n47
Brodie, Thomas, 3n14, 8n27, 32n114, 35n8, 57, 57n17, 57n19, 57n22, 59, 71n80, 72n81, 72n82, 74n1, 78, 82n45, 87, 87nn60, 61, 62, 108n63, 109n63, 127n38
Brown, Schuyler, 45n7
Bruce, F. F., 95n17, 128, 141n52
Brunt, P. A., 73n86
Bühlmann, Walter, 13n51
Butts, James R., 4n15, 34n7, 37n22, 38n23, 60n43, 76n13, 124n33

Cadbury, Henry J., 14n53, 15n58, 25n93, 33(5x), 41n31, 86n57, 103, 122n24
Calvin, John, 22, 46, 89n71, 94n9, 94n11, 95, 96n19, 111n73
Cantalamessa, Raniero, 105n50
Canter, H. V., 86n56
Caragounis, Chrys C., 43n1
Carson, Donald A., 130, 133, 133n22
Casey, Maurice, 35n8
Charette, Blaine, 134, 135
Chevallier, Max-Alain, 71n78, 97n24
Chevallier, Raymond, 56
Cho, Youngmo, 16n64
Christenson, Larry, 105n50
Cichocka, H., 74n2
Clark, Donald, 60n42
Congar, Yves, 106n55
Cribiore, Rafaella, 3n14, 60n42, 61n44
Crone, Theodore M., 137n39
Crowley, Sharon, 20n80, 23n90

Darby, J. N., 95n17, 103

INDEX OF PERSONS

Deere, Jack, 106n54
Delebecque, Edouard, 34n5
Derrett, M., 135n27
Diehl, Johannes Friedrich, 48n22
Dietrich, Wolfgang, 11n41, 46
Dillon, Richard J., 1n3
Dorr, Donal, 132n19
Downing, G., 132n37
Dubois, Jean-Daniel, 8n27
Duckworth, George Eckel, 9, 81n41
Dumais, Marcel, 95n13
Duncan, J., 135n27
Dunn, James D. G., 11n40, 35n8(2x), 105, 112, 134, 138n41, 141n50
Dupont, Jacques, 1
DuPree, Sherry Sherrod, 93

Eagleton, Terry, 70n71
Eckstein, Hans-Joachim, 83n49
Edmunds, Lowell, 57n19
Ehrhardt, Arnold, 5n19, 25n93, 41n31(2x), 71n78, 86n57, 86n58, 97, 103, 122n24, 125n35
Elbert, Paul, 7n24, 18n74, 22n85, 23n92, 25n93, 27n98, 29n107, 35n8, 44n3, 45n11, 48n20, 53n32, 58n27, 59n35, 81n39, 82n46, 82n47, 86n58, 89n72, 93n4, 94n12, 98n27, 100n38, 103n46, 109n65, 110n71, 112n73, 134n27, 135, 145n10, 146n11
Ellis, E. Earle, 25n94, 70n74, 102n43, 109n66, 137n39
Emmett, A., 86n56
English, E. Schuyler, 96n21
Enslin, Morton S., 80n31, 82n45(4x), 109n63(2x), 136n33
Erdman, W. J., 95n17
Eriksson, Anders, 71
Ernst, Josef, 10n39
Ervin, Howard M., 101n42, 128, 129
Evans, C. F., 19n76

Fannon, P., 25n94, 70n74, 109n66
Fantham, Elaine, 73n87
Faricy, Robert, 105n50
Fee, Gordon, 128, 129(5x), 130
Ferguson, John, 135n30, 57n19, 79
Fiore, Benjamin, 5n17, 62n56, 77n17, 124n34
Fitzmyer, Joseph A., 1n3, 15n56, 34n5, 55n3, 55n4, 75n5, 118n8
Fleddermann, Harry T., 50n24, 51(2x), 144n6
Forbes, C., 135n30, 137n39
Franklin, Eric, 5n18, 35n8, 57n21, 71n76, 133n21

Frein, Brigid Curtin, 2, 3n9, 3n12, 81n39, 97n25, 131n14, 139n43
Frenschokowski, Marco, 28n101, 28n102

Gaffin, Richard B. Jr., 113n79, 137n38, 140n47
Gagnon, Robert A. J., 51n28
Gaisser, Julia Haig, 86n56
Galen, 79(2x), 80, 81, 92
Gaventa, Beverly Roberts, 10n36, 12n48
Gennete, Gérade, 21n82, 23n90
George, Augustin, 6n22, 12, 28n102, 71n78, 97, 105n50, 134n25
Gerhardsson, Birger, 56n13
Giangrande, Giuseppe, 79
Giblet, J., 104, 105n49, 134n23, 134n24
Gibson, Craig A., 61n46, 74n2, 75(2x), 76n11, 145
Goldingay, John, 102n43, 132n20
Goodacre, Mark, 35n8
Goodwin, William W., 56n5
Gorman, Heather M., 142n1
Goulder, Michael D., 58
Gräbe, Petrus, 108n62
Graves, Robert W., ix
Green, Barbara, 9n31
Green, Joel B., 104n47
Grudem, Wayne A., 131n11, 137n38, 140n47
Gunkel, Hermann, 60n41, 104, 105n49
Guy, Laurie, 16n65

Hadot, I., 136n37
Hafemann, Scott, 131n13
Haft, Adele J., 9, 81n41
Hagene, Sylvia, 4n16, 11n40, 11n41, 15n57
Hanson, J., 27, 135n32
Härter, A., 86n57
Haya-Prats, Gonzalo, 45n8, 60n41, 134n23, 134n25
Heath, Malcolm, 60n43, 76n13
Hemer, Colin J., ix, 25n93, 41n31, 58n33, 86n57, 86n58, 103, 108n61, 117, 122n24, 125n36, 128, 135n31, 136n35
Hengel, Martin, 92n80, 108n61, 117n5, 130n10, 138n42
Henry, Elisabeth, 9
Hersey, John, 70n71
Hinds, Stephen, 57n19
Hippocrates, 78, 80(6x), 80n36, 92
Hock, Ronald F., 3n14, 9n28, 33n2, 39n27, 68n65, 74n1, 75, 76n13, 81n40, 88n68
Hocken, Peter D., 98n29
Holman, Charles, 97n23, 135n29
Holtz, Traugott, 143
Homer, 9, 37, 42, 62, 68, 76, 79, 80, 81,

INDEX OF PERSONS

Horsley, Greg H. R., 136, 136n35–36
Horst, Peter W. van der, 4n14
Horton, Harold, 99n31
Hovenden, Gerald, 18n71
Howard, Wilbert Francis, 120n16, 131n14
Hude, Karl, 80n36
Hultgren, Stephen, 35n8
Hunger, Herbert, 4n15, 34n7, 42n33, 60n44, 74n2, 104n48

Ingalls, W. B., 86n56
Isaacs, Marie E., 13n49

Jacobsen, A., 82n45, 87
Jaquier, Eugène, 5n19
Jastrow, Robert, 113n79
Jervell, Jacob, 126n36, 131n13, 133, 137n39
Jewett, Robert, 84n53
Johnson, Luke Timothy, 68n68, 126n36
Johnson, William A., 67n61
Jünst, Johannes, 87

Kearsley, R. A., 121n19
Kennedy, George A., 4n15, 13n51, 19n76, 34n7, 42n33, 60n44, 61n45, 69n69, 74n2, 77n21, 90n76, 143n3
Kilgallen, John L., 13n50, 15n58, 136n37
Kilpatrick, G. D., 20n78
Kim, Dongsoo, 122n43
Kim, Hee-Seong, 31, 58, 60n41, 82n45, 90n73, 123n28–29
Kim, Seyoon, 131n12
Kizhakkeparampil, Isaac, 106n55
Klein, Hans, 44n4, 75n7
Knight, Virginia, 79
Kolenkow, Anitra B., 28n103
Köstenberger, Andreas J., 101n42, 132n18
Kremer, Jacob, 138n40
Kudlien, Fridolf, 80n32, 80n34
Kurz, William S., 62n55, 69n69(2x), 77n17, 139n43

Laan, Cornelius van der,, 99n33, 107n57
Lake, Kirsopp, 24n93, 25n93, 41n31, 86n57, 86n58, 103, 122n24, 138n41
Lausberg, Heinrich, 5n17, 14n52, 26n95, 61n44, 74n2, 77n17
Lee, Sang-Whan, 94n11
Lewis, Paul, 93, 94
Liefeld, Walter L., 105n50
Lindemann, Andreas, 35n8
Linnemann, Eta, 16n61
Llewelyn, Stephen R., 56n9, 121n19
Loisy, Alfred, 109n63, 111n73

Luhman, Reginald, 131n12
Lumpe, A., 62n56, 77n16
Luce, Alice, 107

Ma, Julie C., 97n23, 107n56
Ma, Wonsuk, 97n23
MacDonald, Dennis R., 3n14, 71n79, 72
Macgregor, G. H. C., 83n49
Mack, Burton, 88n68
Mainville, Odette, 7n23, 60n41, 95n13
Manson, Thomas W., 59, 60n40, 108
Marguerat, Daniel, 23, 78, 104, 105n49, 110n69
Marrou, Henri Irénée, 3n14, 42n33, 57n16, 60n42
Marshall, I. Howard, 1n9, 14n55, 15n58, 22n89, 40, 97n23, 103, 132n20, 138n40, 139, 139n44
Martin, Francis, 104, 105n49
Martin, Josef, 14n51, 26n95
Martin, Lee Roy, 105n52
Martin, Ralph P., 58, 122
Marx, Werner G., 136n35
Maslakov, G., 62n56, 77n16
May, J. M., 86n56
McKay, John, 94n10
McQueen, Larry R., 20n79
Mealand, D. L., 139n45
Menoud, Philippe H., 25n94, 70n74, 109n66
Menzies, Robert P., 20n79, 45n8, 60n41, 101n40, 101n42, 104, 104n49, 132n18, 137n39, 138n40, 138n41, 140n50
Menzies, William W., 101n40, 104n49, 128, 129, 130
Metzger, Bruce M., 60n41
Meynet, Roland, 31n112
Michiels, Robert, 6n22, 98n26
Millard, Alan, 56n10, 57n16, 78, 121n19
Minchen, Elizabeth, 34n6, 38n23, 42n34
Moessner, David P., 30n111, 75n8
Moltmann, Jürgen, 102
Montague, George T., 12
Morgan, Teresa, 3n14, 42n33, 60n42, 61n44, 76n11
Moule, C. F. D., 120n16, 131n14
Moulton, James Hope, 57n20
Mühlen, Heribert, 132n19
Müller, Paul-Gerhard, 25n94, 70n74, 109n66
Mundle, Wilhelm, 109n63

Nave, Guy D., Jr., 45n6
Neale, D. A., 15n58
Neil, William, 24n93
Newsom, Carole, 9n33
Neyrey, Jerome H., 38n23

INDEX OF PERSONS

Nissan, J., 131n12
Nock, Arthur Darby, 108n61, 136n35
Nordh, A., 77n16

Oberhelman, S. M., 80n32
O'Brien, P. T., 3n11, 10n38
Oehler, Robert, 62, 62n57
O'Fearghail, Fearghus, 30n111
Öhler, Markus, 8n27
Olbrechts-Tyteca, Lucie, 19n75
Oss, Douglas A., 113n79, 140n47
O'Toole, Robert, 7n23

Packer, J. I., 106n55, 130n11
Parsons, Mikael C., 1n4, 5n17, 22n85, 61, 74n1, 78n22
Patillon, Michel, 4n15, 9n33, 13n51, 26n95, 34n7, 37n22, 45n10, 54n34, 60n43, 76n13, 76n14, 77n19–20, 78n23, 81nn42–43 85n54, 86n56, 87n68, 90nn74–76, 91nn78–79, 101n41, 104n48, 124n33,142n1
Pelling, Christopher, 28n101, 67n61
Penella, Robert J., 143n4
Penner, Todd, 5n17, 22n85
Penny, John, 130n8, 132n18, 137n39
Perelman, Chaïm, 19n75
Pesch, Rudolf, 5n19, 12n44, 22n87, 45n8, 47, 48, 54, 110, 125n35
Petts, David, 131n16
Pfister, Manfred, 57n18
Phillips, E. D., 136n34
Pinnock, Clark, , 98n30
Plessis, Isak J. du, 56n7
Plummer, Alfred, 17n68
Pokorný, P., 16n61
Polkinghorne, John, 94n5, 105n51
Porter, Stanley E., 51n25, 58n33, 60n41, 78n24, 121n20
Powers, Janet Everts, 18n71
Poythress, Vern Sheridan, 140nn48–49
Preuschen, Erwin, 87
Price, Bennett J., 5n17, 33n2, 62n55, 77n17, 124n34
Procksch, Otto, 5n19
Prosser, Peter E., 95n14

Quesnel, Michel, 134n23

Rabe, Hugo, 37n23
Race, W. H., 86n56
Rad, Gerhard von, 7–8n26, 82n44
Rambaud, Michel, 68n66
Ramsay, William M., 57, 58n23, 126n37, 138n41

Rea, John, ix
Reicke, Bo, 56n12
Rengstorf, Karl H., 1n3
Riesner, Rainer, 11
Robbins, Vernon K., 88n68
Robeck, Cecil M., Jr., 93n3, 94n11, 137n39
Roberts, W. Rhys, 14n51
Robinson, James M., 50n24, 51n29
Roller, Matthew B., 145
Roon, A. van, 122n22
Rooney, Lucy, 105n50
Runia, Klass, 99n33
Rusam, Dietrich, 2n8
Russell, D. A., 73n87
Russell, E. A., 24n93, 105, 134n24
Ruthven, Jon, 95n16, 96n20, 113n77, 113n79, 130n9

Sanders, James A., 19n77
Saucy, Robert, 113
Scarborough, John, 136n34
Scharten, Elize, 107
Schenk, Wolfgang, 50n24, 51n26, 84
Scherer, Karl, 13n51
Schissal, Otmar, 42n33, 60n44, 77n22
Schmidt, Daryl D., 108n61, 120n15
Schnackenburg, Rudolf, 59, 108
Schneider, Gerhard, 1, 10n38
Schottroff, Louise, 16n61
Schrenk, Gottlob, 17n68
Schubert, Paul, 139n43
Schulz, Siefried, 1n2, 50n24, 51n26, 58, 81n39
Schulze, H., 58n24, 82n45, 123
Schürmann, Heinz, 99n32, 108
Schwanbeck, E. A., 87
Schweizer, Eduard, 24n93, 25n93, 43n2, 60n41, 105, 134, 138n40, 139n46
Sellner, Hans Jörg, 45nn6–8
Seytre, Christian, 96n18
Shalev, Donna, 38n25
Shelton, James B., 18n70, 60n41, 67n60, 74n1, 94, 97n23, 105, 112n76, 132, 134n24, 137n39
Shipp, G. P., 68n65
Sluitter, Ineke, 80, 81n38
Smail, Thomas, 131n15
Smith, Robert H., 135n29
Smith, Wesley D., 80n35
Soards, Marion L., 45n9
Solin, Heikki, 70n72
Soltau, W., 82n45, 88, 109n63
Spengel, Leonard, 4n15, 76n14, 142n1
Spicq, Ceslas, 15n56, 85n55
Stählin, Gustav, 13n51, 69n69, 78n22

INDEX OF PERSONS

Stanton, Graham N., ix, 35n8, 95n15, 134n26
Starr, Raymond J., 67n61
Stegemann, W., 4n15, 60n43, 76n13
Stegman, Thomas D., 78n22
Stenschke, Christoph, 16n67
Sterling, Gregory E., 29n110
Steyn, Gert J., 20n79
Storms, C. Samuel, 99n31, 113n79, 140n47
Strathmann, Hermann, 17n69
Stronstad, Roger, 96n21, 97n23, 101n42, 128(2x), 129(2x), 130(3x), 131(2x), 131n14, 132(2x), 132n18, 133(4x), 134, 134n25, 135, 136, 137, 141n51
Stuhlmacher, Peter, 25n93, 41n31, 86nn57-58, 103, 122n24
Suhl, Alfred, 55n1, 75n4
Sullivan, Francis A., 105, 132, 134n23

Talbert, Charles H., 2, 6nn21-22, 18, 81n39, 139n43
Tannehill, Robert C., 12n47, 39n27, 132n20
Thiering, B. E., 45n7, 82n45, 109n63
Thomas, John Christopher, 16n66, 28n105, 135n27
Thomas, Richard F., 57n19, 79
Thomas, Robert L., 100n34, 137n38
Thompson, M. B., 57n16, 121n19
Thornton, Claus-Jürgen, 55n1, 75n4
Throckmorton, B. H., 14n54, 15n56, 15n59
Theon, Aelius, of Alexandria, 4, 4n17, 5, 6n20, 9n33, 13, 20, 21, 21n82, 22n86, 27, 30n111, 34, 37, 37n23, 39n27, 41, 42, 42n33, 45n10, 60, 61, 62, 68, 70, 74, 76, 76n13, 77, 78, 79, 81, 82, 85, 85n56, 86n56, 90, 90n76, 91, 91nn77-79, 92, 101n41, 104n48, 124, 124n34, 142, 143n3, 145, 147
Toit, Andrie B. du, 83n49
Tolkien, J. R. R., 94
Tucker, Jeffrey T., 142n2
Turner, Eric 40n29, 57n16
Turner, Max, 105, 109n65, 134n23, 137n39, 138n41, 141n50

Tyson, Joseph B., 60n41

Unnik, W. C. van, 3n13, 114n80, 131, 140

Vanderbout, Elva, 107
Vergil, 9(2x), 24, 79
Vielhauer, P., 117, 118, 121, 121n21
Voelz, James W., 68n68
Volkmann, Richard, 26n95

Walker, William O., Jr., 58, 59, 74n1, 82n45, 109n63, 123
Walton, Steve, 71n74, 109n67, 117(4x), 118(4x), 119(8x), 120(6x), 121(4x), 121n21, 122(2x), 123(4x), 124(4x), 126n36, 127(2x)
Warrington, Keith, 97n23
Watson, Duane F., 69n69
Webb, Ruth, 3n14, 61n44, 61n46, 68n62, 68n64, 74n2, 75, 76, 77n19, 143n4
Weber, Giorgio, 80n33
Wedderburn, A. J. M., 118n9, 120n15
Weissenrieder, Annette, 8n27, 28n104, 50n23, 75n9, 79n31
Wendel, Carl, 53n31
Wendt, Hans Hinrich, 111n73(8x)
White, John L., 56n9
Whitmarsh, Tim, 77n22
Wiedemann, Thomas, 86n56
Williams, Charles Bray, 86n59
Williams, C. G.18n71
Williams, Garry J.94n9
Williams, J. Rodman, 100n34, 113n79, 132n19
Witt, R. E., 56n14, 135n30
Wolter, Michael, 16nn62-63, 16n65, 25n93, 103, 122n24
Woodman, A. J., 26n95

Youngblood, Ronald, 100, 100n34

Zahn, Theodor, 25n93, 41n31, 86nn57-58, 103, 122n24

175

Index of Ancient Sources

Old Testament

Genesis

37:7	8
37:9	8
37:10	8
41:2–7	8
41:17–24	8
41:53	8
41:54	8
43:26	8
43:28	8

1 Samuel

2:30–34	8
4:11	8
4:17	8

2 Samuel

7:13	7

1 Kings

2:27	8
8:20	7
8:56	8

2 Kings

10:10	8

4 Kingdoms

5:10	48

Psalms

103:4	18

Isaiah

40	49
44:1–3	48–49
61:1–2	14

Joel

3:1–5	6

New Testament

Matthew

3:11	5
6:10	51
7:7	50
7:28	51
8:5–10	51
8:8	51, 52
8:13	51
11:28	5
21:13	52
28:19–20	53
28:20	5

Mark

11:17	52

Luke

1:1–4	71
1:1–3	123
1:1	1, 5, 7, 124, 132
1:4	2
1:13–17	2
1:26–37	2
1:32–33	7
1:39–44	2
1:45	8
1:57–66	2
1:57	2
1:67–70	2–3
1:68	15
1:69	15
1:71	15
1:77	15
2:1–2	2
2:11–12	2
2:11	14, 15, 25, 82, 143
2:15–20	2
2:30	14, 143
3:1–20	2–3
3:4	49
3:5–6	49
3:6	14
3:8	14
3:10–14	14
3:16	11, 12, 18, 22, 25–26, 44, 82
3:17	18
4:16–21	2, 14
4:18–19	16
4:21	2
4:43	16
5:1	10, 10–11
5:5	11
5:24	15
5:32	14, 15
6:35	49, 53
6:37–38	49
6:46–49	11
7:1–10	51
7:7	51, 52
7:21	16
7:22	16
7:24–27	2–3
7:34	15
7:36–50	15, 84, 142
7:38	120
7:44	39, 120
7:50	143
8:8	11
8:10	16
8:11–15	11
8:11	11
8:21	11
8:24	34
8:25	34
8:50	49
9:2	16, 120
9:15	2
9:22	2
9:24	40
9:25	40
9:44	2
9:60	16
10:3	120
10:9	16
10:11	16
10:20	16, 17
10:25	50
10:28	50
11	53
11:2	51
11:5–13	17
11:5–8	12
11:9–13	12
11:9	50
11:13	2, 10, 12, 22, 44, 63, 103n47, 104
11:20	16
11:28	11
11:39–40	91
12:1–53	120
12:8	15
12:11–12	2
12:49	40
12:51	40
13:3	14, 15
13:5	14, 15
13:16	16
13:32	120
13:35	2
14:13–14	50
14:15–24	16
14:35	11
15	16
15:1–7	144
15:4–6	16
15:4	144
15:6	17, 144, 146

15:7	14, 15, 16, 144–45	1:4	2, 10, 17, 21, 63, 65
15:8–10	144	1:5	2, 10, 12, 17
15:8–9	16	1:8	2, 13, 18, 30, 44
15:8	16, 145	1:9–11	18
15:9	17, 145, 146	1:14	2, 13, 17
15:10	14, 15, 144–45	2	10, 89
15:11–32	16, 144	2:1–31	145
15:24	16, 17, 146–47	2:2	18, 28
15:32	16	2:3	18
16:16	16	2:4	2, 18, 22, 63, 67, 68
16:19–31	15, 16	2:9–11	88
16:30	15	2:11	18
17:3f	14	2:12	19, 39
17:16	40	2:14–16	19
17:18	40	2:17–21	19, 20
17:21	16	2:17	6, 21, 24, 25–26, 27, 28, 139
17:37	39		
18:17	40	2:18	6, 18, 24, 25–26, 27, 45
18:18	40	2:19	28
18:31–33	2	2:21	6, 16, 20, 24, 25
19:1–10	144	2:22–33	19
19:5–10	84	2:30	7
19:9–10	144	2:33–36	46
19:17	53	2:33	3, 19, 20, 21, 23, 44, 46, 63, 65, 95
19:38	2		
20:21	87	2:34–36	19
21:5–36	120	2:36	46, 54
21:6	40	2:37	19, 39
21:7	40	2:38–39	21, 26, 89
22:10–12	2	2:38	vii, 22, 23, 43–54, 64, 65, 110, 129
22:13	2		
22:14–38	120	2:39	22, 23, 26, 44, 64, 65, 129, 139
22:19–20	119, 120		
22:20	119	2:42	24
22:21	40	2:43	28
22:22	40	3:22	11
22:48	40	3:23	11
22:34	2	3:24	8
22:61	2	4:8	67, 68
23:29–30	40	4:12	146
23:31	40	4:29	28
24:27	19	4:30	28
24:44	19	4:31	67, 68
24:47	14, 17	5:12	28
24:48	13, 17	5:19–21	28
24:49	2, 10, 17, 18, 21, 44, 63, 65, 133	5:29	2
		5:31	14
24:53	13	5:32	46
		6:3	64, 67, 68
		6:8	28
Acts		7:37	7
		7:55	67, 68
1:1	5, 97	8:12	11
1:4–5	44	8:15	64

Luke (continued)

8:17	11, 64	15:8	65
8:19	64	15:12	28
8:22	50	15:13–20	33
8:26	46	15:23	118
8:26–29	28	15:28	118
8:30	40	15:29	118
8:31	38	16:3	118
8:36	40–41	16:6–12	28
9:1–19	28	16:30	146
9:6	50	16:31	50, 84
9:13	37	17:1—18:17	123
9:14	37	17:30	15, 146
9:17	30, 64, 67, 68	18:9–11	28
9:21	37	18:23—19:7	88, 122
9:27	28	18:23f	123
10	90	18:23	41, 59, 85
10:1–23	28	19	47–48
10:15	91	19:1	41, 85–86, 103
10:30–33	28	19:2–6	47
10:34	74, 87–92	19:2	41, 48, 65, 85–86, 103
10:35–36	91	19:6	18, 65, 86
10:35	88, 90	19:9	15
10:36	90	19:10	15
10:37–43	92	20:18–35	117
10:38	28	20:18–21	119
10:42	90	20:19	122, 123
10:43	90, 91, 146	20:21	121
10:44	64	20:22–24	119
10:45	46, 64	20:23	3, 121, 137–38
10:46	18	20:24	121
10:47	64, 89	20:25–27	119
11:1–15	28	20:26	121
11:1–2	33	20:28	119, 120, 121, 122
11:9	91	20:28–31	119
11:15	64	20:31	53, 123
11:17	37, 46, 64	20:32–35	119
11:18	15, 91	20:33–35	123
11:24	64, 67, 68	21	118
11:27–28	3	21:8–9	73
12:1–11	28	21:8	27
13:2	119	21:9	27
13:9	67, 68	21:10–11	2
13:20	8	21:18	118
13:23	2, 14	21:21	118
13:26	143	21:25	118
13:27–29	2	21:26	122
13:27	2	21:27–28	3
13:33	2	21:37	39
13:38–39	146	22	118
14:3	28	22:6–11	28
15	59	22:10	50
15:7–9	33	22:17–21	28
		23:4	39
		23:11	28, 139

23:26–30	33	12:13	66
23:23–24	28	13:1	18
23:34	28	14:15	66
24:21	42		
25:3	37		
25:5	37	## 2 Corinthians	
25:9	37		
26:8	42	1:22	62
26:12–18	28	2:15	144
26:27	1	5:5	63
27:21–26	28	7:10	143, 146
27:23–24	2	11:4	63
27:44	2		
28:14	2		
28:31	139	## Galatians	
		2	59
## Romans		2:6	87–88
		2:12	118
1–3	83	3:2	62
1:1	59, 88, 123	3:14	62
1:4	90	3:26	143
1:7	83	5:3	118
1:11	58, 74, 81, 82, 84, 85, 86, 87, 92	5:11	118
		5:16	66
1:16	143	5:18	66
2:4	146	6:15	118
2:9	88		
2:10	88, 90		
2:11	74, 87–92	## Ephesians	
2:16	90		
5:5	63, 84, 85, 88	1:13	63
5:9	83	2:8	143
8:4	66	4:30	63, 66
8:9	66	5:18	63, 66
8:15	63, 85, 88		
8:16	66		
8:26	66	## Philippians	
10:9	74, 81, 82, 83, 84, 86, 87, 92		
		3:1	147
10:11	90	4:4	147
10:12	90		
12	84		
14:9	90	## Colossians	
15:29	84		
		1:14	143
## 1 Corinthians			
		## 1 Thessalonians	
1:18	143, 144		
2:12	62, 84	1:1	121
3:16	66	1:9	144
9:19–23	118	2:9	123
12	84		

1 Thessalonians (continued)

2:12	121
2:14	121
3:1–10	123
4:1–2	122
4:6	121
4:8	62
4:11–12	122

2 Thessalonians

2:10	144

James

5:1	53

Jude

21	53

Extra-Biblical Sources

Aristides

Def. Or.

380	68

Panathenaic Oration

82	68
394	68

Aristotle

Rhetorica

1356b3	145
1356b20	145
1393a27	145
1403a5	145

Cicero

De inventione rhetorica

1.29.27	82
1.34.57—41.77	18

Rhetorica Herrenium

2.18.27—29.46	19
4.49.62	19

Eusebius

Ecclesiastical History

9.7.14.2	49

Herakleopolites

BGU

16 2646, ll. 34–37	48

Hermogenes

Περὶ εὑρέσεως

4.1	145

Homer

Odyssey

11.146	76

Isocrates

Panagyricus

8.4	79
9.1–6	79

Quintilian

Institutio oratoria

1.5.3	81
4.2.31	82
7.2.24	56n11

Seneca

Epistulae morales

84	79

Sirach

33:4	49

www.ingramcontent.com/pod-product-compliance
Lightning Source LLC
Chambersburg PA
CBHW082039230426
43670CB00016B/2711